The Therapeutic State

The Therapeutic State

Justifying Government at Century's End

James L. Nolan, Jr.

NEW YORK UNIVERSITY PRESS

New York and London

NEW YORK UNIVERSITY PRESS
New York and London

Library of Congress Cataloging-in-Publication Data
Nolan, James L., Jr.
The therapeutic state : justifying government at century's end /
James L. Nolan, Jr.
p. cm.
Includes bibliographical references and index.
ISBN 0-8147-5790-1 (cloth : acid-free paper).—ISBN
0-8147-5791-X (paper : acid-free paper)
1. Political culture. 2. Political psychology. 3. Political
culture—United States. 4. Law—United States—Psychological
aspects. I. Title.
JA75.7.N65 1997
306.2'0973—dc21   97-21234
                    CIP

New York University Press books are printed on acid-free paper,
and their binding materials are chosen for strength and durability.

Manufactured in the United States of America

10 9 8 7 6 5 4 3 2 1

To Cathy

Contents

List of Tables

Acknowledgments

I benefited greatly from the input and assistance of many throughout my work on the various stages of this project. In particular, I'm grateful to James Davison Hunter, Gianfranco Poggi, Mark Lupher, and Steven Tipton, whose support and scholarly advice aided in the progress and completion of the work. I'm especially indebted to James Hunter, whose intellectual creativity and scholarly ambition have been sources of inspiration for some time. Finishing the work in a timely manner was also aided by the generous support of the Graduate School of Arts and Sciences and the Postmodernity Project at the University of Virginia.

For input on my law chapters I was aided through discussions with Carter Pilcher and James Nolan, Sr.; research assistance from Jeff Tatum; and helpful guidance and direction from Kent Olson at the University of Virginia Law School. For aid in the aggregation of the National Elections Study data used in Chapter 2 and the Bureau of Justice Statistics survey used in Chapter 4, I have Paul Bergan and Rick Holt at the Social Science Data Center to thank. And for practical tips on developments in education, Bruce Aster offered valuable input.

Helpful during the very final stages of the book project was the support I received from my colleagues in the Department of Anthropology and Sociology at Williams College. I also profited from my association with many during my years at the University of Virginia. Spurred by their own scholarly efforts and practically aided through advice on mine, I have gained much from having, among others, Joe Davis, Beth Eck, Daniel Johnson, Karin Peterson, Kimon Sargeant, and Saundra Westervelt as colleagues. Conversations with others have also helped to clarify my thinking on different parts of the project. Though I cannot here name all who have assisted in this way, I would be remiss not to mention the help I received through discussions with Ty Buckman, Sally Ennis, Chris Jensen, Wade Luhn, Ken Meyers, Scott Roulieau, and Chuck Slater. I owe a special thanks, too, to Anne McIlhaney for reading and commenting on an early draft of the manuscript; to Donna Chenail for her input on a much later draft; and to Niko Pfund at New York University Press for his helpful editorial guidance and advice.

Finally, and most importantly, I thank my wife, Cathy, without whom the completion of the project would have been considerably more difficult, if not impossible. For her companionship, patience with the practical demands of research and writing, willingness to endure many readings of various chapters, and indefatigable support and good humor I am infinitely grateful.

1

The Therapeutic Culture

In the city of Washington, D.C., one walks into a federal district court and finds a judge with microphone in hand, roaming the floor of the courtroom rather than sitting behind her bench. Like a therapist or social worker, she asks personal questions of the offenders turned "clients" before her and encourages them in their battles against drug dependency and other criminal behaviors. In the same city, the mayor has publicly aligned city goals with the goals of recovery. Regularly sprinkling his rhetoric with the language of therapy, Marion Barry advocates a citywide "transformation" and "rejuvenation." After all, Washington's mayor claims, "we, too, need recovery as a city, don't we?"

Appeals to therapeutic themes are not limited to the local level. Just outside the Washington beltway, President Bill Clinton began his presidency in 1993 with a Camp David gathering of cabinet members and therapeutic facilitators. Participants "shared" intimate—and in some cases, embarrassing—aspects of their past lives in an effort to build trust and caring relationships. Similarly, in one of his first acts as Speaker of the House, Newt Gingrich employed the services of a corporate psychologist to help Republicans speak in a language that would resonate with the citizenry.

These examples of government adoption of the ideas, practices, and language of the therapeutic enterprise in the nation's capital raise the question of whether the dalliance between the American political order and the therapeutic cultural ethos is a phenomenon of more widespread proportions. In other words, has the cultural impulse that Philip Rieff called the "triumph of the therapeutic" begun to institutionalize itself into the various functions of the political order? Through investigations of various dimensions of the modern American state, this book assesses on a comprehensive level, the extent to which the therapeutic cultural orientation has become a dominant feature of the American state.

Before turning to theoretical arguments about the state and to investigations into different arenas of state activity, let me first make clear what I mean by the cultural phenomenon of the therapeutic ethos. When I speak of the therapeutic perspective, I am referring not to the psychoanalytic emphasis within the discipline of psychology or to specific psychological or counseling enterprises per se but to a more widespread, cultural ethos or system of moral understanding. To be sure, it can be traced back to a psychoanalytic frame of reference, but it has spilled out into the culture more broadly. As Peter Berger explains, "Psychoanalysis has become a cultural phenomenon, a way of understanding the nature of man and an ordering of human experience on the basis of this understanding."[1]

In other words, the therapeutic perspective has become a taken-for-granted part of everyday life. It provides culture with a set of symbols and codes that determine the boundaries of moral life. The cultural manifestation of the therapeutic ethos, analyzed as it has been by a number of social scientists and cultural critics, has been variously described as "the psychological society,"[2] "the therapeutic culture,"[3] "the triumph of the therapeutic,"[4] "the culture of narcissism,"[5] "the shrinking of America,"[6] "the therapeutic attitude,"[7] "the fall of public man,"[8] and "the rise of selfishness in America."[9] One can derive from this literature several major defining features of the therapeutic ethos. I review these here not to level yet another jeremiad against America's therapeutic culture but to delineate, within specific heuristic categories, the symbolic reference points of this cultural system. This is the necessary first step to prepare for an analysis of the extent to which the therapeutic ethos has penetrated the modern American state.

The Emancipated Self

First, and perhaps most important, the therapeutic ethos, unlike traditional moral orders, is at its heart self-referential. As I discuss in the next chapter, the conditions of industrialized capitalism effectively undermined older forms of moral authority. Consequently, the individual has been left to himself or herself to establish standards of moral interpretation. Where older moral orders looked to a transcendent being, to a covenantal community, to natural law, or to divine reason to provide the substantive basis for culture's moral boundaries, the therapeutic ethos establishes the self as the ultimate object of allegiance. The self has become, as Daniel Bell contends, "the touchstone of cultural judgment." [10]

As such, cultural understandings of the self have been significantly transformed. Where once the self was to be brought into conformity with the standards of externally derived authorities and social institutions, it now is compelled to look within. Alasdair MacIntyre characterizes the situation in this way: "I cannot genuinely appeal to impersonal criteria, for there are no impersonal criteria." [11] In other words, the contemporary cultural condition is such that externally derived points of moral reference are not available to individuals as they once were. Instead, cultural standards for judgment, guideposts for actions, understandings of oneself, and the tools for navigating through social life are likely to be rooted in the self.

This cultural understanding of the self departs from past cosmologies, which called for the denial of self in deference to the authority of social institutions and codes of moral understanding existing outside of the self. Sigmund Freud, in contrast, supplied the analytical tools to conceive of the self as independent of (though in conflict with) these formerly binding moral orders.

Contemporary understandings of the self, however, depart even from Freudian psychoanalysis in the way that it was conceived by its founder. Providing the mechanisms whereby the self could mediate against society rather than overturn it, Freud did not discount the need for socialization. The new psychologies of the self—the work of Carl Rogers, in particular—take a more negative view of the social world. Where Freudian psychoanalysis is essentially a therapy of adaptation, Rogerian client-centered therapy is one of liberation. [12] The former views a binding culture, oppressive though it may be, as something the impulses of the self must struggle against. The latter advocates the replacement of traditional culture with a culture dominated by impulses. No longer is society something the self must adjust to; it is now something the self must be liberated from. As Bell explains, "Where the earlier intention of psychoanalysis was to enable the patient to achieve self-insight and thereby redirect his life—an aim inseparable from a moral context—the newer therapies are entirely instrumental and psychologistic; their aim is to 'free' the person from inhibitions and restraints." [13] Where once the self was to be surrendered, denied, sacrificed, and died to, now the self is to be esteemed, actualized, affirmed, and unfettered.

Arguably, this concept of the self has its roots in the romantic strains of the French Enlightenment. It may have been Jean-Jacques Rousseau who first articulated the notion that has become so popular in the contemporary context, what he called *amour de soi-même*—or as it has been translated into English, "self-esteem." According to Rousseau, self-esteem is a natural disposition that, along with the natural sentiment of compassion, produces virtue in the individual and contributes to the preservation of the society.[14]

The Rogerian conception of the self likewise sees the self as naturally inclined toward good (or as Rogers liked to say, as naturally bent toward becoming trustworthy, constructive, and responsible). Rogers himself recognized how this understanding of the self was a departure not only from traditional religious views of the self but from a Freudian psychoanalytic perspective as well. Where Freudian therapy sought to hold in check the untamed forces of the id, Rogers believed that "the innermost core of man's nature, the deepest layers of his personality, the base of his 'animal nature,' is positive in nature—is basically socialized, forward-moving, rational and realistic."[15]

It is this view of the self—the liberated rather than the adaptive—that is increasingly evident in contemporary American culture. It is not surprising that with such a cultural understanding of the self, more attention is paid to the self. When the individual's basic nature was viewed as less than naturally virtuous, efforts to realize, esteem, and analyze the self would understandably have been less popular. Why would one want to be so familiar with that which was considered evil by nature? If, however, virtue or responsibility rests in the natural goodness of the self, then a greater preoccupation with the self makes perfect sense.

This, generally speaking, is what we see happening in modern America. Social institutions no longer bind and determine the self as they once did. More and more areas of life (vocation, beliefs, sexual identity, etc.) are now areas of choice, determined by the individual self. The therapeutic ethos is thus characterized by a conspicuous self-referencing.

It is only in this context that a magazine called *Self* could flourish. *Self* magazine, first published in 1979, now has a total circulation of more than 1,250,000 readers.[16] Another indicator of the cultural absorption with self is the number of books published on the topic. In

1994, more than 720 books in print had titles that began with the word *self*. There were 619 books under the subject heading "self-help technique," 365 under the heading "self-esteem," 292 under "self-actualization," and 126 under "self-realization." In total, the subjects of at least 2,421 books in print had something to do with the self.[17] This is a fairly substantial increase over the 1978 level, when only 209 titles began with the word *self*, and the 1950 level when a mere 35 titles began with the word *self*.[18]

Observers of America's increasingly therapeutic society have variously depicted the self in the contemporary context as the "imperial self," the "saturated self," the "unencumbered self," the "emotivist self," and the "authentic self."[19] The self has moved to a more central place in American culture. In short, as Philip Rieff observes, "the best spirits of the twentieth century have thus expressed their conviction that the original innocence, which to earlier periods was a sinful conceit, the new center, which can be held even as communities disintegrate, is the self."[20]

The Emotivist Ethic

With the viability of external reference points increasingly undermined and the emergence of the self as the "new center" of the social world, it becomes clear why another feature of the therapeutic ethos has appeared. If one is discouraged from appealing to religious symbols or even to divine reason in the classical sense, one is left with one's own feelings. This emphasis on emotions, or what Alasdair MacIntyre calls the "ethic of emotivism," has become an important trait of the therapeutic culture. The emotivist motif is also salient to contemporary life in that it represents a "high-touch" departure from the "high-tech" harshness of the instrumentally oriented public sphere.

In a certain sense, then, the emphasis on emotions appears to be a reaction against the highly impersonal nature of bureaucratized modern structures. Yet it is probably more accurate to characterize the rationalization of the modern world as the necessary foundation for or precursor to the emergence of therapeutic emotivism. As Richard Sennett observes, "The celebration of objectivity and hardheaded commitment to fact so prominent a century ago, all in the name of Science, was in reality an unwitting preparation for the present era of subjectivity."[21] The objectivity of the industrialized world undermined the authority of traditional moralities, preparing the cultural soil for a more widespread concern with emotions.

Thus, though the therapeutic ethos (and the emotivist ethic in particular) represents an attempt to break out of the Weberian "iron cage" — out of the alienating existence of life in the machine — it does so without referencing back to traditional cultural systems and without challenging the fundamental structure of the capitalist order. Life in the machine has made appeals to these older systems of meaning increasingly implausible. Instead, the individual is encouraged to escape from within and to refer to the language of emotions. The emotivist motif, then, is the "dictum that truth is grasped through sentiment or feeling, rather than through rational judgment or abstract reasoning."[22] It encourages a particular ontology that replaces the Cartesian maxim "I think, therefore I am" with the emotive "I feel, therefore I am." This emotivist understanding of the self shapes the way in which individuals participate and communicate in societal life. In the contemporary context, as Jean Bethke Elshtain observes, "all points seem to revolve around the individual's subjective feelings — whether of frustration, anxiety, stress, fulfillment. The citizen recedes; the therapeutic self prevails."[23]

One feature of this societal concern with the place of emotions is that these feelings, once identified, are to be expressed openly. When this is done correctly, emotions are revealed without constraint or discrimination. As Edwin Schur writes, "Every emotion has value. . . . We must recognize all feelings, express them, open them up to the people around us."[24] Increasingly, this is how Americans communicate. As early as 1975, Thomas Cottle observed that "our entire society seems to be leaning toward more and more divulging and exposing, and less and less confidentiality and withholding."[25] To fail to express is to be in denial or to be dishonest. In this sense, the very notion of honesty is redefined, because the basis for honesty becomes one's willingness to be in touch with and to express one's feelings. It is not honesty in the sense of truthfulness to an objectively measured empirical reality or to an external worldview that enjoins the individual to hold certain things as true and adjust his or her behavior accordingly; nor is it the honesty of intellectual deference to reason or even, in some instances, to conventional protocol. It is honesty defined by the open communication of one's feelings.

This understanding of honesty parallels the cultural shift from "honor" to "dignity" that Peter Berger talks about and the movement from "sincerity" to "authenticity" that Lionel Trilling discusses.[26] The true or real person is the one who begins with the self, as opposed to social institutions outside the self, and "honestly" and "authentically" emotes his or her inner tides outward. In the contemporary context, emotions serve as a new barometer for making decisions, for relating to others, and for understanding oneself. In short, as MacIntyre argues, "emotivism has become embodied in our culture. . . . We live in a specifically emotivist culture."[27] This is not to say that all Americans or even a majority of Americans appeal primarily to their emotions to determine how they should function within society. But it is to say that the social conditions increasingly militate against other forms of moral referencing and self-understanding.

A New Priestly Class

A third major feature of the therapeutic ethos is the emergence of a new elite in the psychologically defined moral universe. Once religious leaders operated with considerable "occupational prestige" and respect in society; but their role has declined along with the cultural systems they represent. As Rieff explains, "The professionally religious custodians of the old moral demands are no longer authoritative."[28] Replacing them are the psychiatrists and psychologists of the therapeutic ethic. These are the ones who understand and can decipher the emotivist language emanating from the authoritative self. Replacing the "pastors of the older dispensation," the psychoanalyst has assumed "the role of a 'secular spiritual guide'."[29]

Bernie Zilbergeld, Ellen Herman, and others have documented the growth of this new "priestly" class, revealing the substantial aggregate influence of psychology on society. For example, between 1968 and 1983 the number of clinical psychologists in America more than tripled, from twelve thousand to over forty thousand.[30] The number of clinical social workers likewise, grew from twenty-five thousand in 1970 to eighty thousand in 1990.[31] In all, by 1986 there were 253,000 psychologists employed in the United States, more than one-fifth of whom held doctoral degrees.[32] The National Science Foundation projected in 1986 that civilian employment in psychology would increase between 27 and 39 percent by the year 2000 a growth rate approximately fourteen to fifteen percentage points higher than that forecast for all other occupations.[33] America has more psychiatrists than any other country in the world. In 1983 there were an estimated ninety thousand licensed psychiatrists in the entire world; one-third of them were in America.[34]

Between 1965 and 1981, the number of annually conferred doctorates in psychology more than tripled while the number conferred in all fields only doubled.[35] In 1986 there were 133 more doctorates in psychology alone than in all the other American social sciences combined. Likewise, in 1993 more bachelor degrees were awarded in psychology than in all other social science fields and in most other natural science disciplines as well.[36] Membership in the American Psychological Association grew from 2,739 in 1940 to 30,839 in 1970 and to over 75,000 in 1993.[37] It has been estimated that some eighty million Americans have now sought help from therapists, with a recent average of around ten million per year doing so.[38] Furthermore, the number of new books published annually in the area of psychology tripled between 1960 and 1980. This rate of increase was higher than that in the book publishing industry generally.[39] Over 325,000 copies of *Psychology Today*, a magazine that began publication fewer than twenty-five years ago, are sold each month.[40] The monumental increase in the psychologization of modern life is also evident in the fact that there are more therapists than librarians, firefighters, or mail carriers in the United States, and twice as many therapists as dentists or pharmacists. Only police and lawyers outnumber counselors, but only by a ratio of less than two to one in both instances.[41]

These psychologists, psychiatrists, counselors, therapists, and social workers have been granted a high level of prestige and social recognition in American society for their ability to help individuals make sense of life in the modern world. They interpret individual behavior and social interactions with an authority that was once conferred on individuals associated with other vocations in American society. Christopher Lasch explains that "the authority of parents, priests, and lawgivers, now condemned as representatives of discredited authoritarian modes of discipline," has been replaced by "medical and psychiatric authority."[42] Thus the priests of traditional moral systems have "given way ... to their logical and historical successors, the psychologizers"[43] of the therapeutic age. The modern individual now turns to the growing supply of "therapists, not priests ... or models of success like the captains of industry . . . in the hopes of achieving the modern equivalent of salvation, 'mental health'." [44]

That a growing number of individuals need this new form of "salvation" is fostered by a social situation in which an increasing number of behaviors are interpreted on the basis of healthiness or sickness, rather than on the basis of whether actions are good or bad, moral or immoral, right or wrong. Many behaviors once interpreted through a religious frame of reference are now viewed in terms of health, which of course makes more essential the role of the therapeutic practitioners. The role of the new priest, as such, depends in part on the redefinition of human behaviors in pathological rather than moralistic categories.

The Pathologization of Human Behavior

Another defining feature of the therapeutic ethos, then, is the growing tendency to define a range of human behaviors as diseases or pathologies. Within the therapeutic enterprise the therapist is, of course, concerned with healing or curing the afflicted patient. As the therapeutic perspective has spilled into the culture more broadly, so has the belief that a growing number of human actions represent diseases or illnesses that need to be healed. Behaviors that were formerly described at face value or interpreted in moralistic terms have increasingly been portrayed as pathologies. "The psychiatrist," as Christopher Lasch observes, "has translated 'everything human' into 'mental terms of illness.' " [45] That many Americans have accepted this pathological redefinition of behavior is evident on several fronts.

One important carrier of this mind-set is the popular self-help group format of Alcoholics Anonymous (AA). Widespread involvement in AA and in treatment hospitals such as the Betty Ford Clinic, CompCare, and Fair Oaks helped foster the now common view that alcoholism and drug use are illnesses that require therapeutic treatment for recovery. A 1987 Gallup poll reported, for example, that 90 percent of Americans believe alcoholism is a disease. [46]

Americans have not always held this view. During the colonial period, when per capita drinking was much higher than it is today, family gatherings at local taverns typically involved much alcohol consumption. However, this consumption was informally regulated by the social fabric of community life, indulged in within the context of eating meals, and generally perceived as a normal part of daily life. The description of rum by the colonial Puritan Increase Mather as "the good creature of God" is just one indication of the more benign role alcohol was believed to play in early American society.[47] When drunkenness did occur, it was the individual, rather than the alcohol, who was seen as the problem.

With industrial urbanization and massive European immigration, consumption of alcohol became disengaged from community regulation. Urban saloons replaced the family taverns. During the nineteenth century, alcohol consumption became the perceived culprit behind a number of social ills. The good creature of God became the "demon rum," and the favored political party among immigrants was denounced as the party of "rum, Romanism and rebellion." The temperance movement, made up of Protestant, middle-class, nativists took on the "evil" of alcohol with great force. By 1920 they were able to secure legally the prohibition of alcoholic consumption in the United States. Opposition to the use of alcohol during this period, however, was largely conceived of in moralistic rather than pathological terms.

Even the original AA fellowship established by Bill Wilson and Robert Smith in 1935, although a mix of "pseudomedical, psychological, and religious"[48] sentiments, arose from the evangelical roots of the Oxford Group. This is certainly evident in AA's well-known twelve steps, where God is mentioned six times and where prayer and meditation, repentance, and public confession and restitution are encouraged. However, it was out of the AA subculture that a view of alcoholism as a disease eventually came forth.[49]

But AA provided only the first step in a longer process of reinterpreting many other behaviors as diseases. Other self-help groups based on the AA model, such as Alateen (AA for teenagers), Narcotics Anonymous (NA), and Parents Anonymous (PA, for parents struggling with abusive behavior toward children), have emerged around the country. Also following AA's lead are the codependency groups CoDependents Anonymous (CoDa), Adult Children of Alcoholics (ACOA), and Al-Anon (for spouses of alcoholics), whose members' identities are based on their dysfunctional or codependent relationship with an alcoholic family member.[50]

Today self-help groups exist for any number of habitual behaviors.

Recovery groups have arisen for gamblers, overeaters, compulsive shoppers, smokers, those involved in compulsive sexual behaviors, and sufferers of agoraphobia (fear of open places).[51] Other self-help groups include Debtors Anonymous, Workaholics Anonymous, Dual Disorders Anonymous, Batterers Anonymous, Victims Anonymous, and Unwed Parents Anonymous, to name only a few.[52]

In addition to the disease labels of those involved in self-help groups, a number of other behaviors have been reinterpreted as illnesses. One indicator of this is the list of disorders in the *Diagnostic and Statistical Manual of Mental Disorders, Third Edition, Revised* (DSM III-R), put out by the American Psychiatric Association. DSM III-R is the most prominent mental health classification system in the United States. It has been "widely accepted in the United States as the common language of mental health clinicians and researchers."[53] A survey of diagnostic experts in fifty-five countries found that seventy-two percent of them used this classification system.[54]

Among the classifications in DSM III-R are "Impulse Control Disorders," which include "Pathological Gambling" and "Intermittent Explosive Disorder." The latter refers to "discrete episodes of loss of control of aggressive impulses resulting in serious assaultive acts or destruction of property."[55] DSM III-R also has diagnostic classifications for "Adjustment Disorders," which are pathological responses to major life changes such as divorce, losing one's job, going to school, or getting married. Included in this category is "Adjustment Disorder with Anxious Mood," which features the symptoms of "nervousness, worry, and jitteriness." The symptoms of "Adjustment Disorder with Mixed Emotional Features" include "a combination of depression and anxiety or other emotions." Someone suffering from this disorder might be an "adolescent who, after moving away from home and parental supervision, reacts with ambivalence, depression, anger, and signs of increased dependence."[56] A son's or daughter's initial departure from home has always involved some degree of anxiety, excitement, or apprehension. A period of adjustment and of getting one's bearings is fairly typical. What is new is the interpretation of one's emotional response to this often difficult transition as a disorder.

Among the so-called personality disorders in the DSMIII-R is "Narcissistic Personality Disorder," which refers to someone who has "a grandiose sense of self-importance"; "Avoidant Personality Disorder," which refers to someone who has a "pervasive pattern of social discomfort, fear of negative evaluation, and timidity"; and "Dependent Personality Disorder," which refers to a person with a "pattern of dependent and submissive behavior." [57]

Not long ago these behaviors were understood quite differently. Someone with Narcissistic Personality Disorder was known as someone who was overprideful or conceited, but not necessarily as someone with a pathology. An individual with Intermittent Explosive Disorder was someone who at best had a bad temper, at worst was considered violent. A person suffering from Avoidant Personality Disorder was a little shy. The victim of Dependent Personality Disorder could have been considered faithful or loyal. And the nervous bride with Adjustment Disorder with Anxious Mood, was said to have cold feet or was simply excited about her wedding. Again, it is not necessarily the behaviors that have changed but the cultural understandings of them.

Among other behaviors pathologically redefined by the DSM III-R is academic underachievement.[58] Perhaps the most popular DSM III-R disorder is "Attention Deficit Disorder" (ADD) or "Attention Deficit Hyperactivity Disorder" (ADHD), which refers to what used to be called hyperactivity or even rowdiness. It generally applies to children who have a hard time focusing on their work, although adults are also now included among those suffering from ADD. This disorder category even has its own self-help group network, Children and Adults with Attention Deficit Disorders (CHADD), which was founded in 1987.

CHADD now has more than twenty-eight thousand members in forty-eight states. Literature put out by some of its chapters list illustrious figures who may have suffered from ADD, including Winston Churchill, Benjamin Franklin, Socrates, and Isaac Newton.[59] "Experts" claim that as many as 3.5 million young Americans suffer from ADD, or up to 5 percent of Americans under eighteen years old. One account of the ADD phenomenon noted that "fifteen years ago, no one had ever heard of ADHD. Today it is the most common behavioral disorder in American children." [60] Again, what has changed is not just the behavior among children but the social definition of behaviors.

Just as physical illnesses often require pharmacological remedies, so, too, do many of these new behavioral pathologies. In addition to participating in self-help groups, many victims of ADD are prescribed the therapeutic drug Ritalin. Use of Ritalin has grown 390 percent in the last four years and has been prescribed for such ADD symptoms as "is easily distracted," "has difficulty following directions," "talks excessively," and "fidgets and squirms in their seats."[61]

The adult parallel to Ritalin is the psychotherapeutic drug Prozac. First introduced on the market in 1988 by the Eli Lilly pharmaceutical company, Prozac now boasts over $1.2 billion in annual sales. It is estimated that over six million Americans have used Prozac. Though officially listed as a remedy to depression, Prozac has also been prescribed for premenstrual syndrome (PMS), panic anxiety, fear of public speaking, gambling, eating disorders, and dysthymia (chronic discontent).[62] The most often reported success of this form of psychopharmacology is its ability to raise an individual's self-esteem.[63]

The increase in the number of individuals for whom Ritalin or Prozac have been prescribed is just one indication of the increasing percentage of Americans who are now considered to have some type of pathology. In addition to the 3.5 million sufferers of ADD, it is believed that anywhere from twenty to thirty million Americans are alcoholics and that more than eighty million Americans suffer from some type of codependent or coalcoholic disease. Moreover, more than thirty million Americans are said to have anorexia or bulimia. Add to this obesity and some eighty million Americans suffer from eating disorders. Additionally, many of the 30 percent of Americans who still smoke reportedly suffer from cigarette addiction, and as many as fifty million Americans suffer from depression or chronic anxiety.[64] The National Association on Sexual Addiction Problems estimates that nearly twenty-five million Americans suffer from sex addictions, and the National Council of Compulsive Gamblers claims that twenty million Americans are "addicted to games of chance."[65]

The 1977 President's Commission on Mental Health found that one-quarter of all Americans suffer from "severe" emotional distress and that thirty-two million Americans need psychiatric help. By another estimate, 20 percent of Americans claim to suffer from a diagnosable psychiatric disorder, costing society $20 billion annually. Add to this drug and alcohol addictions and the estimated cost is more than $185 billion a year.[66] It would seem that everyone has some disease or illness. Leaders in the codependency movement and other psychological enterprises appear to make just such a case. John Bradshaw, for example, insists that 96 percent of American families are dysfunctional in one way or another. "In modern parlance, we are all," as Martin Gross observes, "to some extent sick."[67]

The important point here is not that everyone is sick or that everyone understands himself or herself to be sick. Certainly, many would find these sweeping pathological reclassifications a bit excessive. What is important to recognize is that it is increasingly acceptable, on a cultural level, to understand oneself and to speak of oneself according to these categories. Such an understanding of the world is particularly appealing given the alienating, or to use Max Weber's apt phrase, disenchanting, conditions of a citizenry disengaged from the rationalized and impersonal world of politics, a condition that Elshtain refers to as a "politics of displacement." The therapeutically derived sickness view of the world provides a type of moral understanding or cultural explanation for this condition. As Elshtain explains, "Politics in our time is displaced and a therapeutic worldview, one which constitutes the subject as a client or a patient, as well or ill, as neurotically miserable or happily fulfilled, is part and parcel to a politics of displacement."[68] Within this cultural condition, then, the sickness, disease, and addiction concepts serve as increasingly acceptable symbolic reference points.

Appeals to these reference points are often subtle. Consider, for example, the way in which Americans offer pathological interpretations of a range of social behaviors. It is not uncommon to hear of someone who is obsessive-compulsive, is in denial, has repressed things from the past, suffers from low self-esteem, is acting out, has an inferiority complex, is going through a midlife crisis, or comes from a dysfunctional family. The pathological reinterpretation of human behavior has become an observable tendency within American society. Stanton Peele contends that "no other nation has taken the implications of disease theories of behavior as far as the United States or applied the disease model to as many new areas of behavior."[69]

The concern about whether one is happy and healthy now challenges in importance whether one is good or bad or even right or wrong. It is not just that behaviors have changed, though in some instances this may be the case; what has also changed is how behaviors are defined in American culture. How Americans view alcoholism and other behaviors is a reflection of our cultural values, of the reigning zeitgeist. We are, as Herbert Fingarette explains, victims of our beliefs just as those in the past were "victims of their beliefs."[70] To call Americans victims of their beliefs is particularly appropriate in the contemporary context, where the victim mind-set increasingly has become part of the way we understand ourselves and our relationships with others.

Victimization

The tendency for individuals and groups to understand themselves as victims of their abusive pasts or of the oppressive social environment that surrounds them appears to be on the rise.[71] The victimized mentality, of course, closely relates to the central place of the self and the growing cultural proclivity to interpret behavior in pathological terms. The self is not the perpetrator but the victim of a disorder. Implicit in the very definition of a disease is the belief that it is not the individual's fault but that someone or something else is to blame. As Stan Katz and Aimee Liu, authors of *The Codependency Conspiracy,* explain, "The diseased person is cast as a victim of the infectious agent, a person who is powerless over his or her disease and has no responsibility for its onset."[72] Just as a patient with acquired immune deficiency syndrome (AIDS) is a victim of human immunodeficiency virus (HIV), so, too, are those within the self-help culture victims of their codependent relationships: this is how leaders in the movement portray it. For example, Melody Beattie, author of *Codependent No More,* argues, "Alcoholism and other compulsive disorders turn everyone affected by the illness into victims."[73]

But if not the "victim," then who is to blame for whatever the "illness?" For the codependent, it is usually the alcoholic family member. Likewise, the alcoholic is a victim either of a biological predisposition, inherited from alcoholic parents, or of an abusive past. This victim predilection is, in a certain sense, the conflation of the various traits of the therapeutic culture with what Mary Ann Glendon has described as "rights talk." The sick self not only speaks with the language of emotions but blames someone else for infringing on his or her rights to health and happiness. One can be a victim in several respects. First, one can be a victim of one's disease, as discussed above. Second, one can be a victim of discrimination because of one's disease. And finally, one can be a victim of discrimination because of a number of other character traits, regardless of whether or not one is "sick."

In premodern moral orders, pain, suffering, and injury were viewed as a part of life. They were understood to contribute toward the refining process that helped the individual to surrender self and grow in virtuous character. A misfortune was viewed not as the fault of another but as the consequence of fate or divine allowance. This was the basic understanding of pain and suffering within classical and Judeo-Christian traditions. Marcus Aurelius, for example, in his *Meditations,* viewed as impious the "man who is afraid of pain," and it was because of Job's highly virtuous life that the God of ancient Judaism allowed him to suffer so greatly. Previous moral traditions provided interpretations for small inconveniences and for larger calamities: they were an expected part of the natural order of things. With the undermining of traditional cultural systems and the advance of science and technology, "society began to lose its belief in both the inevitability of suffering and the need for stoicism in the face of adversity." [74] Less evident today are what Weber described as the theodicies that provided cultural explanations for suffering and death.

With the devaluing of these older moral orders and the greater cultural emphasis on the self and on individual rights, Americans today are more inclined to blame someone or something else for whatever difficulties they face. Indeed, today many groups claim the status of victim, for any number of reasons. They are victims because of their race, gender, sexual orientation, physical or mental impairment, and so on. Even Evangelical Protestants, the ones some blame as the malefactors of their victimhood, have recently taken up the victim banner. Decrying "intolerance" and "religious bigotry," some politically active Evangelical Christians portray themselves as victims of the discriminating views of the media and the "cultural elite." [75]

This is not to say that most persons, on the level of individual consciousness, necessarily think of themselves in this way, though the cultural climate may encourage cognitive understandings of oneself to move in this direction. Again, the important point here is that the language of victimhood is increasingly visible in American culture, which makes appeals to it, in spite of one's cognitive disposition, more likely.

This might help explain why Senator Bob Packwood, after being accused of sexual harassment by more than a dozen former associates and employees, publicly committed himself for alcoholism treatment; why Washington, D.C., mayor Marion Barry, after being caught smoking crack cocaine in an FBI sting operation, claimed to be the victim of racist white federal agents and later turned himself in to a clinic for alcoholism treatment; why Richard Berendzen, former president of American University, after being caught making a number of obscene phone calls, blamed his behavior on his abusive childhood and checked himself in for psychiatric treatment; and why Michael Deaver, former aide to President Ronald Reagan, attempted to defend himself against perjury charges by arguing that "his memory had been clouded by alcoholism." [76]

The victim mentality has provided the basis whereby individuals have defended a number of interesting actions. In a Pennsylvania school district, a man was fired from his job for consistently arriving late to work. He sued his former employers, arguing that he was a victim of "chronic lateness syndrome" and thus had no control over his tardiness. [77] An American foreign service officer in Uruguay was dismissed after engaging in public sex acts with several local prostitutes. The officer claimed that his dismissal constituted discrimination toward his handicap of "acute alcohol addiction" and a "schizoid personality disorder." [78] Two Marine Corps officers claimed that they were the victims of discrimination when they were discharged for being, as they claimed, "chronically overweight." [79] In Orlando, Florida, a man was given a bad haircut, which led to a "panic-anxiety attack." The victimized patron sued his hairdresser for depriving him of his "right to enjoy life." [80] After twenty-six years of marriage, a man brutally beat and killed his wife. His defense was that he was the victim of husband abuse and of his culture (one that discouraged divorce). The jury agreed and convicted him of manslaughter rather than first-degree murder. [81]

Granted, these are extreme examples. But the fact that individuals can plausibly invoke the language of victimhood is indicative of its greater visibility and availability today than in the past. Thus, as Robert Hughes observes, "The all pervasive claim to victimhood tops off America's long-cherished culture of therapeutics." [82]

The Therapeutic Ethos

The therapeutic ethos—with the victim pathologies of the emotivist self interpreted for us by the priestly practitioners of the therapeutic vocations—offers itself as a replacement to traditional moral codes and symbols, worn out by the effects of modernization. In Bourdieuian terms, it is a form of "cultural capital" that has, in the contemporary cultural context, a high exchange rate. This is not to say that traditional ideological systems have no cultural value. But, given the apparent strength of the therapeutic impulse, it would seem that even those who align themselves with traditional cultural systems or who view with skepticism some of the sensational extremes of the therapeutic culture are sometimes compelled to exchange the symbols associated with the older moral orders for the stronger currency found in therapeutic ideals.

The therapeutic ethos is a system of meaning that is right for the times. As Peter Berger writes, "If Freud had not existed, he would have been invented."[83] Modernization and the various processes associated with it helped prepare the cultural soil for the germination and widespread fruition of therapeutic tendencies. A brief review of the major social processes commonly associated with modernization helps illustrate this point.

Consider, first, what social scientists refer to as "structural pluralism," or the historically unique societal arrangement of a defined bifurcation between the private life of domesticity and family and the public world of industry, work, and large-scale bureaucratic institutions.[84] Sociological accounts of this modern arrangement point not only to the significance of the physical distance between work and home but to the cultural distance between a highly rationalized, impersonal, and alienating public realm and a private world of religious practice, "brotherly love," family, sexuality, and identity—one effect of which is the privatization of traditional moral systems.

The therapeutic ethos provides an ostensible antidote to the tensions created by this arrangement. That is, it offers to reintegrate the disparate private and public spheres effected by the processes of modernization. As Berger observes, the therapeutic ethos occupies "an unusually strategic position in our society" in that it can "accompany the individual in both sectors of his dichotomized life."[85] The private therapist who counsels the individual on his failing marriage or sexual identity problems speaks the same basic language as the business consultant who gives seminars on conflict resolution and stress management within the work environment. It is a worldview that cuts across the public and private, offering the individual a unifying cosmology. The therapeutic ethic, as such, is uniquely constituted to relieve this dichotomized modern condition, or at least to make it less cognitively dissonant.

Another feature of modernization that undermined the plausibility of traditional codes of moral understanding and prepared the way for the therapeutic ethic is what social scientists refer to as "cultural pluralism," or the joining together of individuals and groups from a variety of cultures, bringing with them the various belief systems and customs represented within each.[86] As a consequence of massive immigration to America's growing urban areas, beginning in the early nineteenth century and continuing into the twentieth century, individuals and groups from a wide range of cultural backgrounds were brought into close proximity to one another. The coexistence of diverse cultural systems challenged the hegemony of the moral codes and symbols that had traditionally provided the boundaries for American cultural life and legitimated the early American state. Questions of what constituted the common good subsequently became increasingly problematic and, at times, issues of significant cultural discord, not just between various religious sects but between those with more progressive orientations and those with more traditional religious sensibilities.[87]

Again, the therapeutic code of moral understanding is uniquely suited to assuage the tensions of modern pluralism. It is both a derivative of the modern "scientific" discipline of psychology and quasi-religious in nature. With the cultural authority granted science through the process of modernity, it makes sense that a new cultural system would have to be rooted in some kind of scientific enterprise. Yet the language, organization, and personal nature of the therapeutic ethos are also reflective of religious sentiments, usefully absent their sometimes divisive and sectarian qualities. Thus this ethic transcends the modern chasm between science and religion and offers to those from culturally diverse faith and nonfaith communities a religion-like system of collective meaning.

Consider, finally, the modern process of rationalization. The increasingly rationalized and bureaucratic tenor of the state and other social institutions played an important role in devaluing the plausibility of older systems of collective meaning.[88] Rationalization, or the shift from substantive rationality to functional rationality, made irrational those elements of life that could not be subjected to empirical observation, uniformed criteria of utility, and routinized bureaucratic processes. Such an orientation, with its disregard for the mystical and magical dimensions of social life, eventually made less plausible the appropriation of traditional moral codes to justify societal institutions. Though the plausibility of belief has been challenged, the need to believe or to make meaningful sense of the world, as Weber and others contend, remains. Life in the machine is too harsh, but the once-dominant cultural systems, undermined as they have been by the processes of rationalization, cannot be resurrected as plausible remedies to this modern condition. The therapeutic model, however, with its unique synthesis of scientific and religion-like qualities, offers itself as the most suitable antidote to the difficulty of life in a highly mechanistic world.

Though sometimes portrayed as a reaction against utilitarian capitalism, the therapeutic cultural impulse does not directly challenge or threaten the utilitarian orientation of the capitalistic order. To the contrary, the therapeutic ethic appears to complement the utilitarian ethic. It offers to soften the harshness of life in the machine without removing the machine. In fact, it is often defended as a viable source of action because of its purported efficacy. Though these two dispositions seem intuitively disparate, they may actually be complementary.

Both orientations, for example, embody the perceived limitlessness with which those in the modern world approach life. The utilitarian perspective tells us that the natural world has no limits, that we can control it and re-create it. The therapeutic ethos tells us that our psyches have no limits, that, in the vernacular of Friedrich Nietzsche and Richard Rorty, we can re-create ourselves. Both the internal and external worlds are mutable and open to transformation. Thus, though seemingly antithetical, the therapeutic and utilitarian orientations may actually be different sides of the same coin. The therapeutic cultural system may actually be providing a capitalistic order and its commitment to technology a well-suited cultural complement.

Drawing on Daniel Bell's terms, the axial principle of the economy, "efficiency," neatly coexists with the axial principle of the culture, "self-realization." Embodied in this system, then, are the unlikely bedfellows of the therapeutic and utilitarian orientations. Philip Rieff alludes to this interesting harmonious coexistence when he argues that "psychological man, freed from all suspicions of divinity, can continue to work efficiently in all kinds of institutions, but without permitting his feelings to be entrapped by institutional service." [89] The therapeutic orientation provides a personalized remedy to a highly impersonal, rationalized, bureaucratic system, but without fundamentally altering the system.

Again borrowing from Bell's analytical framework, we recognize that the axial principles of the economy (efficiency) and of the culture (self-realization) do not exist in isolation from the axial principle of the polity, namely, "legitimacy." That is, historically, the state has drawn on the cultural symbols that prevail in a particular social context to legitimate itself to society. Given the dominance of the therapeutic ethos in American society, I anticipate finding elements of this cultural impulse in state efforts to legitimate itself in the late twentieth century. Before investigating this proposition through analyses of various arenas of state activity, I discuss in the next chapter, in greater detail, the theoretical concept of state legitimation. In addition to devising an analytical approach that takes seriously the important place of culture in the ongoing process of state legitimation, I also review those codes of moral understanding that legitimated the early American political order. Finally, I review in Chapter 2 empirical evidence that highlights the apparent gravity of the American state's legitimacy problem.

Having considered the theoretical concept of legitimation, I turn in Chapters 2–7 to an investigation of the extent to which the therapeutic cultural ethos has infused the modern American state, thus offering the state an alternative source of legitimation.

2

Legitimation of the State

Standing on the floor of the United States House of Representatives on March 21, 1995, Congressman Robert Clement expressed a concern many in America have come to share: a pronounced disquietude about the credibility of the American political order. "Mr. Chairman," Clement started, "I believe restoring America's trust in government is the single greatest challenge facing this Congress. The American people are perilously close to losing their faith in this institution and its members' ability to effectively govern." [1] Congressman Clement was echoing a theme touched on two years earlier by the first lady of the United States, Hillary Rodham Clinton, when she told a crowd in Austin, Texas, that "all of us face a crisis of meaning" and that "the signs of alienation and despair and hopelessness" can be seen "popping through the surface." We need a system, Clinton argued that "gets rid of micromanagement, the regulation and the bureaucracy, and substitutes instead human caring, concern, and love." This sentiment was similarly articulated in 1979 by President Jimmy Carter, when he spoke of the "general disrespect for government" and the "crisis of confidence" that "strikes at the very heart and soul and spirit of our national will."

All three of these public figures noted the distance and disillusionment Americans experience in relationship to the late twentieth-century American political order. The views expressed in all instances are indicative of what social scientists have described as the problem of state legitimation, which refers, in part, to the way in which the policies, practices, and behaviors of the state are somehow incongruous with the disposition of the culture. Be it a crisis, a problem, or a deficit of legitimation, what the literature generally depicts is a modern state that is failing to justify itself vis-à-vis the interests, orientation, and expectations of society.

Theoretical Considerations

In the social scientific literature it was Max Weber who first spoke of legitimacy in relationship to state authority, in his typological depiction of charismatic, traditional, and legal-rational forms of domination. Weber's conceptualization has provided the analytical framework for most analyses of state legitimation since and has generated no small measure of confusion regarding the concept.[2] As Weber is most commonly interpreted, societies have evolved from political orders based on charismatic and traditional types of legitimation to a modern state legitimated primarily on legal-rational grounds, where laws are accepted because of their having been established according to particular procedures.[3] As understood from this theoretical vantage point, the very process or "accustomed manner" by which a law is enacted engenders confidence in its legitimacy.[4] The law, as such, is self-legitimating. Jürgen Habermas, among others, takes issue with Weber (and Niklas Luhmann) on this point, questioning the viability of legal-rational authority detached from any form of moral or philosophical justification.[5] According to Habermas, legal-rationality cannot stand alone as an independent source of legitimacy: "A procedure can . . . legitimize only indirectly, through reference to authorities which, for their part, must be recognized."[6] Habermas believes Weber's assumption that legal-rationality stands as an "independent, morally neutral . . . legitimating force" has simply "not stood up" to historical verifiability.[7]

Though a number of scholars have persuasively questioned the viability of proceduralism absent the important role of moral justifications,[8] it is David Beetham who most clearly deciphers the confusing elements of Weber's ideas on legitimation and offers a revised typological framework that adequately stresses the symbolic or justificatory component of state legitimation. According to Beetham, Weber's three terms—*charismatic, traditional,* and *legal-rational*—actually represent components of legitimacy, rather than historically specific ideal types. He argues that throughout the history of political arrangements, legitimate power has been based on three features: *validity* (the way in which state actions are sanctioned by written laws), *justification* (the cultural symbols that justify these laws), and *consent* (the manner in which subordinates demonstrate their adherence to authority). Thus legal-rationality approximates just one component of legitimation, namely, what Beetham calls "validity." Without accompanying sources of justification, legitimation is not complete. As Beetham explains, "On its own, legal validity is insufficient to secure legitimacy, since the rules through which power is acquired and exercised themselves stand in need of justification."[9]

That this reformulation opens up the possibility for a uniquely cultural interpretation of political legitimation is evident in the way it so agreeably blends with the theoretical model of cultural analysis put forth by Peter Berger and Thomas Luckmann.[10] According to Berger and Luckmann, culture and social institutions exist in a dialectical relationship with each other. The collective values of culture are externalized, or poured out into the world (a component of the dialectical process that approximates Beetham's idea of justification). These externalized cultural sentiments are institutionalized or objectified into social structures (in this case, the state); or, in Beetham's terms, they are written into law, thus making valid corresponding state authority. Finally, the institutionalized laws and government policies act back on society. They are consented to (Beetham's phrase) or internalized (Berger and Luckmann's). And this, of course, is not a static process. The dialectical relationship continues as culture and, correspondingly, social institutions change and influence each other.[11] Figure 1 summarizes the cultural approach to the dialectical process between the state and culture put forth here.

As understood within this model, the symbols and moral codes that permeate a given culture invariably objectify themselves into society's

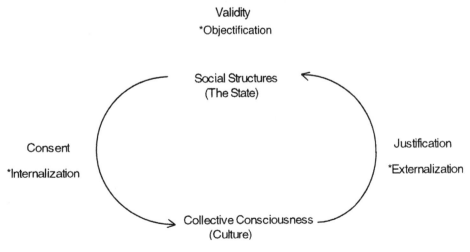

Validity
*Objectification

Social Structures
(The State)

Consent

*Internalization

Justification

*Externalization

Collective Consciousness
(Culture)

Fig. 1. State Legitimation

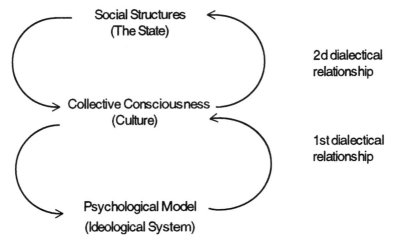

Fig. 2. The Two Dialectical Relationships of Legitimation

structures, including the state. However, the relationship between the state and the culture is just one of the dialectical processes that is occurring in the larger drama. Another dialectical relationship exists between culture, or the collective consciousness, and a "psychological model," which could also be called an ideological system.[12] Just as social structures shape and are shaped by the culture, the culture influences and is influenced by particular ideological systems or psychological models. These models, once created and adopted by the culture, are in turn institutionalized into social structures.

Understood in this way, Chapter 1 highlighted one dimension of the latter dialectical relationship, that is, the impact of a psychoanalytic ideological system on American culture. The next part of this chapter reviews the ideological systems of meaning that once more profoundly informed American culture. The primary concern of this book, however, is with the former dialectical relationship—the relationship between the state and the culture—which will be the focus of Chapters 3–7. Figure 2 illustrates the coterminous dialectical relationships.

If the literature on the modern state has neglected considerations of the substantive influence of culture on political legitimation, most cultural analyses have neglected systematic empirical investigations into the changing language of large-scale institutions such as the state. By merging the two theoretical paradigms this work aims to fill these gaps.[13]

When I speak of state legitimation, then, I conceive of it as necessarily containing a value or ideological component. Consistent with Beetham's reformulation of Weber's typology and in keeping with Berger and Luckmann's parallel understanding of the term, *legitimacy* here refers to *the cultural ideas and value systems that undergird the practical functions of the state*. Specifically, I focus on the sources of legitimacy that give moral and philosophical justification (or "normative dignity") to the laws, policies, and programs of a given state system.

Though Beetham's tripartite typology is useful for conceptual purposes, the distinction between "justification" and "validity" is not always so clear in the practical realities of the modern state. Oftentimes actual laws—particularly court rulings but even statutory language—contain within them justifications for the existence of the given law; the same applies to certain government programs. As such, the types cannot be easily separated. Often represented in a single legal document, policy statement, or program are both dimensions of Beetham's heuristic formula. As noted above, the major focus of this book is on the first part of the dialectical process: the externalization of cultural sentiments and their institutionalization into the legal and political processes of the state. In Beetham's terms, then, I focus on the justification and validity components of the legitimation formula, the changing laws and programs of the state and the "master symbols" that are invoked to justify them.[14]

It should be noted that the Beetham-inspired reconceptualization does not necessarily call into question the general movement that Weber identifies toward the increasingly instrumental shape of the social order generally and the political order specifically. Beetham himself concedes that

> the Weberian concept of "rational-legal" authority, or procedural correctness in the creation and application of legal rules, may effectively characterize the distinctive mode and temper of modern officialdom in contrast to traditional types of administration, but it cannot provide us with a sufficient criterion or account of political legitimacy in the modern world. For that we need some understanding of the principles and beliefs that give the rules their justification.[15]

The problem with the ideal typical evolution toward legal-rationality, then, is not whether it occurred but whether it signifies a transformation in types of political legitimacy. Even when legitimacy is conceived as it is by Beetham, it is not unrelated to the shift in the mode of administration that Weber identifies.

Thus, though Weber's evolution toward legal-rationality may not appropriately signify a shift in types of legitimacy, it and the concomitant processes of cultural and structural pluralism discussed in Chapter 1 are relevant to understanding how former legitimations have been undermined and how the cultural conditions were established for the emergence of distinctly new ideological impulses, such as the therapeutic ethos. Again, framing the analysis of state legitimation in this way allows the researcher to compare the different sources of legitimation that have historically been employed to justify the American state. Toward this end, I turn now to a brief consideration of the cultural systems of collective meaning that preceded the emergence of the therapeutic culture in American society.

Older Sources of Legitimation

If there is disagreement about the analytical substance of legitimacy in post-Weber considerations of the topic, there is general agreement that the state is in a current condition of crisis, or at least of "legitimation deficit." A legitimation deficit arises when older sources of justification have been undermined, that is, when the philosophical reasons for state authority have been made implausible.[16] Given this condition, the problem of legitimation remains and is, in fact, intensified.

According to Habermas, the modern state must—"like the pre-capitalist state—be legitimated, although it can no longer rely on residues of tradition that have been undermined and worn out during the development of capitalism."[17] What, specifically, were the sources of legitimation that justified the state prior to the rationalizing and secularizing influences of modernization?

In attempting to answer this question, I turn more to the political philosopher than to the sociologist to describe the substance of the political ideas (or the sources of legitimation) that once justified the American state. Sociological treatments of legitimacy seldom move beyond the realm of abstract theory and even less often delineate those sources of legitimation that have served to justify state laws and actions. Considerations of these ideological systems are presented not as an argument that early American participants in societal life were all Enlightenment philosophers, Christian believers, or classical republicans or as an attempt to critique their truth value but as an effort to unpack the substance of the philosophical ideas from which cultural symbols and codes were constructed and that, in turn, served as a basis for state legitimation. A brief overview of the forms of legitimation that have been "undermined and worn out" is necessary to set the stage for understanding why the therapeutic cultural ethos would arise as an alternative code of moral understanding in the last decades of twentieth-century America.

According to Hannah Arendt, throughout most of human history political arrangements were legitimated by external authorities or externally derived codes of moral understanding:

> Historically, we know of a variety of sources to which authoritarian rulers could appeal in order to justify their power: it could be the law of nature, or the commands of God, or the Platonic ideas, or ancient customs sanctified by tradition, or one great event in the past, such as the foundation of the body politic. In all these cases, legitimacy derives from something outside of the range of human deeds; it is either not man-made at all, like natural or divine law, or has at least not been made by those who happen to be in power.[18]

In the early American social arrangement, it appears that three ideological systems were drawn on to construct the moral boundaries of American cultural life. The cultural manifestations of these philosophical systems, in turn, provided the basis of legitimation for the various institutions of America's political order. Though there was considerable overlap among these forms of justification, one could argue, for the sake of analytical clarity, that the three sources—classical republicanism, Lockean liberalism, and Protestant Christianity—joined in a historically unique fusion to legitimate the nascent American state.

For years, historians and political philosophers have highlighted and sometimes debated those sources of legitimation that most profoundly influenced the American founding fathers and provided the philosophical foundation of legitimacy for America's political institutions. Taken in sum, this body of literature demonstrates both the salience of the three ideological systems in early American political thought and the complexity with which they joined together in legitimating the American state.

Louis Hartz and Daniel Boorstin, for example, asserted in the 1950s that Lockean liberalism was the greatest influence on early American political life.[19] In the 1960s, Gordon Wood and Bernard Bailyn instead focused on the variations of classical republicanism that contributed toward the philosophical foundation of the American state.[20] In the 1980s, Joyce Appleby and John Diggins criticized the republicanism argument and sought to reassert the central influence of liberalism.[21] However, both Diggins and Wood also contended that a particular Christian ethic had an important influence on early American political arrangements. A defense for the centrality of republicanism was reasserted in the 1980s by J. P. A. Pocock, who reiterated earlier arguments he had made on the subject.[22] More recent works, however, show that both republicanism and liberalism, in combination with Protestant Christian ethics, blended in a historically unique fashion to legitimate the early American state.[23]

Because the extent to which these various ideologies have historically legitimated the American state has been considered elsewhere,[24] only a brief overview of each is put forth here. Doing so provides the necessary background for understanding the novelty and significance of new forms of legitimation.

Civic Republicanism

Classical republicanism generally refers to the ideas of self-government (or direct participation in the common rule of society); a self-sacrificial commitment to the common good; and the individual cultivation of such civic virtues as dignity, fortitude, simplicity, restraint, temperance, frugality, honor, and independence. Classical republicanism has its roots in the philosophies of the ancient Greek and Roman Stoics. According to the early Greek Stoics, humans were to be guided by Reason, the divine Logos that ordered the cosmos and imposed on the individual the rigorous requirement of cultivating certain demanding virtues.

Later, in the Roman period, Stoicism, in addition to stressing an austere individual philosophy, placed emphasis on civic duty, social responsibility, and equality among all human beings and had an important impact on the Roman political arrangement. Recall, for example, the central republican ideals embodied in Plato's well-known cave simile, where the philosopher-king, having ventured from the darkness of the cave and been enlightened by discovery of "the good," is compelled by a sense of duty to return to the cave for the sake of the whole society.

The ruler returns not for the sake of personal benefit but out of a commitment to the common good. And he rules not because of a love for power—indeed, in Platonic political thought, only those who do not love power should get it—but out of a sense of civic duty. As such, the Roman ruler's authority rested not in his individual power but in an external source—the sky of ideas outside of the cave—which legitimated his authority. The good, in the Platonic sense, is not arbitrary or even historically contingent but an immutable standard of measurement, relevant to all ruling orders.

Another important feature of classical republicanism is the authoritative power of tradition. Romans strongly paid homage to the very foundation of the Roman civil order, evident, for example, in the mythological potency of the generative story of Romulus and Remus. Foundation, for the Romans, had a sacred quality that legitimated political leadership throughout the period. As Arendt holds, "At the heart of Roman politics, from the beginning of the republic until virtually the end of the imperial era, stands the conviction of the sacredness of foundation, in the sense that once something has been founded it remains binding for all future generations."[25] Thus, for the Romans, legitimation rested in the idea of the good revealed through reason and in the foundational authority of tradition.

Civic republicanism was revived in the Italian Renaissance by Machiavelli, then in the eighteenth century by Montesquieu and the American founding fathers. Machiavelli, like the Stoics, underscored the importance of sacrifice, honor, strength, and patriotism and saw the cultivation of such virtues as necessary to maintain the independence and liberty of a self-governing citizenry. However, he departed from the republican tradition that viewed harmony as essential to a civic order. Instead, he believed that conflicts and factions could strengthen a republic. He also held to, though transformed, the republican notion of tradition or foundation. Whereas, for the Romans, foundation rested in the past, Machiavelli seized on it as something that could legitimate the making of a new civil order. Thus the foundation of Roman tradition became for Machiavelli the foundation of modern revolution.

Arendt observes that the violence of the French and other European revolutions were characteristic of Machiavelli's understanding of revolution, while the American Revolution was qualitatively different. The political arrangement that followed the Declaration of Independence relied in large measure on the charters and state constitutions that were ratified prior to the Revolution. As such, there was some semblance of foundation that rested in the past, in the Roman sense, rather than in the "initiating of a whole new order of things" in the Machiavellian sense. Because of this distinction, and the fact that America was separated from the European development of the nation-state, Arendt believes the American founding fathers "remained closer to the original Roman spirit."[26] Also highlighting the early American kinship to Roman republicanism, James Kloppenberg observes, "Neither Montesquieu nor James Madison nor John Adams subscribed to a version of republican virtue that elevated the will to combat fortune above the individual's responsibility to adhere to the moral law."[27]

Thus classical republican ideals had a significant influence on American culture and provided the early governing order with an important source of legitimation. John Adams spoke of a "Republican Spirit among the People," and of the classical writers he stated, "They will convince any candid mind, that there is no good government but what is republican."[28] Edmund Pendleton accused Virginians during the 1776 convention of "treading upon the Republican ground of Greece and Rome."[29] And George Washington, seen by many as the prototype of classical republicanism, was sometimes compared to Lucius Quinctius Cincinnatus, the Roman patriot who, in 458 b.c., left his farm to lead Rome against the Aequi and Volscian invaders, only to return to his home sixteen days after securing victory to resign from his position as dictator. Washington's dutiful military leadership and resistance to personal political power were seen to resemble Cincinnatus's life. In 1776, Landon Carter lamented that more were not like Washington, who "was not so much in quest of praise and emolument" as he was "of real good to [his] fellow-creatures."[30] Thomas Jefferson and James Monroe, among other early American leaders, also paid great personal costs to dutifully serve the public good.[31]

Republican ideals clearly played an important part in the formulation and adoption of the U.S. Constitution. The Federalist James Madison, for example, argued in favor of the Constitution and the structure of representative democracy established within it during Virginia's 1788 ratifying convention but recognized that the formula would succeed only with the continuance of republican virtues among the citizenry:

> But I go on this great republican principle, that the people will have virtue and intelligence to select men of virtue and wisdom. Is there no virtue among us? If there be not, we are in a wretched situation. No theoretical checks—no form of government can render us secure. To suppose that any form of government will secure liberty for happiness without any virtue in the people, is a chimerical idea. If there be sufficient virtue and

intelligence in the community, it will be exercised in the selection of these men. So that we do not depend on their virtue, or put confidence in our rules, but in the people who are to choose them.[32]

Civic republicanism, however, was not the only ideological system that informed early American consciousness and legitimated the American Constitution. Lockean liberalism was another important philosophical source that informed the early American political order.

Lockean Liberalism

There is really little doubt that the Lockean ideas of individual natural rights, personal liberties, limited state, and philosophical naturalism were near center stage of America's political origins. Lockean liberalism justified government's role on the basis that, through a social contract, it protected the natural rights of free and equal individuals and that, if the government failed to ensure these rights, a revolution was justified (an understanding of government authority clearly evident in the Declaration of Independence).

However, it is a mistake to understand Locke's ideas of natural rights and liberties apart from his understanding of natural law, for as Kloppenberg asserts, "his concept of individual liberty dissolves if it is removed from the context of divinely established natural law."[33] Like Machiavelli and Montesquieu's republicanism, the legacy of Locke's natural law theory extends back as far as the Greek and Roman Stoics. According to the Stoics, providence provided a universal natural law that was immutable and everlasting. It corresponded with right reason and was applicable to all humans. As the Roman Stoic philosopher Cicero explains:

> There is in fact a true law—namely right reason—which is in accordance with nature, applies to all men and is unchangeable and eternal. By its commands it summons men to the performance of their duties; by its prohibitions it restrains men from doing wrong. Its commands and prohibitions always influence good men but are without effect upon the bad. To invalidate this law by human legislation is never morally right, nor is it permissible ever to restrict its operation, and to annul it wholly is impossible.[34]

In the Middle Ages, natural law was reconceived in Christian terms. From the patristics to Thomistic thought in the thirteenth century, ancient natural law theory became reinterpreted within a theological frame of reference. Transcendent truth became the ultimate source of natural law. As Adam Seligman explains, "The sources of natural law were no longer seen to be immanent in the workings of the world, but the subject of divine will."[35]

In the seventeenth century, Hugo Grotius, the founder of modern natural law theory, proposed a rationalized version of the principle that in a certain sense returned it to its pre-Christian origins. Though Grotius still made mention of God, the *divine* origins of natural law were a less central and more derivative feature of the principle.[36] And though Scottish enlightenment thinkers such as David Hume would extend this less theologically based understanding of natural law even further beyond its transcendent moorings, one still finds an interesting synthesis of natural rights with natural law in the work of John Locke. As Seligman explains, Locke's emphasis on individual rights and privileges was understood in the context of "a specific Christian, if not Calvinist, reading of man's relation with God."[37] According to Locke, human authority "must be conformable to the law of nature, i.e. to the will of God, of which that is a declaration, and the fundamental law of nature being the preservation of mankind, no human sanction can be good or valid against it."[38]

Given this understanding of Locke it is not surprising that some interpreters of America's philosophical origins would see Hobbes and the Scottish commonsense philosophers as the most important sources of liberal thought influencing the American founding fathers. Thomas Hobbes, along with David Hume, Francis Hutcheson, and Adam Smith, postulated a more materialist understanding of the natural order, arguing that, with the proper mechanisms in place, a good society would emerge from the actions of citizens motivated only by self-interest. Seligman, for example, believes that "it was very much on Humean—rather than solely Lockean—principles that the liberal individualism of the United States of America was to be based."[39] However, the more mainstream view is that the Scottish Enlightenment was a secondary influence to Lockean liberalism.[40] Even those who do argue for the greater influence of the Scottish commonsense philosophers agree that when this was joined with America's third major source of influence, Protestant Christianity, the result approximated a Lockean type of liberalism.

From either perspective—be it Locke's understanding of natural rights in conjunction with a transcendent understanding of natural law or a more secularized notion of individual rights juxtaposed against a pervasive Protestant ethos—the end result in early America was a situation in which individual liberties, rights, and privileges were given preeminence but were held in check by certain Nature-imposed notions of duty. Jefferson, for example, understood individualism in this sense. The self-interested individual, though free, was compelled by a sense of public duty that prevented him or her from oppressing another. Jefferson believed that Nature imbued the individual with a "moral instinct," an instinct that mitigated unfettered self-interest:

> Self-love, therefore, is no part of morality. . . . It is the sole antagonist of virtue, leading us constantly by our propensities to self-gratification in violation of our moral duties to others . . . nature hath implanted in our breasts a love of others, a sense of duty to them, a moral instinct, in short, which prompts us irresistibly to feel and to succor their distresses.[41]

Thus, though the Enlightenment ideals of individual natural rights, freedom, limited government, and equality informed early American understandings of the role of the state, they were joined with a concern for responsibility, public duty, and civic virtue among the citizenry. Emphasis on the latter part of this formula was evident even within some theories of natural law, particularly within Lockean understandings of the principle, but was also informed by the third source of legitimation, namely, Protestant Christianity.

The Early American Protestant Ethos

Peter Berger observes that religion has historically "been the most widespread and effective instrumentality of legitimation."[42] Indeed, Plato's emphasis on Reason replaced the varied Greek gods, which previously had given meaning to the social and political arrangements of Hellenistic culture. The Roman Empire was later legitimated by the Christian God during Constantine's fourth-century reign. In the medieval period, as is well known, a ruler's authority was his divine right; to oppose the king was to oppose God. Even at the outset of the modern era, as Ernst Cassirer observes, "the divine origin of the state was generally acknowledged,"[43] so much so that Machiavelli, though he offered a new political formula, did not challenge it in his political writings. Moreover, it was from state-endorsed religious establishments that the early American settlers fled in the sixteenth and seventeenth centuries. In short, as Robert Bellah and Phillip Hammond note, "through most of Western history some form of

Christianity has been the established religion and has provided 'religious legitimation' to the state." [44]

In early American life, Protestant Christianity provided an important source of political legitimation. Many of the colonies were nothing less than politically organized religious establishments. State laws required that officeholders be Christian believers—a practice that extended in some states even into the early decades of the nineteenth century. In the forming of the Union, however, the federal government did not establish a particular religious sect. Still, Protestant Christianity was an important cultural source of state legitimation. So pervasive was the influence of Christianity (along with civic republican ideals) that Samuel Adams could declare America a "Christian Sparta." [45]

But how could the authoritative structures of the Christian religion coexist with the seemingly antithetical impulses of Enlightenment-inspired individualism? In large measure, this was due to the particular breed of Christianity that was established on the eastern shores of the North American continent. The Calvinism of the early American Puritans emphasized a conspicuously more individualistic form of Christianity than existed in the Catholic, Anglican, and Orthodox establishments of Europe. The Puritan form of Reformation theology challenged the authority of the clerical priest with its contrasting emphasis on the priesthood of every believer. Moreover, it undermined the sacramental theology of the Eucharist as a means of grace, which again shifted understandings of what constituted religious faithfulness away from practices within the church to individual, personal piety. The additional features of an individualist soteriology and a redirected emphasis on the Scriptures (*sola scriptura*) over the authoritative traditions of the church further served to allow this breed of Christianity to coexist, though tenuously, with liberal individualism.

If the prevailing Protestant ethos of early America united with liberal ideals in its concern for the place of the individual, it joined with classical republicanism in its emphasis on virtue and civic responsibility. Commitments to personal piety and to the common good were seen as duties enjoined on the individual by God. As such, religion was understood as the necessary glue that allowed for the coexistence of liberalism and classical republicanism. The experiment was seen as possible only inasmuch as a Protestant worldview prevailed within the culture. John Adams, for example, observed in 1789, while he was vice president, "We have no government armed with power capable of contending with human passions unbridled by morality and religion. Our constitution was made only for a moral and religious people. It is wholly inadequate for the government of any other."[46] Similarly, in his farewell address as president, George Washington stated that "of all the suppositions and habits which lead to political prosperity Religion and morality are indispensable supports."[47]

Though Christianity informed the civic arrangement of early American political life, it did so without becoming the state-established religion in any formal way. Rather, it was seen to provide, on the cultural level, restraints to the possible excesses of liberal individualism. But this did not mean it had no impact on political life. As Alexis de Tocqueville notes in his early nineteenth-century observations of American political and cultural life, "From the beginning politics and religion contracted an alliance which has never been dissolved."[48] Not yet, anyway.

Again, it was an alliance that depended not on the formal institutionalization of Christianity as a state-sponsored religion but on the habits of the people. Tocqueville writes: "In the United States religion . . . directs the customs of the community, and, by regulating domestic life, it regulates the state."[49] Thus religion, though formally distinct from the federal state, had great political consequences. In short, it was held "to be indispensable to the maintenance of republican institutions."[50]

Revelation and Reason

The coexistence of the varying philosophical tendencies is evident in America's original political documents. Consider, for example, Jefferson's well-known reference to "the laws of nature and of nature's God" in the Declaration of Independence. Here, as elsewhere, he gives weight not only to the Lockean ideals of individual rights and liberties but to the religious sources that give these import. Consider, too, his words "We hold these truths to be self-evident, that all men are created equal, that they are endowed by their Creator with certain unalienable Rights, that among these are Life, Liberty and the pursuit of Happiness." The slight adjustment to the Lockean rights of life, liberty, and property is combined with an acknowledgment of a Creator who endows them with significance.

It is wrong to consider the early American nation-state a theocracy, although the individual colonial establishments prior to the Revolution might be characterized in this way. It is likewise wrong to consider the early understanding of a separation between church and state to mean that religion had no role in informing the establishment of America's political institutions. The cultural salience of Protestantism was viewed as an important ingredient of the larger political experiment. Likewise, it is as wrong to argue that Enlightenment liberalism was the only source that informed early American political philosophy as it is to claim that it played no role in legitimating the nascent American state.

Instead, what informed the establishment of America's governing institutions was a complex and unique conflation of three independent yet interrelated sources, one stemming from Jerusalem and two from Athens—what Seligman calls the twin pillars of revelation and reason. Together, according to Seligman, they "formed the basis of legitimacy upon which the civil republic rested and by which national identity was defined." [51] It was a "unique, fragile and historically contingent balance between them that infused the original notion of civil society with its overwhelming saliency, but which today can no longer provide the ground for contemporary arguments for civil society." [52] It cannot because each has largely been delegitimized as a plausible source of justification for state laws, policies, programs, and actions. The modern understanding of the separation between church and state, informed as it has been by Jefferson's problematic "wall of separation" metaphor, views religion as relevant only to the private sphere of life.[53] Moreover, ideas of duty and responsibility from the civic republican tradition have, as Mary Ann Glendon observes, largely been replaced with greater concern for individual liberties and rights.[54] And one need only consider the hostility with which the media and other cultural pacesetters ridiculed legal advocacy of natural law in the context of Clarence Thomas's Supreme Court confirmation hearings to realize the extent to which external bases of authority (even those partially derived from Enlightenment ideas) are increasingly viewed as obsolete. It should also be noted that the rapid expansion of the American state (a development that will be taken up in the next section of this chapter) represents a marked departure from the liberal notion of limited government.

Beetham argues that the rules of power will lack legitimacy when "changing circumstances have made existing justifications for the rules implausible." [55] This is what we see happening in the American situation. The salient sources of early American legitimation no longer inform the public consciousness as they once did. In Robert Bellah's words, the covenant has been broken. Undermined by the processes of modernization, the sources of legitimation that once informed the culture and justified the institutions of the American state are not available in the way in which they previously were. They have been, as John Schaar observes, "gravely weakened, leaving obedience a matter of lingering habit, of expediency or necessity, but not a matter of reason or principle, and of deepest sentiment and conviction." Schaar sees the United States in the vanguard of the movement toward a legitimation crisis, where all that remains are "the eroded forms of once authoritative institutions and ideas" and the "hollow winds of once compelling ideologies." [56]

State Expansion

While the older sources of legitimation have been undermined, the state has continued to expand—a development that, according to Habermas, further intensifies the legitimacy problem: "The expansion of state activity produces the side effect of a disproportionate increase in the need for legitimation." [57] The reason for this, according to Habermas, is that as the state advances into new realms of societal life, it takes over areas of culture that were once regulated and legitimated locally and informally—that were, in his words, "self-legitimated." By taking over these realms, state action cannot be solely mechanistic, though this is commonly a part of it. Additionally, certain values, principles, or systems of belief must give guidance to and justification for the state's expanded role. In other words, as the state enters into realms of society once left to local and private regulation, the purposes for acquiring this new authority must be justified. Why should the state be active here, toward what end, and based on what guiding philosophies?

It is well known that the American state has continued to expand—even, much to the chagrin of some fiscal conservatives, during the 1980s, when the rhetoric of the Reagan administration advocated a downsizing of the federal bureaucracy. [58] According to some economists and state theorists, government expansion is an inevitability. Thus, in spite of the well-meaning efforts of politicians to restrain growth, the very character of the modern state is to propel itself into an increasing number of dimensions of societal life. [59] Whatever the cause, this certainly is what has happened to the modern state generally and to the American political order in particular. One indicator of the government's continued expansion is the enormous growth in federal budget outlays, which have increased steadily—from $92 billion in 1960, to $196 billion in 1970, to $591 billion in 1980, to approximately $1.475 billion in 1993. Even adjusting for inflation, this represents a net growth in expenditures of well over 300 percent between 1960 and 1993. Total federal expenditures represented a substantial 23.9 percent of the gross domestic product (GDP) in 1993, up from 18.2 percent in 1960.[60]

Though growth in the number of federal civilian employees has been more moderate, it, too, has expanded over the years, from 2.4 million in 1960 to 3.1 million in 1991.[61] Add to this state and local government employees and the rate of growth is more pronounced.[62] The total number of government employees grew from 8.8 million in 1960 to 18.7 million in 1992. The greatest growth, however, has come not in increased government employment but in a variety of federal expenditures, ranging from aid to state and local governments for assistance in health care and other costs, to expensive defense procurements, to an enormous expansion in social welfare benefits. Annual national defense outlays, for example, increased from $53.5 billion in 1960 to $332.5 billion in 1992.[63] In 1984 the Department of Defense spent more in one hour than the whole government spent in 1800.[64] Beginning with Franklin Roosevelt's New Deal initiatives in the 1930s and continuing over the next fifty years, the federal government increased social welfare spending at exponential rates. (See Appendix 1 for measurements of government growth between 1960 and 1990.)

One of the most pronounced areas of growth is in health care. The cost of Medicare alone increased from $6 billion in 1970 to $133 billion in 1993.[65] The cost of federal food programs likewise grew, from $9 billion in 1980 to $21 billion in 1992.[66] Total federal budget outlays for Social Security increased from $30 billion in 1970 to $304 billion in 1993.[67] Given this kind of expansion, it is no surprise that revenues have not kept up with the pace of government growth. The federal debt, which exceeded $4 trillion in 1992, was about $0.9 trillion as late as 1980. Between 1980 and 1992 the debt increased over 400 percent, with an average growth rate of 13.2 percent each year.[68]

This growth has resulted in the federal bureaucracy's involvement in an increased number of areas of domestic life that once were left to the regulation of state, local, and private authorities. By some estimates, approximately half of all American families receive some form of payment from the Treasury Department.[69] Theodore Caplow observes that the growth of the state is the most important change that has occurred in the American political apparatus in the second half of this century. He argues that the American state has expanded into a wide range of areas previously left outside the auspices of federal authority, including "education, health care, workplace conditions, the regulation of sexuality, crime control, the preservation of historic structures, the encouragement of the arts, the care of the handicapped, the design of automobile engines, and scores of other new interventions." "In most instances," Caplow explains, "federal controls were superimposed on the existing state and local controls." [70]

The important point here is that with the expansion of the state, the problem of legitimacy is intensified. Areas that were formerly "self-legitimated" by cultural systems distinct from government regulation are now in need of legitimation for the very reason that the state has assumed a new regulatory role. In Habermas's words, the "boundaries" of the political system vis-à-vis the cultural system have been redefined. Because the state exercises authority over areas previously regulated by nonstate authorities, the political system's purposes and policies must be justified in ways that were previously not necessary. As such, the problem of legitimacy is made all the more acute.

Public Disenchantment

Given the delegitimation of former moral systems and the American state's continued expansion into more areas of societal life, it is not surprising that we would find growing public distrust and frustration with the American political system. The increasing apathy and frustration of the electorate is evidence of a decline in the third component of legitimation, namely, consent. Lack of participation and expressions of alienation are indicators of the state's failure to engender trust and confidence from the citizenry. With the state's continued expansion and the implausibility of older sources of legitimation, the ingredients are just right for a legitimation shortage, a condition that should manifest itself in lower levels of confidence in the various institutions of the modern state.

Accounts of public attitudes toward government reveal that the level of esteem with which Americans regard their political apparatus is noticeably on the decline. Daniel Yankelovich first reported in 1977 that "trust in government declined dramatically from almost 80% in the late

1950s to about 33% in 1976."[71] He also found that an increasing number of Americans feel alienated from the political process and that a large majority say they don't trust those in positions of leadership as much as they used to.[72] Other studies have found similar trends. Perhaps the most important work in this regard is S. M. Lipset and William Schneider's 1983 *The Confidence Gap*. Pointing to the nationally demoralizing events of the unpopular Vietnam War, the Watergate scandal, the Kennedy and King assassinations in the 1960s, and growing public frustration with high inflation and unemployment rates, Lipset and Schneider observe that trust in the government and belief in its efficacy steadily declined between 1960 and 1980. Though their findings are compelling, their work is more than fifteen years old. Below I consider data from a 1996 national survey conducted by the Gallup Organization and sponsored by the Post-Modernity Project at the University of Virginia, as well as longitudinal data from the American National Elections Survey and the Bureau of the Census, to analyze further the levels of participation and confidence in the operations of the American state.

One of the most important indicators of a problem with consent is the declining voter turnout rate in national elections. Between 1960 and 1988, voter participation rates steadily declined in each presidential election, with the single exception of a small 0.5 percent increase between 1980 and 1984. Overall, the percentage of the electorate voting in presidential elections declined from 62.5 percent in 1960 to 50.1 percent in 1988. Voter participation did increase in 1992, to 55.2 percent. This was the highest presidential-year participation rate in twenty years. Arguably, the increased participation was partially due to the unprecedented number of votes for a third-party candidate. Evidence we consider later in this chapter suggests that the nineteen million plus votes cast for Ross Perot were, for many, a protest vote against "politics as usual."[73] That the higher-than-normal rate in 1992 did not represent a new trend in increased voter participation was confirmed in the 1996 presidential election, where less than 49 percent of the voting age population cast ballots—the lowest voter participation level in more than seventy years.

Voter participation in off-presidential-year elections is even lower. In 1990, less than one-third of the voting age population cast votes for a candidate running for a seat in the House of Representatives, the lowest rate in thirty-five years. The level increased several percentage points in 1994, to just over 36 percent, but still remained significantly below the "peak" years of 1962 and 1966, when 45.5 percent of the voting age population cast votes in congressional elections. (See Appendix 2.) It should be noted further that 49 percent for a presidential year and 36 percent for an off-year congressional election are remarkably low percentages compared with voter participation in other democracies and speak to the growing frustration and alienation with which the electorate views America's political institutions.[74]

Such disillusionment is illustrated even more profoundly through an analysis of longitudinal data from the American National Elections Survey (NES). According to a number of indicators, public approval of the American government has steadily declined over the years. Consider, for example, measures of public trust in the government. In 1958 over 75 percent of the American population believed that government could be trusted to do what is right "most of the time" or "all of the time." By 1980 only 25.7 percent believed this to be the case. Levels of trust increased during the four years between 1980 and 1984, then declined again to 28.2 percent in 1990. (Tables illustrating this and other trends discussed below can be found in Appendix 3.)

Whether the catalyst it was the Iran-*contra* scandal, the savings and loan crisis, or the continuing escalation of the national debt, the public's initial enthusiasm with the Reagan revolution began to wane after 1984—and with it, confidence in the political institutions symbolized by Reagan's leadership. Declining public trust in government is also evident in the level of confidence (or lack thereof) in the intelligence and judgment of political leaders. In 1958, nearly 60 percent of Americans believed those running the government knew what they were doing. By 1980, confidence in political leaders, according to this measure, had declined to 35 percent.[75]

Decreased confidence in the judgment of government officials is no doubt due in part to the greater visibility, if not greater reality, of corruption among America's political leaders. Beginning with the Watergate scandal in the early 1970s, the corrupt deeds of political figures have become more public and appear to have increased dramatically. For example, the number of government officials indicted and convicted for corrupt acts rose from 43 in 1975 to 470 in 1985 and to 665 in 1990.[76] In 1989 the Speaker of the House, Jim Wright, was forced from office because of questionable financial dealings. Seven years later Wright's nemesis, Congressman Newt Gingrich, assumed the Speakership of the U.S. House of Representatives for a second term, only to face a reprimand and a $300,000 fine for ethical lapses. In the late 1980s, five senators from both parties (the so-called Keating five) were implicated for involvement in the savings and loan failure.[77] The House bank scandal, in which it was discovered that a large number of representatives were regularly reimbursed for overdrawn checks, also served to lower the public's esteem of Congress and prompted the early retirement of many members in 1992.

Such acts of public disfavor have certainly influenced the views of the electorate toward those who govern them. Consider a final measure of trust. In 1964, nearly three out of four Americans thought that "not many" or "hardly any" of the people running the government were crooked. By 1980, just over half of Americans believed the same. Again, between 1980 and 1984 this measure of trust increased, but by 1990 it had returned to its lowest level ever, with only 50 percent of Americans believing that not many government officials were crooked. Stated another way, nearly half of the American population believes that "quite a few" government officials are crooked.

With such low levels of trust in the government, it is not surprising that we would find Americans experiencing a growing sense of disconnect from their political institutions. Over the years, respondents to the NES were asked whether they thought the government was run by a few big interests, looking out for themselves, or for the benefit of all. In 1964, only 29 percent of respondents said that government "is pretty much run by a few big interests." Sixteen years later 70 percent of Americans believed this to be the case, and by 1992, three out of four Americans believed government is run by a few big interests—the highest level since the NES began asking the question.

Measurements of government responsiveness also indicate that public satisfaction with the country's political leadership is on the decline. In 1964, more than 43 percent of those surveyed said Congress paid attention "a good deal of the time" to those who elected them. By 1980, only 17 percent believed this to be true. Americans also increasingly believe that those whom they elect to Congress quickly lose touch with their constituency: in 1980 more than 75 percent believed this to be the case, compared to only 55 percent in 1964.

One final measure of responsiveness (what the NES describes as a measure of political efficacy) speaks to the alienation that the electorate experiences in relationship to their elected officials. Respondents were asked whether public officials care about what they think. Arguably, responses to this question indicate the distance between the values and beliefs held by the general public and those symbolized by political leaders. In 1960, only 26 percent of Americans thought public officials did not care what they thought. By 1990 this number had increased to 64.2 percent. With this question, as with others, the larger trend toward growing dissatisfaction slightly shifted direction in the early 1980s but then moved back to levels even higher than those reflecting the electoral disenchantment evident in the 1970s and before.

Results from the 1996 "In a State of Disunion" survey, sponsored by the Post-Modernity Project at the University of Virginia and conducted by the Gallup Organization, add further support to the trends found in the NES data. Here it was found that levels of public confidence in government in the United States are precipitously low. Sixty percent of respondents said they had little or no confidence in the government. Even more (64 percent) had little or no confidence that government officials tell the truth. When asked about particular branches and levels of government, the overwhelming majority of respondents claimed to have only "some" or "very little," rather than "a great deal" or "quite a lot," of confidence in the various government entities. Americans are least confident in the U.S. Congress, with three out of four responding that they have only some or very little confidence in the American legislative body. (See Appendix 4.)

Respondents were also overwhelmingly negative toward the government when presented with various specific assumptions about the political world. For example, 66 percent of Americans agreed or mostly agreed that though the system of government may be good, the people running it are incompetent. Sixty-three percent believed that the federal government controls too much of our daily lives. A full 78 percent agreed or mostly agreed that political leaders are more concerned with managing their images than with solving our nation's problems. Still more (79 percent) believed that politicians are more concerned with getting reelected than with doing what is right. Four out of five Americans agreed that political events today seem more like entertainment than something to be taken seriously. And so the story goes in a host of possible objections. The majority of Americans believe that elected officials don't care what they think, that the United States is run by a close network of special interests, and that most Americans don't have a say in what the government does.

Thus measurements of participation, trust, and perceived government responsiveness overwhelmingly reveal that America's confidence in its political order continues to decline. This evidence suggests that a deficit of legitimation is indeed acute, and that, in Beetham's terms, the consent dimension of legitimation is in a precarious condition.

The Therapeutic Alternative

Let me summarize what has been considered up to this point. An important and too often overlooked component of theories on state legitimation is a focus on the significant influence of the changing cultural codes of moral understanding that justify the laws, functions, and policies of the state. Recognizing that the state and culture exist in a dialectical relationship with each other, we considered the substance of the cultural codes that once undergirded and gave meaning to the state. In the American situation, the state was historically legitimated by a unique conflation of the generative moral models rooted in Athens and Jerusalem. With the undermining of these cultural systems by the processes of modernization, the door has opened for the introduction of alternative sources of state legitimation. The continued expansion of the state and the evident disillusionment of Americans with its governing institutions make all the more acute the need for legitimation. Because of the devaluation of former cultural codes of moral understanding and the rise of the therapeutic cultural system, the conditions are ripe for the infusion of the latter into the various programs and policies of the American state.

In short, I propose the following: the erosion of the older sources of state legitimation, along with the continued expansion of the state, make particularly poignant the problem of legitimation and particularly pregnant the need for a new source of legitimation. Because of the strength of the therapeutic consciousness in American culture, and because of the apparent need for alternative sources of state legitimation, I argue that we should find evidence of the therapeutic ethos beginning to institutionalize itself into the American state. In the next several chapters, then, I consider various aspects of the state (both historical and contemporary) with an eye for the cultural symbols and codes that justify its policies, actions, and programs.

3

Civil Case Law

Certain dimensions of civil case law offer an avenue for measuring the extent of the state's adoption of the therapeutic ethos. As discussed in Chapter 1, an important component of the therapeutic perspective is the emphasis on feelings, where individual subjectivity and emotivism have challenged the modern notions of scientific objectivity and rationalism. If emotivism, as one aspect of the therapeutic ethos, has replaced more rationalized and scientific understandings of "empirical" reality, and if the dialectic between cultural consciousness and societal structures is playing itself out as has been theoretically proposed, then evidence of emotivism should be finding its way into the court decisions of America's judicial system.

Personal Injury Law

Tort or personal injury law, an area of civil case law that expanded with the rapid development of the industrial revolution in the United States, presents itself as a viable means of considering the possibility of such an infusion. A tort can generally be defined as a wrongful act, injury, or damage for which a civil action can be brought. In addition to personal injury, tort law involves such acts as libel, slander, trespassing on private property, and defamation. Personal injury law, however, is clearly the most important in terms of the number of cases the courts have handled. As one legal scholar explains, "Personal injury cases, statistically speaking, are what tort law is all about."[1]

Prior to the onset of industrialism in the United States, personal injury law, as we know it today, essentially did not exist. "American tort law," as Lawrence Friedman explains, "to all intents and purposes, began in the 19th century."[2] Its relative absence prior to the growth of the railroad industry in particular is itself evidence of the dominance of prior sources of legitimation. The traditional sources of legitimation discussed in Chapter 2 provided the moral codes for understanding suffering or injuries, and these codes of understanding did not involve the perceived need to receive monetary compensation for an injury. During this period, as Friedman posits, "people were . . . more likely to ascribe calamities to fate, chance, [or] divine intervention."[3] Based upon this perspective, the victim of a negligently inflicted injury would not think to blame another party with the anticipation of receiving some form of monetary reward but would accept the difficulty as a part of his or her lot in life. Ultimately, providence or fate, rather than an individual or group, was responsible for allowing the damaging incident to occur. J. Rainer Twiford, writing for a journal advocating the advancement of the behavioral sciences in American law, laments this previous historical condition, where "explanations of emotional disturbance were dominated by religious and moralistic dogma."[4]

With the onset and growth of industrialism and its accompanying influences this all changed, and tort law began to grow. As Friedman argues, "Tort law was the bastard child of technology."[5] As industrialization expanded and along with it the influences of rationalization, the individual and cultural perspective on injury changed profoundly. The early development of personal injury law was emblematic of the advancement of instrumental rationality throughout society. Where once an injury was understood as fate, it became understood as a matter that was caused by another and that should be redressed by a measurable sum of money. In fact, the whole idea of "workmen's compensation," a program developed to insure against personal injury costs in the industrial environment, was originally based on the calculated perspective that within the productive capacities of a business, the costs of accidents could be predictably factored in as expenses that insurance would cover. Thus the very conception of injury or suffering was placed within a new framework of understanding. As James Willard Hurst explains, "matter-of-fact engineering of a social relation" replaced "moralistic judgments on it."[6] Or as Twiford puts it, "Scientific elucidations of behavior replaced mystical nomenclature."[7] As such, industrial rationalization served to redefine injury, making it a predictable business expense rather than a consequence of the will of the transcendent.

But through the second half of the nineteenth century, accidents only rarely led to legal claims; and even when they did, the plaintiff seldom received any compensation. It was still a legal culture of low liability.

"Most people got nothing or very little in the way of settlements."[8] In the twentieth century, this slowly changed as tort law began to expand, both with respect to the number of claims and to the amounts of compensation granted. Certainly, this itself is an interesting development that says much about the increasingly litigious nature of American society. But what is most interesting about the development of personal injury case law in the twentieth century is the nature of the claims with which the courts have been primarily concerned.

To document the development of personal injury case law during the twentieth century, I use what is called the Century and Decennial Digest System.[9] This legal data system contains documentation of all published federal and state case law from the seventeenth century to the present. Utilizing the system, a researcher can find abstracts of all published American decisions on a specific point of case law since the 1600s.[10]

In the Digest, in the general area of personal injury claims, is a section under the heading "Damages" that refers specifically to emotional or mental injuries ("Mental Suffering"). I counted the number of cases in this section for each time period, beginning with the first volume and continuing up to the present, and compared these with the number of cases in the categories of pecuniary (financial) loss and physical injury. Given my theoretical presuppositions, I expected to find a recent increase in the volume of cases that dealt with emotional damages. And this is precisely what I found.

A look at Table 3.1 reveals that the number of emotional injury cases[11] (the third bar on the scale) during each ten-year period remained fairly steady until around 1960. After this time, the number of court cases dealing with claims for emotional damages rose at an extraordinary rate. In fact, during the 238–year period between 1658 to 1896 (which is not represented in the table because it does not fit within the ten-year period increments of the other sets of volumes) only twenty-nine published cases fell under the heading "mental suffering." Contrast this with the five-year period between 1986 and 1991, where there were 1,058 published cases.

Consider, too, the difference between the number of emotional damage cases in the ten-year period between 1957 and 1966 (244) and the number of cases in the ten-year period between 1977 and 1986 (1,504), an increase of over 600 percent. What makes this development even more interesting is the comparison between emotional damage cases and the aggregate growth of Digest cases in the areas of pecuniary and

TABLE 3.1
Personal Injury Cases,
Decennial Digest (20th Century)

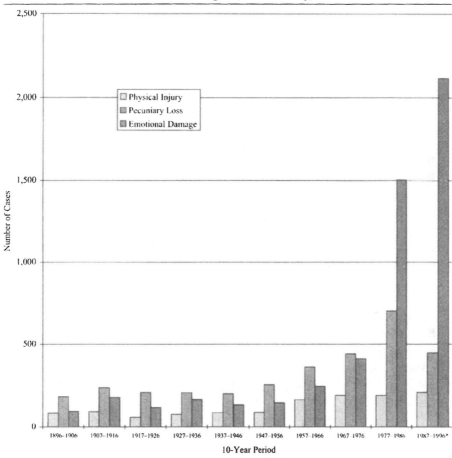

*The number of cases in this period (1987–1996) was estimated by doubling the number of cases published in the first five years of the period (1987–1991). This table indicates the number of published appellate opinions abstracted in the Digest under the specified headings for the various types of damages.

physical damages. As with emotional damages, the number of cases in these areas of tort law remain fairly steady for each ten-year period from 1896 until 1960. Similar to the emotional damages category, 1960 marks a noticeable upturn in the number of cases in each ten-year period (particularly with respect to pecuniary damages). By comparison, however, the number of cases listed in the area of emotional damages dwarfs the number of cases listed in these other two categories.

Another look at Table 3.1 shows, for example, that between 1976 and 1986, two and a half times as many cases were listed in the area of emotional damages as were listed in the area of pecuniary damages (1,504 as compared to 602). This increase is particularly noteworthy given the fact that until 1976 there were always more pecuniary than emotional damage cases. In fact, for every ten-year period between 1896 and 1976 there were, on average, seventy-five more cases dealing with pecuniary damages than there were cases dealing with emotional damages. Table 3.1 also shows that in the ten-year period between 1976 and 1986, eight times as many court cases listed in the Digest dealt with emotional damages as dealt with physical damages.

The recent difference in the volume of cases for each of these categories is even more pronounced when one looks at the number of cases for every five-year period since 1976. In 1976 the editors of the Decennial Digest began publishing its volumes every five years rather than every ten years, because of the growing number of published cases generally. Looking at Table 3.2 we see that between 1987 and 1991 (the most recent compilation of published cases) there were actually close to 5 times as many emotional as pecuniary damage cases, compared to 2.5 times as many between 1976 and 1986, and more than 10 times as many emotional as physical damage cases, compared to 8 times as many in the former time period. (See Table 3.1.)

Thus the expansion of emotional damages in recent years as compared to pecuniary and physical damages, reflected in the Digest, is even more pronounced when five-year rather than ten-year increments are considered.

Because the majority of cases in the Decennial Digest are appellate-level cases, evidence presented in Tables 3.1 and 3.2 may not be representative of legal activity in a more general sense. Arguably, the growth in the area of emotional damages, as represented in these data, is largely due to changes in the court standards used to determine the viability of emotional damage claims. As such, more cases show up at the appellate level because of greater uncertainty regarding the law rather than because of the total volume of emotional damage claims in the general caseload. Even if this were the only reason for the conspicuously larger number of emotional injury cases listed in the Digest, it would not undermine my thesis. The questions still remain: Why are the standards changing, and in what direction are they changing? Are they moving in a direction that is in keeping with the elevated status of emotions

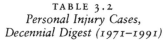

TABLE 3.2
Personal Injury Cases,
Decennial Digest (1971–1991)

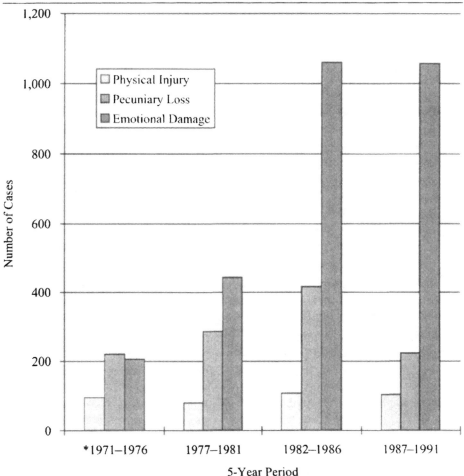

*The number of cases of this time period (1971–1976) was calculated by taking one-half the number of cases that were published between 1967 and 1976 for each category. Recall that after 1976, Digests were published every five years.

characteristic of the therapeutic culture? These questions will be taken up in turn.

But first, are these data really inconsistent with what is happening at the lower court level? Is the comparative aggregate growth in court concern with emotional damage issues reflected in Tables 3.1 and 3.2 simply attributable to court adjustments over legal standards (the important story this tells notwithstanding)? Trends at the trial court level seem to indicate that evolving standards are not the only factor effecting a greater caseload of emotional and mental distress claims at the appellate level; for here, too, we find an expansion in the volume of emotional damage claims that exceeds the growth of civil adjudication generally. Unfortunately, there is no data system with the same historical and geographical scope as the Decennial Digest for lower court cases. The systematic collection of trial court data is rather difficult, making analysis of trends at this level of American jurisprudence nearly prohibitive. The scarcity of trial court data represents a sizable gap in the general area of sociohistorical legal research.[12] However, the compilation of jury verdict reports in several jurisdictions is helpful in getting some sense of the nature of recent trends in personal injury case law at the trial court level. I consider here collections of jury verdict reports from California and New York.[13]

A compilation of California cases put out by Juris Verdictum Press, called *O'Brien's Evaluator,* comprises a majority of southern California trial court cases, as well as a smaller percentage of northern California cases.[14] It also includes some cases that were settled outside of court (that is, before a court verdict was reached). According to *O'Brien's Evaluator,* the total number of annual trial court cases in this region that involved some type of emotional, mental, or psychological damage claim rose during the fourteen-year period between 1981 and 1994. In 1981, only 27 of these types of cases were listed; by 1994, there were 280. More generally, between 1981 and 1983 fewer than eighty such cases were reported each year. Between 1984 and 1991 there were more than one hundred, and between 1992 and 1994 there were more than two hundred.

Analysis of a collection of New York jury verdict reports compiled by the Moran Publishing Company *The New York Jury Reporter* reveals a similar, though less dramatic, increase in the total number of emotional/psychological injury cases reported each year. Between 1981 and 1988, fewer than 100 such cases were reported each year (with the exception of 1985, when there were 107). Between 1989 and 1994 there were more than 100 cases reported each year. The total number of reported psychological/emotional injury cases, as revealed in this source of data, grew from 49 in 1981 to 145 in 1994 (the largest number of such cases reported in *The New York Jury Reporter*).

The increase in the number of such cases, as represented in Table 3.3,

TABLE 3.3
Psychological/Emotional Injury Cases,
New York and California (1981–1994)

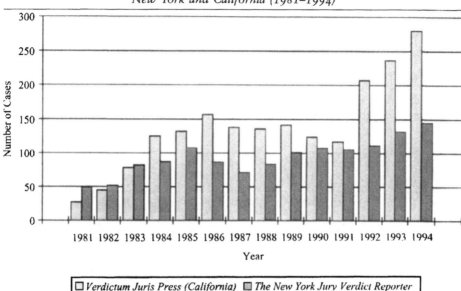

□ *Verdictum Juris Press (California)* ■ *The New York Jury Verdict Reporter*

SOURCES: Information based on *The New York Jury Verdict Reporter* for 1981–1994, compiled by the Moran Publishing Co., Islip, New York; and *O'Brien's Evaluator* for 1981–1994, Juris Verdictum Press, Claremont, California.

is more pronounced than the growth of personal injury cases generally. Table 3.4, below, shows the percentage of psychological/emotional injury cases relative to the total number of personal injury cases as reported by each data source. According to the collection of California cases compiled by Juris Verdictum Press, in 1981 only 4 percent of all cases involved some type of emotional distress or emotional injury claim. Between 1989 and 1990, this level grew to around 21 percent, then dropped to 17 percent for the years 1992 and 1993. The level rose again, 21 percent, in 1994. For every year during this time period, with the exception of 1981, the plaintiffs won the majority of these cases.

In New York, the percentage of emotional injury cases relative to the total number of personal injury cases in this data set also increased during this time period—from 5 percent in 1981 to 11 percent in 1993 and 1994. For each year during this period, New York plaintiffs won the majority of these cases—with the average being around 74 percent.

Comparisons between these developments and those evident at the

TABLE 3.4
Psychological/Emotional Injury Cases
as Percentage of Reported Personal Injury Cases,
New York and California (1981–1994)

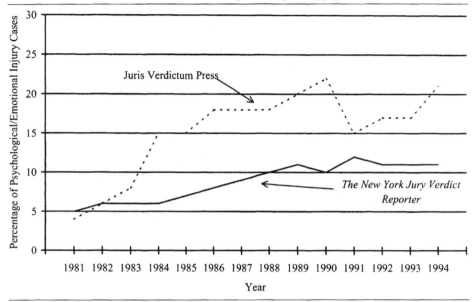

SOURCES: Information based on *The New York Jury Verdict Reporter* for 1981–1994, compiled by the Moran Publishing Co., Islip, New York; and *O'Brien's Evaluator* for 1981–1994, Juris Verdictum Press, Claremont, California.

appellate level are limited because of the varying time scales and the fact that the jury verdict reports go back only fifteen years, as opposed to over one hundred years in the case of appellate-cases. Therefore it is not possible to compare the aggregate growth of trial court cases to the more long-term development considered in the appellate cases above. Nonetheless, the growth in the fourteen-year period between 1981 and 1994 reveals that the number of emotional damage cases, relative to the total number of personal injury cases, is on the rise. Both at the trial court and the appellate level, cases with a central emotional or mental suffering component have generally increased. Both levels of civil adjudication, then, reveal increased legal activity around plaintiff concerns for emotional and mental well-being.

But what is the significance of these developments? What does it mean that more individuals are making claims based on how, in some manner, their feelings have been hurt or injured? That more legal activity would center on *mental, psychic,* or *emotional* (all terms used within legal scholarship to describe nontangible injuries) concerns makes perfect sense given the cultural context in which the claims are made and the court cases are decided—evidence that offers support to the proposition that the prevailing therapeutic ethos is objectifying itself into the state's legal apparatus. The courts are presently more inclined to recognize and give credence to the belief that emotions are central to one's personhood. If emotions are becoming the rubric through which individuals perceive life, then it makes sense that a historical consideration of *personal* injury would increasingly find emotions at the center of a person's self-identity. In such a context it is not surprising, then, that *personal* injury would increasingly mean *emotional* injury.

What has largely been considered thus far, though, is the volume of cases in each area. Evidence from New York and California reveals that a majority of recent trial court cases have gone in favor of the emotionally distressed plaintiff. With respect to the appellate-level cases, however, we have looked only at the number of cases, not at the outcomes. Yet it is at the appellate level that the doctrinal standards for determining the viability of emotional damage claims are set. Here the guiding parameters for trial court decisions are established. The questions are then: Have court standards changed at the same time that emotional injury cases have expanded? If so, in what direction have they changed? Have they evolved in a direction commensurate with the elevated status of emotions evident within the therapeutically oriented culture? To answer these questions, it is important to consider the substantive nature of the cases and the guidelines the courts have used for making these decisions.

The Doctrinal History of Emotional Damage Cases

Parasitic Tort

Through the first twenty-five years of this century, most courts did not allow recovery for emotional distress unless it was accompanied by some form of physical injury. If the mental or emotional distress was not concomitant with a physical injury (either as a consequence of it or as a precursor to it), no recovery for damages was granted. And even when a physical injury was present, there was still no guarantee that the emotional suffering would be recognized as compensable. In any respect, the vast majority of the early emotional damage cases were really only corollaries to some kind of physical injury.[15] For this reason, allowance of recovery for emotional distress was treated as a "parasitic tort."

The California court, for example, established emotional damages as a parasitic tort in its 1896 *Sloane v. Southern California Railroad Company* case. Here it was held that "mental suffering constitutes an aggravation of damages when it naturally ensues from the injury now complained of," but unattached to some physical injury, it held no right to relief.[16] The parasitic tort standard was also applied in a 1903 Illinois court ruling that rendered compensable the mental anguish a plaintiff suffered from being physically injured on a defective sidewalk.[17] And a 1910 Kentucky court ruled that a negligently injured employee was entitled to damages "fairly compensating him for mental suffering proximately resulting from the injury."[18]

But without some form of physical injury (and in many cases, even with it), the court would not consider emotional damages compensable. Consider, for example, a 1911 Iowa case where the court ruled against a plaintiff who, because of the negligence of a travel agent in promptly forwarding her steamship ticket, was forced to remain and labor at the port site until the ticket arrived several months later. The court refused compensation of resulting disappointment because the plaintiff suffered no physical injury.[19] Likewise, in an 1897 Massachusetts case, a plaintiff brought suit against a defendant who, after an altercation with her father, threw a rock through the plaintiff's window. The court ruled against compensating the plaintiff's subsequent fright and emotional distress because she was not physically struck or touched.[20]

The historical justifications offered by the courts for refusing recovery of emotional damages absent some form of physical injury tell much about the prior cultural resonance (or lack thereof) of the therapeutic ethos and of the conspicuously modern allegiance to notions of empirical measurability and verifiability. Relief was often denied based on the stated reasons that (1) allowing recovery would lead to a flood of litigation, including many fraudulent claims; (2) emotional distress was not significant enough to warrant independent legal protection; and (3) standards for measuring the extent or the monetary basis of such intangible injuries could not easily be determined.[21] Thus, within the modern worldview of the industrial era, the injury had to be somehow measurable, and the emotional dimension of the human personality was not viewed as substantial enough to merit legally imposed remuneration.

From this perspective, American courts frequently cited the dictum, offered by Lord Wensleydale in a nineteenth-century English case, that "mental pain or anxiety the law cannot value, and does not pretend to redress, when the unlawful act complained of causes that alone."[22]

The Impact Rule

Over time, however, state courts began to carve out exceptions to their general refusal to grant compensation for independently caused emotional damage. For example, some state courts made exceptions in cases of negligent mishandling of corpses and negligently transmitted false telegrams.[23] Another, more subtle exception developed within the legal concept of the "impact rule," which is essentially a derivative form of the physical injury requirement. According to this standard, an emotional damage was compensable only if some type of physical impact or contact transpired. This measure was used to determine the genuineness of the claim.

Though the impact rule was usually used to limit recovery in emotional damage claims, courts sometimes allowed very slight impacts to justify redressing emotional injuries. For example, recoveries have been made for emotional damages when the impact was only a slight blow,[24] an electric shock,[25] the jostling of occupants in an automobile,[26] dust in the eye,[27] or the passing of smoke through the nostrils.[28] In many cases, no matter how "slight, trifling, or trivial the contact," emotional damage claims could be made.[29] Bending the impact rule in this way, some state courts moved toward a position of greater empathy with the plight of emotionally affected victims, but they did so without really altering the standards of personal injury case law. This stretching of the letter of the law became rather absurd in some cases. Consider, for example, the Georgia court ruling that the evacuation of a horse's bowels into the lap of the plaintiff was an "impact" justifying recovery for emotional damages.[30]

These examples notwithstanding, the main theoretical purpose and practical application of the impact rule was to maintain a definable standard that limited emotional damage claims.

The Zone of Danger

Beginning in 1928, some state courts offered another exception whereby plaintiffs could recover for emotional damages. In *Palsgraf v.*

Long Island Railroad, a New York judge introduced what has come to be known as the "zone of risk" or "zone of danger" rule.[31] Under the zone-of-danger standard, a plaintiff could be compensated for a negligently inflicted emotional injury if he or she was in close proximity the site of an accident. For example, if a father was with a child in the street and the child was hit by a negligently driven automobile, the father could recover for emotional distress because he was in the "zone of danger." The defendant would be liable in this case because the father was within an area where he feared for his own physical well-being. Under this standard, however, if the father was watching the occurrence from a "safe" distance—say, through the window of his home—he could not recover for damages, because he was not in the "zone of danger."

Based on this standard, a mother who was not present at the scene of the accident where her ten-year-old son was struck by a motorcycle could not recover for the emotional shock she experienced on first seeing her son's injuries in the hospital several hours after the accident;[32] but a daughter who witnessed her mother's death while with her in an automobile accident could recover for emotional distress.[33] The 1980 *Vaillancourt* case illustrates the fine line between being within or outside the zone of danger. Here the court ruled that the mother whose baby died during delivery (allegedly because of medical malpractice) could recover for emotional distress because she was within the zone of danger and was "subject to reasonable fear for her own safety" at the time of the negligent act, but the father, who was also present, could not, because the negligence did not threaten his personal safety.[34]

For many courts, being in the zone of danger did not in itself justify recovery for emotional damage. It was often also required of the plaintiff that he or she evidence certain physical injuries as a consequence of the emotional trauma. This so-called physical manifestation requirement was also introduced as a means of limiting fraudulent claims. Based on this requirement, a plaintiff in a 1958 South Carolina case could recover for emotional distress following a car accident because the stress manifested itself physically in a "skin rash, weight loss and fevers,"[35] but a woman in a North Carolina case could not recover for the emotional distress that resulted from being negligently misinformed that she was pregnant with twins because she failed to allege physical manifestations of her distress.[36] Thus, for many courts, the zone-of-danger rule was qualified with the physical manifestation requirement.

The Zone of Emotional Distress Risk

Up until the late 1960s, federal and state courts relied on either the zone of danger or the impact rule as the outside boundary for determining the viability of emotional damage claims, with the more recent cases favoring the zone of danger over the impact rule. Thus the basic, albeit increasingly elastic, standard that some form of physical injury was necessary for the compensation of emotional damages was sustained. Judicial sympathy toward the emotional concerns of plaintiffs, however, began to accelerate in 1968, with the important California Supreme Court decision of *Dillon v. Legg*.[37] In this case, a mother witnessed her daughter being hit and killed by a car while walking in a crosswalk. A second daughter, who was not physically injured but who was also in the crosswalk, could, according to the zone-of-danger rule, recover for emotional distress. The mother, who was only a few more yards away on the sidewalk, could not, although she allegedly suffered emotional distress from having witnessed the accident.

The California court, even though it had adopted the zone-of-danger rule, just a few years earlier, decided to abandon it in order to justify compensation for the mother. Instead, the court relied on the concept of "foreseeability," or what has also been called the "bystander proximity" doctrine.[38] The court argued that determination of emotional injury cases should be based on whether the emotional distress was caused by a "foreseeable risk." And the standard for determining this, as proposed in *Dillon,* was to be based on:

1. whether the plaintiff was located near the accident in contrast to one who was a distance away from it;
2. whether the shock resulted from a direct emotional impact on the plaintiff from the sensory and contemporaneous observance of the accident, in contrast to learning of the accident from others after its occurrence; and
3. whether the plaintiff and the victim were closely related, in contrast to an absence of any relationship or the presence of only a distant relationship.[39]

Thus, whereas the zone-of-danger standard was based on whether or not one stood in an area where a physical injury could have occurred, *Dillon* established a zone where an *emotional* injury could have occurred. As one legal scholar notes, *Dillon* effectively created a "zone of emotional distress risk."[40] As such, the court granted greater credence to emotional claims allegedly caused by the negligent actions of another.

The California court's adoption of the foreseeability standard was seen within the legal world as a radical liberalization of personal injury case law and a significant step away from its longstanding refusal to view as compensatory emotional damage claims independent of some form of physical impact or injury. After *Dillon,* a number of legal scholars analyzed the importance of the new standard, the reaction of other state courts to it, and the likelihood that it would become the majority standard.[41]

Emotional Damages—An Independent Tort

Interestingly, just two years after *Dillon,* a Hawaii court extended the legal parameters for emotional damage claims still further and set the issue on a whole new level.[42] In *Rodriguez v. State,* the court took the final step by permitting a general negligence case of action for the infliction of emotional distress completely independent of any physical injury. In *Rodriguez,* the home of a resident in Hawaii was damaged by a flood. The plaintiff sued the state for the emotional distress that resulted from this property damage—damage that allegedly should have been prevented by the road maintenance of state employees. The court could have ruled in favor of compensating emotional damages as a "parasitic tort" to negligent injury to property but instead took the opportunity to establish the negligent infliction of an emotional damage as an independent cause. The court made reference to the precedented exceptions for the negligent handling of corpses and false telegrams as the basis for what it believed should be a general rule: that is, liability for negligent actions causing emotional distress independent of the need for some other tort.

Rodriguez invoked the foreseeability concept introduced in *Dillon,* but instead of basing it on the three stipulations cited in that case, it introduced the "reasonable person standard." This means that the court must consider whether "a reasonable man, normally constituted, would be unable to adequately cope with the mental stress engendered by the circumstances of the case."[43] According to this standard, it is up to a judge or a jury to determine who is a reasonable person and what circumstances this person should be able to endure adequately. Thus, with this case, the focus for determining the validity of an emotional damage claim was shifted to a conspicuously subjective level, leading some legal scholars to fear a situation where "courts may be faced with the impossible task of redressing all injuries that juries subjectively believe are compensable."[44] And, for the first time, a state court recognized as a general rule that plaintiffs could receive compensation for having been injured emotionally when no other tort violation was involved.

In 1980, the Supreme Court in California followed suit in *Molien v. Kaiser Foundation Hospital.*[45] In this case, a married woman was told by medical practitioners that she had contracted syphilis. It was later discovered that this was a false diagnosis. In the interim, however, the wife was subjected to further medical tests; the marriage was put in jeopardy because of the suspicion of extramarital affairs; and despite efforts to salvage the marriage (including counseling), the couple eventually filed for divorce. These emotionally disturbing activities all were alleged to have stemmed from the false diagnosis. The court found that, though there was no actual physical injury involved, the psychological injuries incurred through the couple's "loss of consortium" were grounds enough for an award for damages. In this case, the court held that "the unqualified requirement of physical injury was no longer justifiable." Like *Rodriguez, Molien* recognized the severity and credibility of psychological injury on the same level as physical injury.

Since 1980, California courts have set some restrictions on the scope of *Molien.*[46] Nevertheless, since *Rodriguez* fifteen other states (including California) have followed the trend of allowing emotional damage claims apart from physical injury, and a number of legal scholars believe it is just a matter of time before this becomes the majority position among all state and federal courts.[47] A number of other states either have come very close to accepting this position or have, for the time being, maintained the physical injury requirement, but only over strong dissents within court decisions. This occurred, for example, in a 1989 case in Georgia, one of the few states still employing the impact rule. The dissenting opinion expressed agreement with "the handful of courts that allow a cause of action to recover for serious emotional distress without regard to whether the plaintiff suffered any physical injury or physical illness."[48] Similarly, a dissent in a 1988 Rhode Island case argued that "the time has come to abandon the rule that denies all recovery for negligently inflicted emotional injury when that injury lacks any physical manifestation."[49]

Recovery of Emotional Damages in the New Legal Climate

As a result of these developments, a large variety of emotional damage claims have been ruled compensable by state and federal courts—decisions that would have been viewed as highly implausible even forty years earlier. For example, a family in Hawaii recovered $1,000 in compensation for the emotional distress incurred from the negligent death of their dog, Princess. Princess, a nine-year-old female boxer, died when the state negligently transferred her to a private veterinary hospital. On hearing the news, all family members "cried, except the father." The trial court "found that the entire family was preoccupied with Princess's death for two to three weeks after hearing the news, suffering serious emotional distress." [50] Explaining this distress in court, the plaintiffs offered testimony "relating to the background of their relationships with Princess, the role Princess played in their daily routine, and their respective feelings and the type of loss which each felt upon hearing the news of the dog's sudden death." [51] The court employed the "reasonable person" standard set forth in *Rodriguez* and drew on the following jury instructions, offered in a 1972 court decision, for determining the amount of compensation: "In making an award of damages for emotional distress and disappointment, you should determine an amount which your own experience and reason indicates would be sufficient in light of all of the evidence." [52] Thus the extent of the subjectively realized emotional injuries of a plaintiff are to be determined by the subjective perceptions of a judge or jury.

In a California case, property owners received $200,000 in compensation from Firestone Tire and Rubber Company to redress their "fear of cancer." [53] The fear allegedly stemmed from plaintiffs having consumed drinking water contaminated by toxic chemicals that a Firestone plant dumped in an adjacent landfill. What is interesting about this case is that there were no physical signs of injury from the property owners having ingested the water, nor was it certain that the plaintiffs would get cancer in the future. They were compensated because of their "fear that they will develop the disease . . . respondents fear cancer now. Their fear is certain, definite, and real." [54]

The reification of the subjective is also evident in a 1986 Alabama court case in which an automobile owner, after complaining about the repairs done on his car, was treated tersely by the mechanic. The court ruled that the owner was entitled to recover for the mental suffering that resulted from the mechanic's "rude and insulting language." [55] Recovery for emotional damages was also granted in a 1983 Michigan court case in which the court ruled that apartment tenants were entitled to damages for "emotional stress, embarrassment, and humiliation" that they suffered after being locked out of their apartments, when owners negligently changed the locks on the apartment doors and unintentionally failed to supply these tenants with new keys. [56]

A New York City woman recovered $315,000 in damages for emotional distress resulting from an unsuccessful abortion. Three weeks after visiting the abortion clinic, the woman gave birth to a stillborn fetus. The jury found the clinic negligent for failing to inform her that the abortion was unsuccessful. [57] In yet another case, a Minnesota court ruled that a passenger on a TWA flight could recover $50,000 for the emotional injury suffered when the commercial airliner dove thirty-four thousand feet in a tailspin before pilots recovered control of the plane. [58] Damages have also been awarded for emotional distress associated with "asbestophobia," [59] being trapped in an elevator, [60] and the negligent handling of a deceased poodle's funeral service. [61]

The above-cited cases do not, of course, represent decisions made only under the independent tort standard. Nonetheless, that some other tort, in addition to an emotional injury, is the ostensible basis for making a claim tells a very interesting, if not more profound, story. One discovers that in many of these cases, what is really at issue in court deliberations is the viability of the emotional injury claim over and above any other stated tort. A review of several trial court cases from the jury verdict reports helps illustrate this point.

In a 1992 medical malpractice case, a fifty-nine-year-old woman contested that years of Talwyn injections to relieve back pain had resulted in the hardening and atrophy of her upper buttock muscles. The defendant in this case conceded malpractice but contested the damages. The plaintiff's expert witness testified that her client "seemed unable to integrate the alteration to her appearance into her self image, causing the surgical corrections to become an emotional obstacle." She further testified that "it is reasonable for a person having a traumatic cosmetic disfigurement to have an emotional overlay." In this case the jury awarded the plaintiff $450,000 in damages, all for pain and suffering. [62] The substance of the plaintiff's arguments strongly suggests that what was at issue was her emotional response to her injury. In the body of the case, there is no reference made to actual physical suffering.

In another case, a woman was prescribed antidepressants by a psychiatrist to treat chronic headaches. The plaintiff in this case claimed that, over a period of two and one-half years, the drugs caused her behavior to deteriorate and to become "manic." During this time she lost her job, her husband, and her house. What is interesting about this case is the nature of the defense. The plaintiff didn't sue just for medical malpractice but for being betrayed by the psychiatrist and for the emotional injuries she incurred as a consequence of this betrayal. A psychiatrist and a psychologist, who based their diagnoses on standards outlined in the DSM III-R ("the foremost authority on mental disorders and diseases of the mind"), gave expert witness on behalf of the plaintiff. They argued that she "developed post-traumatic stress disorder as a result of feeling betrayed by [the defendant] because of his refusal to identify her manic behavior." They went on to explain why someone would be so traumatized by such a betrayal: "If someone feels betrayed and injured emotionally by the acts of another it is logical to assume that some form of emotional trauma will result." She was awarded over $8 million in damages, $3 million of which was for pain and suffering. In this case, again, the injury was "tangible" at face value, but as recorded in the jury verdict report, the defense was based largely on feelings of betrayal rather than on the physical consequences of a faulty drug prescription.[63]

A final example from a 1994 New York case illustrates the palatability of emotions over and above other types of torts. In this case the plaintiff sued his employer, Shell Oil Company, for giving him a negative employee evaluation. The plaintiff, who was openly homosexual, believed his employers suspected him of having AIDS and that he was discriminated against for this reason. Moreover, he contended that "the employee evaluation caused him emotional distress and that he resigned from the company because of the evaluation." Interestingly, the court found that the employee evaluation was "not slanderous or libelous" but that it "did cause plaintiff emotional distress." In other words, the court found that the evaluation was not based on discriminatory motives; therefore Shell Oil was not found liable for punitive damages, and the plaintiff was not awarded any money for past lost earnings. But because it was found that the plaintiff suffered emotional injury from the evaluation, he was awarded $45,250 in compensatory damages for his emotional harm and $10,000 and $5,000, respectively, in punitive damages against the two supervisors who made the evaluation. The only injuries compensated in this case were emotional, even when the contested cause for the emotional trauma did not hold up.[64]

To summarize, the state courts have moved from a situation where personal injuries were scarcely acknowledged in the judicial system, to a legal climate where tangible and measurable injuries (i.e., physical injury and pecuniary loss) received limited compensation, to a judicial focus where the courts have been willing to consider and compensate a large volume of personal injury claims, among which is the sizable and expanding category of emotional injuries. The evolution within the courts from the parasitic tort to the impact rule, the zone of danger, the zone of emotional risk (*Dillon*), and ultimately the independent tort standard illustrates the extent to which the courts have increasingly accepted the viability of emotional damage claims—and, more generally, how they have granted greater credence to the place of emotions in societal life. The majority of the states now abide by either the *Dillon* (zone of emotional risk) or the independent tort standard, with only a small minority still holding to the impact rule (See Table 3.5.)[65] It is important to recall that the twenty-eight states following either the *Dillon* or the independent tort standard have done so only since 1968. And as indi-

TABLE 3.5
Current State Court Standards for Awarding Emotional Damage Claims

Rule	Impact rule	Zone of danger	*Dillon*	Independent tort
States	Arkansas	Alaska	Arizona	Alabama
	District of Columbia	Colorado	Florida	California
		Delaware	Iowa	Connecticut
	Georgia	Idaho	Massachusetts	Hawaii
	Indiana	Kansas	Michigan	Illinois
	Kentucky	Maryland	Nevada	Louisiana
		Minnesota	New Hampshire	Maine
		Mississippi	New Mexico	Missouri
		New York	Pennsylvania	Montana
		North Dakota	Rhode Island	Nebraska
		Oklahoma	Wyoming	New Jersey
		South Carolina		North Carolina
		South Dakota		Ohio
		Tennessee		Oregon
		Utah		Texas
		Vermont		Washington
		Virginia		
		West Virginia		
		Wisconsin		
Total	5	19	11	16

cated earlier, legal scholars believe the movement within the courts is toward a majority acceptance of the independent tort standard.

The movement depicted here toward greater judicial recognition of the emotivist self is not limited to personal injury torts. Similar trends have also developed in the areas of defamation,[66] invasion of privacy,[67] and sexual harassment,[68] to name only a few. In the last of these, the U.S. Supreme Court adopted the reasonable person standard in the 1993 *Harris v. Forklift* case. In the majority opinion, Justice Sandra Day O'Connor argued that a sexual harassment case is valid "so long as the environment would reasonably be perceived, and is perceived, as hostile or abusive." Thus *Harris*, like *Rodriguez,* placed the determination of emotional harm on a clearly subjective level, leaving it to the juries to determine the reasonableness of the person vis-à-vis the environment and circumstances. The conclusion in *Harris* led Justice Antonin Scalia to note, although he voted with the unanimous majority, that the decision "lets virtually unguided juries decide whether sex-related conduct engaged in (or permitted by) an employer is egregious enough to warrant an award of damages." The general development in all of these areas of tort law leads one to conclude with Rodney Smolla that "courts are increasingly willing to recognize the legitimacy of protecting emotional and mental tranquillity from injury."[69]

Legal Recognition of Cultural Pressure

These emerging judicial trends within personal injury law and other torts are important steps in elevating emotions in the law to a level logically consistent with the kind of authority that they are granted within the culture more generally. And it is interesting to note that this legal trend is a fairly recent phenomenon. One learns from reading these cases that legal practitioners and scholars, though perhaps unfamiliar with the theoretical works of Philip Rieff, Peter Berger, Daniel Bell, and the like and perhaps disinclined to attribute legal changes to external social forces, sometimes seem cognizant of the pressure put on them by a therapeutically oriented culture.[70]

Twiford, for example, observes that "public attitudes toward emotional vulnerability and mental illness" are among the factors that "explain modern trends in court decisions."[71] More specifically, Smolla sees a parallel in the expansion of emotional injury claims and the growth of the "me-generation," the concern with "psychic well-being" and with "nurturing the inner self" in American culture.[72] And Stanley Ingber argues that these cultural features have had very real ramifications on jurisprudence. He believes that the "cultural focus on the need for 'inner peace' and the value of psychological therapy" results in a societal perception that psychic and emotional injuries are just as real as any other type. Subsequently, society demands that "the tort system should provide some method of redress to victims of such injuries."[73] These observations illustrate the extent to which, within the legal culture, there is some cognizance of culture's influence on the direction of trends in American tort law. Given America's cultural orientation and the pressure it places on legal structures, it is not surprising that court decisions would justify evolving standards in accordance with psychology's elevated status.

Indeed, the expansion of liability for emotional injury has often been justified, in various court decisions, based on "advances in the medical and mental health sciences."[74] Consider, for example, the assertion in *D'Ambra v. U.S.* that "today the psychiatric sciences have reached such a high degree of sophistication that the genuineness of a claim can be well explored prior to the end of a trial."[75] The court's recognition of psychology's growing cultural authority is also evident in *Taylor v. Baptist Medical Center*, where it was held that requiring some form of physical manifestation would be "adherence to procrustean principles which have little or no resemblance to medical realities."[76] In *Sinn v. Burd*, the court acknowledged just how far it has come on this matter: "It has been long assumed that medical science is unable to establish that the alleged psychic injuries in fact resulted from [an] accident. . . . Advancements in medical and psychiatric science throughout this century have discredited these hoary beliefs."[77] Likewise, in *James v. Lieb*, the Supreme Court of Nebraska stated that "while physical manifestation of the psychological injury may be highly persuasive, such proof is not necessary given the current state of medical science and advances in psychology."[78]

Given the court's increasing sympathy toward the emotionally injured victim and its growing deference to "advances" in psychology, it is not surprising that the personnel offering expert testimony in emotional injury cases are increasingly comprised of those who have been identified as the "new priests" of the therapeutic age, namely, the ever-expanding professional class of psychologists and psychiatrists. A study of Arizona trial court cases found that in 79 percent of the sample's emotional damage cases, the plaintiff called a psychologist and/or a psychiatrist to testify as an expert witness.[79] Likewise, in the collection of cases from the *New York Jury Verdict Reporter* considered here, 53 percent of all cases making some type of emotional damage claim employed one or more psychologists or psychiatrists to testify as expert witnesses. Interestingly, lawyers in plaintiff verdict cases were more likely to have called a psychologist or psychiatrist to give expert testimony (55 percent of such cases) than they were in the cases where the defense was victorious (47 percent of the cases). Also testifying in some recent personal injury cases are economists, who, along with psychologists, provide juries with "objective" criteria for determining the monetary value or "hedonic value" of loss of life enjoyment. The standards are arrived at through use of the DSM III-R and economic calculations.[80]

Given the growing presence of psychologists and psychiatrists in personal injury case law, it is worth investigating the extent to which the new "high priests" have been allowed by the courts to offer expert testimony more generally. How long have these cultural "carriers" been delivering the rationales of psychotherapy to the courts? When did the states confer upon psychologists the status they currently enjoy, particularly as it concerns their role in legal proceedings?

Psychologists as Expert Witnesses

For years the courts have allowed expert witnesses to testify in both criminal and civil cases. Those testifying have typically included physicians, surgeons, and even psychiatrists. The last of these were considered experts because of the legitimacy conferred upon them by a medical degree. Judicial acceptance of *psychologists* as expert witnesses, however, is a fairly recent phenomenon. Prior to the 1940s, no state court directly affirmed the admissibility of psychological expert testimony.[81] This changed in 1940, when a Michigan court allowed a psychologist to testify regarding the sanity of the defendant in a manslaughter case. Interestingly, the court justified the psychologist's testimony by citing those aspects of his expertise that approximated conventional medical practice; for example, it was argued that he knew "about the anatomy of the brain, having studied physiological psychology and neurology," and that he gave "diseases of the brain special study." Therefore it could not be held that "his ability to detect insanity was inferior to that of a medical man." [82] Acceptance of an expert psychologist in this case reveals both a deferential tipping of the hat to the older paradigm of scientific medicine and significant movement to the newer, therapeutic paradigm.

Four years later, a Minnesota court followed Michigan's lead. Unlike the Michigan case, where the expert held a Ph.D. in psychology, the expert witness in the Minnesota case held only a master's degree. He had, however, been employed as a psychologist for the state Bureau of Psychological Services for eight years. Since *Hawthorne* and *re Masters,* all other state courts have allowed psychologists to testify as expert witnesses. Table 3.6 indicates the decade in which each of the fifty states and the District of Columbia first admitted the expert testimony of psychologists.

The *American Law Reports* predicted correctly in 1961 (when only nine states admitted psychologists as expert witnesses) that the subject of the psychologist's role in criminal and civil case law "may be considered an embryo which will grow into a body of law." [83] Since that time the forty-two remaining states all have decided to allow psychologists to testify as expert witnesses. It is interesting that the "increasing tendency to call [the psychologist] as an expert witness" was anticipated in 1961. Even more interesting is that this expectation was understood to be related to the "growing . . . use of the psychologist in present society." [84]

TABLE 3.6
Decade When States First Admitted Psychologists as Expert Witnesses

1940s	1950s	1960s	1970s	1980s
Michigan	Connecticut	Missouri	Georgia	Arkansas
Minnesota	New Jersey	District of	Rhode Island	Maine
	New Mexico	Columbia	Pennsylvania	Montana
	New York	Virginia	Massachusetts	Nebraska
	Ohio	California	Indiana	Kansas
	Texas	Oklahoma	Colorado	Delaware
		Louisiana	Alaska	Nevada
		Florida	Arizona	New Hampshire
		Illinois	South Dakota	North Carolina
		Maryland	Tennessee	South Carolina
		Oregon	West Virginia	Alabama
			Kentucky	Idaho
			Mississippi	Vermont
				Wyoming
				North Dakota
				Hawaii
				Utah

Thus, as with the justification for expanding the scope of emotional damage claims, the admittance of the expert psychologist to the witness stand was facilitated by psychology's growing authority in society more generally.

Indeed, a reading of the court cases in which the psychologist first ascended to the status of expert reveals the extent to which America's therapeutically oriented culture has influenced the state courts. Here one sees the manner in which increasing authority has been conferred upon the practitioners of the therapeutic enterprise. For example, when an Oregon court first allowed a psychologist to testify as an expert witness, it did so based on the rationale that "clinical psychology has become established and recognized as a profession whose members possess special expertise." In this case, the court observed that the "courts . . . have lagged in recognizing the expertise of an evolving profession,"[85] a condition it sought to remedy by allowing the psychologist into the courtroom. With similar reasoning, an Illinois court first allowed the expert psychologist to occupy the witness stand because of the "increasing recognition of psychology's contributions to an understanding of human behavior."[86] And in 1959 a New Mexico court announced its enlistment with this embryonic legal movement in these terms: "We adopt the modern trend of authority in allowing a properly qualified psychologist to give his opinion as an expert."

The legitimacy of the psychologist can also be noted in the expansion of state licensing of psychologists. As with the establishment of the psychologist as an expert witness, state licensing of psychologists is a fairly recent phenomenon. In 1946, Connecticut was the first state to pass legislation for the licensing of psychologists; in 1977, Missouri became the fiftieth state to enact such legislation. (See Table 3.7.)

Often, state courts justified the admittance of psychologists as expert witnesses on the basis of the licensing statutes passed by their state legislature. Somehow licensing codes gave credence to the idea that the psychologist was a legitimate expert. As one legal scholar explains, "Legal definition and regulation seem to be a prerequisite to expert status in courts."[87] It is not surprising, then, that legislative adoption of licensing codes generally preceded the practice of allowing psychologists to testify as expert witnesses.

It is also evident that legal passage of licensing codes followed psychology's elevated status in society generally. This certainly is evident in Florida's law regulating psychology, which states, "The Legislature finds

TABLE 3.7
Decade When States Adopted Licensing Statutes for Psychologists

1940s	1950s	1960s	1970s
Connecticut	Georgia	Colorado	West Virginia
Montana	Minnesota	South Carolina	Massachusetts
Kentucky	Delaware	Alabama	Ohio
Michigan	Tennessee	Idaho	Pennsylvania
	Utah	Illinois	Iowa
	Arkansas	Nevada	Vermont
	Washington	New Mexico	South Dakota
	New York	Oregon	Virginia
	California	Louisiana	Missouri
	Florida	Arizona	
	Maryland	Oklahoma	
	New Hampshire	Wyoming	
		Mississippi	
		New Jersey	
		Alaska	
		Hawaii	
		Kansas	
		Maine	
		Nebraska	
		North Carolina	
		North Dakota	
		Indiana	
		Rhode Island	
		Texas	
		Wisconsin	

that as society becomes increasingly complex, *emotional survival is equal in importance to physical survival*" (emphasis added). Since psychology assists the public "primarily with emotional survival," then, "the practice of psychology" should be regulated by the state.[88] Also recognizing psychology's growing cultural status, Robert Schulman observed in 1965 that "psychology has become a specialty comparable to law or medicine." He expressed concern, however, that "statutory regulations have not followed and kept pace with this development."[89] At the time, only twenty-seven states had passed licensing statutes; but within another twelve years, all fifty states would have done so.

If one could depict such a development in linear terms, the historical evolution would look something like this: psychology's elevated status in society led to the adoption of state codes regulating the practice of psychology, which in turn led to the use of psychologists as expert witnesses in court proceedings. That such a development cannot be so neatly delineated is clear. Nonetheless, the process whereby states have adopted legal codes and invited psychologists to testify as expert witnesses is evidence of the state's recognition and embracing of the practitioners of the therapeutic culture. In other words, it offers support to the proposition that the tenets of a therapeutically oriented culture are becoming institutionalized into the legal processes of the modern American state.

Thus the elevation of the emotivist self, evident in the evolution of personal injury case law, has emerged at approximately the same time that the expert psychologist has found his or her way into the American courtroom. The purpose of documenting these historical developments is not to show a correlation between the two per se; that is, it is not being argued that personal injury case law evolved as it did because of the inclusion of psychologists in trial situations, though there may be some kind of relationship here. (Recall the high percentage of psychologists found among those testifying as expert witnesses in personal injury cases.) What these developments do illustrate is the extent to which aspects of the therapeutic culture have become institutionalized in American jurisprudence—a development that has proceeded even in spite of what, on the surface, appear to be countervailing cultural trends.

Litigation Reform: Therapeutic and Utilitarian Defenses

Consider, for example, initiatives by legislators in California and other states to limit compensation for emotional injuries in workers' compensation cases. Largely directed toward reducing fraud and combating costs to businesses, legislative reform efforts in the 1980s and early 1990s, among other things, made it more difficult for employees to recover for emotional distress on the job.

California state court standards for determining the viability of emotional distress in workers' compensation cases evolved historically in a manner similar to the one traced in this chapter: that is, psychological injuries have, over time, been taken more seriously by the courts, as have the *subjective* determinations of the injured.[90] This process culminated in the important 1982 *Albertson's Inc. v. WCAB (Bradley)* case, where the court ruled in favor of the psychologically distressed worker on the following grounds: "The proper focus of inquiry, then, is not on how much stress *should* be felt by an employee in his work environment, based on a 'normal' reaction to it, but how much stress *is* felt by an individual worker reacting uniquely to the work environment."[91]

As with the history of emotional damage cases generally, the quantity of workers' compensation stress-related cases grew as the court standards expanded. Between 1980 and 1988, the number of stress cases increased seven times. In 1987 alone, the California insurance industry paid out an estimated $176 million in settlements.[92]

In reaction to these developments, insurers and business employers joined together in the 1980s to lobby for reform of the workers' compensation system, and one of their primary targets was the so-called subjective nexus test set out in *Albertson's*. Though effective in limiting therapeutically based claims, reform efforts were more probusiness and proeconomic efficiency than they were antitherapeutic.[93] In fact, the passage of the 1989 and 1991 reform bills in the California legislature, though oriented toward objectifying the workers' compensation system, actually institutionalized an important instrument of the therapeutic community: namely, the DSM III-R. According to the California Labor Code, an injury was to be diagnosed "using the terminology and criteria of the American Psychiatric Association's *Diagnostic and Statistical Manual of Mental Disorders, Third Edition-Revised* or the terminology and diagnostic criteria of other psychiatric diagnostic manuals generally approved and accepted nationally by practitioners in the field of psychiatric medicine."[94] Thus, in their efforts to objectify the standards of workers' compensation mental stress cases, California lawmakers actually affirmed the legitimacy and expertise of therapeutic practitioners in determining the viability of an emotional injury. As with efforts to determine the objective "hedonic" value of loss of life pleasure, then, workers' compensation reform actually brought together the cultural inclinations of therapy and economics.

Tort Reform

Efforts to reconcile these two impulses within contemporary legal culture were also evident in recent congressional debates over reforming the civil litigation system. Consider, for example, the debate over tort reform in the first session of the 104th Congress. As part of the Republican "Contract with America" agenda three tort reform bills passed the House in March 1995. Respectively, they would limit punitive damage awards in product liability and other civil litigation cases; make it riskier for litigants to initiate lawsuits (in some instances forcing the losing party to pay its opponent's attorney fees); and make it harder for dissatisfied investors to sue companies (in so-called strike suits). Included in the first of these bills was a provision to limit awards for noneconomic damages (such as pain and suffering, loss of consortium, and emotional distress) in medical malpractice suits. It would seem that such legislative efforts offer a challenge to the kind of developments documented in this chapter, and in certain respects they do.

The only bill to pass through the Senate in May 1995, however, was a much-narrowed version of the product liability bill. The Senate bill placed a cap on punitive damage awards in product liability cases at two times the amount of compensatory damages (which would include economic and noneconomic losses) or $250,000, whichever was greater. In May 1995, the Clinton administration threatened to veto even this narrowed-down version of tort reform, fearing it would limit the rights of the victims to sue.

It is important to note that what largely fueled the debate over tort reform was not a question about the legitimacy of emotional injuries but rather concern over the expanding expenses businesses and corporations face in handling increasing litigation costs generally. Emotional damages were an issue only inasmuch as they, like other areas of tort law, were perceived to contribute toward rising legal expenses. Thus, economics were behind the political fight, not any a priori philosophical problems with the legal status of emotional injuries. As some commentators observed, "The political debate has largely been driven by financial interest." [95]

The final Senate bill placed no limitations on emotional or noneconomic injuries.[96] It limited awards only for punitive damages, that is, awards that penalized a company or business for producing a faulty (and potentially injurious) product. The criterion for determining the limits of punitive damages was based, in part, on the amount of noneconomic damages recovered, a standard that implicitly validates the latter. Interestingly, in the debate over the matter, Republican senator Slade Gorton, a sponsor of the bill that was ultimately approved by the Senate, argued in favor of the legislation by emphasizing the fact that it placed no limits on the victim's ability to recover compensatory awards but only on the amount of punitive awards the defendant would be required to pay: "Punitive damages, of course, are damages awarded to punish the defendant, rather than to compensate the victim either for the victim's economic or noneconomic emotional damages. As such, they are a troubling concept in our system of law." [97] What was troubling to Gorton, then, was punishing businesses above and beyond the compensation victims received for economic and noneconomic injuries.

Similarly, Republican congressman Henry Hyde, in his defense of the House version of the products liability bill, argued the following:

> Punitive damages are not designed to compensate for losses. They are designed to punish wrongdoers, not compensate victims. The provisions in H.R. 956 do not affect, in any way, a victim's full recovery of complete economic damages, such as medical costs and lost wages, or noneconomic damages, such as for pain and suffering and emotional distress. [98]

As with discussion about the Senate version of the bill, Congressman Hyde defended the House version on the particular grounds that it *did not* alter a plaintiff's ability to recover for emotional damages. Thus the one piece of legislation, among the various tort reform bills, that finally passed Congress was defended in part on the basis that it did not limit the types of claims discussed in this chapter.

Even the Senate amendment specifically aimed at capping noneconomic damage awards (which was ultimately voted down by the legislative body) was defended on the basis that it limited the monetary gain of lawyers, not plaintiffs. As Arizona senator Jon Kyl, the sponsor of the amendment, argued, "The loser will be the attorney who is trying to get the great jackpot here, the big bonanza, of earning something like $300,000 for one hour of work. That will be the loser, not the claimant, with this particular cap." [99] In fact, Kyl went so far as to argue that the claimant would actually "do as well or better" if the measure were approved. [100] Thus, even a measure aimed directly at limiting noneconomic damages was defended on the grounds that it would not affect the ability of an individual victim to recover for psychological or emotional injury. Once again, at issue in discussions over the Kyl amendment was not the legitimacy of noneconomic damages but the need to establish some measure for predicting expenses in this realm of civil law. As Senator Kyl explained, "No one can put a dollar amount on how much pain and suffering it is when someone is injured. What we are saying is there should be a predictable sum that at least represents the absolute top." [101]

Thus, without denying the viability of emotional injuries, members of Congress attempted to introduce some tangible measurements for determining costs, fusing once again the therapeutic with the utilitarian orientations. Whether complementary or in tension, these were the two languages to which legislators appealed. Proponents of tort reform, such as the California legislators who revamped the workers' compensation system, opposed certain excesses in civil jurisprudence (including the expansion of awards for emotional injury) not on philosophically driven disapproval of the validity of therapeutically legitimated complaints but on concern with the growing expense of litigation. No arguments were made for resurrecting previous cultural understandings of injury. In the end, the congressional tort reform efforts of 1995 offered only a very limited challenge to the expansion of the therapeutic impulse in America's legal system, a challenge rooted in economic interest rather than in any principled critique of the place of emotions in personal injury law. In other areas of the state, as we will see, similar efforts to reconcile the therapeutic and utilitarian impulses are also evident.

Whatever their relationship to the utilitarian ethic, it is apparent that the various qualities of the therapeutic ethos discussed in Chapter 1 have significantly infused themselves into the legal system. Today the court looks upon the emotivist self with greater empathy than it ever has in its history, and therapeutic practitioners, with unprecedented "expert" authority, provide the courts with psychologically inspired interpretations about human behavior, motives, criminal activity, and truthfulness. In both instances, legal changes were justified through appeals to the elevated status of psychology in society generally. In the next chapter, we will investigate the extent to which similar changes have occurred in another area of American jurisprudence, namely, in various dimensions of the criminal justice system.

4

Criminal Justice

In considering the infusion of the therapeutic ethos into America's criminal justice system, one is reminded of several highly publicized cases. In January 1994, Lorena Bobbitt was acquitted of maliciously wounding her husband because she was deemed temporarily insane by the jury. A host of psychologists and psychiatrists aided her defense in their arguments that she "suffered from a psychotic episode," from "depressive disorder, post traumatic stress syndrome and panic disorder," and that, "flooded by a wave of emotions" and under the influence of an "irresistible impulse," she struck out at the "instrument of torture" that had caused her anguish. Also at the beginning of 1994, the lawyers of Lyle and Eric Menendez, employing a similar defense strategy, were able to secure mistrials as a consequence of deadlocked juries. These sons of a wealthy Beverly Hills couple based their defenses on the argument that they were victims of "mental, sexual and emotional abuse" and were thus justifiably compelled to murder their parents.

In the Bobbitt and the Menendez trials, the defendants claimed the role of the victim, used the new high priests of the therapeutic age to interpret and decipher the gravity and complexity of their mental and emotional states, and publicly understood their situations in pathological rather than legal-rational terms. Indeed, Lorena Bobbitt's defense attorney proclaimed, after the verdict was announced, that "this is a giant step forward for Lorena in the healing process," instead of something like "We are all glad that the law was upheld and justice prevailed."

Recent therapeutic defense strategies have also been based on such pathologies as overindulgence in junk food (the so-called twinkie defense), too much television watching, alcoholism, PMS, and postpartum depression.[1] ADD, discussed in Chapter 1, has reportedly been used in some fifty-five criminal defenses.[2] The therapeutic influence on criminal law, however, is not limited to curious defense strategies and the unusual diseases that ostensibly justify criminal action. One might speculate that the arguments employed in these cases and the surprising verdicts appear as anomalies within the world of criminal law. Exploration into recent developments within the criminal justice system reveal, however, that the rationales advanced in these apparent aberrations actually persist on a wider and deeper, albeit less sensational, level.

Drugs and Crime

When one considers the various offenses that make up the sum of crimes committed in the United States, it is hard to get around the evident centrality of drug offenses. One reason drug crimes remain at the fore-front of societal consciousness is the media's persistent attention to drug-related violence in America's turbulent inner cities. Certainly, recent political declarations of a full-fledged "war on drugs" have also served to draw public attention to this area of criminal law.

Empirical evidence suggests that these political and journalistic preoc-cupations are not without foundation. The growing level of criminal and law enforcement activity surrounding illegal drugs indicates that an important avenue for broaching the field of criminal law more generally is through a consideration of the drug problem. This assessment makes clear that drug offenders occupy an ever-increasing percentage of arrests, court cases, and prison spaces. In 1992 there were over one million arrests for drug offenses in the United States, an increase of 7 percent from the 1991 level and 57 percent from the 1983 level.[3] Two-thirds of the 1992 drug arrests were for possessing drugs and one-third for selling and manufacturing illegal substances.

It is no surprise, then, that America's prisons and jails are increasingly filled with drug offenders. In 1989, close to one of every four jail inmates was serving time for a drug offense, up from one of ten in 1983.[4] Likewise, in 1991, 21.3 percent of the prison population in the United States were serving for drug-related offenses, an increase of 8.6 percent from 1986.[5] In New York State this level is even higher: according to Richard Girgenti, director of New York's Criminal Justice Services, al-most 50 percent of all prison commitments in the state of New York stemmed from convictions on drug offenses.[6] In the federal prison sys-tem, drug offenders make up an even higher percentage of the total

prison population. It has been reported that as many as 61 percent of
federal prison beds are occupied by drug offenders.[7]

The relationship between crime and drugs, however, is even more
widespread than these percentages indicate. Many inmates, though not
serving time for a specific drug offense, are in prison because of their
involvement in drugs. In a 1991 Justice Department study of twenty
participating cities, for example, more than half of the arrestees tested
positive for illegal substances.[8] Other studies have similarly found a high
correlation between criminal activity and frequent drug use. A 1989
survey conducted by the Bureau of Justice Statistics found that more
than 75 percent of jail inmates reported some drug use in their lifetime,
more than 40 percent reported having used drugs within the month prior
to committing their offense, and 27 percent reported being under the
influence of drugs at the time of their offense.[9] In this same survey it was
also found that 13 percent of the inmates had committed the offense for
which they were presently incarcerated in order to obtain money to
purchase drugs. This percentage was even higher among cocaine and
crack users, 39 percent of whom had committed their offense to get
money for drugs.[10]

Again, the strength of this relationship is more pronounced at certain
local levels. In Manhattan, for instance, 75 percent of those persons
arrested in 1990 tested positive for illicit drug use.[11] A 1989 National
Institute of Justice study found that in the cities of Los Angeles, New
York, Chicago, Philadelphia, and New Orleans, more than 60 percent of
all male arrestees tested positive for cocaine use alone. When other drugs
were included, the percentages were, of course, still higher.[12] According
to recent research conducted in the Miami area, it was "conservatively"
estimated that "80 percent of those booked on felony charges at the
Dade County Jail were under the influence of a drug other than alcohol
at the time of arrest."[13] A mid-1980s study of substance abusers in
Miami found that 573 drug users, in a period of only one year, committed an astounding "6,000 robberies and assaults, 6,700 burglaries, 900
auto thefts, 25,000 acts of shoplifting, and 46,000 other larcenies or
frauds."[14]

Looking at this phenomenon from the perspective of drug treatment
providers, one likewise finds a strong correlation between drug use and
other criminal activities. A number of studies have found that the majority of people in drug treatment have committed serious crimes. A na-

tional study conducted by the Drug Abuse Reporting Program (DARP), for example, found that 87 percent of those in drug treatment had previously been arrested and 71 percent had been in jail or prison before entering treatment.[15] Another study found that about 60 percent of those entering publicly funded residential treatment programs in the United States had committed one or more crimes for economic gain in the year before treatment.[16]

All this is to say that to consider the judicial and law enforcement response to drug crimes is to get at the very heart of criminal activity in the United States. The question relevant to this project is: Based on what perspective are officials approaching the drug problem? In other words, how are government and law enforcement officials dealing with drug crimes, and what legitimating philosophy are they invoking to guide and justify their efforts?

The Historical Antecedents to Therapeutic Justice

When President Bill Clinton announced his national drug strategy at a Maryland prison on February 9, 1994, he may have provided a clue to the shifting emphasis in approaching the drug problem. His plan to spend $13.2 billion was an increase of over $1 billion from the previous fiscal year's level. The vast majority of this increase was designated for "treatment." Eventually, $1 billion would be designated in the proposed budget exclusively for America's Drug Courts. Though this would have been the largest national expenditure on the so-called drug war in U.S. history, efforts to stop drugs at the border, an important part of the drug strategy during the Reagan and Bush years, were actually cut by $94 million. Instead of putting more resources into cutting the "supply" of drugs, the Clinton plan allocated money to cut the "demand" through such means as treatment and education. Though the treatment approach to the drug problem is not completely novel, history informs us that it is a relatively new development in America's criminal justice system.

Prior to the mid-1960s, there were only two public drug treatment facilities in the United States: one in Lexington, Kentucky, and one in Fort Worth, Texas. Both public service hospitals were built in the 1930s and, for the thirty-plus years thereafter, were the only institutions serving prisoners with histories of narcotics abuse. Thus, for the majority of

U.S. history, the criminal justice system and the providers of drug treatment existed independently of each other.[17]

The door was opened for greater collaboration between these two entities when, in 1962, the U.S. Supreme Court ruled in *Robinson v. California* that drug addiction was not in itself a crime and that a state could compel offenders to undergo drug treatment.[18] Four years later Congress passed the 1966 Treatment and Rehabilitation Act, which gave the courts statutory authority to commit drug offenders involuntarily to residential and outpatient treatment programs as an alternative to incarceration. With these changes, the stage was set for the conflation of criminal law and therapeutic drug treatment. A number of organizations and agencies sprang up to fill this opening.

Treatment Alternatives to Street Crime

The most important of these organizations is TASC—Treatment Alternatives to Street Crime.[19] TASC was formed out of a 1972 joint effort between the Law Enforcement Assistance Administration (LEAA); the Special Action Office for Drug Abuse Prevention (SAODAP); established by the Nixon White House; and the Division of Narcotic Addiction and Drug Abuse (DNADA)[20] of the National Institute on Mental Health. Recognizing the strong correlation between drug use and crime and believing the application of treatment modalities to be an effective means of stopping drug abuse, these groups joined together for the purpose of determining how they might "link treatment and the judicial process."[21] Subsequently, they commissioned the establishment of TASC.

The first TASC project opened in Wilmington, Delaware, in August 1972. Selected arrestees, charged with nonviolent offenses and who tested positive for narcotics use while awaiting trial in jail, were given the option of treatment "diversion." Those who volunteered for TASC were referred and escorted to a treatment program within the community. TASC followed, monitored, and reported back to the court on the "client's" progress. Successful completion of the treatment program usually resulted in dismissed charges.

Within the next year, thirteen TASC sites were initiated in eleven different states.[22] By 1978, the LEAA of the Department of Justice had funded seventy-three projects in more than twenty-four states. During this initial six year period, more than thirty thousand offenders were diverted to treatment through TASC, at a cost of over $35 million.[23] In 1982, when federal TASC funds expired, many TASC programs continued under state and local auspices. Before federal dollars were withdrawn in 1982, there were 130 TASC sites in thirty-nine states, and by August 1991, there were 178 programs in thirty-two states.[24] TASC remains the largest and most respected organization of its kind. Its purpose was and is to serve as a link between the traditional functions of criminal justice and the treatment community. Instead of incarceration, the courts can choose to put drug offenders in a diversion program. TASC serves as the neutral middleperson who will place a defendant in an appropriate drug treatment program, then monitor and report back to the court on his or her progress.

Such services offered to the drug offender take place in a "clinical" rather than a "correctional" setting. It is clear, in reading literature on TASC programs, that the TASC people are very conscious of the philosophical differences between a traditional adjudicative perspective and a treatment one. Consider the differing approaches, for which TASC purports to provide a bridge:

Justice System	*Treatment System*
Legal sanctions	Therapeutic relationship
Community safety	Changing individual behavior
Punishment	Reducing personal suffering[25]

TASC personnel recognize that these are fundamentally variant perspectives with potentially conflicting orientations. The nomenclature used within each system is indicative of the disparate frameworks employed for looking at the drug problem. Again, TASC sees itself as a bridge, joining together the divergent perspectives represented in the following terms:

Corrections Term	*Treatment Term*
Offender	Client/patient
Prison	Residence
Surveillance	Counseling
Sentence	Treatment phase
Criminal behavior	Disease
Completion of sentence	Recovery[26]

It goes without saying that the treatment orientation fully typifies the therapeutic perspective discussed in Chapter 1. Drug users are clients or patients instead of offenders; they have a disease rather than a disposition to commit crimes; they need to be treated rather than punished, and they must be helped toward recovery rather than serve a sentence. Their behavior is understood in pathological rather than legal-rational terms. Matthew Cassidy, associate executive director of TASC, perhaps puts it best:

> TASC provides an objective and effective *bridge* between two groups with differing philosophies: the justice system and community treatment providers. The justice system's legal sanctions reflect community concerns for public safety and punishment; whereas the treatment community recommends therapeutic intervention to change behavior and reduce the suffering associated with substance abuse and related problems.[27]

TASC seeks not necessarily to fuse the two orientations but to supplement traditional adjudication with treatment services. The whole idea of diversion means that the offender/client is diverted to a different track for a certain period, often in conjunction with parole, before reporting back to the courts. With TASC as the link, the courts themselves do not get involved in treating the drug user. The distinction between the once-separate entities of corrections and treatment, however, became less clearly delineated with the emergence of the Drug Court.

Courtroom Therapy

The Dade County Drug Court

The first Drug Court was initiated in Florida in 1989. It is probably no coincidence that it began in a state that had more TASC programs than any other state in the country. Though these are separate initiatives with no formal organizational ties, the Drug Court represents the natural next step in the process begun by TASC. Some Drug Courts, in fact, still use TASC as their treatment provider. The Drug Court, however, unlike TASC, actually fuses the entities of traditional adjudication and therapeutic drug treatment. That the Drug Court represents an important progression from TASC's more limited linking role was underscored by one TASC official's reaction to Washington, D.C.'s Drug Court. Susan Timber, with TASC in New York, observed the Washington Drug Court in action and was surprised by the judge's treatment-like approach to dealing with offenders. She expressed concern that "judges should do judging, we do treatment. . . . Let TASC do the treatment part."[28] Timber's protest notwithstanding, the Drug Courts do assume a more therapeutic approach to handling drug offenders, with judges assuming responsibility for what was once the sole responsibility of treatment providers.

The first Drug Court was started in Dade County's Eleventh Judicial Circuit (Miami), the eighth largest court in the country. It arose in response to Dade County's increasing number of drug arrests, its overcrowded jails, and the high recidivism rate of its already adjudicated drug offenders. The idea emerged after a one-year effort led by Florida associate chief judge Herbert M. Klein to coordinate a plan for relieving the overcrowding in the Dade County criminal justice system. Out of this effort Florida introduced a new type of court, one that brought the therapeutic perspective into the courtroom itself. Defendants assigned to this court enter into what looks like a group therapy session rather than a traditional criminal courtroom.[29]

Defendants eligible for the Drug Court are offered the choice of a court-monitored drug treatment program instead of incarceration. The diversion, which is expected to last twelve months, involves a three-phase program that includes acupuncture, regular urinalysis drug testing, individual and group therapy sessions, and regular trips back to the Drug Court, which is overseen by Judge Stanley Goldstein. Goldstein, a former Miami police officer and prosecutor, was hand-picked to run the Drug Court. Preparation for his role in this unique judicial setting required special drug treatment training. Goldstein is a colorful figure in the courtroom who speaks personally and candidly with those assigned to his purview.

The Dade County Drug Court has received national attention for its innovative and unconventional nature and because of the belief that it is less costly and more effective than traditional means for handling potential drug felons. CNN, PBS, several local television stations, and all three major television networks have run lead stories on the court. Scores of large newspapers have featured articles on the court including the *New York Times,* the *Washington Post,* and the *Los Angeles Times.* The court's notoriety intensified when Janet Reno, Florida's former state attorney and a strong supporter of the Drug Court, was appointed attorney general of the United States by President Bill Clinton in 1993. In the early part of 1994, the court also received public attention when Hugh Rodham, a public defender in the Drug Court and the brother of First Lady Hillary Rodham Clinton, ran for one of Florida's U.S. Senate seats.

In the beginning, the program only accepted first-time drug offenders. Today, however, arrestees are accepted regardless of how many times they have been charged with a drug offense. To be eligible, the arrestee must have been charged with either a possession or a purchasing offense. Ineligible are those who have been arrested for drug trafficking, who have a history of violent crimes, or who have more than two previous nondrug felony convictions.[30]

Treatment Phases

Once committed to treatment, the client goes to one of Dade County's drug treatment clinics and begins the process of moving through the program's three phases: detoxification, stabilization, and aftercare. In the first phase—which is expected to last two weeks but can last as long as six—the drug offender undergoes acupuncture treatment. Acupuncture ostensibly serves as a calming agent that reduces the craving for drugs and makes the drug offender more amenable to conventional forms of treatment. Acupuncture treatment is not a mandatory part of the overall treatment program, though it is estimated that about 85 percent of the clients elect to use it. This treatment modality was discovered when Dade County officials toured Lincoln Hospital, a drug treatment center in New York City. Dr. Michael Smith, director of the facility, had been treating drug patients with acupuncture for over ten years.

Also in phase 1 of the treatment program, the client is assigned to a primary counselor who is "a licensed addiction treatment professional."[31] The counselor tracks the daily urine specimens, submitted by the client and tested by the clinic, for traces of drug use. He or she also offers the client individual and group counseling and prepares a treatment plan tailored toward the offender's individual needs. To ascertain what these needs are, the counselor takes the client through what is called a "psychosocial assessment":

> Typically, the psychosocial assessment includes information about the client's history of substance abuse involvement and previous treatment; social, economic and family background; educational and vocation achievements; mental health problems; and arrests, convictions, and sentences (based on court records). If necessary, counselors can refer clients for psychological testing.[32]

Clients are allowed to move on to phase 2 only with Judge Goldstein's approval. Court rules require that the client attend all twelve of his or her scheduled counseling sessions and come up negative for drugs in seven consecutive urine tests. However, as with many aspects of the program, these are not hard and fast criteria. Goldstein has much flexibility to adjust the rules as he views appropriate for each case.

The emphasis in phase 2, stablilization, is on helping the client maintain his or her abstinence from drug use. In this phase of the program, the client attends individual and group counseling sessions. The client also participates in fellowship meetings like the twelve-step meetings of Alcoholics Anonymous and Narcotics Anonymous, either at the clinic or elsewhere in the community. The client continues to submit urine specimens for testing of drug use but does so less frequently. Some also continue to attend twice-weekly acupuncture sessions.

Phase 2 is supposed to last fourteen to sixteen weeks but may be as short as two months or as long as a year. If a client has difficulty staying off drugs, the Drug Court judge may transfer him or her back into phase 1. As in the first phase, the client in phase 2 periodically reports back to the Drug Court, usually once every thirty days. If the client has difficulty staying within the boundaries of the program, the judge may assign him or her to "motivational jail"—two weeks in the local jail, where 146 treatment beds are reserved for use by the Drug Court. Approximately 60 percent of the successful clients spend at least two weeks in the jail, which, incidentally, is more time than a first- or second-time drug offender going through the normal adjudication process typically spends in jail.

In the final phase, aftercare, the client reports to one of the Miami-Dade community colleges instead of the treatment clinic, where educational and vocational goals are pursued. The purpose of this stage is to help clients make a transition back into the community as productive citizens. Clients are given help in attaining job training skills, preparing for passing a General Education Development (GED) test, applying for financial aid, and so on. Many enroll in regular classes offered at the community college. During this phase, clients still return to court every thirty to sixty days and undergo urinalysis monitoring. Many clients continue to attend fellowship meetings, while some, particularly those who have relapsed into drug use, participate in formal individual counseling. Phase 3 is expected to last thirty-six weeks, which would make the planned time period for the entire program about twelve months.

Clients who successfully complete the program have their arrest record sealed.

The Drug Court Movement

Since Dade County started its Drug Court, in 1989, more than six thousand suspected felons have entered the program. Officials from foreign and American court systems routinely visit the Drug Court. In December 1993, more than four hundred judges, directors of treatment programs, and other law enforcement officials from around the country attended a national Drug Court conference in Miami. The conference was held "because," as one Drug Court reports, "there has been widespread interest in the program as a major meaningful addition to the arsenal in the war on drugs."[33]

More than one hundred other courts in the United States have either begun special Drug Courts, similar in some respect to the Dade County model, or are in the process of creating them. At the end of 1992, only nine Drug Courts were in place in the United States. (See Table 4.1.) Most of these courts sent envoys to Florida to watch and study the Dade County Drug Court. Since 1992, the number of Drug Courts has grown. Beyond those listed in Table 4.1, other cities have implemented Drug Courts, including Boston, Denver, San Francisco, Atlanta, Seattle, and Tacoma, Washington. Still other counties are in the planning stages for or in the process of starting Drug Courts. (See Table 4.2.)

Those counties implementing such programs have employed the same innovative features as the Dade County model: acupuncture, diversion, intensive counseling, the possibility of dismissed charges, urinalysis testing, court monitoring of treatment clients, and redefined roles in the courtroom. Dade County and other courts have recently expanded or considered expanding the model to nondrug charges as well, such as domestic violence, burglary, and prostitution cases.[34] Los Angeles judge Steven Marcus, for one, is enthusiastic about this development. He believes that violators should be offered the option of treatment for a number of small crimes, including "prostitution, bad check writing, and some drug sales cases." According to Judge Marcus, offenders "should be offered treatment instead of incarceration—in the same way Drug Courts offer it to drug addicts"—because their violations stem from what he believes to be the same root problem, namely, "low self-esteem."[35]

TABLE 4.1
Locations and Starting Dates of Drug Courts in the United States
(in existence for at least one year as of July 1995)

Date started	Location	Judge
1989	Dade County, Florida	Judge Stanley Goldstein
1991	Berrien County, Michigan	Judge Ronald Taylor
1991	Broward County, Florida	Judge Robert J. Fogan
1991	Multnomah County, Oregon	Judge Harl H. Haas
1991	Oakland, California	Judge Jeffrey Tauber
1992	Clark County, Nevada	Judge Jack Lehman
1992	Kalamazoo, Michigan	Judge William Schma
1992	Maricopa County, Arizona	Judge Susan Bolton
1992	Mobile, Alabama	Judge Kitrell Broxton
1993	Beaumont, Texas	Hon. Walter Sekaly, Magistrate
1993	Kansas City, Missouri	Judge Donald L. Mason
1993	Pensacola, Florida	Judge John Parnham
1993	Travis County, Texas	Judge Joel Bennett
1993	Washington, D.C.	Judge Bruce Beaudin
1993	Bakersfield, California	Judge Frank Hoover
1993	Cook County, Illinois	Judge Michael Getty
1994	Eugene, Oregon	Judge Gregory Foote
1994	Baltimore, Maryland	Judge Joseph H. H. Kaplan
1994	Tallahassee, Florida	Judge Philip Padovano
1994	Okaloosa County, Florida	Judge John Parnham
1994	Escambia County, Florida	Judge Keith Brace
1994	Wilmington, Delaware	Judge Richard Gebelein
1994	Little Rock, Arkansas	Judge Jack Lessenbery
1994	Los Angeles, California	Judge Steven Marcus
1994	Tampa, Florida	Judge Donald Evans
1994	Key West, Florida	Judge Richard Fowler
1994	Louisville, Kentucky	Judge Henry Weber

Though all the Drug Courts approximate the Dade County model in some way and share the same general philosophy, format, and goals, they vary according to a number of factors, for example, funding levels, community support, cooperation from the state's district attorney's office, the age of the program, and so on. Some, like Dade County, are preadjudicative—that is, defendants are diverted to the program before making a plea. Others, such as the Broward County, Florida, court, may be postadjudicative, in which defendants must plea guilty before entering the program.[36] Others, such as the Oakland, California, and Maricopa County, Arizona, courts, are based on a point system in which various degrees of compliance are rewarded with reductions in parole terms and/ or court fines. Some courts offer treatment in conjunction with parole, whereas others view the treatment program as an alternative to parole. Some Drug Courts provide in-house treatment for clients, while others contract with a local clinic to provide the treatment part of the program. Some still use TASC for diverting clients but maintain greater judicial oversight throughout the treatment process.

Eligibility criteria also vary among the courts. Some, such as Broward County, accept only first-time drug offenders. Other courts, such as the Portland, Oregon, Drug Court, accept drug offenders with any length of conviction history. Dade County has expanded its eligibility criteria from only first-time drug offenders to drug offenders with any number of prior drug felony arrests. The scope of eligibility often depends on the availability of financial and staff resources.

It should be noted that the term *Drug Court* has been used to refer not only to courts with a strong emphasis on diversionary treatment, like the Dade County model, but also to courts implementing case management and expedition programs. For some Drug Courts, case management is the only emphasis. Only Drug Courts with some form of a treatment component, however, are listed in Table 4.1 and considered in this analysis. Thus use of the term *Drug Court* in this study refers only to treatment-oriented Drug Courts.

The growing number of Drug Courts has led some to conclude that a movement is taking place within the criminal justice system. This certainly seems to be the case in the state of Florida as advocates and observers speak of the Drug Courts as inspiring a "revolution" in the way Florida handles drug cases. Not only does Florida have more Drug

TABLE 4.2
Drug Courts in the United States
(as of May 1995)

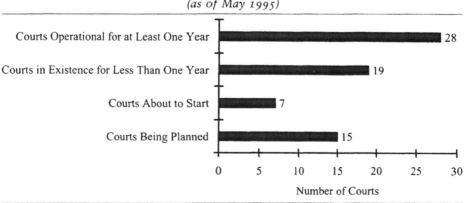

SOURCE: Drug Court Resource Center (a program of the Bureau of Justice Assistance at the American University), *Summary of Drug Court Activity by State* (Washington, D.C.: U.S. Department of Justice, 1995).

Courts than any other state in the United States, but aspects of the Drug Court were institutionalized on a statewide level when, in April 1993, Florida made it statutory law that a court could dismiss a defendant's offenses upon successful completion of a treatment program.[37] In October 1993, the Florida legislature made the Drug Court format legal for processing offenders caught purchasing or possessing illegal drugs other than cocaine.[38]

Such developments are not limited to Florida. The National Institute of Justice, for example, reports that "the Dade County Court appears to have spearheaded a growing mini-movement in American courts."[39] With equal anticipation, Diane Magliola, director of the treatment component of Texas's Travis County Drug Court, believes that the growing number of Drug Courts nationwide represents "a revolution . . . a movement from the top down."[40] Likewise, Judge Jeffrey Tauber of the Oakland Drug Court claims that "interest in the Drug Courts is sweeping the nation."[41] Indeed, the already mentioned Clinton crime bill originally included $1 billion designated for financing Drug Courts throughout the country.[42] A coalition of some twenty-two Drug Court judges assisted in lobbying for this allotment. Clearly, the Drug Court movement is a significant development in the criminal justice system, with important implications for the present analysis.

To begin with, the Drug Court model more fully fuses the historically disparate functions of traditional adjudication and therapeutic drug treatment. The format draws together these two entities, which were only "linked" with TASC and which were essentially independent before that. Washington, D.C.'s Drug Court implementation plan speaks to the former separation of the criminal justice and treatment communities:

> Traditionally, both in the District of Columbia and across the nation, the criminal justice community and the treatment community have not seen themselves as having much in common. The perception has been that the two communities do not share goals, terminology, or even a basic understanding of the nature of addiction. . . . In short, the relationship between courts and treatment programs was dichotomous and dysfunctional.[43]

The D.C. project, along with the other Drug Courts, however, represents "an innovative approach to integrating substance abuse treatment into the criminal justice system."[44] With this emerging alliance, the very nature of the criminal justice enterprise is altered. The result is a courtroom heavily influenced by the perspectives and practices of therapeutic treatment.

Personalized Justice

One important consequence of this new marriage is the personal nature of the court. Recall the proposition that the therapeutic perspective presents itself as a likely candidate for state legitimacy in that it offers to make personal the impersonal nature of a highly rationalized system. Indeed, one of the selling features of the Drug Court is its very personal orientation. As Tim Murray with the Dade County Drug Court explains, the Drug Court is "a very personal experience in an impersonal system."[45] Judges in the various programs seem to take a genuine interest in the individual lives that come before them, thus cutting through the atmosphere of distance and alienation typical of a traditional criminal courtroom. Once in the Drug Court program, the defendant always relates to the same court personnel—the same judge, district attorney, and public defender. In the Drug Courts, there is a much higher level of personal interaction and accountability than in the traditional criminal court.

Particularly noteworthy is the personalized nature of the relationship between judge and defendant. Dr. Alex Stalcup, a physician and adviser to Judge Jeffrey Tauber of the Oakland Drug Court, believes that it is this feature of the Drug Court that has made all the difference. "This intervention is human," says Stalcup. "They have to encounter Jeff [Tauber], respond to him, say something, do something. This is a very new definition of diversion."[46] Judge Tauber, who, in his role as a Drug Court judge, reportedly "dispenses praise and blame like a stern but attentive father,"[47] offers the following as guidelines to which the Drug Court judge should adhere:

> Express your belief that they can (and will) succeed if they work at it. . . . Be less the dignified, detached judicial officer. Show your concern, as well as your toughness. Treat the offender as a person and an individual (i.e. never *voir dire* offenders as a group). Don't lecture the offender, but engage him or her in conversation. . . . Make a connection. . . . Impress upon them the importance of their case to you, your deep and abiding interest in them, and the very real consequences of success or failure.[48]

According to Tauber, the Drug Court judge is to assume "the role of confessor, task master, cheerleader, and mentor; in turn exhorting, threatening, encouraging and congratulating the participant for his or her progress, or lack thereof."[49]

Judge Goldstein of Dade County certainly functions within these parameters. He can be both encouraging and supportive, and often invites defendants to his bench, where he carries on private conversations with them. Consider, for example, this interchange with a client:

> John! Looking good, John! Come over here! [Goldstein leans over his bench, shakes the man's hand warmly.] You going to school still? Get your GED yet? All right, seven out of seven clean, good attendance. You in phase III now? Okay. See me back here in 30 days.[50]

Goldstein often takes on a fatherly role, speaking of his clients as children whom he desperately wants to see succeed. One defendant, who had been in treatment for nearly nine months, said this of the Dade County Drug Court:

> Everyone in there believed in me so much. I believe in myself now. If I ever feel like I'm going to backslide, I call the judge to talk. I have no family, no one to believe in me. But Judge Goldstein believed in me. He saved my life. That whole courtroom saved my life.[51]

The personal connection between defendant and Drug Court officials is also evident in Judge Robert Fogan's Broward County court. Judge Fogan believes that society needs to "put an arm around those who are suffering from addiction."[52] In the Broward County Drug Court, according to Fogan, "we try to build self-esteem. I'm talking in terms of treatment, love and care."[53] A defendant named Dawn, for example, got "a donut and applause from everyone in the courtroom" for having completed 130 days of drug-free living. Fogan told Dawn, "you're doing well, and we're proud of you."[54] Others are given key chains or bumper stickers for successful court appearances, and program graduations are celebrated by the court with special invitations, diplomas, T-shirts, coffee and cake. Fogan tells the story of one graduate who, the day of his graduation, left the following message on the judge's voice mail: "Judge, I graduate today, the first time I've been sober in 30 years. . . . It's 5 a.m. and I'm so excited I can't sleep. I want to be appropriate. Please call me back and tell me—is it okay to hug the judge?"[55]

Judge William Schma of Kalamazoo Michigan's Drug Court also gets personal with those who come into his court. On a biweekly basis, the judge calls participants before his bench to discuss informally how they are doing and how they are progressing through the program.[56] He tells one defendant, for example, how good she looks, and he asks how her children are doing.[57]

Judge Steven Marcus of the Los Angeles Drug Court similarly assumes a personal and caring posture toward those who come into his court. It is August 5, 1994, and a defendant named Valerie is scheduled to come before the judge. Earlier in the day, at the treatment center, she had talked about how she was a little nervous about seeing the judge because, in her words, she "had not been doing too well," meaning that a lot of her drug tests had been positive. When her name comes up, Judge Marcus recognizes Valerie and asks how she is doing. She responds by saying she is doing well, that her children are fine, and that she had recently brought them to visit the treatment center. Judge Marcus responds, "We want you to be happy. You always seem happy. That is an amazing quality about you. I'm glad you're happy. I'm glad about your children." Even though Valerie had come up positive on all of her urinalysis tests from the previous two weeks, he gives her another chance, assigns a new court date, and implores her to do better. "I'm going to try to do better," she replies. She leaves the courtroom, and Judge Marcus calls up the next Drug Court client. The personal encounters continue. "Don't let me down," he urges one. "I'm going to give you a break," he tells another.[58]

Marcus informs a new client about the rules and philosophy of the Drug Court. With the client's permission, he waives his right to a speedy trial and tells him about Impact House, the Los Angeles drug treatment facility. Judge Marcus lets the client know that he is there to help him personally:

> If there is a problem going on, we can talk about it. You've got to come back to my court. In the beginning I want to see people often. I want to help you. I want to talk to you. The D.A. wants to help you. Normally, she wants to put you in jail.[59]

The Clark County, Nevada, Drug Court is very explicit about the personal role to be assumed by the judge. Consider, for example, this excerpt from the court's statement of purpose: "The purpose of the Drug Judge is to be a combination authority and father figure, a psychologist, social worker and judge."[60] When defendants appear before the Drug Court judge, he "tells them how terrific they are" if they are doing well in the program or "discusses with them what the problem is" if they are turning up drug-positive urine tests.[61]

Treatment

The personalized nature of the Drug Court format, however, is not confined to the courtroom. It is perhaps even more pronounced in the court-regulated treatment dimension of the program. Here clients receive one-on-one and group therapy on a regular basis. In addition, clients participate in AA and NA twelve-step groups in the local community and in the treatment facility. Treatment programs are specifically designed to meet the individual needs of the client. Consider the following program goals concerning treatment for the client:

Drug Court	*Program Goal or Description*
Mobile, Alabama	"To ensure treatment interventions meet each offender's needs."
	"To provide defendant-specific services for redressing the factors which aid and support the addiction."
Los Angeles, California	"Develop measurable Treatment Plans to address client goals and objectives appropriate to individual client needs and preferences."
	"Treatment will be tailored to meet individual needs and will address the ethnic and cultural issues as well as the special needs of this target population."
Maricopa County, Arizona	"Treatment subjects include the disease concept of chemical dependency, with the goal of improving participants' emotional, social, and individual growth and awareness."
Portland, Oregon	"The program . . . is tailored to the participants' needs."
Broward County, Florida	"Because of the resources BARC (Broward Addictions Recovery Center) has at its command, treatment

for Drug Court defendants can be individualized and modified, as defendant needs require."

Denver, Colorado

"The Treatment Program is individually tailored to meet individual needs . . ."

It is probably not surprising that the treatment component would be personal and directed toward the needs of the individual. Therapeutic intervention, by definition, is highly focused on the individual's needs and concerns.[62] Drug treatment providers go to great lengths to make the treatment "client-centered," to borrow Carl Rogers's term. The Broward County treatment facility, for example, makes provision for "culturally sensitive programs geared to African Americans and Hispanics, with special support services to address their specific needs, . . . and a Women's Group which women can choose to attend."[63] Similarly, treatment providers in Denver, Colorado, are "required to attend special sessions conducted by the Drug Court on cultural diversity and motivational interviewing."[64] The treatment service in Kalamazoo, Michigan, provides support for "housing, child care, and personal and family subsistence."[65]

Not surprisingly, the actual content of the counseling is also very personal and strongly reflective of the various elements of the therapeutic ethos discussed in Chapter 1. Much emphasis, for example, is placed on feelings. Consider the following introductory testimonial to a large "Feelings" section of a program workbook used by counselors with clients in Los Angeles's Impact treatment program:

I remember how frustrated I became early in treatment. My counselor would say, "How do you feel about that?" I'd begin my answer by saying "I think . . ." or "I believe . . ." or some other answer which did not deal with feelings at all. I just couldn't get it. What was the big deal about feelings? What did feelings have to do with my dependency? There were two feelings I knew for sure; high and higher. Well, now I'm beginning to realize that I have been covering up my real feelings for a long, long time. A few months ago I couldn't have recognized a real feeling if it had danced a tango on my nose. Now I'm beginning to be more sensitive to my feelings. I have a lot of sadness inside of me today. I'm also confused and afraid. The feelings aren't comforting but at least they are real and that tells me I'm coming back to life.[66]

Clients are helped in the process of identifying and acting on their feelings in a number of different ways. They are told, for example, that "feelings, by themselves, are not wrong or right. They are just a part of you." Moreover, they are instructed that "if you do not learn to accept and express your feelings honestly and appropriately, you may be tempted to use the temporary, ineffective and damaging alternative of mood-altering drugs."[67]

Clients appear to take this emphasis on feelings to heart. Discussion in group counseling (which, in Los Angeles, was specifically called a "feelings processing group") and in AA and NA group meetings often focuses on feelings. Consider the following remarks from one AA meeting: "I have feelings now. I always want to cry. I just feel good. . . . I'm starting to like myself."[68] A woman responded immediately after with an affirmative statement about the role of feelings.

> I could identify with [person making first statement]. When I first started coming I also cried. My tears were tears of joy . . . once I got in touch with my feelings and put a name to that. It feels good that I have learned to give back what was freely given to me. . . . Please keep coming back. The program works.[69]

One man talked about how he rediscovered feelings when he became sober. Like the taste of food, it was something that alcoholism had prevented him from truly acknowledging and enjoying:

> I've been sober for one year. I was in heavy denial. I went to see a psychiatrist. I was a daily drinker. This program is not about quitting. It's about staying sober. I don't know. It works somehow. . . . Feelings—that was a trip. Eating—that was a trip. Eventually things fall into place.[70]

Another talked specifically about his feelings of anger: "I have a problem with justified anger. I've been thinking about anger toward others. I knew that I would feel better once I shared that with somebody."[71]

There is also a strong emphasis on self-esteem within the various treatment programs. In Los Angeles, clients are encouraged to replace "shameful thoughts" with statements such as "I am a good person. I have unique and special gifts from my Higher Power" and "It is okay when people disagree with me or act as if they don't like me. I know I'm okay."[72] In fact, self-esteem is often seen as the root of the client's drug problem. "For some addicted people low self-esteem may have begun long before they took their first drink or first drug. Bad feelings may have come from bad childhoods."[73] To build their self-esteem, clients are encouraged with various exercises. In one, they are told to complete the sentence "I like myself because . . . " with five statements. In another, they are to list behaviors they like about themselves. In another, they are to list attainable goals that are "right for you."[74]

It is important to note, however, that the intensity of treatment and court oversight is much more pronounced in the Drug Court than it was with TASC, with the greatest changes being not so much in the nature of treatment, which not surprisingly embodies the therapeutic approach, but in the courtroom itself.

The Transformation of Roles

A remarkable feature of the Drug Court is the transformed roles of the various actors in the courtroom drama. The more personal Drug Court judge has been variously described as a therapist, a social worker, a counselor, and a psychologist. The judge often engages the defendant directly, while the attorneys "literally and figuratively take a step back."[75] But the judge's role is not the only one transformed in this novel setting. Also converted are the traditionally adversarial roles of the district attorney and the public defender. Consider, for example, these instructions offered by Judge Jeffrey Tauber of the Oakland Drug Court: "A successful Drug Court Judge depends on the willingness of you and your staff to work as a team. Prosecuting and defense attorneys avoid confrontation in court and work together to sell the program to potential offenders."[76]

This change is particularly pronounced in the case of the district attorney. Instead of trying to prosecute the defendant, the district attorney becomes part of the Drug Court team trying to help the defendant toward recovery. He or she assumes a highly conciliatory role. As Jose L. Fernandez, a prosecutor in the Dade County court, observes, "In this court all of us are public defenders, really."[77] In fact, in Dade County not only the judge but also the prosecuting and defending attorneys have received special drug treatment training. Not all district attorneys have accepted this role so easily. There was much controversy in Broward County when Broward state attorney, Michael Satz resisted the alteration of his role and what he viewed as the undermining of his authority.

John Goldkamp, director of the Crime and Justice Research Institute and professor of criminal justice at Temple University in Philadelphia, has written, with Doris Weiland, the most exhaustive assessment of Dade County's Drug Court. Goldkamp and Weiland describe the transformed roles of the conspicuously therapeutic courtroom scene:

> The unusual role of the judge, thus, is best understood in the context of the unorthodox, non-adversarial and team-oriented roles played by the other criminal justice officials in the courtroom, roles designed to support the judge's role and to contribute to the treatment progress of the drug-involved felony defendants coming through the Court. The priority is given to defendants' treatment progress, and transactions in the courtroom seem, at times, more to resemble "psychodrama" or "therapeutic community" treatment modalities than normal criminal proceedings. Most noticeable are the transformed roles of the prosecutor and defender. The prosecutor in the courtroom shifts between communicating strong encouragement for defendants who appear to be making progress to raising the prospects of reinstating formal prosecution of charges when defendants do not seem to be participating appropriately in treatment. The defender seems clearly supportive of the opportunity Drug Court provides and also plays a role that appears more "therapeutic" in nature than adversarial.[78]

Also affected by the new arrangement are parole officers, many of whom likewise have been trained in drug therapy to assist in the treatment process. At other times, the role of the parole officer is replaced by state-contracted treatment providers. Not all parole officers have been immediately amenable to their redefined roles. In Oakland, for example, "several probation officers said they resented trading familiar tasks like writing reports for new ones like running group counseling sessions and having their discretion eroded."[79] In this case, however, it was reported that "they quickly found their new roles more satisfying than the old ones and the results inspiring."[80]

One of the most important role transformations is that of the defendant. In many courts defendants are referred to as "clients" or "members." The typical process in the court is to have new divertees sit in the "audience" while clients already in treatment are brought before the judge. Successes are applauded—literally, by everyone in the court—at the judge's beckoning, while those with positive urine tests are implored to try harder or are given two weeks in jail. Perhaps what is most significant about the client's new role is that his or her behavior is viewed in an altogether new manner, which leads to another important feature of the Drug Court.

The Pathologization of Crime

Another common theme evident in these various Drug Courts is the redefinition of criminal behavior. Where once drug offenses were commonly understood as crimes or legal infractions, they are increasingly interpreted as illnesses or pathologies. Certainly, that those caught using or purchasing drugs are considered "clients" or "members" rather than "offenders" or "defendants" is one sign of this paradigm shift. Articulations from those involved with the Drug Courts indicate that this shift in nomenclature is more than empty symbolism. Elizabeth Campos, assistant public defender in the Oakland Drug Court, speaks for many when she says, "This is the first program I have seen that really treats the war on drugs as a medical problem and not just a criminal problem." [81] Drug Court advocates argue not only that drug-abusing behavior is an illness rather than a crime but, correspondingly, that the means of correcting the behavior is treatment, not punishment.

Judge Fogan of Broward County, for example, says that he "fervently believes that addiction is a disease, and that prison is no cure." [82] Moreover, he claims that one "can be addicted to drugs and alcohol and be a decent person. The use of drugs is a sickness. It's something that should be treated, not punished." [83] Similarly, one of the foundational presuppositions of the Portland Drug Court is the belief that "if drug use is the problem drug treatment is the answer." [84]

Just as recovery from any other illness takes a long time, so, it is believed, does recovery from drug abuse. Based on this understanding, the Drug Court personnel often express the need for patience with relapses, setbacks, and slow progress among their clientele. Though such a perspective on drug abuse may not be new to those familiar with the treatment perspective, it certainly is new in the criminal court. Traditional adjudication would not be sympathetic toward this philosophy. As Goldkamp and Weiland explain:

> It is likely that the criminal justice perspective would set forth conditions that the defendant would agree to and then expect those conditions to be met. In the event of non-compliance, defendants would risk having program participation revoked and be susceptible to adjudication of their charges in a normal setting and, quite likely, experience pretrial detention in the interim. [85]

Such impatience with noncompliance, however, is not in keeping with the treatment perspective—in fact, quite the contrary. A treatment perspective, as Goldkamp and Weiland explain further, "would understand that . . . the road to progress is likely to be very difficult, with initial failures routinely to be expected." [86]

Because "relapse is a part of recovery," as understood within the Portland Drug Court, "people dealing with addicted defendants need to appreciate that" and need to have "the tolerance and patience that give an addicted defendant a real chance." [87] Or, as Stanley Goldstein of Dade County argues, the Drug Court program "must allow for participants to make mistakes . . . it is unrealistic to think that a drug addict can break free of addiction overnight . . . it can sometimes take two years or more." [88] Similarly, the Oakland Drug Court recognizes that "drug abuse is a debilitating disease, that relapse and intermittent progress are a part of most successful drug rehabilitations; that as drug addiction is not created overnight, it cannot be cured overnight." [89] In short, as Judge Schma of the Kalamazoo Drug Court argues, "You've got to be willing to put up with relapses." [90]

The nascent Los Angeles Drug Court is very conscious of the shift from a traditional, adjudicative to a therapeutic, treatment perspective regarding the nature of drug behavior and the need for patience with relapses. "The Drug Court will differ from the current diversion program through a philosophical change towards relapse, which is viewed as part of the treatment process. A dirty drug test or failure to report for a treatment session will not result in automatic termination from the program." [91]

Thus an important trait of the Drug Court is the institutionalization of a treatment perspective toward the recovering "patient." Where once drug offenses were seen as legal infractions that needed to be punished, they are increasingly viewed as illnesses that need to be treated.

The themes considered thus far—in particular, the personal nature of the court and the pathologization of criminal behavior—represent aspects of the Drug Court that purport to soften the criminal justice system. They are the "kinder and gentler" dimensions of the phenomenon here considered. These more personal and caring features fit well within the larger theoretical proposition that the attractiveness of the therapeutic alternative rests in its promise to alleviate the harshness of a highly impersonal, bureaucratic system. What is interesting, however, is that in seeking to gain public acceptance of the Drug Court format and philosophy, the courts do not rely exclusively on the sensitive, emotivist emphasis. Indeed, often employed with this is one of the defining features of the rationalized system the Drug Court format purports to soften: the utilitarian ideals of efficiency and cost-effectiveness.

The Utilitarian Argument

Drug Court proponents consistently argue that adoption and expansion of Drug Courts will save the state money. Moreover, it is often argued that court-monitored diversion programs "work" in getting drug offenders off of drugs and out of the crime cycle. One of the most common arguments in this regard is the assertion that putting offenders through treatment is much less costly than putting them in jail or prison. Consider, for example, the arguments below, which were advanced by representatives of the various Drug Courts.

Drug Court	*Argument*
Dade County, Florida	"Compared with $17,000 to keep a drug offender in county jail, the treatment program costs about $600 per year. . . . It's cost-effective and it appears to work."[92]
	"The program costs about $1.2 million; that translated into about $500 to $700 a person a year, roughly the cost of jailing an offender for nine days."[93]
Clark County, Nevada	"Economically, it presently costs us $1,000 to put a person through the Drug Court program for a year; it costs approximately $18,000 a year to keep a person in the Clark County Detention Center, and approximately $24,000 a year to put them in state prison. Putting them in the detention center or state prison does not get them off drugs. Our program does."[94]

Broward County, Florida	"Treatment works better and is less expensive than punishment. In Florida, the cost of adding one person to the prison system is $37,000 for the first year, much higher than the $1,000–a-year price tag for rehabilitation programs."[95]
Berrien County, Michigan	"During the first quarter of the 92–93 grant year, seventeen defendants were deferred into treatment versus incarceration. Of the seventeen, thirteen were jail bound, and four were prison bound. If you were to estimate a ninety day jail sentence, the cost to the County would have been $35,000 for the first quarter alone. The treatment alternative represents an important savings to our County."[96]
Mobile, Alabama	"In 1992, the average cost per inmate to maintain offenders . . . was $9,312. . . . The average annual cost per inmate housed in . . . jail [was] $11,257. . . . The proposed program is expected to accommodate 600 defendants. . . . The estimated cost is $1,665."[97]

It is further argued, also from a conspicuously utilitarian perspective, that the Drug Court saves money by eliminating the need for expensive trials; by opening up jail and prison space (which can be rented to other state agencies for further savings); by avoiding state-funded foster care for children of incarcerated offenders; and so on. Perhaps the most important argument is the belief that the treatment program helps clients to quit drug use and concomitant criminal activities, which, in turn, relieves the overburdened criminal justice system. In other words, treatment ostensibly reduces the recidivism rate, which ultimately reduces state outlays. Clients graduating from the Drug Courts, it is argued, will be less likely to return to drugs and crime. It is this argument that is most palatable to defenders of more traditional adjudicative processes. The question remains, however, whether this actually is the case.

Whether or not these programs are effective per se is beyond the scope of the present analysis. However, this issue does warrant consideration here, on the grounds that the varying interpretations of efficacy turn out to be further evidence of the infusion of the therapeutic perspective. It appears that even the framework one uses for evaluating success in preventing crime depends on whether one subscribes to a traditional criminal justice or a therapeutic drug treatment perspective. A discussion of the different analyses of the Drug Courts will embellish, and, it is hoped, clarify this point.

The Problem of Efficacy

On the surface, the arguments that treatment reduces recidivism appear very plausible and demonstrative of the Drug Court's efficacy. Though long-term assessments of the effectiveness of these programs are limited due to the relative novelty of the Drug Courts, initial findings regarding recidivism rates appear fairly impressive. According to an in-house study conducted by Judge Jeffrey Tauber of the Oakland Drug Court, for example, implementation of the Fast, Intensive, Report, Supervision, and Treatment (FIRST) program resulted in a 46 percent reduction in the average number of rearrests per drug offender for the 24–month time period following diversion (from .97 rearrests per offender in a 1990 sample to .52 rearrests per offender in a 1991 Drug Court sample).[98] Pointing to similar success rates, Dade County officials—as reported by the National Institute of Justice (1993) and the American Bar Association (1993)—claimed that the rearrest rate among drug offenders in Dade County's Eleventh Circuit Court prior to the Drug Court was 60 percent. For those who successfully completed the Drug Court program, by contrast, the recidivism rate reportedly dropped to somewhere between 7 and 11 percent. Dade County officials also asserted that 60 percent of those diverted to the treatment program successfully completed it.

Judge Harl Haas of the Portland, Oregon Drug Court also reports a lower recidivism rate among participants. In a 1994 overview of several Drug Courts by the UCLA Drug Abuse Research Center, Haas claims that of the 122 who graduated from Portland's Drug Court program between November 1992 and April 1993, only 6 percent were rearrested. By contrast, of the 246 defendants terminated from the program, 24 percent were rearrested. The Beaumont, Texas, Drug Court likewise reported in a 1994 program guide that of the 114 clients who had entered their program since December of 1992 only 7 percent had been rearrested.

Studies conducted by agencies outside the Drug Courts, however, are less encouraging. A Rand Corporation study of the deterring effects of urinalysis drug testing among Maricopa County, Arizona, drug offenders randomly selected four tracks of offenders and submitted them to either (1) no drug testing; (2) infrequent random drug testing; (3) scheduled (biweekly) urinalysis testing; or (4) drug testing with treatment. After a six-month follow-up of cases originally assigned in March 1992, Rand found that the rearrest rates for the first two categories were actually lower (18.24 percent and 20.42 percent, respectively) than the rate for Drug Court-assigned offenders, which was 21.91 percent. Those with scheduled drug testing had the highest rearrest rate at 27.52 percent.[99]

Likewise, in a study conducted by W. Clinton Terry, professor of criminal justice at Florida International University, no real differences were found between the recidivism rates of those who completed and those who dropped out of Broward County's Drug Court treatment program. Only a 4 percent difference in the number of felony rearrests and a 1 percent difference in the number of misdemeanor rearrests were found between the two groups. In both cases, the lower rates were for those remaining in the treatment program, but the differences were not statistically significant.[100] Terry concludes from the findings that "there appears to be little difference between persons remaining in the program and those who have not."[101]

The most comprehensive studies have been conducted with data from the Dade County Drug Court, which is no surprise, given that it is the oldest of America's Drug Courts. Two evaluations in particular offer fairly thorough assessments of the Dade County Drug Court; the above-mentioned Goldkamp and Weiland study and a 1993 American Bar Association (ABA) study. A close look at these sheds some light on the apparent discrepancy between the reported success rates advanced by the various courts and the more underwhelming findings published by outside agencies.

To begin with, the ABA study acknowledges the high success rate cited by Murray and others regarding the efficacy of Dade County's

Drug Court; that is, 7 percent recidivism rate, down from the 60 percent rate before the Drug Court was established. However, data collected by the ABA contradicts these findings:

> In contrast, our data show only a small, and statistically non-significant, decrease in felony rearrests when comparing defendants whose cases were assigned to Drug Court with similar defendants whose cases were disposed prior to the Drug Court. . . . Among offenders who were sent to the Drug Court, 20% were rearrested for a drug offense and 32% were rearrested for any felony offense within one year of the sampled arrest. Among pre–Drug Court defendants, 23% were rearrested for a narcotics offense and 33% for any felony offense within one year.[102]

The ABA study also used a one-way analysis of variance to determine whether Drug Court participants were rearrested later than non–Drug Court participants. Again, they found little difference between the samples. Drug offenders sent through the Drug Court were rearrested, on average, 324 days after their first court appearance, whereas drug offenders sentenced prior to the Drug Court were rearrested, on average, 319 days after their first court appearance.[103] The study thus concludes that there is "no discernible effect of establishing the Drug Court and its attendant treatment program on decreasing crimes committed by drug offenders in Dade County."[104]

Interestingly, Goldkamp and Weiland's data reveal similar findings. One would not, however, get that impression from an initial reading of the report. This research project, cofunded by the State Justice Institute and the National Institute of Justice, is a very extensive analysis of the Dade County program, with a final report of over 160 pages. To determine the efficacy of the Drug Court, participants who were admitted to treatment between August and September 1990 were compared with five other sample groups, including two groups admitted in 1987 (one made up of felony drug offenders and one made up of felony nondrug offenders) and three groups admitted during the same time period as the test sample (one made up of nondrug offenders, one of drug offenders ineligible for assignment to the Drug Court, and one of eligible offenders who chose not to enter the treatment program).

It is the final group—those assigned but not admitted to the Drug Court treatment program—that offers the most appropriate comparison group. The two 1987 two groups are less fitting comparisons, not only because they are from another time period but also because one is made up of felony nondrug offenders and the other, though made up of felony drug offenders, includes both those who would and those who would not be eligible for the Drug Court. The 1990 Drug Court sample includes only those eligible for the Drug Court (those with less serious criminal histories). Of the three 1990 comparison groups, the felony nondrug group is, of course, qualitatively different. Arguably, successful recovery from drug abuse is not an issue in these cases. The group of ineligible drug offenders is problematic in that these offenders are ineligible for the very reason that they have more serious criminal histories. Of the three 1990 comparison groups, then, the third—those "assigned but not admitted" to the Drug Court (identified as "Sample II" in the report)—is the most appropriate for a comparison with the 1990 Drug Court cases. Goldkamp and Weiland come to the same conclusion:

> Sample II, consisting of similar felony drug defendants entering the process during the same period of time as Drug Court defendants and with similar criminal charges and prior record attributes, was designed to play a special role in the assessment of the impact of Drug Court. . . . As a proposed "natural" control group, under ideal conditions this sample would offer the most appropriate available comparison of relevant outcomes to identify the impact of the Drug Court.[105]

However, when comparing rates of recidivism, both in terms of the number of rearrests and the time elapsed between admittance and rearrest, Sample II is excluded from the main analysis. In fact, in the "Executive Summary" and in the eleven-page synopsis of the report put out by the National Institute of Justice, this group does not show up at all.

In the larger *Final Report,* the comparison between the Drug Court group and Sample II is buried in an appendix at the end of the report. Looking at it, one discovers that the rearrest rate during an eighteen-month observation period was actually higher for Drug Court participants than for those in Sample II—33 percent compared to 30 percent. Moreover, it took less time, on average, for offenders in the Drug Court sample to get rearrested (235 days) than it did for offenders in Sample II (261 days).[106] These findings correlate very closely with those in the ABA study: recall that the ABA study found a 32 percent rearrest rate among Drug Court defendants.

However, Goldkamp and Weiland exclude this sample, based on the later discovery that eighteen defendants from Sample II "should possibly have been included in the treatment cohort."[107] At another point they propose, in a manner both unclear and seemingly contradictory, that as many as forty of the eighty-nine defendants in Sample II may have entered treatment sometime after the 1990 August–September test period. Still, even in this worst-case scenario, more than 60 percent of the entire sample did not enter treatment, and even those who ostensibly did were in treatment for a shorter part of the eighteen-month observation period than were those in the Drug Court sample. Because Sample II was the most "appropriate available comparison" group, it is important, even with only 61 percent not having been exposed to any treatment, that this group was found to have a lower recidivism rate than the Drug Court group.

When compared to the other groups, though, the Drug Court shows a lower recidivism rate. But this is to be expected. The Drug Court sample represents those defendants most likely *not* to be rearrested. They were selected as eligible for the Drug Court because of criminal histories with fewer infractions. None of the other groups (with the exception of Sample II) had defendants who were selected according to such a criterion of eligibility. Goldkamp and Weiland themselves admit that defendants "with no or just one prior arrest or conviction more often recorded favorable program outcomes than defendants with more extensive histories."[108] This is precisely why it does not make sense to compare Drug Court participants with any group other that those eligible according to the same criterion, namely, Sample II. Thus the Drug Court addresses those least likely to be rearrested and most likely to complete the treatment program. What explains the success, then, is the nature of the defendants, not the program. It should also be noted that, regardless of what comparison groups are used, the 33 percent recidivism rate does not come close to the 7 percent rate initially reported by the court.

Goldkamp and Weiland also discover the "curious finding" that "defendants who need treatment the least (because they have little or no drug involvement) last longest in the program."[109] Such a finding seems more obvious than curious and would explain why, when comparing those who finish or remain in the program with those who do not, one finds the former rearrested less frequently than the latter. This would explain the success rate of Portland's Drug Court as offered by Judge Haas, in the previously noted overview by the UCLA research center. Again, those who are least likely to be rearrested are those most likely to complete the treatment program. Yet it is this very finding that Haas has offered as evidence for his Drug Court's "success" rate.

Another commonly reported finding regarding Dade County's Drug Court is that most who enter the treatment program finish it. Before the Goldkamp and Weiland study came out, it was reported that as many as 90 percent completed the program. Since the Goldkamp and Weiland study, however, and based on its findings, the court has been reporting a 60 percent completion rate among Drug Court divertees. Yet a close look at the study reveals that even this 60 percent completion rate may be misleading. Goldkamp and Weiland actually discover at the outset that only 34 percent of those diverted to the Drug Court "successfully completed diversion according to court records."[110] It is only through some interesting reconceptualizations that they arrive at the 60 percent figure, and it is here that one discovers the important influence of a therapeutic mode of interpretation.

The favorable completion rate was raised from 34 to 46 percent when the "cases still active" column was collapsed into either the favorable or the unfavorable category. The authors make this adjustment for the following reason: "Defendants who had active or open cases at the end of 18 months either should be counted as provisionally having recorded favorable outcomes, or be counted as having unfavorable outcomes, if they had absconded from the program and had not returned to active participation."[111] In other words, a defendant who, after eighteen months, was still in what is supposed to be a yearlong program was to be considered favorable, even when his or her remaining in the program was likely due to relapses and noncompliance with the treatment program. In fact, Goldkamp and Weiland report elsewhere in the study that 37 percent of these continuing cases had been jailed (in motivational jail) at least once.[112] This seems to mitigate the position that such cases should be considered successes or favorable outcomes. Here it is important to recall, however, the treatment perspective that relapses and setbacks are part of the process of recovering from a disease. As such, this statistical adjustment represents the replacement of a traditional criminal justice standard of measurement with a therapeutic treatment one.

Another adjustment is made to reach the 60 percent level when the Goldkamp and Weiland, as they put it, adopt "yet another assumption that has been argued from the drug treatment perspective."[113] In this case, they exclude from the total sample forty-two defendants who had dropped out of the program within the first three weeks of admission, because "some minimum period of program participation . . . should be required before it is reasonable to evaluate the impact of the program on defendants' behavior."[114] Recall that what is being measured here is the percentage of defendants who successfully complete the program, a standard of measurement that should call into question the practice of removing from the sample those who do not complete the program.

How such a seemingly questionable adjustment is rooted in a "drug treatment perspective" is not immediately clear. On further reflection, though, the reasoning seems to be based on the assumption that the treatment program is inherently beneficial to the life and well-being of the client. Thus the longer one is exposed to it, the better off one is. Perhaps this makes it a distinctively drug treatment perspective, in that it intuits the usefulness of therapeutic processes regardless of whether a client responds to them or whether they are efficacious. But isn't this what is being tested? In this case, subjective intuition appears to supersede empirical validation. Does the therapeutic perspective mean that one can adjust the standards of empirical measurement to line up with intuition? Perhaps.

In spite of this rather precarious adjustment of the data (one that reduced the total sample size from 326 to 245 defendants), it is the 60 percent favorable outcome rate that has been offered by the court and cited in media accounts of the program's success. What is important about the difference between the 34 percent and 60 percent favorable outcome levels, for the present analysis, is that the reason for adjusting the data is the replacement of a traditional criminal justice standard of measurement with a therapeutic drug treatment one.

Could it be that such liberty in adjusting measurements would explain the discrepancy between the low recidivism rates reported by the courts (6, 7 and 9 percent) and the much higher rates found by external agencies? In other words, how were these reportedly low rates of recidivism arrived at? In trying to answer this question, the ABA study reveals that the 7 percent rate offered by Dade County really refers to those who entered the treatment program and then stayed in it, which is only a percentage (between 30 and 50 percent) of the total number of defendants who were actually diverted to the program. The ABA did find the rearrest rate of those who entered the program and stayed in it for over a month to be 8 percent, as compared to the 7 percent reported by the court. However, as the study points out, "it needs to be emphasized that those who actually enter the program are a select group . . . and that these defendants are those likely to be *least* disposed to commit new crimes, having demonstrated a motivation to treatment." [115] In other words, defendants most predisposed to refrain from criminal behavior and most willing to comply with the demands of criminal justice officials are selected out, and based on this sample, a low rearrest rate is reported. This adjustment, as with the adjustment in the rate of successful completion, seems precarious from a traditional criminal justice or scientific empirical perspective but is somehow justified by a therapeutic orientation.

Goldkamp and Weiland are cognizant of the tension between the two perspectives and realize that each has different performance expectations and different measures of effectiveness. Consider the following differences identified by the authors:

	Criminal justice	Drug treatment
Expectation of performance	Formal roles (judges, probation, prosecutor, defense, etc.)	Counselors/treaters
	Probation-like supervision or monitoring	Access to community based on treatment needs
	Enforcement of conditions of provisional liberty	Expect failure and slow progress
	Sanctions for failure including revocation, incarceration	Flexibility and adjustment
Measure of effectiveness (Outcome)	Reduced current future/caseload	Reduced abuse
	Abstinence	Abstinence
	Reduced crime	Increased skills[116]

Clearly, the expectations and measures of effectiveness differ greatly between the two groups: traditional criminal justice sanctions failures, whereas treatment expects failures and setbacks; traditional criminal justice enforces compliance, whereas treatment is flexible and adjusting; traditional criminal justice measures the reduction in crime, whereas treatment is concerned with increased performance and skills. Recognizing the difficulty of reporting results satisfactory to both perspectives, Goldkamp and Weiland posit that "adopting one measure or another is really a policy decision that should most appropriately be made by the various participants in the court system operating the program." [117] It appears that in the case of Dade County, the treatment perspective has prevailed. But Dade County is not alone.

The Terry study of the Broward County Drug Court also recognizes the emerging salience of the treatment perspective in evaluating program success. Terry observes:

The question of success based upon rearrest information is an approach arising from within the context of criminal justice issues. *An equally viable approach* would be to examine the question of success from the standpoint of substance abuse and treatment, for, after all, this is a population of substance abusers. An effort is being made this year to collect this type of information. (emphasis added) [118]

Terry himself seems to move in the direction of the treatment perspective when he concludes — though he found no real difference in rearrest rates between Drug Court and non–Drug Court participants — that "there is absolutely no question that the Drug Court is having a very positive effect upon the lives of many people." He believes this because, at "the personal level, one is moved when hearing the individual success stories of persons who have turned their lives around as the result of the Drug Court." [119] In essence, then, Terry ignores the more positivistic, empirical data in deference to more subjective, anecdotal accounts. Based on similar reasoning Goldkamp and Weiland include in their report anecdotes about individuals who participated in the Dade County Drug Court.

The Portland Drug Court also moves away from a traditional criminal justice measure of success when it argues that though defendants not graduating from the treatment program may not have succeeded in a certain sense, they still have

encountered a system that focused on their needs and gave them an opportunity to learn what a drug free life felt like if even for a few months, weeks or days. Many of these folks have acquired, through S.T.O.P., the knowledge and the tools that will help them make it when their time of commitment comes. [120]

Again, it is presupposed here that the mere exposure to treatment, regardless of whether it got someone off drugs or kept them from committing future crimes, is beneficial. The intuited belief that the therapeutic approach is the right approach stands up even against more traditional understandings of failure.

Judge Lawrence Terry of San Jose, California's emerging Drug Court also advocates the drug treatment perspective. He believes that such objective criteria as urinalysis testing do not take into consideration the human realities of the recovery process; rather a lot of time needs to be spent "reeducating judges about what success is." [121]

Discussion

To summarize, the therapeutic perspective not only has been infused into the processes of criminal justice, as evidenced in the development and expansion of the Drug Court model, but has also colored the evaluation of Drug Court success rates. Though recidivism rates may not have decreased, the individual "needs" of the client are being addressed—and this, from a therapeutic treatment perspective, constitutes success. As such, the treatment approach, which originally was only linked to the criminal justice system through TASC, was brought into the courtroom with the Drug Court.

With redefined courtroom roles, this new court is team-oriented rather than adversarial. It is much more personal than the traditional criminal court. Moreover, it treats the defendant as a patient and offers to assist him or her in the recovery process. Public advocacy of the Drug Court does not rely exclusively on the pertinence of these more soft and caring traits but also draws on the modern industrial principle of efficiency and cost-effectiveness. Thus the Drug Court is defended with both emotivist and utilitarian arguments. On one level these appear to be two sides of the same coin: the program is sensitive to the individual's needs and feelings, and it works. On closer examination of the substantive basis of the efficacy argument, however, it appears that the more subjective, emotive perspective has superseded it, or at least redefined what is meant by "it works."

Prison Therapy

What have been considered so far with respect to the criminal justice system are activities in the courtroom—specifically, diversion alternatives to incarceration. Before moving on to other dimensions of the state, it is worth briefly considering what happens to those who are incarcerated. Are therapeutic practices being introduced within the prisons and jails as well?

As with preadjudicative diversion processes, therapeutic treatment programs in prisons were rather scarce until the 1960s. Up until the mid-1960s only inmates assigned to the previously mentioned Lexington and Fort Worth prison hospitals received any form of narcotics abuse treatment. The door was opened for more extensive drug treatment in prisons with the 1966 passage of the Narcotic Addict Rehabilitation Act (NARA), which mandated in-prison treatment for drug offenders convicted of violating federal laws. It was only well after NARA that drug treatment and other counseling programs were instituted on a more widespread level within America's prison systems.

Using raw data on state correctional facilities from surveys conducted by the Bureau of Justice Statistics in 1974, 1979, 1984, and 1990, I was able to examine longitudinally the growth of prisoner involvement in counseling and treatment programs.[122] As indicated in Table 4.3, the number of prisoners involved in some type of counseling program increased dramatically in the time period examined. The overall number of prisoners in counseling programs in 1990 (218,534) is 141 times greater than the number enrolled in 1974 (1,544).

Not surprising, when considering the growth of counseling programs according to type of program, one sees the greatest increase in the area of drug treatment. The number of inmates involved in drug treatment increased from 13,765 inmates (5 percent) in 1979 to 81,506 inmates

TABLE 4.3
*Prisoners Enrolled in Counseling Programs
in State Correctional Facilities*

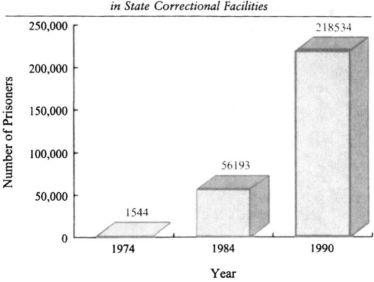

SOURCE: U.S. Department of Justice, Bureau of Justice Statistics, "Census of State Adult Correctional Facilities," 1974 and 1984, and "Census of State and Federal Adult Correctional Facilities," 1990, made available by the Inter-University Consortium for Political and Social Research, Ann Arbor, Michigan.

(11.8 percent) in 1990. There have been increases in other areas as well. See Table 4.4.

Even when one takes into consideration the rapid growth in the number of prison inmates generally, the total percentage of inmates involved in some form of treatment has still increased significantly. As shown in Table 4.5, the percentage of inmates involved in some type of counseling or treatment increased from 1.3 percent in 1974, to 14.4 percent in 1984, to 31.6 percent in 1990. Included in Table 4.5 are only those prisoners involved in alcohol treatment, drug treatment, or psychological/psychiatric counseling.

Recent research indicates that the level of inmate involvement in treatment and counseling programs continues to rise. A 1991 survey of

TABLE 4.4
*Prisoners Enrolled in Counseling Programs
according to Type of Program* *

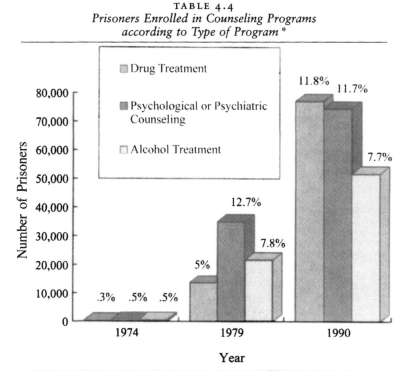

* Percentages in the chart represent the percentage of the total inmate population in state correctional facilities enrolled in a particular counseling or treatment program.
SOURCE: U.S. Department of Justice, Bureau of Justice Statistics, "Census of State Adult Correctional Facilities," 1974 and 1979, and "Census of State and Federal Adult Correctional Facilities," 1990, made available by the Inter-University Consortium for Political and Social Research, Ann Arbor, Michigan.

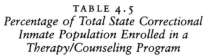

TABLE 4.5
*Percentage of Total State Correctional
Inmate Population Enrolled in a
Therapy/Counseling Program*

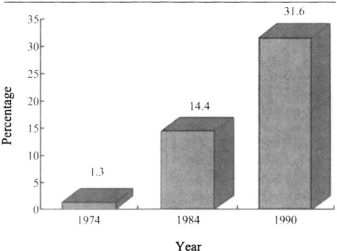

SOURCE: U.S. Department of Justice, Bureau of Justice Statistics, "Census of State Adult Correctional Facilities," 1974 and 1984, and "Census of State and Federal Adult Correctional Facilities," 1990, made available by the Inter-University Consortium for Political and Social Research, Ann Arbor, Michigan.

the state correctional population found 13.4 percent of inmates (93,600) to be in drug treatment.[123] This is an increase of more than 12,000 from the 1990 level, when 11.8 percent of state prison inmates (81,506) were in drug treatment. (These figures, like those in Tables 4.3 through 4.5, represent the number of offenders in treatment at the time the survey in question was conducted.)

When previous inmate involvement in prison treatment programs (not just involvement at the time of the survey) is taken into account, the more recent levels are even higher. In 1991, for example, 32.7 percent of state prison inmates had participated in a drug abuse treatment program at some point since admission to their most recent prison sentence.[124] When types of treatment other than for drug abuse are also taken into account, the level of inmate involvement is still higher. The 1990 census of state correctional facilities, for example, found that more than 42 percent of state prison inmates were involved in some form of counseling, be it for drug dependency, alcohol dependency, psychological/psychiatric conditions, life skills, parenting, or employment.[125] A

1991 survey found that 22 percent of state prison inmates participated in group counseling alone.[126] The types of treatment vary among the fifty state prison systems. Table 4.6 identifies the most common treatment programs used in the prison systems and the number of states that employ each.[127]

Developments in the criminal justice world indicate that these types of prison treatment programs continue to expand. In 1987, for example, the Bureau of Justice Assistance of the U.S. Department of Justice initiated and funded a program called Project REFORM to help state prisons develop and expand comprehensive drug abuse treatment strategies. In the two years after the project was initiated, eleven states received assistance from Project REFORM. Eight of these states (Alabama, Connecticut, Delaware, Florida, New Mexico, New York, Oregon, and Washington), in a period of only eight months, either implemented or expanded a total of more than six hundred different treatment programs. Table 4.7 indicates the various types of programs initiated or expanded on by these states during this eight-month period.[128]

Therapeutic Communities

Of these various programs, one of particular interest and importance is the therapeutic community (TC) model, which is basically an extension and amplification of the twelve-step model of AA and NA. The first drug treatment programs to open after the 1966 passage of NARA were

TABLE 4.6
Prison Treatment Programs in the Fifty States

Number of states	Treatment program
50	Group counseling, i.e., Narcotics Anonymous, Cocaine Anonymous, or Alcoholics Anonymous self-help groups meeting once or twice a week and small groups, led by a therapist, meeting occasionally during the week
48	Individual counseling, where an inmate meets with a therapist (usually a psychiatrist or counselor) occasionally during the week
30	Intensive residential program, often based on the therapeutic community (TC) model
39	Preliminary assessment procedures with newly sentenced inmates
24	Family counseling/therapy
44	Some form of short-term (35–50 hours) drug education programming

TABLE 4.7
Implementation of State Prison Drug Programs

Type of program	# Implemented	# Expanded
Assessment and referral	39	33
Drug education	36	82
Drug abuse resource centers	44	27
Self-help groups (e.g., AA and NA groups)	20	62
Urine monitoring programs	11	4
Prerelease counseling and/or referral	74	54
Postrelease treatment programs with parole or work release	39	10
Isolated unit (milieu) treatment programs	77 (implemented or expanded)	
Therapeutic community treatment programs	8	0

unit-based treatment programs that followed the TC model. These initial programs were established in 1968 at federal institutions in Terminal Island, California; Alderson, West Virginia; Milan, Michigan; and La-Tuna, Texas. By 1978 there were thirty-three such programs in federal institutions.[129]

TCs were equally popular in the state prison systems. The 1979 survey of state prisons discussed above found that 32 percent of all prison programs that year were based on the TC model. Thus 42 percent of all inmates involved in treatment in 1979 were part of a TC. The trend in the early 1980s was toward greater use of low-intensity therapy—AA and NA self-help groups, individual and group counseling, and so forth—as opposed to the more intense and comprehensive TC-type treatment programs. However, after mid-1980s studies by Harry Wexler et al. and Gary Field of TC programs in New York and Oregon reported high rates of success in reducing drug abuse and rearrests among clients, interest in TCs was revived in the criminal justice world.

TCs are long-term, comprehensive treatment programs that generally last between six and eighteen months. Treatment in the TC is intense and holistic in nature. Selected inmates live together in a separate unit. The projects are staffed by former drug addicts and by professionally trained counselors, who impose community responsibility through a strictly regimented program, a reward system, and intense therapeutic intervention. TCs are essentially twenty-four-hour-a-day treatment programs. The type of counseling offered within TCs varies among programs, with group therapy sessions or encounter groups being the most common. Table 4.8 shows the different modes of treatment used in a TC and the percentage of programs that employ them, based on a National Institute of Drug Abuse (NIDA) survey of TC programs in 1979.

In recent years, both federal and state prison systems have expanded or established new comprehensive drug treatment units of this type. Two flagship TC models, New York's Stay'n Out and Oregon's Cornerstone programs, were started between 1976 and 1978. High success rates reported from these projects have spawned the initiation of other TCs throughout the prison system. For example, an effort was made in 1988 to expand TC treatment programs in federal prisons. By January 1991, five TC units, each handling between 100 and 125 offenders per year, had become operational. A number of others were started in the federal Bureau of Prisons in the next two years.

In the state prison systems, one sees a similar trend. In October 1990, for example, the California Department of Corrections started Amity Righturn, a TC-model treatment program at San Diego's R. J. Donavan Correctional Facility. At any time two hundred male inmates are enrolled in this program, which lasts between nine and twelve months. Components of Amity Righturn's treatment program include the twelve-step recovery programs of AA, NA, and Cocaine Anonymous (CA); individual counseling; and "expressive therapy."[130] In June 1990 three other drug abuse treatment units, with therapeutic intervention approaches even more intense than the typical TC models, were initiated on a pilot basis in Butner, North Carolina; Tallahassee, Florida; and Lexington, Kentucky, each serving between 90 and 150 inmates per twelve-month period.[131]

Just as the Drug Court has expanded in recent years to include nondrug offenders, so the TC model has expanded to include inmates serving for crimes other than drug offenses. Particularly popular has been the application of the TC approach to sex offenders.

The Common Themes of Prison Therapy

The main form of therapy, within TCs and otherwise, is the encounter group or group therapy session. Within TCs, encounter groups can meet as often as five times per day. In low-intensity prison therapy programs, though the groups meet less often, they are still the main treatment modality, as indicated in Table 4.8. Even the military-styled "boot camps," a new form of incarceration used by some states to treat young

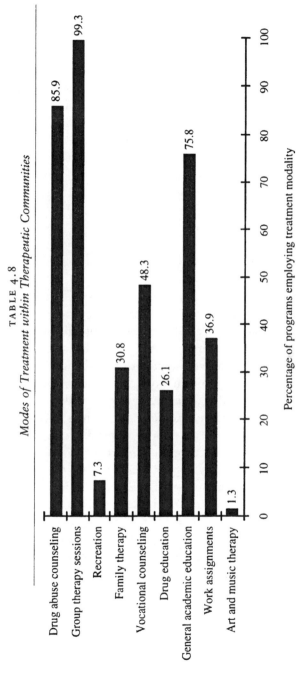

TABLE 4.8
Modes of Treatment within Therapeutic Communities

Percentage of programs employing treatment modality

SOURCE: Based on data from 149 TC programs surveyed in a national study of prison treatment programs reported in NIDA's Treatment Research Report *Drug Abuse Treatment in Prisons* (Washington, D.C.: U.S. Department of Health and Human Services, 1979).

felony offenders, have a strong therapeutic dimension: here, too, group therapy is a major element of the overall program.

It is not surprising that most of these groups, as well as the individual counseling programs, are led by the therapeutic practitioners identified in this study as the new priestly class of the therapeutic culture. A study of drug treatment in jails found the following distribution of mental health and social services personnel coordinating jail treatment programs: "psychologists (19 percent), psychiatrists (8 percent), social workers (31 percent), and drug specialists (30 percent)."[132] Similarly, a survey of state prisons found that within the treatment programs, 21 percent reported the availability of psychologists, 4 percent had psychiatrists, 81 percent included full-time counselors, and 25 percent employed part-time counselors. It would be interesting to know what type of training the counselors, over half of whom hold advanced degrees, received. This information, however, is not reported in the results of the survey.[133]

The content of therapeutic instruction advanced by these practitioners includes several common themes. As reported by Douglas Lipton, Gregory Falkin, and Harry Wexler therapeutic counseling in prisons typically focuses on "problems, feelings, attitudes, and behaviors." The goals of the sessions are to "improve the inmate's self-image, sense of personal responsibility, and ability to function in a socially acceptable manner." Different therapists employ different counseling styles. They may include "traditional psychotherapy, transactional analysis, behavior modification, and reality therapy." Variations depend on the training of the counselor and the "needs of the inmate patient."[134] Though there may be stylistic variations, what appear consistent are the emphases on the primacy of self and the centrality of emotions, the view of the inmate as a patient in need of healing, and the assumption that abusive and victimized pasts predispose one toward crime. Consider, for example, this description of New York's Stay'n Out TC encounter groups: "Encounter groups and counseling sessions are more indepth and focus on the areas of self-discipline, self-worth, self-awareness, respect for authority, and acceptance of guidance for problem areas. . . . Debate is encouraged to enhance self-expression and to increase self-confidence."[135]

A focus on the emotivist self is also evident at Washington, D.C.'s new 256-person TC-type facility, Unit 57–A, where inmates, after getting up at 5:30 A.M., participate in a fourteen-hour day of "counseling appointments, academic classes, spiritual-awareness groups and recreation." [136] Therapy is intended to help inmates get in touch with their pasts and their feelings, in order to discover why they are disposed toward criminal behavior. The following is a *Washington Post* account of how the program functions.

One inmate, a Melton Roach, Jr., is admonished by Unit 57–A's staff because he "is suppressing personal feelings and shortcomings that have contributed to his drug use and criminal behavior." [137] His assertion that his apparent lack of self-expression is a result of having "learned to control his emotions" is dismissed as a denial of what is really inside him. According to the unit's staff, Roach, though a model prisoner in many respects, has a problem because he is not in touch with his feelings; he "cannot tell when he is depressed or angry." One staffer, attempting to help Roach, tells him, "Your feelings are who you are. . . . They determine the motivation for your actions." Accompanying the strong emphasis on navigating life through one's emotions is the conspicuous focus on the self. Melton Roach tells unit staff that one reason he wants to get out of prison is to help care for his mother and son. Yet he is instructed that it is too early to focus on caring for others. Instead he is told, "You have to get yourself together first." [138]

Often individuals resistant to facing their pasts are regarded as unwilling to progress toward healing. Melton Roach was viewed in this way; so was Arnie Hall, a seventeen-year-old criminal at Giddings State Home and School, a maximum-security correction facility near Austin, Texas. In 1993, Arnie participated is a special sixteen-week program of "grueling talk therapy" with twenty-three other young offenders. Arnie Hall participated in encounter groups with three therapists and seven other teenage killers. During these sessions, questions were directed at Arnie in an effort to "peel back the layers of his past." His mother abused drugs and his stepfather was an alcoholic. Therapists were unable to get Arnie to feel remorse for his crime. "You're cutting off your feelings," shouted one therapist during a session. "Your mom was shooting up just like your victims," shouted another. "Were you taking it out on all of them because of her?" Reportedly, Arnie failed not only his inquisitors but also himself. He didn't crack enough under the "psychodrama" designed to "undo defenses and allow introspection." [139]

The offender's past is also emphasized in Illinois's Menard Psychiatric

Center for criminal sex offenders. According to Michael Dolan, a Menard prison psychologist, "Rapists think in distorted ways because many of them were severely abused as children and had no one to turn to—thus absorbing the violence and hatred." During a group therapy session at Menard, Dolan challenges an inmate named Jack, who was sexually abused as a child, to recognize his parents' part in his sex crimes. Jack replied, "I'm the one who's here. It's my problem." "Wait a minute," Dolan responded. "Your problem is you're in here because you sexually assaulted kids. Their problem is they jacked you around and screwed you up—that's their problem. . . . Why do you put it in reverse?" [140]

Prison officials claim that offenders often deny that they have been abused. Barbara Schwartz, director of the sex offender program at Twin Rivers prison outside Seattle, for example, states that "sometimes it takes years to get that out of them." [141]

Related to the belief that understanding the abuses of one's childhood is the starting point for understanding the crimes of one's adulthood is the view that a person's disposition toward criminal activity is a sickness. In both cases, external influences caused or at least fostered one's proclivity toward crime. Like the Drug Courts, prison counseling programs often take into consideration elements of the treatment view of criminal behavior. The controversy surrounding Avenal's Adult Diagnostic and Treatment Center in New Jersey, a comprehensive TC-type facility for sex offenders, is evidence of the increasingly common perception that criminal offenses are really illnesses that need healing.

Avenal, which costs the state $17 million annually, requires inmates to get recommendations from therapists to be eligible for parole. The therapy program at Avenal centers on "group counseling each week, and additional counseling in specialized areas like victim empathy, anger management and substance abuse." [142] Interestingly, Avenal has been criticized for not being therapeutic enough. State senator C. Louis Bassano, for example, believes that health care personnel should be in charge of the prison:

> A person who has good credentials when it comes to running a prison is great at an ordinary prison, but at Avenel you're dealing with a unique situation. . . . The inmates have an illness, and you need people sensitive to that problem. The public may say, "Lock them up and throw away the key," but you can't. These people come back into society eventually. In most cases, they can be treated so it won't happen again. [143]

Clearly, not all criminal justice officials share this view. As with the Drug Courts, there is tension between those holding to a more traditional criminal justice perspective and those who advocate a more therapeutic treatment perspective.

The Problem of Efficacy Revisited

Again, this tension necessarily poses problems for interpreting the efficacy of prison therapy programs. According to Lipton, Falkin, and Wexler, "Most research studies of the effectiveness of individual counseling have shown little evidence of success in reducing recidivism (and other negative behaviors)." From a traditional criminal justice perspective, this would indicate program failure. These authors also observe, however, that "positive psychological changes have been demonstrated," a statement that from a treatment perspective, would represent success.[144]

Reviewing a number of studies of drug treatment in prisons, Carl G. Leukefeld and Frank M. Tims similarly conclude that "limited research evidence currently exists to support the effectiveness of drug abuse treatment in prisons, including the most traditional forms of drug abuse treatment such as drug education, self-help groups, individual counseling, group counseling, and milieu therapy."[145] Yet this does not necessarily discredit the importance of such programs. Again, one's conclusion depend on the paradigm within which one operates. Leukefeld and Tims are cognizant of these differences and of the potential tension between them:

> The chronicity and relapsing aspects of drug abuse often make the effectiveness of drug abuse treatment difficult to understand. Viewed from a health perspective, treatment should be followed by "cure" and no further drug abuse. Viewed from a correctional perspective, recidivism should be reduced and drug abuse ended. These goals are compatible but frequently are implemented differently, often causing tension.[146]

Thus, as with the Drug Court, determination of program efficacy itself has been influenced by the therapeutic perspective. Inability to alter recidivism rates does not necessarily mean a program is ineffective. According to a therapeutic interpretation of human behavior, which recognizes the influences of one's past and the length of time it takes to recover from an illness, success is interpreted differently.

Discussion

Both in the courtroom and in prisons and jails, it is evident that therapeutic processes are expanding. It is clear, too, that the therapeutic model as implemented in these contexts is not a neutral forum for handling offenders. The structure and philosophy of therapeutic intervention carry important ideas about the roots of criminal behavior, about how to treat offenders, and about how long such a process should take. From TASC to the Drug Court to therapy processes in prisons, the disparities between a traditional criminal justice view and a therapeutic treatment view are evident. It has been shown that the therapeutic treatment perspective not only has made advances within the processes of criminal justice but has even begun to influence how the effectiveness of these various programs are measured.

Given these developments, how does one reconcile the irrefutable advancement of therapeutic practices with the increasingly popular "tough on crime" rhetoric of contemporary politics? Arguably, a number of factors explain growing political calls for such anticrime measures as a larger police force, a "three strikes and you're out" policy for repeat felons, boot camps for juvenile offenders, the reinstitution of prison chain gangs, and the removal of weight-lifting equipment from prisons. Not least among these factors is the public perception that America's criminal justice system is not working, and that public policy toward criminal behavior has been too soft.

Do these tough on crime political impulses offer a counterforce to the type of developments reviewed in this chapter? In part, they do. The Republican reconstruction of the 1994 crime bill sought to replace appropriations for the Drug Courts and other prevention programs with funding for new prisons and the institution of stiffer penalties for repeat felons. Such political opposition to treatment programs indicates that there may be limits to public tolerance of therapeutic practices in the criminal justice system. However, in important respects the tough on crime orientation does not directly oppose therapeutic developments. The nature of the Drug Courts and prison therapy programs considered in this chapter make clear that therapeutic intervention is not synonymous with a "soft" approach to crime. Drug Court participants often spend more time in the criminal justice system than do similar offenders who go through the more traditional adjudication process. Moreover, participants in the Drug Courts and prison therapy groups are often subject to greater intrusiveness into their private lives than are other prisoners and criminal defendants, in that judges and counselors delve into personal matters once largely left outside the purview of the courts and prisons.

It was, in fact, on this point—the greater intrusiveness of the courts— that Drug Court judges successfully lobbied the Republican-controlled Congress to reconsider support for the Drug Courts.[147] As mentioned earlier, the 1994 crime bill authorized a total of $1 billion for the Drug Courts over a period of five years. After the Republican takeover of Congress, the House rescinded the $29 million of this amount that was appropriated for the 1995 fiscal year. After lobbying efforts by Drug Court judges, however, the House specifically identified the Drug Courts as one of the programs for which federal block-grant dollars could be used. Moreover, the Senate reduced the rescission of Drug Court dollars to $17 million in its version of the revised crime bill, thus reinstating over $10 million of the Drug Court's 1995 fiscal-year dollars. In the end, a sum of $18 million was allotted to the Drug Courts when the 1995 fiscal-year budget finally passed through Congress and was signed by President Clinton. As Judge Ronald Taylor of the Berrien County, Michigan, Drug Court had correctly anticipated, federal dollars for fiscal year 1995 would be "covered one way or another."[148]

In the final analysis, then, "tough on crime" measures do not necessarily mean antitherapeutic measures. Funding for the Drug Courts was, at least partially, sustained because of the courts' observably intrusive orientation, as well as its ostensibly utilitarian value. The conflation of the tough with the therapeutic approach to crime is also evident in the introduction of boot camps for juvenile offenders. According to one report, boot camps, which were first initiated in 1983 and are now established in thirty states, feature not only "military drills and hard labor" but "substance abuse treatment."[149] A Bureau of Justice Statistics study similarly reports that boot camps or "shock incarceration" programs "use physical or mental challenges to build self-esteem and self-control—modeled after 'challenge' programs such as Outward Bound."[150] Initial findings from yet another study found that 58 percent of boot camp programs identified "drug treatment" as a "primary element in their programs."[151] Thus therapeutic intervention is often a major part of the military-styled boot camps, a program most often known for its regimented, hard-hitting approach. In this scenario, as with the Drug Courts, the presence of therapeutic drug intervention does not equate with a soft approach to crime. Hence the tough-on-crime orientation of the mid-1990s political climate may more accurately be understood to coexist with therapeutic programs than to stand in opposition to them.

Arguably, given the fundamentally utilitarian nature of the "Contract with America" agenda, the coexistence of these two impulses is a subset of the larger phenomenon observed in this chapter, of the conflation of therapeutic and utilitarian languages. After all, the most often repeated claim by those favoring reform is that the present criminal justice system "does not work." Variations in the meaning of efficacy notwithstanding, the emotivist ethic is conflated with the utilitarian perspective in public advocacy of the therapeutic process within the world of criminal justice. In other words, the implementation and advancement of therapeutic processes are supported on the dual basis that these processes work and that they are more personal and sensitive to the needs of clients. Empirical evidence that calls into question program efficacy (as interpreted in a more traditional sense) has, in some instances, been ignored or disregarded, particularly in the case of the Drug Courts. This would seem to indicate that the efficacy argument is used chiefly as an aesthetic appeal to the persistent (though perhaps waning) resonance of utilitarianism in American society. However, that the defenses of these therapeutically oriented programs have to draw on the language of utilitarianism to be taken seriously is significant and may say more about how the two perspectives necessarily coexist than it does about the triumph of the therapeutic over the utilitarian orientation.

As with the tort reform efforts considered in the previous chapter, then, recent tough-on-crime political declarations may have more to do with an enduring utilitarianism than they do with a principled opposition to the therapeutic ethos (or its institutional manifestations). Though the two orientations can be conflictual, they can also, as is evident in the cases of the Drug Courts and the boot camps, exist simultaneously. Whether complementary or conflictual, these are the prevailing languages to which politicians and criminal justice authorities appeal to guide and defend their programs.

Evident in the advancement of the Drug Court and therapeutic prison programs, then, are both dimensions of the legitimation equation being investigated here. With respect to the validity component, state power is valid inasmuch as it is advanced through these approved judicial programs. Furthermore, the programs are justified or defended through appeals to both utilitarian and therapeutic ideals.

That court officials are changing programs in a manner that they believe reflects the disposition of the culture was made glaringly apparent in one judge's plea to a gathering of more than five hundred participants at a national Drug Court conference. In advocacy of what he called "therapeutic jurisprudence," Judge Thomas Merrigan stated:

> If we don't change what we are doing in the next few years, and if we don't change how we go about serving the community with more relevancy, with more meaning, we are going to find that in twenty-five years, we have become irrelevant in the minds of the public. They will no longer consider us meaningful. . . . So, for me, it's not an option. For me, what we are doing is . . . reinventing justice, and we are doing it in a way that is relevant to what are the needs in the community.[152]

Evident in Merrigan's defense of the Drug Courts is a clearly articulated concern with the perceived erosion of the judicial branch's legitimacy, and the belief that what will engender confidence anew is the institutionalization of therapeutic ideals and practices.

We turn now to America's educational system, to investigate the presence of similar legitimating themes in this important institution of the American state.

5

Public Education

Though education, in the contemporary context, is clearly an important institution in the American state apparatus, this has not always been the case. It was not until after the efforts of nineteenth-century common-school crusaders that universal free education became a reality in the United States. To say that the state was not involved in education prior to that time, however, would be misleading. Even before the widespread institutionalization of compulsory public education, the state governments were involved in varying degrees with supporting and shaping the direction of America's schools. As David Tyack, Thomas James, and Aaron Benavot explain, "In one form or another, government has always been in the classroom." [1] Still, the state's role has certainly expanded over the years, which makes public education an interesting case study for this project. Recall Habermas's assertion that continued state expansion exacerbates the problem of legitimation—that is, as the state enters into new realms of society, the problem of justifying its presence is made all the more acute. Inasmuch as education represents an area where the state has continued to expand its authority, it offers itself as an interesting forum for investigating the problem of legitimacy.

Considered here, then, is not the expansion of state control over education—a development well documented elsewhere—but of the sources of legitimation to which educators and legislators have appealed for justifying the state's expanding role. Offering themselves as avenues for documenting this phenomenon are the various legal directives that have guided school policy over the years and the changing content of curricula and other educational materials used in the classroom. [2] In many instances, the two are directly related to each other. State and federal laws have often specified what could be taught and even, in some instances, how it should be taught. Taken together, these avenues point to the sources of legitimation to which politicians, parents, and teachers have appealed for justifying the state's involvement in education.

Specifically, this chapter focuses on that part of education which is concerned with the inculcation of values or morals. Any historical treatment of education in America necessarily begins here, because this was the primary focus of the schools in early American history. And though this component of education has clearly changed and is less integrated into the totality of the pedagogical process, it remains an important feature of American education. Because my concern is with the notion of legitimacy, values education represents the obvious place where cultural codes of moral understanding or the sources of legitimacy are most observable.

The Colonial Period

Until the 1830s, education in the United States was organized at the local level, where the structure of the school and the content of instruction varied from district to district. Schools were funded through a combination of state assistance, tuition and fees, and local property taxes.[3] Schools were not centrally organized; they were not compulsory, nor were they universally free. Inasmuch as the individual state polities provided oversight for the schools, the support was justified by its purported aim to ensure the inculcation of traditional religious ideals.

Consider, for example, the following statute passed by the legislative authority of Massachusetts in 1671:

> It being one chief project of Satan to keep men from the knowledge of the Scripture . . . to the end that learning may not be buried in the graves of our forefathers, in church and commonwealth, the Lord assisting our endeavors; it is therefore ordered by this court and authority thereof, that every township within this jurisdiction, after the Lord hath increased them to the number of fifty householders, shall then forthwith appoint one within their towns to teach all such children as shall resort to him to write and read.[4]

Similarly, the General Assembly of Maryland passed an act in 1723 to make provision for "the liberal and pious education of the youth of this province."[5] South Carolina's 1712 prescription for who could teach in a Charleston school was likewise based on concerns about the advancement of the Christian religion. The statute provided that

> the person to be master of the said school shall be of the religion of the Church of England, and conform to the same, and shall be capable to

teach the learned languages, that is to say, Latin and Greek tongues, and to catechise and instruct the youth in the principles of the Christian religion, as professed in the Church of England.[6]

Even when state involvement in education was resisted, the rationales for doing so were based on religiously derived legitimations. For example, in 1670 the British commissioners of plantations issued to several governors of the English colonies the conditions of their respective jurisdictions, including questions about provisions for educating children. Sir William Berkeley, governor of Virginia at the time, wrote in response, "I thank God that there are no free schools nor printing, and I hope we shall not have these hundred years; for learning has brought disobedience, and heresy, and sects into the world, and printing has divulged them, and libels against the best government. God keep us from both."[7] Thus the available sources of legitimation for government action (or inaction) were derived from a conspicuously religious ideological system.

Not surprisingly, then, any mention of education in the various state constitutions was of the same nature. Consider, for example, Massachusetts's Constitution, ratified in 1789, which called for the "support and maintenance of public Protestant teachers of piety, religion, and morality";[8] or the New Hampshire Constitution, framed in 1784, which provided state support for "public protestant teachers of piety, religion, and morality," believing that "morality and piety, rightly grounded on evangelical principles, will give the best and greatest security to government."[9] As Lawrence Cremin observes, "Piety and good character were the stated requirements for teachers everywhere, with piety defined as religious orthodoxy in most of the colonies."[10] The religiously understood basis for education was also evident in the Northwest Ordinance, issued in 1787, which declared that "religion, morality, and knowledge, being necessary to good government and the happiness of mankind, schools and the means of education shall forever be encouraged."[11]

Thus, though there was no centrally administered public educational system, the states did give some direction and provide some support for schools during this period, and justifications for doing so were based on a religious—indeed, Protestant Christian—basis of legitimation. An example of more direct government involvement in education at the beginning of the nineteenth century—a case that foretold greater state participation in America's schools—was New York's support of the Public School Society, established in 1805. The purpose of the society was to provide schools for the poor children in New York City. who could not attend private, usually denominationally sponsored, schools in the city. Consistent with the state mandates reviewed above, New York justified state support for the society with its promise to implant in children's minds "the principles of religion and morality" and to assist them in cultivating the "habits of industry and virtue." [12] And though the society was nonsectarian, the content of instruction was in keeping with the religious sentiments evident in early state statutes.

Consider the following excerpt from a teacher's manual used in the primary grades of the Public School Society schools:

Teacher. My dear children, the intention of this school is to teach you to be good and useful in this world, that you may be happy in the world to come. What is the intention of this school?

T. We therefore first teach you to "remember your Creator in the days of your youth." What do we first teach you?

T. It is our duty to teach you this, because we find it written in the Holy Bible. Why is it our duty to teach you this?

T. The Holy Bible directs us to "train you up in the way you should go." What good book directs us to train you up in the way you should go?

T. Therefore, my children, you must obey you parents.

Scholar. I must obey my parents . . .

T. You must obey your teachers.

S. I must obey my teachers . . .

T. God always sees you. (*Slowly, and in soft tone.*)

S. God always sees me.

T. God hears all you say.

S. God hears all I say.

T. God knows all you do.

S. God knows all I do.[13]

The content of instruction, though nonsectarian, was clearly Protestant in orientation and resembled the materials used in non-state-sponsored schools. The most popular of these was the *New England Primer,* first published by Boston's Benjamin Harris in 1690. Contained in the *New England Primer,* along with the alphabet and the syllabary were the Lord's Prayer, the Apostles' Creed, various proverbs, and many other selections from the Bible. Children were admonished in the *Primer* with maxims such as "He who ne'er learns his ABC, forever will a blockhead be." The ABC's were learned through such religiously informed rhythmic couplets as "In Adam's fall / We sinned all. Heaven to find / The Bible mind. Christ crucify'd / For Sinners dy'd."[14] As such, the content of the curriculum corresponded directly with the statutory declarations regarding the purpose of education.

And though direct government involvement in the schools was limited during this period, the ideological seeds were sown for a society-wide public education system. Thomas Jefferson, Benjamin Rush, and Noah Webster were among those in the colonial period who advocated the establishment of universal free education, or what came to be called "common schools." Strong opposition to higher taxes and preference for local autonomy led Americans largely to resist such efforts through the end of the eighteenth century and into the first couple of decades of the nineteenth century. It was only after the enormous social changes that accompanied the processes of industrialization, massive immigration, and urbanization during the nineteenth century that communities began to recognize the possible merits associated with the establishment of common schools.

Universal Free Education

With the opportunities accompanying the growth of industrial capitalism in the United States, the flow of immigrants into the states increased dramatically after 1830. During the 1820s, fewer than fifteen thousand typically immigrated to the United State each year. Between 1832 and 1850, in contrast, the annual rate was usually more than one hundred thousand, with new arrivals in the 1840s typically numbering more than two hundred thousand per year. Between 1830 and 1850, the total U.S. population expanded from thirteen million to roughly twenty-three million.[15] A large percentage of these immigrants were Catholic. In the 1830s, for example, some 600,000 Catholics immigrated to the United States; in the next two decades, in excess of 4,200,000 arrived on American shores. By the 1880s, Catholics represented 12 percent of the American population, whereas less than a century earlier they had comprised only about 1 percent of the total population.[16] It perhaps goes without saying that this influx of Catholics challenged the demographic and ultimately cultural predominance of Protestantism.

Most of these immigrants settled in the growing urban areas of the industrializing Northeast and Midwest. In fact, the number of individuals living in towns or cities with more than twenty-five hundred inhabitants increased three times as fast as did the general U.S. population during the same period. Between 1830 and 1860, the proportion of people living in communities of twenty-five hundred or more rose from less than one in ten to about one in five; that is, whereas less than 10 percent of the population lived in cities with twenty-five hundred or more residents in 1830, more than 20 percent did so by 1860.[17] In 1800, only six cities in the United States had more than ten thousand inhabitants; by 1850, the number of cities had increased to more than sixty.[18]

The social changes that accompanied these large demographic shifts became issues of much concern to America's middle-class Protestant establishment, particularly with respect to the growing labor class in the urban areas. As Mustafa Emirbayer notes, "Respectable citizens expressed heightened concern over the social volatility of the 'laboring classes'; they pointed with growing alarm to such immoral and disruptive behaviors as brawling, rioting, drunkenness, prostitution, vagrancy, licentiousness, and juvenile delinquency."[19] Widespread public concern with these conditions opened the door for the advancement of the common-school ideas first introduced by Jefferson and Rush at the end of the eighteenth century.

Common-school crusaders, fearing the disruptiveness of growing and diversely populated urban areas, saw a unified educational system as a means whereby fundamental American values could be passed on to children. It was believed that only by instilling in children the values of good citizenship could the Republic be preserved. On a broader cultural basis education became viewed as a potential social force that could serve to assimilate and Americanize the diverse, expanding, and "disruptive" population of immigrants in America's industrializing cities.

Thus the social conditions were ripe for the state to establish and administer a more centralized public educational system. And although state-controlled education was proposed as a remedy to the problems associated with these larger social changes, it, too, was not spared the impact of industrialization and the concomitant influence of rationalization. As Carl Kaestle explains, the "same ethos of efficiency, manipulation, and mastery" that affected other nineteenth-century institutions likewise influenced the schools. The introduction of an educational bureaucracy, centralized control, and the training of teachers in the new "normal schools" served to make the institution "in some respects like a factory."[20] Classes were, for the first time, divided into a stratification of different grade levels for various age groups: courses became special-ized (that is, different teachers taught specific subjects); and the format of instruction became more uniformly standardized.

In large measure, justifications for government-sponsored education continued to be based on a traditional religious code of moral under-standing. However, because of growing cultural pluralism, the establish-ment of a common school necessarily involved appeals to the symbols that resonated throughout the society as a whole. Thus religious ideals were expressed in a much less sectarian fashion and were joined in a unique mix with other ideological systems—a fusion of cultural legiti-mations approximating those discussed in Chapter 2. Educational theo-ries during this period, and concomitant justifications for the develop-ment of the common schools, were, as Emirbayer explains, "the product of a complex synthesis of multiple world-views. Classical republican, evangelical Protestant, and liberal individualist ideals were all selectively and creatively drawn upon by mid-nineteenth century respectables." [21]

This was certainly evident in public arguments for support of the common schools offered by Horace Mann, who had become during that time the "most powerful figure in American education" [22] and the lead-ing spokesman for a more inclusive and less sectarian approach to education. Consider, for example, the following statement written by Mann and issued by the Massachusetts Board of Education in 1847:

> I believe in the existence of a great, immutable principle of natural law, or natural ethics, —a principle antecedent to all human institutions and incapable of being abrogated by any ordinances of man, —a principle of divine origin, clearly legible in the ways of Providence as those ways are manifested in the order of nature and in the history of the race, —which proves the absolute right of every human being that comes into the world to an education; and which, of course, proves the correlative duty of every government to see that the means of that education are provided for all. ... The will of God, as conspicuously manifested in the order of nature, and in the relations which he has established among men, places the right of every child that is born into the world to such a degree of education as will enable him, and, as far as possible will predispose him, to perform all domestic, social, civil and moral duties, upon the same clear ground of natural law and equity, as it places a child's right, upon his first coming into the world, to distend his lungs with a portion of the common air." [23]

In the same statement, then, Mann appealed to Providence and the will of God; to natural law and the rights of the child; and to the importance of performing "domestic, social, civil and moral duties," and he did so to justify government's duty to provide education "for all." As such, each of the three legitimating themes identified in Chapter 2 was invoked in some form to justify expanded state involvement in the education of America's children. Gone were the more conspicuously Protestant legitimations evident during the colonial period. Again, the growing diversity of American culture, fostered by immigration and urbanization, made defenses for state education rooted in sectarian Protestant theology increasingly unpalatable to the citizenry at large.

The result was the advancement of a public school system that was self-consciously less guided by the specific tenets of a Protestant Christian ideological system. Consider, for example, the fate of the previously considered Public School Society in New York. Under pressure from Catholics, the New York legislature in 1842 removed control of the schools from the society, which had overseen them for more than thirty years, and placed it under the auspices of a newly created board of education. Subsequently, the specifically Protestant emphasis of the early society schools was neutralized. As the legislative act states:

> No school . . . which shall be organized under this act, in which any religious sectarian doctrine or tenet shall be taught, inculcated, or practiced, shall receive any portion of the school moneys to be distributed by this act, as hereinafter provided; and it shall be the duty of the trustees, inspectors, and commissioners of schools in each ward, and of the deputy superintendent of schools, from time to time, and as frequently as need be, to examine and ascertain, and report to the said board of education, whether any religious sectarian doctrine or tenet shall have been taught, inculcated, or practiced in any of the schools in their respective wards.[24]

By the end of the nineteenth century, forty-one of the forty-eight existing states passed similar statutes forbidding sectarian influence within the common or public schools.[25] The legislative directives were aimed not only at prohibiting sectarian control of schools but at forbidding the use of sectarian instructional materials in the classroom. An 1875 Arkansas statute held, for example, that "no teacher employed in any of the common schools shall permit sectarian books to be used as a reading or textbook in the school under his care."[26] Similarly, an 1895 New Hampshire statute held that "no books shall be introduced into the public schools calculated to favor any particular religious sect or political party."[27]

In some cases, provisions against sectarian control of the common schools were made part of a state's constitution. For example, the following provision became part of California's Constitution in 1879: "nor shall any sectarian or denominational doctrine be taught or instruction thereon be permitted, directly or indirectly, in any of the common schools of this state."[28] Interestingly, what led to the adoption of this and related constitutional requirements was a fracas over use of the *McGuffey Readers* in California's schools.

The *McGuffey Readers* were a major feature of American education during the nineteenth century. It is estimated that more than 120 million copies of the *Readers* were sold between 1836 and 1920.[29] However, like the *New England Primer* that preceded it, the *McGuffey Readers*, particularly the earlier editions, contained lessons based heavily on a Protestant ideological system. Consider, for example, Lesson 37 of the *Eclectic First Reader* (1836):

> At the close of the day, before you go to sleep, you should not fail to pray to God to keep you from sin and harm.
>
> You ask your friends for food, and drink, and books, and clothes; and when they give you these things, you thank them, and love them for the good they do you.
>
> So you should ask your God for those things which he can give you, and which no one else can give you.
>
> You should ask him for life, and health, and strength; and you should pray for him to keep your feet from the ways of sin and shame.
>
> You should thank him for all his good gifts; and learn, while young, to put your trust in him; and the kind care of God will be with you, both in your youth and in your old age.[30]

With the changing cultural climate, use of the traditional readers became a matter of some controversy, as occurred in California as part of a larger battle over which political body—the state legislature or local authorities—would control education in the state. The Board of Education stopped using the *McGuffey Readers* in 1875, replacing them with the more progressive *Pacific Coast Readers* published out of San Francisco. The conflict between the courts, the legislature, and the Board of Education over use of the *Readers* continued for another four years and culminated in the passage of an amendment to the California Constitution that effectively removed the *McGuffey Readers* as the state-mandated textbook for use in California's common schools.[31]

The removal of the *McGuffey Readers* as the sponsored text series in California's common schools, the usurpation of control of the Public School Society schools in New York, and the introduction of antisectarian laws all are indicative of the growing implausibility of an educational system based on the precepts of Protestant Christianity. During the common-school era, legitimations for the state's increased involvement in education were based on a mixture of moral reference points, with an identifiable leaning toward the ideals of civic duty and virtue within a classical republican system of moral understanding. Even the content of the *McGuffey Readers* moved in this direction in later editions.[32]

Mann, along with other important figures in the common school movement such as John Pierce of Michigan, Calvin Stowe of Ohio, and Henry Barnard of Connecticut, promoted a form of instruction that stressed the development of the republican traits of good citizenship. Such notions of republican virtue had existed in American culture from its earliest days. However, with the neutralizing of the distinctive characteristics of the previously hegemonic Protestant system of moral understanding, the republican ideals of good citizenship and commitment to the common good became all the more prominent.

Emphasized in state government directives were republican and industrial-era virtues such as moderation, truthfulness, frugality, patriotism, industry, temperance, and promptness. Consider, for example, this late-nineteenth-century statute passed by the Massachusetts legislature, which encouraged teachers to "impress on the minds of the children . . . the principles of morality and justice, and a sacred regard for truth; love of country, humanity and universal benevolence; sobriety, industry and frugality; chastity, moderation and temperance; and all other virtues which ornament human society."[33] Similarly, an 1897 statute in the state of Washington held:

> It shall be the duty of all teachers to endeavor to impress on the minds of their pupils the principles of morality, truth, justice, temperance, humanity and patriotism; to teach them to avoid idleness, profanity and falsehood; to instruct them in the principles of free government, and to train them up to the true comprehension of the rights, duties and dignity of American citizenship.[34]

These state codes illustrate how the American schools shifted away from a strictly Protestant basis of education to a more complex fusion of less sectarian Protestantism with civic republicanism and Enlightenment-based ideas of individual rights. Emphasis on the last of these is certainly evident in the public justifications offered for the common school. Recall how Mann's defense of universal free education was based, in part, on an "absolute *right* of every human being that comes into the world to an education."

It was this emphasis on the child's right to education that justified the introduction of compulsory attendance laws in many states in the latter part of the nineteenth century and that would become the greater focus of state educational efforts in the years thereafter. Paradoxically, then, initial steps by Mann and others to disassociate pedagogy from the specific tenets of particular Protestant dogmas eventuated in the development of an educational system that looked nothing like what the reformers had intended. Over time, the liberal emphasis on the rights of the individual and on the need to foster the naturally good instincts of the child would become a more prominent feature of governmental declarations about the purpose of education. Again, these leanings became more pronounced in public defenses of compulsory attendance statutes introduced in the last decades of the nineteenth century.

Compulsory Education

The first state to pass a compulsory attendance law was Massachusetts, in 1852. By the turn of the century, thirty-two states had passed compulsory education laws, and by 1910, all but a handful of Southern states had done so.[35] The introduction of compulsory attendance laws represented the natural next step in the expansion of state authority in education. Not only would the state provide universal free schools, as was successfully accomplished in the first part of the nineteenth century, but now it would insist that children attend them. Like the common schools, compulsory attendance laws were initially resisted. Opponents argued against them on the grounds that they interfered with the rights and liberties of parents, that they would be difficult to enforce, that they were un-American, and that they granted new powers to the government.

Without denying the further abrogation of parental authority by the government, advocates defended the laws by appealing not only to notions of public duties — the republican themes popular in defenses of the common school — but to the idea of the child's individual rights. The latter, in large measure, served as the basis for this new demonstration of state authority. As Tyack, James, and Benavot explain, "The theory behind compulsory attendance laws introduced new assumptions about the authority of the state in education. One was that the child had 'educational rights' that must be protected by the state and could not be denied by parents."[36] This basic line of reasoning was certainly evident in the defense of Connecticut's 1872 compulsory attendance law offered by B. G. Northrop, secretary of the Board of Education of the state of Connecticut at the time. Northrop claimed that "the child has rights which not even a parent may violate. He may not rob his child of the sacred right of a good education."[37] Responding to those who may have thought education was unnecessary, Northrop argued, "Those who need education most and prize it least are fit subjects for coercion."[38]

Similarly, a report put out by the United States Bureau of Education in 1914 responded to the contention that such laws violated the rights of parents by stating, "Has the helpless child no sacred rights? Has the State not some privileges?" Again, state privilege (or power) was justified on the grounds that it fulfilled a child's natural rights. The report claimed further that "when the State compels the parent to send his child to school, it is simply compelling the parent to put the child in possession of his own rightful inheritance . . . his right to the benefit of what the State has collected and set apart for him."[39]

These arguments for the sacred rights of the child were joined by appeals to ideas of duty; but even here, the notion of duty was used in a slightly different way. Because the "State needs the intelligent services of that child," it was argued, it must prepare him or her through education. It was as if education served the purpose of preparing the child for effective use in the machinery of the state. As the 1914 U.S. Bureau of Education report articulates:

> In a democracy, such as ours, the primary object in educating the people is to make good, intelligent, loyal, and prosperous citizen-sovereigns. . . . If our Government is to achieve and maintain that eminence among the powers of the earth to which we pledge our faith, it must secure for itself an intelligent, efficient, and orderly citizenship. Intelligence and efficiency lie at the very foundation of any people's greatness. Intelligent and efficient citizens are a State's fundamental asset.[40]

As such, it was the state's "duty . . . to see that the child is fitted for its part."[41] Similarly, a report issued by the Illinois superintendent of public instruction in 1868 advanced the following maxim: "That a State has a just moral claim upon so much of the property of the people as may be required to educate its children, and fit them for usefulness as good citizens—involves the idea of compulsion in the last resort." [42] Capturing both of the forms of legitimation that typically undergirded defenses of compulsory attendance laws, John Ireland of Minnesota argued the following at a 1890 National Education Association meeting about the issue:

> I unreservedly favor state laws making instruction compulsory. Instruction is so much needed by each citizen for his own sake and for that of society that a father who neglects to provide for his child's instruction sins against the child and against society, and it behooves the state to punish him. [43]

Thus compulsory education extended the authority of the state still further. It was largely justified on the grounds that education helped prepare useful and efficient citizens and served the rights and needs of children. The latter would become the more predominant concern in the next period of American educational history.

The Progressive Era

With compulsory public schools instituted on a society-wide basis, issues of state authority and concomitant rhetorical legitimations became centered not so much on state control of the schools but on control over the type of education that should take place in the schools. As is commonly known, the Progressive Era, or the approximate period in educational history between the beginning and the middle of the twentieth century, saw the further extension of the individual-rights emphasis in education that was detectable at the end of the nineteenth century. At the ideological center of these efforts were the ideas of the educational theorist and reformer John Dewey.

Like the efforts of nineteenth-century reformers, progressivist efforts at the turn of the century and beyond developed in response to a perceived need to bring about radical reform in society. Some of the same societal processes that had sparked reform during the common-school era precipitated the actions of progressive reformers in the early part of the twentieth century. A second wave of immigrants, continuing industrialization and urbanization, rapid growth in transportation, and technological advancements in communication all served to alter further the nature of community, family, and traditional processes of socialization. As in earlier times, these social shifts brought changes that many saw as highly problematic. Immigrants were still viewed by many as a "distinct national menace" who led native-born Americans into "idleness, crime, and error." [44] As before, education was considered an agent of reform, a forum through which children would be made into useful American citizens.

In certain respects, Dewey and other progressivists were reacting against the highly rationalized nature of education that became established in the latter part of the nineteenth century. Dewey viewed with disdain the routinized practices of rote memorization and mechanical recitation of math tables, as well as the formal behavioral etiquette rigidly enforced in the schools. But Dewey's work was not just an antithesis to rationalization. Indeed, in many respects his educational goals represented a full endorsement of rationalism. For one thing, he strongly advocated practical training in manual skills. According to Dewey, the student should not just learn abstract ideas from a textbook but should realize the practical experience of working with his or her hands, pragmatic skills relevant to life in an industrialized society. In 1919, for example, Dewey celebrated the introduction of new curricula that not only taught "the scientific laws that . . . brought about the changes in society" but substituted "real work—which itself teaches the facts of life—for the study and memorization of facts after they have been classified in books." [45] He also observed approvingly that the educational system was just beginning to recognize that such "training is necessary for the man who works with his hands . . . [and] that control of the material things of life is knowledge." [46]

The effects of rationalism were also evident in Dewey's rejection of religion as a necessary part of public education. Instead, he embraced the modern notion that what was true was only that which could be empirically measured, observed, experienced. For example, Dewey stated in his 1930 "Credo" on religion that "faith in its newer sense signifies that experience itself is the sole ultimate authority," and that we should surrender the "supernaturalism and fixed dogma and rigid institutionalism with which Christianity has been historically associated." [47] Instead, Dewey believed that "science and the scientific method would solve all human problems." [48]

Dewey's alignment with empirical science, however, was joined with new ideas about the nature of children and about the teacher's responsibility to meet children's psychological needs. Deweyian educational philosophy was self-consciously child-centered. "Everyone," Dewey held, "has a right to demand an education which shall meet his own needs, and that for its own sake the State must supply this demand.[49] According to this philosophical understanding of education, then, the state's involvement was justified on the grounds that it fulfilled the rights and needs of the child.

Less evident in progressivist theories were the former legitimations based on classical republicanism and Protestant Christianity. That this shift was not isolated in the philosophy of an individual educational theorist is evident in the changes of some state laws delineating the duties of the public schoolteacher. Consider, for example, Virginia's public education statute as first instituted in 1887:

> Provision shall further be made for moral education in the public schools to be extended throughout the entire course. Such instruction shall be imparted by reading books and text-books inculcating the virtues of a pure and noble life. The text-books shall be selected as are other text-books by the State board of education.[50]

In 1928 this language was emended to read as follows:

> The entire scheme of training shall emphasize moral education through lessons given by teachers and imparted by appropriate reading selections.[51]

Gone were the specific state instructions to inculcate the virtues of a pure and noble life.

A similar law enacted in Florida in the latter part of the nineteenth century read as follows:

> Every teacher is directed . . . to embrace every opportunity to inculcate, by precept and example, the principles of truth, honesty and patriotism and the practice of every christian [sic] virtue. To require the pupils to observe personal cleanliness, neatness, order, promptness and gentility of manners, to avoid vulgarity and profanity, and to cultivate in them habits of industry and economy, a regard for the rights and feelings of others, and their own responsibilities and duties as citizens.[52]

In 1951 this statute was repealed. In its place, new language was attached to an adjacent statute regarding health and the dangers of alcohol and drugs, as follows:

... and provided further, that any child whose parent shall present to the school principal a signed statement that the teaching of disease, its symptoms, development and treatment, and the viewing of pictures or motion pictures or such subjects conflict with the religious teachings of their church, shall be exempt from such instruction, and no child so exempt shall be penalized by reason of such exemption.[53]

Again, these changes demonstrate a departure from reliance on former sources of legitimation. (And that instructions regarding student behavior were shifted to a section on health is itself telling, and likely to be related to the larger societal process of reinterpreting behaviors in pathological rather than moral terms.)

Though progressivists still drew arguments from the complex mixture of cultural systems evident in the common-school era, the scales were clearly tipped in the direction of individual freedom. Indeed, Dewey's followers went beyond Dewey's own understanding of freedom. Whereas, for Dewey, freedom was "achieved though the exercise of intelligence," for some of his "less discriminating" disciples, "intelligence [was] achieved through the exercise of freedom."[54] The telos moved from obedience to externally imposed moral and intellectual demands to the realization of internally derived needs and experiences.

Although there is little question about the profound effect Dewey's work had on American education, there remains some question about how far-reaching his influence was on actual educational practices in the schools. Dewey, for example, observed in 1902 that though his ideas had "become the commonplace of pedagogic writing and of the gatherings where teachers meet for inspiration and admonition," it was the conservative who still "retained actual control of school conditions.[55] This, of course, would change in the thirty-plus years after Dewey's turn-of-the-century observation—but to what extent?

While Dewey's influence on state educational practices did become more visible over time, progressivist ideas were usually instituted at the local school board rather than at the state level. Consider, for example, a 1916 account of developments in the public schools of Gary, Indiana. Under the leadership of Superintendent William Wirt, the Gary schools were reorganized to form "a genuine children's community, where the children's normal healthy interests [were] centered." Offering to "take the place of the old household and rural community life which provided for our forefathers," the Gary schools provided "well-balanced facilities of work, study, and play" and placed greater emphasis on "doing the things that have meaning to . . . children."[56]

Similarly, as a result of a 1919 Board of Education mandate, the Winnetka, Illinois schools were reorganized according to progressivist themes. According to Carleton Washburne, superintendent of the Winnetka school district at the time, "The Winnetka schools were reorganized to provide for individual progress, a large measure of individual instruction, and considerable emphasis on socialized and self-expressive activities."[57] The self-expressive activities were ungraded exercises that grew "out of the children's interest" and were apparently the main focus of educational activity, occupying "about half of each morning and half of each afternoon."[58]

That the state turned to progressivist ideals to legitimate its involvement in the content of instruction was also evident, in some instances, at the federal level. Consider, for example, state justification for educational programs within the Civilian Conservation Corps (CCC), established in March 1933 as one of the earliest and most popular New Deal initiatives. In 1940 the American Council on Education noted that more boys entered the CCC than entered American colleges and universities as freshmen each year. By 1941, more than 2.5 million young men had been enrolled in the corps. In 1935, C. S. Marsh, director of the CCC, noted the influences of progressivist ideas on the American educational landscape, specifically the shift toward greater concern with the individual: "The individual is the center of interest; our grave concern is the development of his power and his individuality." Marsh saw the "educational philosophy underlying the CCC Educational Program [to be] in full consonance with this current movement."[59]

Among the objectives of the CCC was a commitment "to develop in each man his powers of self-expression, self-entertainment, and self-culture." The forms and content of instruction were not "imposed from above" but were oriented toward meeting "the immediate needs and interests of the people." In short, Marsh saw the CCC as in complete philosophical and practical agreement with the "modern philosophy of . . . education," namely, "that not only the individual shall be fitted to live in his own world, but that his immediate needs and interests shall be made the dominant concern."[60]

Thus, more than fifteen years after Dewey lamented the slow progress of his ideas, he could write that his educational philosophy was becoming "transmuted into reality" and that schools based on his experimental models were "rapidly coming into being in large numbers all over the country."[61] The legacy of Dewey's success represents an important transition point in the focus of education. Though it was, in some respects, a reaction against certain features of a more rationalized educational system, it also fully welcomed other aspects of rationalized science, along with certain psychological ideals and practices. Dewey himself recognized how the "arguments of science and psychology" reinforced the "educational changes which took place."[62] A 1930 *New Republic* article, not fully sympathetic with progressive education, noted these two dominant tendencies within progressive educational philosophy: "One emphasizes the need of making education a direct preparation for life; the other emphasizes the importance of full and free development. The former prides itself on its application of scientific method to the problem of the curriculum; the latter poses as the champion of childhood's right to live a life of its own."[63]

With the undermining of traditional cultural systems in education, the child was instructed toward the end of self-realization—a development, however, that did not involve a rejection of the scientific method. Such emphases left the child with little more than his or her subjective feelings as a basis for moral reasoning. The evolution toward this self-determining basis for values was, as noted above, more evident in theory than in practice. It would, however, become more explicit in the later decades of the twentieth century, though under a different guise. Late-twentieth-century educational philosophies, however, clearly stem from the progressive educational themes of the first half of the twentieth century—a movement that was itself the logical end of changes that began in the nineteenth-century reform efforts of common-school crusaders.

As both Kaestle and Emirbayer observe, it was the process of sectarian disengagement initiated by the common-school reformers that started this process. The logic was the same: "If Puritan is too narrow, try Protestant; if Protestantism offends, broaden it to Christian; if Christianity alienates, mute spirituality in a secular faith for the schools. The strategy was to be inclusive by being uncontroversial."[64] Thus, though uncontroversial, the legitimating basis for public education was fundamentally altered. It evolved to fit the changing conditions of a more pluralistic industrial society. As Robert Michaelsen writes, "At this juncture, what seemed to be needed was a 'common faith' which would emerge from the democratic community . . . from life together, not from a transcendent entity or a historic tradition."[65]

The Cosmopolitan Era

The advance of progressive education in the United States appears to have sputtered to a halt in the 1950s. By the mid-1950s, as Richard Hersh, John Miller, and Glen Fielding write, "the progressive education movement had all but died." [66] This may, however, be overstating things a bit. The emphasis of Dewey's progressive ideas did take a beating in the 1950s. With the Soviet launching of the Sputnik satellite, Americans became fearful that their educational system was failing, that children were not being adequately instructed in the academic basics, and that the Soviets were surpassing Americans in intellectual and technological prowess. The experiential, subjective, and individualistically oriented practices of the Progressive Era were blamed for these failings. President Dwight D. Eisenhower, for example, advised educators in the late 1950s "to abandon the educational path that, rather blindly, they have been following as a result of John Dewey's teaching." [67] But the backlash against Dewey was short-lived. In retrospect, it appears to have been more of an aberration than a sea change in the direction of education.

By the early 1960s, as H. Warren Button and Eugene Provenzo note, "conservative criticism waned." [68] What emerged in its place were essentially, the central themes of progressive education, though garbed in new nomenclature. That the Supreme Court ruled in the early 1960s that prayer and Bible reading in public schools were unconstitutional is just one indication of education's continued departure from traditional sources of legitimation. [69] These rulings are also indicative of the state's usurpation of authority over not only the structure of the educational system but the content of instruction as well.

Similar changes were also being codified at the state level. Consider, for example, the changes in Idaho law regarding the "duties of teachers." A statute first instituted in 1893 mandated teacher duties according to republican and industrial-era themes:

> Every teacher shall ... keep himself or herself without reproach, and endeavor to impress upon the minds of the pupils the principles of truth, justice, morality, patriotism and refinement, and to avoid idleness, falsehood, profanity, vulgarity and intemperance; give attention during every school term to the cultivation of manner. [70]

This law remained on the books until 1963, when it was repealed and replaced with the following:

> In the absence of any statute or rule or regulation of the board of trustees, any teacher employed by a school district shall have the right to direct how and when each pupil shall attend to his appropriate duties, and the manner in which a pupil shall demean himself while in attendance at the school.[71]

Absent in the 1963 replacement of the earlier law are instructions regarding the inculcation of the republican virtues of patriotism, temperance, and the like. Interestingly, the new Idaho law, like the revised Virginia law considered earlier, is more procedural and neutral. Neither really appeals to any source of legitimation. As such, they provide no clues as to the emergence of a new form of state legitimation. What replaced the Protestant and republican codes of moral understanding can, however, be detected in changes in various curricula, an area of education that itself increasingly came under the control of the state.[72]

In considering of instructional materials in what some have called the "cosmopolitan era" (the 1960s, 1970s, and early 1980s), one finds a fuller realization and advancement of ideas introduced during the Progressive Era. The developmental psychology models of Lawrence Kohlberg and Jean Piaget became the philosophical centerpieces for understanding how children develop morally. And though these models provided a framework for conceptualizing the natural process of moral development, it was actually the "values clarification" approach that was popularly used to help children advance on the path of moral growth.

The concept of values clarification assumes that the way to instruct children in morality is to help them "find the things that they value." In so doing, a student will "learn to set and achieve goals that will bring meaning and satisfaction to their lives."[73] Values clarification first emerged on the landscape of moral education with the 1966 publication of *Values and Teaching* by Louis Raths, Merrill Harmin, and Sidney B. Simon. The architects of the values clarification approach see the operation of clarifying one's values as a three-stage process: first, the child is to choose his or her values; second, the child is to prize those values, that is, cherish them and publicly affirm them; third, the child is to act upon his or her values.[74]

Though the authors of *Values and Teaching* claim that values clarification is not therapy, the process bears a striking resemblance to the client-centered therapy model of Carl Rogers. Both values clarification and client-centered therapy aim to help students/clients become more positive and self-directed. In both genres, the student/client is to be treated in an accepting and encouraging environment, where predetermined norms are not moralized onto the student/client and where interchanges are "emotional-affective" rather than "rational-intellectual." [75] Finally, in both situations the teacher/therapist assumes a role of valuing the student/clients ideas and feelings, of not giving advice, and of seeking to understand the situation from the perspective of the student/client. Alan Lockwood, for one, believes that "the similarities between client-centered therapy and values clarification are significant enough to conclude that values clarification is, in essence, a form of client-centered therapy." [76] As such, values clarification, at the least, represents the precursor to a more conspicuous adoption of the therapeutic ethos in American education. Regardless of whether values clarification represents a full appropriation of the therapeutic perspective as characterized in this book, it certainly indicates a departure from previous forms of moral instruction.

Proponents of values clarification, in fact, celebrate its distinctiveness from more traditional approaches to moral education. Leland and Mary Howe, for example, believe that the answer for helping children in the schools is not to "try to teach values through such means as moralizing, lecturing, reward and punishment, or any other methods which attempt to impose values externally." Efforts to impose such externally derived standards of morality will only compound the child's frustration and "lead ultimately to resentment of the well-meaning teacher." [77] The Howes believe that students should instead be helped to "prize and act upon their own freely chosen values." [78] With a similarly celebratory tone regarding the demise in the authority of previous moral codes and symbols, Maury Smith writes:

> Most of us still feel the effects of the Puritan and Victorian eras, when values were defined primarily in terms of moralistic "shoulds" and "should nots." Values clarification as a methodology considers this moralistic stance to be an imposition upon the individual of predetermined values, and it seeks instead a method whereby individuals can discover their own values. [79]

Though values clarification was popular in the 1960s and 1970s, the use of this specific approach did not last. In today's educational world, values clarification has been largely discredited. In the early 1980s, public concern over the academic condition of education resurfaced in a fashion reminiscent of the 1950s reaction to the Sputnik launching. In 1983 the National Commission on Excellence in Education issued *A Nation at Risk,* a condemning report on the condition of American education. The report found scholastic aptitude test (SAT) scores to have been steadily declining since 1963, that 13 percent of all seventeen-year-olds were functionally illiterate, and that American children ranked near the bottom in international achievement competitions with children from other industrialized countries.

As in the 1950s, the response to the reports of low achievement in the 1980s translated into demands for greater private and government spending on education, a stronger emphasis on academic rigor, and training in more sophisticated use of technology. The American business community, for example, invested heavily in the educational system, though with limited and discouraging results.[80] Missing in both the 1950s and the 1980s, however, were calls to return education to previous codes of moral understanding—a course of action that would be difficult, given the larger social changes in American society.

Thus, though there have been varying emphases in the content of academic instruction, the movement away from traditional sources of legitimation has continued. Just as the progressive ideologies advanced by Dewey and others reemerged in the 1960s and 1970s under a different nomenclature, the values clarification approach of the cosmopolitan era reemerged in the 1990s cloaked in new terminology.[81] The changes originally set in motion by the common-school reformers of the nineteenth century have resulted in the detachment of instruction from traditional cultural systems—in particular, from educational philosophies based in Protestant religion and civic republicanism—and the cultivation of an environment where new forms of legitimation can be advanced to provide a philosophical basis for instruction in the schools.

Before turning to a consideration of the influence of the therapeutic ethos on public American education in the contemporary context, a small qualification is warranted. The historical overview offered here touches on the highlights of legal changes and educational philosophies in U.S. pedagogy from the beginning of the American experience to the 1980s. To be sure, this sweeping review misses the nuanced qualities of instruction distinct to specific districts, schools, and teachers. Nonetheless, the larger changes are those generally agreed upon in historical accounts of American education, and they reveal an evolution that helps make sense of the type of themes that pervade the educational arena in the 1990s.

Therapeutic Education

A number of indicators reveal that the therapeutic ethos has triumphed in American education. The popular, albeit controversial, "outcome-based education" or "performance-based education" programs fully employ the feeling, self-esteeming emphasis of the therapeutic culture. Child behavior once interpreted as unruly or hyperactive is now given the pathological label of Attention Deficit Disorder (ADD). Adopting the "expert" view that 5 percent of the overall population of children have ADD, schools look for a corresponding number of students who should evidence ADD symptoms and offer interesting explanations for the recent rise in the number of ADD cases.[82] Students diagnosed with this "illness" are prescribed regular doses of Ritalin, in some cases even over the objections of their parents.[83] But these more controversial matters are really just the tip of the iceberg. Investigation into contemporary legal directives and the substantive nature of instruction within the schools indicates that the therapeutic cultural impulse has triumphed in American public education on a more widespread basis.

This is certainly evident in Rita Kramer's work on America's education schools. In visiting education schools around the country, Kramer discovered almost everywhere a pronounced emphasis on helping prospective teachers become, in essence, therapists:

> Wherever I went . . . I found a striking degree of conformity about what is considered to be the business of schools and the job of teachers. Everywhere I visited . . . I heard the same things over and over again. And failed to hear others. Everywhere, I found idealistic people eager to do good. And everywhere, I found them being told that the way to do good was to prepare themselves to cure a sick society. To become therapists, as it were, specializing in the pathology of education.[84]

The main means by which teachers are to "cure" their students is through the promotion of self-esteem. Kramer discusses the ubiquitous nature of this concept within educational training:

> What matters is not to teach any particular subject or skill, not to preserve past accomplishments or stimulate future achievements, but to give to all that stamp of approval that will make them "feel good about themselves." Self-esteem has replaced understanding as the goal of education.[85]

Along with self-esteem, Kramer found emotions to be a fundamental concept passed on to those preparing for the teaching vocation. As she explains, "Many if not most of these teachers talk about things like feeling, warmth, empathy more than they do about skills, training and discipline." [86]

An analysis of the state's involvement in today's schools reveals, on several levels, that the government plays an important role in guiding, or at least affirming, the presence of these themes in America's schools.

School Counselors

One area where this can be found is in state regulations regarding counselors in public schools. Many state boards of education mandate not only that schools have a certain number of counselors per number of students but that a certain percentage of a school counselor's time be devoted to direct individual and group counseling exercises. Moreover, in many instances the states provide guidelines for what counselors should discuss when meeting with students. Not surprisingly, the content of the counseling intervention, as required by the different states, bears the recognizable traits of the therapeutic ethos as it has been depicted in this project.

In Montana, for example, the school counselor is to assist the student in developing "a positive self-image, personal initiative, and physical independence" and in refining his or her ability to "identify and express feelings." In Massachusetts, according to state standards, the counselor is to counsel "students and others in such a way as to encourage self-exploration, self-understanding, and self confidence." And in Texas the school counselor is to "provide appropriate counseling and guidance for the changing social, emotional, psychological, and academic needs of students" and to "support the efforts of teachers and parents in promoting the student's self-esteem, academic readiness, social and interpersonal sensitivity and skills," among other things.

In many states, counselors are required to integrate the substance of developmental counseling exercises into the content of classroom instruction. Often this is to happen through regular classroom visits, as well as input into the development and selection of curricula. For example, Missouri school counselors are to spend 35 percent to 45 percent of their time "within the curriculum delivery component (structured, developmental experiences presented systematically through classroom and group activities)." Likewise in Pennsylvania, school counselors are to be in "consultation and follow-up with the school staff and administration on the application of psychological principles and knowledge to the curriculum and to classroom instruction." The South Carolina Department of Education requires that its public school counselors do the following:

> Conduct classroom guidance activities in each teacher's class and/or systematically conduct developmental counseling groups for each grade level throughout the year; consult with and/or provide resources to teachers to facilitate their instruction of counseling content and to infuse counseling content in the regular education curriculum.

Listed in Table 5.1 are state regulations concerning counselor-student ratios, as well as selected examples of the content of counseling services as regulated by state departments of education.[87]

As is evident in the various task descriptions, "self-esteem" is regarded as a significant component in school counseling efforts. That this theme is a major part of general classroom instruction is also apparent from other vantage points. Before turning to a closer look at the place of self-esteem and other therapeutic symbols in today's classrooms, I digress for a moment to consider the extent to which the self-esteem concept has been advanced on a more comprehensive basis within both education and other state institutions. So prominent has self-esteem become that proponents speak of its advancement as no less than one of movement proportions.

The Self-Esteem Movement

One of the vanguards in the movement to integrate the concept of self-esteem with education and other dimensions of the state can be found in California's state legislature. Under the leadership of Assemblyman John Vasconcellos, chairman of California's Ways and Means Committee, the state's governing body appropriated $735,000 in 1987 for the establishment of a self-esteem task force to consider the relevance of self-esteem to a wide range of social problems. Three years later, the task force concluded its study and produced a report with recommendations on how the government could promote self-esteem throughout the state.[88] Since the report's release, more than sixty thousand copies have been distributed, nearly all of California's fifty-eight counties have established task forces on self-esteem, and the California legislature has considered several bills directed toward implementing some of the report's recommendations.

For example, in October 1991 the California legislature passed A.B. 795, a bill designating $70,000 to the California's Teacher Credentialing Commission to develop a self-esteem curriculum within the state's teacher training programs. The California legislature has also considered an initiative that would create a state self-esteem "ombudsperson" and another that would create funding (about $200,000) for a nonprofit organization to advance the work of the task force.[89]

A number of grassroots self-esteem organizations have sprung up around the state that now receive some form of public funding. The "I'm Thumbody" program in Kern County; the Children's Self-Esteem Enhancement program in Chico; the California Self-Help Center at the University of California, Los Angeles (UCLA); the Foundation for Self-Esteem in Culver City; the "Student Support Center: Healing Your Feelings" program in Los Angeles; the Esteem Team program in San Rafael; the Promoting Learning and Understanding of Self program in the Irvine Unified School District; and the "Who I Am Makes a Difference" program in San Diego County are only a handful of the dozens of self-esteem programs that receive state funds.[90] There are, in fact, more than 250 programs in California that have self-esteem components.[91]

California's self-esteem efforts were bolstered by Governor Pete Wilson's public endorsement of the movement. Wilson met with the members of the task force in January 1991 and affirmed the importance of their accomplishment in "simply allow[ing] people to feel good about themselves."[92] He also declared February "Self-Esteem Month" in California. The California task force also spawned the development of a National Council for Self-Esteem, which has sixty-six chapters in twenty-nine states.[93] Plans are even underway by the national council to publish a quarterly *Journal of Self-Esteem*.

A number of other states have followed California's example. Maryland, for example, was the second state to establish a task force on self-esteem. In May 1990, Governor William Schaefer appointed a twenty-three-member task force for the purposes of promoting self-esteem among young people, making available information on existing self-esteem programs, and trying to improve the self-esteem of state employees.[94] Members of the task force included cabinet secretaries, school officials, lawyers, and academics. The effort reportedly received a tremendous amount of support. One participant claimed that "never before

TABLE 5.1
Counselor Regulations in State Public Schools

State	Counsel:Student ratio	Selected task descriptions
Alabama	1:400 (K–12)	60% of time to be spent in direct counseling services (i.e., conducting large group guidance sessions on topics such as self-esteem study skills, career information, financial aid, etc.).
Georgia	1:221–690 (9–12)	Conducts and evaluates classroom guidance activities related to . . . the developmental level of the students, i.e., motivation, self-esteem, test-taking, interpersonal relations, problem solving, etc.
Hawaii	—	Personal guidance and counseling may include, but need not be limited to, sex education, drugs and narcotics, moral and spiritual education and values, mental health and behavior.
Idaho	1:400	
Indiana	—	The services shall seek to promote the development of human potential and shall assist the individual in developing confidence and a growing sense of responsibility for his own decisions and self-direction.
Louisiana	1:450	
Massachusetts		The effective school psychologist knows: developmental psychology, psychology of learning, and principles of behavior. . . . The effective school psychologist . . . counsels students and others in such a way as to encourage self-exploration, self-understanding, and self confidence.
Missouri	1:401–500 (minimum standard) 1:301–375 (desirable standard)	The guidance curriculum adequately addresses identified student needs/competencies in career planning/ exploration, knowledge of self and others and educational and vocational development. . . . Elementary school counselors spend 35%–45% of time within the curriculum delivery component (structured, developmental experiences presented systematically through classroom and group activities).
Montana	1:400 (K–12)	Guidance: Learner Goals (1) By the end of the primary level, the student shall have had the opportunity to: (a) Develop a positive self-image, personal initiative, and physical independence; (b) Experience security in his/ her school environment; and (c) Be able to identify and express feelings.
New Hampshire	1:500 (elementary) 1:300 (middle and high school)	
North Carolina	—	Uses appropriate counseling processes and techniques for individual and group sessions to meet developmental, preventive, and remedial needs of students.
North Dakota	1:450 (secondary) 1:500 (elementary)	
Oklahoma	1:450	Counseling services shall be provided to students, in group or individual settings, that facilitate understanding of self and environment. The counseling services shall provide a planned sequential program of

		group guidance activities that enhance student self-esteem and promote the development of student competence in the academic, personal/social, and career/vocational areas.
Pennsylvania	—	Consultation and follow-up with the school staff and administration on the application of psychological principles and knowledge to the curriculum and to classroom instruction.
South Carolina	—	Conduct classroom guidance activities in each teacher's class and/or systematically conduct developmental counseling groups for each grade level throughout the year; consult with and/or provide resources to teachers to facilitate their instruction of counseling content and to infuse counseling content in the regular education curriculum.
Tennessee	1:350 (secondary 1:500 (elementary)	Aid children in academic development through the use and interpretation of test scores, improved self-concept, and early identification and attention to problems that are deterrents to learning and development.
Texas	1:500	The counselor shall: 1) provide appropriate counseling and guidance for the changing social, emotional, psychological, and academic needs of students . . . 3) support the efforts of teachers and parents in promoting the student's self-esteem, academic readiness, social and interpersonal sensitivity and skills.
Vermont	1:300 (secondary) 1:400 (elementary)	
Virginia	1:500	
West Virginia	1:350 (high school) 1:400 (secondary) 1:500 (elementary)	The school counselor shall work with individual pupils and groups of pupils in providing developmental, preventive and remedial guidance and counseling programs to meet academic, social, emotional and physical needs.
Wyoming	—	Services include . . . staff-development for building . . . district staff to help them understand student behavior and to learn intervention strategies which will assist student to practice self-fulfilling behavior.

in the history of Maryland and any of Maryland's commissioned task forces . . . have they had such an incredible amount of response. . . . Phones were totally blocked. . . . People were calling and mailing, begging, begging . . . to get on this task force." [95] In April 1990 more than five hundred participated in Maryland's first statewide conference on self-esteem.

The Maryland task force counted one thousand ways in which citizens were already working to improve self-esteem among their "fellow students, government workers, business executives and cellmates." [96] The task force also worked closely with businesses investigating ways that self-esteem improved work habits and productivity. In July 1990, Maryland personnel secretary Hilda Ford began the effort to improve self-esteem among the state's employees by directing eighty thousand of them "to smile when they do their jobs." She also started a "Yes We Can" campaign, aimed at getting employees to improve the way they listen to and serve Maryland's residents. Buttons, notepads, and twenty-four hundred posters with the "Smile" or "Listen" themes were passed out in state offices.[97]

Virginia also established a task force to promote the importance of self-esteem. As of the summer of 1990, the Virginia legislature had spent $17,850 studying self-esteem with the purpose of discovering ways to reduce the number of school dropouts. The task force initially came up with two hundred ways in which individuals could improve their self-esteem. This number was later reduced to thirty. The recommendations included such suggestions as "Take time to praise others when they do a good job. . . . Share good news to enhance others' ability to achieve. . . . Don't be too critical."[98] Each year between 1990 and 1994 Virginia's ad hoc committee on self-esteem sponsored statewide conferences on the subject.

Louisiana is yet another state whose legislative body started a task force on self-esteem. In 1990 the state created the Louisiana Commission on Promoting Esteem (COPE). One year later, the state adopted a Building Self-Esteem program for schools throughout the state. The commission planned to implement self-esteem programs in every school in the state by the 1993/94 school year.[99]

Similarly, in 1991 the Illinois legislature considered the Self-Esteem Act, which would set up a self-esteem task force based on the California example.[100] Such task forces have also been established in Kentucky, Washington, Michigan, Oregon, and Florida. Additionally, governors or legislators in other states, including Hawaii, Missouri, Mississippi, and Arkansas, are considering efforts to further the self-esteem movement. For example, in 1990, then Arkansas governor Bill Clinton enthusiastically received a personal copy of the California task force's final report from John Vasconcellos. The governor declared that "America is ripe for and looking for a new preventive approach to our major social concerns" and spoke of the "self-esteem endeavor" as "significant and timely."[101] Later that year, Clinton introduced Vasconcellos at a Democratic Leadership Council meeting in New Orleans and praised the task force's report as "a remarkable document" and encouraged all in attendance to talk to Vasconcellos about getting a copy.[102]

When I asked Assemblyman Vasconcellos about recent advances in the self-esteem movement, he responded by saying that

> the whole notion of self-esteem has become much more legitimate. Whereas when we started, people talked about it in therapy offices, now it's . . . in the newspaper everyday. It's about kids, or girls in school, or seniors, or models, or whatever. I think the word has become regularized, and the notion has become accepted by three-quarters of the society.[103]

With its growing acceptability, Vasconcellos noted the self-esteem movement's subsequent influence on a number of realms of societal life, particularly in education:

> With that, it is seeping its way into the culture, and into the schools, schools especially. There was a survey done here a year or so ago. About three-quarters of the schools in California have some self-esteem component: goals, staff development, parental involvement, parental self-esteem, students, or whatever else. . . . Now, it is kind of in the mainstream, so it kind of seeps around. The director of Drug and Alcohol Abuse for the state [of California] is a former chair of the task force on self-esteem. He is incorporating it into the drug and alcohol prevention programs around the state. The prison director has been looking at it in terms of prison systems.[104]

A look at state laws in all fifty states reveals that Vasconcellos's assessment of self-esteem's widespread acceptance and institutionalization is on the mark. By the middle of 1994, some thirty states had enacted a total of over 170 statutes that in some fashion sought to promote, protect, or enhance the self-esteem of Americans. The majority of these (around seventy-five) are, not surprisingly, in the area of education. There are additionally at least twenty self-esteem-related statutes in health care, over forty in welfare or social services, and approximately sixteen in the area of corrections or criminal justice.

Hawaii, for example, passed a law commissioning its health and education departments to "establish a statewide teenage health program designed to enhance self-esteem." Utah appropriated $100,000 in fiscal year 1993/94 "to be used for a gang prevention and intervention program designed to help at-risk students stay in school and enhance self-esteem and intellectual life skills" and another $60,000 "to increase the self-esteem and physical, intellectual, and life skills of students with disabilities through a holistic integrated arts program." A Minnesota labor law establishing employment opportunities, was instituted on the grounds that "work is an integral factor in providing a sense of purpose, direction, and self-esteem necessary to the overall physical and mental health of an individual." And on the belief that "self-esteem and self-discipline are key elements in helping inmates develop employable skills and positive work habits," North Carolina initiated a pilot program in six correctional facilities "to determine whether an inmate study course based on developing positive mental attitudes through self-esteem and self-discipline will affect the incidence of institutional disciplinary infraction and recidivism."

As mentioned above, the influence of self-esteem is most pronounced in the area of education. Florida's Department of Education, for example, was mandated by state code to "revise curriculum frameworks, as appropriate, to include building self-esteem." Among the educational standards identified in a Georgia statute was the "promotion of high self-esteem." An Illinois law requires its state Board of Education to distribute to "all school districts" a curriculum that emphasizes "life coping skills, self-esteem, and parenting skills of adolescents and teenagers." According to a 1993 Iowa statute "Each school board [in the state of Iowa] shall provide instruction in human growth and development including instruction regarding human sexuality, self-esteem, stress management, interpersonal relationships, domestic abuse, and AIDS." The stated intent of a 1994 Massachusetts law was to "ensure . . . that each public school classroom provides the conditions for all pupils to engage fully in learning as an inherently meaningful and enjoyable activity without threats to their sense of self-esteem." Louisiana made provision for "any public elementary or secondary school in Louisiana to offer instruction in . . . self-esteem." And a Wisconsin statute directed schools to provide "instruction to pupils in communication . . . stress reduction, self-improvement and self-esteem." (These and other examples of self-esteem-related statutes are listed in Appendix 5.)

Assemblyman John Vasconcellos, and others involved in the self-esteem movement in California, have even proposed national self-esteem legislation.[105] Though the proposal has yet to make significant progress in the legislative process on Capitol Hill, it has received support from several senators and members of Congress, including Pete Domenici, Sam Nunn, Pat Schroeder, and Maxine Waters.

A number of other high-profile national political figures have publicly endorsed the self-esteem movement. For example, former secretary of Housing and Urban Development (HUD) Jack Kemp, after meeting with two advocates of national self-esteem legislation, commended their efforts and declared that "the promotion of self-esteem is unambiguously at the core of a healthy nation."[106] Likewise, Chairman of the Joint Chiefs of Staff Colin Powell, after receiving an award from the County of Los Angeles Task Force to Promote Self-esteem and Personal and Social Responsibility, wrote that "the campaign to raise and to maintain the self-esteem and personal and social responsibility of all Americans is a vital one."[107] Similarly, former first lady Barbara Bush wrote that "self-esteem has everything to do with how well all human beings live and work. We are painfully aware that low self-esteem is closely related to substance abuse and the toll it takes on a person's life and livelihood."[108]

Though there has yet to be instituted a national self-esteem legislative package on the same scale as the California and Louisiana initiatives, a number of bills have been enacted into federal law that in some way offer to help build or protect the self-esteem of Americans. In 1994, twenty-two federal codes in some fashion addressed the matter of self-esteem. Consider, for example, a 1994 federal code, directed toward strengthening bilingual education programs in schools. The statutory language defends bilingual programs, in part, on the grounds that "instructional use and development of a child's non-English native language promotes student self-esteem."[109] Another federal code directed toward the "strengthening and improvement of elementary and secondary schools," offers assistance for "programs designed to enhance and raise self-esteem, self-confidence, independence, and responsibility among students."[110] Yet another provides guidelines for a federally sponsored teaching demonstration program, which calls for "strategies for the prevention and detection of high risk behavior . . . and for the enhancement of self-esteem among adolescents."[111]

Since 1981, the federal government has issued over 120 regulations from thirteen different federal agencies that in some manner speak of the importance of self-esteem. Sixty self-esteem-related federal regulations have been issued by the Department of Health and Human Services (HHS), twenty-eight by the Department of Education, and seven by the Department of Justice.

HHS, for example, issued a regulation on May 12, 1994, that outlined the priorities of a Runaway and Homeless Youth Program. Establishment of facilities and programs was justified in part on the rationale that "low self-esteem is a major problem among this population." According to the regulation, "Half (49 percent) have a poor self image."[112] In May 1993 the federal government issued a regulation promoting education and counseling programs among adolescent American Indians and Alaskan Natives. The programs were to include "recreational therapy activities that enhance self-esteem, self-sufficiency and team building."[113] A 1990 regulation on the operation of the federally funded Head Start program explained that "Head Start . . . offers disadvantaged children a variety of learning experiences designed to help them grow in curiosity and self-esteem."[114] Issued in 1991 was a regulation directed toward modernizing the distribution of Social Security benefits, which asserted that for "recipients in high-cost areas the reduction in benefits only puts them further behind economically. This makes them more dependent on others for their support, and often lowers their self-esteem."[115]

Perhaps the most curious federal regulation justified in relation to self-esteem was a 1993 HHS regulation that reclassified the date for federal approval of silicon inflatable breast prostheses. The importance of the devices was defended on the basis of research that had "shown that women seeking breast enlargement are individuals who feel physically inadequate, with doubts concerning their femininity and desirability. Inner concerns about lowered self-esteem and a poor self-concept are expressed as depression, lack of self-confidence, and some degree of sexual inhibition." The federal regulation further claimed that in-depth interviews with 10 patients and a written questionnaire completed by 132 patients showed that those who went through with the breast implant procedure experienced an "enhancement of self-image, improved self-esteem, and a high level of satisfaction."[116]

As with the aggregate of state self-esteem laws, a significant number of the federal self-esteem regulations are directed toward the education of America's children. For example, a 1992 federal regulation issued from the Department of Education concerning research in educating individuals with disabilities asserted, "The keys to change are programs, parents, and education or rehabilitation professionals that emphasize independence more than the performance of basic social and vocational skills. The development of individuality, self-esteem, goal oriented behavior, assertive behavior, and decision making ability are also critical outcomes."[117] Another federal regulation, issued in 1992 by the Department of Education on the problem of substance abuse among people with disabilities, asserted that while "little is known about the characteristics associated with substance abuse in persons with disabilities, researchers have found that self-esteem, mood, premorbid personality, and self-destructive behavior appear to be important variables."[118] Finally, a 1981 federal regulation on promoting bilingual education stated the following:

> It is also hoped that activities supported under this program will increase the self-esteem of the minority group children served by the project and will cultivate in all project participants—children, teachers, principals, and parents—a better understanding of special educational needs of the minority group children.[119]

(Other examples of federal self-esteem legislation are listed Appendix 5.)

Emotive Education

In addition to emphasizing self-esteem, state and federal codes underscore the importance of emotions within the educational process. A California code, for example, speaks not only to the problem of low self-esteem among students but also to concern with students' "emotional and physical problems" and "feelings of alienation."[120] Another California code affirms the role of teachers in addressing schoolchildren's "intellectual, social, emotional, physical and cognitive needs."[121] Similarly, an Iowa statute codified the establishment of a program "designed to detect children's physical, mental, emotional, or behavioral problems that may cause learning problems" in elementary and secondary schools.[122] A Massachusetts law calls for the "promotion of physical and emotional well-being and a positive school environment."[123] A Minnesota statute on early-childhood family education programs requires that programs include "activities designed to detect children's physical, mental, emotional, or behavioral problems."[124] And according to a Tennessee statute, among the "complex problems which lead Tennessee children to drop out of school" and that educators are encouraged to "combat" are "poor self-esteem" and "emotional distress."[125]

Just as, in the earlier periods of American educational history, the substance of instruction in the schools followed the basic parameters of state injunctions, so, today, the themes evident within the various state codes and regulations can be found in the curriculum guidelines issued by the various state departments of education and in the most commonly used values-oriented curricula within the schools. Interestingly, where in earlier periods, particularly in the colonial era, values were an integral feature of the entire pedagogical process, today instruction on values is most commonly found in health textbooks—a development that says something about the growing tendency to view behaviors in pathological rather than in traditional moral terms. In any respect, the same emphases found in the state codes and in the orientation of America's education schools are, not surprisingly, pronounced within classroom instruction. And again, the most ubiquitous of these themes is self-esteem.

Self-esteem in the Classroom

The Commission on Values-Centered Goals for the District of Columbia Public Schools issued a report identifying the five most important values it believed the D.C. schools should seek to inculcate among students. The first of these was "self-esteem." Educators in the District's public schools were thus encouraged to "emphasize building students' self-esteem as a central ingredient of the curriculum at all instruction levels and in all subject matter areas where applicable." [126]

Likewise, one of the central goals of the Virginia *Family Life Curriculum* is to help students "develop a positive self-concept," and one of the criteria for evaluating the curriculum's success is whether the child "is aware [of] and understands self." [127] This is also the main point of the 1990 California Department of Education report titled *Toward a State of Esteem: The Final Report of the California Task Force to Promote Self-esteem and Personal and Social Responsibility,* which served as the basis for the introduction of values curricula in California and other state schools. The California task force sees self-esteem as so imperative to moral education that it believes "course work in self-esteem should be required for credentials and a part of ongoing in-service training for all educators." [128]

Consistent with these guidelines, the most popular educational curricula used in today's public schools place a great deal of emphasis on the role of self-esteem. This is certainly the case in the *Character Education Curriculum,* put out by the Character Education Institute (CEI) and used in over forty-five thousand American classrooms and more than 430 cities. CEI assumes that "self-concept" is "the most significant factor in a student's personality." [129] Similarly, according to American Guidance Service (AGS), an organization that claims a clientele of more than 150,000 educators, its DUSO (Developing Understanding of Self and Others) program "is first and foremost an educational program, recognizing the relationship between self-esteem and achievement." Its goal is to "help children see themselves as capable and worthwhile people." [130]

The Washington, D.C.-based Community of Caring group, whose *Growing Up Caring* curriculum is used in forty-nine states and in more than five countries outside the United States, likewise sells its programs on the basis that they help students "experience heightened self-esteem and self-awareness." [131] The third of four stated principles guiding the philosophy of the *Being Healthy* curriculum, put out by Harcourt Brace Jovanovich and used in all fifty states, is "to emphasize positive self-concept and high self-esteem." As the teacher's guide to the curriculum states, "*Being Healthy* promotes the idea that the healthier a person becomes, the better the person will feel about himself or herself." [132] The stated mission of the Pasadena-based Thomas Jefferson Center—an organization whose programs have been used in two thousand U.S. schools, serving approximately thirty-four thousand classrooms and reaching over one million students—is to "write, promote and disseminate curriculum and training programs for schools and families to teach . . . self-esteem." [133] Christine Baroque, a spokeswoman for the center, states, "The program provides the instruction for a strong self-concept which is essential to a truly successful life." [134]

Instructions within the various curricula consistently encourage children to think highly of themselves. McGraw-Hill's *Health: Focus on You*, a curriculum used in all fifty states devotes the first section of its first-grade health curriculum to mental health. The instructions in the "Feeling Good about Yourself" section are as follows: "You can feel good about yourself. You can like yourself. Always do your best. Do not worry when you make mistakes. Be kind to yourself. Know that you are important." [135] Similarly, the first part of Scott, Foresman and Company's *Health for Life* curriculum is titled "How Can You Improve the Way You See Yourself?" In this section children are told, "You are special. Realizing that you are a unique human being can help you feel good about yourself. Feeling good about yourself is important." [136] The emphasis is repeated in curriculum after curriculum. The first of DUSO's three main sections is titled "Developing Understanding of Self." Similarly, the first main section in *Me, My World, My Future,* a curriculum put out by Spokane-based Teen Aid and used in all fifty states by more than one hundred thousand parents and teens, is on "Valuing Self."

Self-esteem Activities

Toward the end of raising students' self-esteem, a number of interesting activities are employed. The *Growing Up Caring* curriculum, for example, encourages students to write a letter to themselves, telling themselves how special they are. Consider the following instructions for this particular self-esteem exercise:

> Imagine that you need to be convinced of your worth as a person. Write a letter to yourself. Tell why you are special. Include all your good points. Think of the talents you have that could be developed. Mention your values. End the letter, "Love," and sign your name.[137]

The CEI *Curriculum News* reports on what is called "The Me Activity." Employing this activity, sixth- and seventh-grade children reportedly raise their self-esteem by cutting out magazine pictures that symbolize their individual character traits and pasting these on construction paper cut to form the word *me*. The activity is celebrated as one that gives students a "better understanding of themselves."[138]

Similarly, the *Me, My World, My Future* curriculum encourages students who are feeling down to talk to themselves in order to build themselves up: "When you talk to yourself, say positive things that help you believe you can succeed. 'Negative messages' will only result in self-doubt and a lack of confidence. Positive 'self-messages' could be, 'I know I can do this . . . I did well on that exam . . . I have what it takes to succeed!"[139] Elsewhere in the same curriculum, students with low self-esteem are encouraged to seek affirmation from those around them. If this is not occurring in their lives, they are told to give themselves "positive feedback." In this regard, students are told, "Concentrate more on building yourself up—or sending yourself frequent positive messages and noting the many good things that you do. Maybe set a weekly goal for yourself and when you achieve that goal 'pat yourself on the back' with a snack, extra TV time, or a phone call to a friend."[140]

The Thomas Jefferson Center also provides exercises in its curriculum for helping students develop higher self-esteem. Students are encouraged, for example, with exercises geared to help them "accept their likes and dislikes . . . to accept their strengths and weaknesses . . . to like themselves ... to take care of themselves." [141] Additionally, students are encouraged to "think of ways to reward themselves." [142] A whole unit in the center's *How to Be Successful* curriculum is devoted to "Self-Talk," the same kind of self-initiated positive feedback reviewed above.

Responsibility Redefined

Interestingly, self-esteem is sometimes discussed in conjunction with the idea of responsibility. The California self-esteem task force report, for example, is titled *Toward a State of Esteem: The Final Report of the California Task Force to Promote Self-esteem and Personal and Social Responsibility,* and it reportedly was able to get through the California legislature only when the term *responsibility* was attached to the legislative package. On the face of it, responsibility would seem to be a check on the individualistically oriented idea of self-esteem. One imagines responsibility to refer to those duties and obligations that are externally imposed on the self. It calls to mind the civic republican ideal of commitment to the common good. Even responsibility, however, has been redefined in the context of contemporary moral education. Its point of reference, like self-esteem, is to the self rather than to the common good.

Consider, for example, the meaning of responsibility in this selection from CEI's "Character Education and the Teacher":

> Students who are most likely to become responsible citizens are those who have a good self-esteem; hence, those students who accept responsibility, increase their own self-esteem. Have you ever thought less of yourself when you did what you were supposed to do? You may not like having to fulfill your duties and obligations, but when you do, you realize that you are responsible and your respect for yourself increases. [143]

Notice that the reason given for fulfilling one's duties is that doing so will raise one's self-esteem. Ultimately, the appeal here is not to others or to the common good but to the self.

This notion of responsibility is similarly portrayed in the Grade Seven edition of the *Health: Focus on You* curriculum. Consider the following instruction under a section titled "Responsible Friendships":

> One of the requirements for forming good friendships is being a friend to yourself. This is the reason a good foundation for forming friendships with others is learning to spend quality time alone. Here are some important questions to ask yourself. Are you a good friend to yourself? ... [144]

The section ends, "Your best choice of a friend is someone who wants you to take care of your health, do well in school, be responsible, and obey your parents or guardian. This is what is meant by 'A friend is a gift you give yourself.' The gift of friendship can improve the quality of your life." [145] Thus friendship is advocated on the basis that it ultimately profits the self. It starts with being a good friend to yourself and ends with a friend being a gift to yourself.

Washington D.C.'s Commission on Values-Centered Goals offers the most glaring example of this redefined and self-focused notion of responsibility. The fifth of the five values that the commission determined should be emphasized in the schools was "responsibility to self and others." According to the commission's September 1988 report (cited previously), this means "to help students revere the gift of healthy bodies and minds, appreciate the interdependence of all things, behave compassionately toward others and learn by example and experience that unselfish service is a key component to self-gratification." The irony here is exquisite—unselfish service for the sake of self-gratification.

Emotivism in the Classroom

State reports and curriculum guidelines also place a great deal of emphasis on the place of emotions. This is spelled out most conspicuously in the California Department of Education's self-esteem task force report. The basic premise offered in the report is that "all feelings are honorable. . . . By themselves, feelings are neither good nor bad. They are clues to our most crucial concerns, our deepest commitments, our needs, and our wants." An exercise offered in the report is indicative of the centrality with which emotions are to be viewed:

1. Turn your attention to how you are feeling. What part of your body feels what?
2. Recognize to yourself that this is how you are feeling, and give it a name. If you hear an inner criticism for feeling this way, just set it aside. Any feeling is acceptable.
3. Let yourself experience the sensations you are having. Separate these feelings from having to do anything about them.
4. Ask yourself whether you want to express your feelings now or at some other time. Do you want to take some other action now or later? Remind yourself that you have choices.[146]

Similarly, the criteria for successful instruction according to Virginia's *Family Life Curriculum* are based in part on whether the student "has a feeling of belonging" and "talks about feelings and emotions and understands positive ways of dealing with them."[147] Major parts of Virginia's guidelines are devoted to understanding emotions. Students are taken through sections that consider such matters as "dealing with emotions," "forces that affect emotions," and characteristics of emotional maturity."[148] In one exercise, teachers have students view "a film on feelings and emotions" and discuss "how the class members have dealt with these feelings and emotions."[149]

In keeping with these state curriculum guidelines, emotions are an important part of the popular values educational curricula. It is remarkable how the various curricula consistently instruct students to arrive at understandings of themselves and of their relations with others through an analysis of their own feelings. A CEI teacher's instructional manual, for example, states that "learning to express themselves freely yet being careful to consider the feelings of others, too, may well be the most important social skill developed in students."[150]

Students are regularly told that their feelings are an important aspect of their being. Moreover, they are actually guided through various exercises designed to help them better understand, categorize, express, and act on their feelings. This is certainly the case in the DUSO program, where a whole unit is devoted to "Understanding and Expressing Feelings." In it are sections titled "To be conscious of feelings," "To clearly express one's feelings," and "To act on one's feelings with courage."[151] Another unit is devoted simply to "Understanding Feelings," which includes the following sections: "To see how feelings influence choices," "To discriminate between real and imagined fears," "To select appropriate ways to express feelings."[152] One DUSO exercise used to help students understand and act on their feelings is the "Feeling Word Activity."[153] In this exercise, students view a dialogue between two characters (puppets) and are then asked to identify and discuss how one of the characters feels. Within the curriculum there are a total of forty-one such "feeling word activities."

In the same vein, Quest International, an organization that has implemented curricula in more than twenty thousand schools in twenty-two countries and whose *Skills for Adolescence* curriculum has been used in more than eleven thousand U.S. schools, claims that "we can understand ourselves only when we know how we're really feeling."[154] On this premise, it states as its goals for Unit Three of its *Skills for Adolescence* curriculum:

1. To understand that young adolescents experience a wide range of common feelings and that these feelings are normal.
2. To explore appropriate ways to communicate feelings.
3. To examine the range of emotions and learn positive responses to outside influences.
4. To learn how to perceive troubling emotions such as anger and frustration as positive challenges.
5. To learn how positive emotions promote feelings about oneself and others.[155]

In a later section of the same curriculum, students are helped to develop a "feelings vocabulary." In another section, they are asked to make a "rainbow of feelings" display to illustrate the range of emotions that are experienced by individuals.[156] In still another section, student are asked to assign their current emotional state to a "Feelings Continuum." Consider the following instructions from the latter, where the teacher is to ask students:

> How are you feeling? Think about it for a moment. What's been happening to you today that might affect how you feel? I'd like a few volunteers to come up to the Feelings Continuum and write your initials on the line closest to the way you're feeling right now.[157]

In the *Skills for Adolescence* curriculum, students are also told to fill out an "Emotion Clock" worksheet, where they are to "remember the day's feelings as well as they can."[158] In another section they are asked to make a "Scrapbook of Emotions." For this exercise, they are given five sheets of paper. Choosing at least five emotions from the "feelings rainbow," they are to begin each paper with sentences such as "I feel delighted when . . ." or "I feel excited when . . .".[159]

A first-grade health textbook put out by McGraw-Hill tells students, "You can show your feelings. Your face can show your feelings. Your body can show your feelings." Based on these statements, students are asked, "How do you show your feelings?" They are instructed further that "sharing your feelings helps you be healthy. You can share feelings in different ways. Some ways are better than others. One good way is to talk about them."[160] For this section, teachers are instructed to test comprehension by telling students to "make faces" and "use their bodies to demonstrate being afraid, happy, sad, and angry." [161]

Educators justify the importance of emotions, in part, because of their integral relatedness to self-esteem. As stated in *Me, My World, My Future*, "Coming to a better understanding and appreciation of ourselves should include a look at our emotions or feelings." Likewise, "identifying feelings, dealing with them and acting appropriately is very helpful in building self-awareness." [162] The California self-esteem task force report states that "by expressing our authentic feelings, we also gain more awareness of our deeper selves." [163] Similarly, the *Growing Up Caring* textbook tells students that how they handle their emotions has a direct effect on their sense of self-worth: "If you don't express emotions or if you dump them on others, you feel guilty or down on yourself." [164]

Evidence of Assimilation

Thus, from a number of vantage points, the emotivist self is central to the aims of contemporary education. The various curricula considered above emphasize the importance of emotions and self-esteem in a manner that is commensurate with the weight given these themes in state statutes and regulatory codes. Because of the decisive emphasis on self-esteem within education, it is not surprising that students have begun to take the idea of its importance to heart.

In a study conducted by University of Michigan psychologist Harold Stevenson, American schoolchildren were found to rank far ahead of students in other developed countries in "self-confidence about their abilities." This healthy self-concept, however, did not seem to translate into actual performance. A comparison of math and science achievement by schoolchildren in twenty countries showed Americans ranking near the bottom, below those with less developed self-concepts. [165]

Likewise, in 1989 a standardized math test was given to thirteen-year-olds in six different countries. Korean children scored the highest on the test while Americans scored the lowest, behind Great Britain, Canada, Ireland, and Spain. On the test, the children were asked to respond to the statement "I am good at mathematics." Only 23 percent of the Korean children answered yes to this statement—the lowest percentage of the six countries—whereas 68 percent of the American children answered yes, a higher percentage than for any other country. [166]

A 1992 Gallup poll asked Americans what factors they think are important in motivating a person to work hard and succeed. Of those polled, 89 percent said that self-esteem (the way people feel about themselves) was a "very important" factor, whereas only 49 percent thought responsibility to a community was a "very important" motivational factor. The same survey found that 63 percent of Americans believe that the time and effort being spent on promoting self-esteem is worthwhile.[167]

Along with the increasing support for and progress of self-esteem programs on both the state and national levels, the movement has received its share of criticism. Articles in *Newsweek,* the *New Republic,* and *U.S. News and World Report* have expressed skepticism about the movement. Moreover, the efforts of the California task force specifically and the self-esteem movement generally have been regularly lampooned in Gary Trudeau's *Doonesbury* comic strip. Yet even these criticisms are evidence of the movement's progress as the critics are concerned for the very reason that the movement is gaining prominence. Christopher Lasch, though leery of the concept of self-esteem, admitted that "it commands automatic assent in many quarters and . . . provides much of the rationale for the expansion of the welfare state." [168] Andy Mecca, former chairman of the California Task Force to Promote Self-esteem, once remarked that Trudeau's criticism actually aided the movement. "It provided an international landscape." [169] Vasconcellos likewise believes that Trudeau "made this obscure little thing out in California suddenly become a national figure.[170] John Leo, writing in *U.S. News and World Report,* agrees with this assessment: "The conception of self-esteem as a public policy issue is not a lotus-land joke, nor a California-only phenomenon. It is an idea that has quietly taken hold all around the country. The self-esteem movemement, in fact, is a social force of some strength, particularly in the schools." [171] Evidence considered in this chapter would certainly add empirical substantiation to this observation.

Arguably, recent politically charged support for "school choice," school voucher systems, and Goals 2000 (with its emphasis on high academic standards) would suggest that many Americans are disgruntled with the public education system. No doubt, some of this frustration is directed at the growing presence of therapeutic themes and the concomitant de-emphasis on academic basics in the schools.[172] Support for programs like Goals 2000 indicate that Americans may be growing impatient with education's therapeutic orientation. Senator Joseph Lieberman, cosponsor of a school voucher bill for low-income families, speaks for many when he argues: "It is clear that public schools are not working for all students."[173]

However, most discussions of education reform in the contemporary context focus more on the problem of declining academic abilities (e.g., declining SAT scores, low rankings in international test competitions) than they do on the a priori problem with a therapeutic approach. In contemporary critiques and prescriptions, the perceived problem is not so much with foundational philosophical emphases (i.e., the moral dimension of education) as it is with the efficacy of the system. Again, in Senator Lieberman's words, the "schools are not working." Those in the business community who invested in America's educational system in the aftermath of the 1983 *Nation at Risk* report, for example, rallied not against therapeutic, child-centered practices but against declining literacy and lack of preparedness for the business world, and they saw as the solution the investment of more dollars into the public schools.[174] Other reform ideas similarly offer more utilitarian, market-oriented remedies. The answer rests, it is argued, in better use of market forces, technology, interactive CD-ROM educational applications, access to the Internet, and the like.[175] What is largely missing from these reform initiatives, however, is discussion about the philosophical moorings of education. As such, challenges to therapeutic themes and programs, if any, are usually indirect. When the missing "moral" element of reform efforts is considered, the emphasis once again is often on therapeutic ideas, rather than on resurrecting the kind of foundational themes evident in the earlier periods of America's educational history.[176]

One could also argue that public disillusionment with and abandonment of public schools is evidence of a rejection of education's therapeutic orientation. But for all the legislative activity and expressed public disenchantment, enrollment in the public schools is actually on the rise. In 1985, thirty-nine million students or 88 percent of U.S. school-age children were enrolled in America's public schools (kindergarten through twelfth grade). In 1990 this number had risen to forty-one million, or 90 percent of school-age children, and in 1995 to forty-five million or 91 percent of school-age children.[177]

Thus, whether Americans on the whole are pleased or displeased with public schools, this is where the majority of children are educated. Even if children do switch to private or home schooling, the question remains whether the content of instruction will be substantively different from that which is in the public schools. As Alan Ehrenhalt observes, school-choice policy ultimately presents "families with the essentially empty freedom of choosing between competing schools that scarcely differ among themselves."[178] Melinda Wagner's study of private Christian schools in Virginia illustrates this claim. She found the self-esteem theme to be just as present in the schools that she observed as it is in the public schools.[179] As such, even if voucher systems and other school-choice programs are initiated, it is likely that children will be exposed to similar therapeutic themes. But until these programs become legislatively approved and institutionalized, the vast—indeed, the increasing—majority of U.S. children are still educated in the public schools, with self-esteem as the central pedagogical tool.

What I have largely focused on thus far in the area of education are the changing laws and practices within state educational systems. In this regard, I have found self-esteem to be a central pedagogical concern. Because of the prominence of the self-esteem concept in education and elsewhere, I turn now to a fuller consideration of the way in which advocates defend its relevance to educational and other types of government policy. In other words, I focus more specifically on the justifications offered for the political advancement of the self-esteem principle. Here, too, we find the interesting coexistence of appeals to both therapeutic and utilitarian ideals.

In a State of Esteem

Self-esteem: A Public Panacea

In observing the substantive claims of the self-esteem movement in the area of education specifically and in the modern state generally, we find that several important themes emerge. To begin with, self-esteem is understood as a "social vaccine," promising to remedy a host of social ills. For example, the Louisiana COPE (Commission on Promoting Esteem) program states:

> The legislature . . . recognizes that the root cause of many of our major social problems, including, but not limited to, crimes of violence, chronic alcoholism and drug abuse, spousal and child abuse, teenage pregnancy, poverty and chronic welfare dependency, and homelessness, are due to

lack of healthy self-esteem and sense of personal and social responsibility.[180]

The California task force report makes a similar claim:

> Self-esteem is the likeliest candidate for a social vaccine, something that empowers us to live responsibly and that inoculates us against the lures of crime, violence, substance abuse, teen pregnancy, child abuse, chronic welfare dependency, and educational failure. The lack of self-esteem is central to most personal and social ills plaguing our state and nation as we approach the end of the twentieth century.[181]

In addition to its pertinence to the laundry list of social ailments listed above, self-esteem is said to be relevant to the workplace[182] and to such problems as AIDS, hunger and homelessness, physical disabilities, and racism.[183]

The self-esteem solution also offers itself as a remedy to the tension created by life in a rigidly dichotomized modern world. In other words, along with the other features of the therapeutic ethos noted in Chapter 1, the concept of self-esteem offers to resynthesize the split between private and public life. As California assemblyman Vasconcellos explains:

> The task force was not trying to mandate but trying to illuminate, you know, give people a recognition of this [self-esteem] being important, so that they can take it into their own lives and develop it. In that sense, everything private has become public.[184]

Recall, too, the California task force's claim that "the lack of self-esteem is central to most *personal* and *social* ills plaguing our state and nation" (emphasis added).

In another example, the Maryland Task Force on Self-esteem, in its work with businesses, highlighted and extended such government policies as elder care plans, family leave policies, and cafeteria benefits because these policies recognized the "wholeness" of the individual and the importance of his or her private family life in the context of public business life. Jackie Miller, director of Strategies for Change and consultant to Governor William Schaeffer in the development of the Maryland Task Force on Self-esteem, has argued that

> 90 percent of the benefit programs [in American businesses] act as if families don't exist, that employees just exist all on their own and that they just came from nowhere, that they don't have parents, they don't have children, they don't have any kind of siblings.[185]

Hence she was pleased with the Maryland task force's emphasis on governmental policies that recognized the importance of the individual's private life.

Self-esteem's Sacred Appeal

One of the most pronounced differences between the public and private realms of life in modern American society is the continued importance of religion in the latter realm and its undermined relevance in the former. The common public understanding of this division is embodied in the concept of a strict wall of separation between church and state in America. When asked whether the sometimes religious-sounding self-esteem concept might represent a breach in this wall, Andy Michael, a former aide to Assemblyman Vasconcellos, responded:

> I agree that church and state should be separated ... But ... we have gone too far ... Religion fits under some spiritual context but religion is dogmatic. Often it is very set in its rituals.... And "spiritual" is much more of an individual expression of your connection with other people in the world. So I don't see that the self-esteem movement, because it doesn't put up the name of one great being like Allah or God, as being what we're talking about. What we're talking about is the quality of the individual.[186]

In other words, religion is a subset of spirituality. Spirituality should not necessarily be separated out from the public realm, but religion should be. Self-esteem is a type of spirituality, but its focus is on the centrality of the individual. Therefore it is valid in both the private and public spheres and should not be exiled from the public realm in the same way that religion is.

When I posed the same question to Assemblyman Vasconcellos, he had more difficulty differentiating self-esteem from religion:

> Well, it is not a religion in one sense. It is not a religion in a sense that we think of religion. It is a belief system. I think it's an ontology. It is a theory of being. It is a theory of knowing. It is an epistemology. It is that. It is certainly a theory of psychology.... In an analytical, logical sense ... it is not a religion. But in a broader sense, it is a belief system that informs life and decisions. So I don't know quite how to distinguish that.[187]

When asked if self-esteem, like religion, should be separated from the public realm, the assemblyman asserted that it should not. Speaking specifically about education, Vasconcellos asked, "But it is a question of what a teacher should do in the classroom. If they treat a child so the child is good, and encourage them to develop self-esteem, is that to be forbidden?"[188] Thus, though Vasconcellos is reluctant to deny outright self-esteem's religious nature, he also believes that it should be allowed in the public schools.

The various educational curricula considered in this research likewise view self-esteem as a form of spirituality. In the "Spirituality and Self-Worth" section of *Growing Up Caring,* for example, we are told that "the idea of spirituality is not religious in itself. It is an inner quality of being. Spirituality is the part of yourself that allows you to know you are alive and to feel the wonder of being alive." This, according to the curriculum, "is why spirituality and self-worth are closely related."[189] The California task force also closely associates spirituality with self-esteem:

> As I come to a fuller appreciation of my own worth, I grow in confidence, in my sense of adequacy, and in my capability to live responsibly and effectively. This personal growth contributes to an emotional and spiritual warmth which becomes part of my sense of myself and my relationship with others.[190]

The nourishment of our spirits is inextricably linked with self-esteem. To nourish the self is to grow spiritually. "Experiencing our spiritual side is part of being human. Nourishing our spirit is necessary if we want healthy self-esteem."[191]

Thus, though religion should be separated from public institutions like education, spirituality need not necessarily be, especially when it is understood to mean the esteeming of the self. The self offers to reunite public and private life because it is socially accepted in both realms, where religion is not. Given its acceptability to both spheres of life, it purportedly provides a reintegration of the strict separation between the two.

Though the idea of spirituality is invoked, it is clear that the self-esteem philosophy is a move away from traditional religious ideas. John Vasconcellos speaks of a time at a conference when he heard articulated two visions of human nature: a more "constrained vision," which referred to humans as basically evil, and an "unconstrained vision" which espoused a belief in the innate goodness and perfectibility of humans. The former Vasconcellos associated with the writings of Adam Smith, Thomas Hobbes, and Frederick Hayek and the latter with the work of

Jean-Jacques Rousseau and John Locke. Historically, religion has been a major advocate of the former and has spoken of the importance of self-sacrifice, restraining self, dying to self, controlling self, and of submitting the self to external sources of authority. Yet, as Vasconcellos explains, the self-esteem movement unequivocally embraces the latter view of human nature. He writes, "It is the latter vision—that human beings are innately inclined toward good and that free, healthy people become constructive and responsible—which underlies the philosophy and work of what has been called the self-esteem movement." [192]

It is evident, then, that when speaking of a sacred dimension of life, the self-esteem activists are referring not to an external authority—be it a god, divine reason, or commitment to a community—but of the self. In religious verbiage, the self is the new sacred, the new object of worship. The sense in which the self is to be regarded as the new sacred, rather than traditional religious notions of the sacred, is evident in this statement by Jackie Miller:

> We don't mean religion when we talk of spirituality. We are not here to deny or say that Judaism or Christianity or Catholicism or that Muslims don't have a place. This is not what this is about. But what we're talking about is just human dignity. And it really transcends any kind of religious separateness. Just general esteem of the self, and ... the esteem and elevation of the human being to a place of dignity. [193]

Likewise, the California task force report states that "spirituality refers to experiencing ourselves in relationship to the universe." Among the ways that this can be understood are "relating ... to the God within, to our divinity, or to our higher consciousness." To enter into the spiritual realm is to "connect with our inner resources, our place in the world, and the sacredness of life." [194] Thus, though the language of the movement is rhetorically deferential to religion, the substance of the self-esteem philosophy is antithetical to traditional religious understandings of the self in relationship to society and, in fact, offers the self as the new sacred.

Self-esteem's Scientific Appeal

The movement also purports a close association with science. The therapeutic ethos, generally speaking, finds its roots in the "scientific" discipline of psychology, particularly in psychoanalysis. Self-esteem's relevance to the modern state is ostensibly based on the findings of research conducted by social scientists in California. A book titled *The Social Importance of Self-Esteem* contains the compiled results of these various studies. The purpose of the effort was to "analyze and clarify our intuition regarding the importance of self-esteem" and to "establish self-esteem at the center of our social science agenda." [195]

Though the study is trumpeted as a foundational work in the self-esteem movement, it showed that there is very little association between self-esteem and the various social problems studied, much less any causal relationship. So dubious were the purported connections between self-esteem and the various social ills that one task force member refused to sign the final report, arguing that "the Task Force's interpretation of the U.C. professors' academic findings understates the absence of a significant linkage of self-esteem and the six social problems." [196] Likewise, Neil Smelser, in the introduction to *The Social Importance of Self-esteem,* confesses that "the news most consistently reported is that the associations between self-esteem and its expected consequences are mixed, insignificant, or absent." [197]

When confronted with these discrepancies, Vasconcellos dismissed them on the grounds that objections come from "those who only live in their heads, in the intellectual," and stated that the importance of self-esteem was confirmed by "our intuitive knowledge." [198] Of the one dissenter to the task force's report, Vasconcellos stated, "The dissenter was a guy who does brain research, and his whole life is in the laboratory and in the statistics, and since it didn't fit in that model, he fought it vigorously." [199] Vasconcellos explained further:

> I had a colleague here who at one point said of self-esteem, "I can't measure it. I'm an engineer." And I said, "you're missing the best part of life ... you can't measure the most important things in life. You can't measure love, you can't measure affection. You can get at it, but you can't directly. Self-esteem is in that category." We have got to try to understand it, identify it, understand its causes and its effects. But to relegate all of our belief into a statistical formula—I don't want to recommend that. [200]

Yet Vasconcellos also pointed to a Harvard scholar who was doing work that showed "academically and scientifically that we're not programmed to be warlike but cooperative." [201] With respect to the findings in the University of California collection of studies, Vasconcellos admitted that there were problems with the empirical substantiation of self-esteem's positive influence on behavior but asserted nonetheless, "We all know it in our gut that it is true." [202]

Such a response and its subjective disregard for empirical substantiation itself reflects a therapeutic understanding of the world. Intuition prevails over logic or reason. Thus, just as the "success" rates of the Drug Courts were reinterpreted according to a treatment perspective, here a therapeutic interpretation of the data supersedes a more positivistic one.

Rationalism: Resisted or Reaffirmed?

Just as Dewey rejected aspects of rationalism while simultaneously embracing others, so do self-esteem advocates. The promoters of self-esteem regularly speak out against the "disempowering" and "depersonalizing" effects of bureaucratic rationalization. Their philosophy offers to soften the severity of life in the state machinery. However, in so doing, it does not challenge the capitalistic system outright but, actually, affirms it. That is, it uses both the language of emotivism (the need for fulfillment, self-actualization, personal affirmation, and restoring human dignity, etc.) and the language of utilitarianism (cost-effectiveness, productivity, and marketability).

The strong reaction against the impersonality of the rationalized modern world is a common theme in the self-esteem literature. Clearly, the self-esteem philosophy sees itself as a cushion to the harshness of life in the machine. For example, in speaking of the progress of the movement in California's governmental agencies, Andy Michael makes this claim:

> We have been working in the state government arena, working with a number of agencies to implement self-esteem strategies in their own work places so that when we work with clients or customers or the public, we are treating them with respect so that they don't feel disempowered, like a lot of people do after dealing with the DMV [Department of Motor Vehicles] or welfare or whatever. [203]

Similarly, Leroy Foster, chairman of the Siskiyou County, California, Self-esteem Task Force, speaks of the need for humans who have become "machines to be reborn back into a spirit. We need to reclaim our value of humanness." [204] When asked specifically whether she thought the institutions in modern American society were overly repressive, Jackie Miller responded:

Oh absolutely! You know, it is so frustrating. Everyone wants to do a good job. So you come into the workplace . . . and how do you really feel when you walk in and there are guidelines and there are rules and there are walls of policies and procedures manuals? . . . And then there are confines and performance appraisals to dictate what you will do. . . . I mean, it is very, very limiting and does squelch any attempt at self-actualization, self-realization, and it does break the spirit.[205]

Likewise, the California task force report *Toward a State of Esteem* expresses regret that in American society, "indications of worth are dispensed on the basis of production and achievements."

Based on the same type of rationale, the Character Education Institute holds that "students should not . . . feel that acceptance depends on their achievement, but that they are worthwhile persons regardless of their accomplishments." For this reason CEI discourages teachers from grading lessons from their curricula: "Students are less willing to express themselves orally or in writing if they feel they are being evaluated. Since Character Education is about their ideas and feelings, it is strongly urged that no grades or marks be placed on any of the students' work that is a result of the lessons."[206] On similar grounds, Leroy Foster reminded conference attendees at Virginia's Third Annual Self-esteem Conference in October 1992 that "we are human beings, not human doings."

Thus it is clear that the self-esteem movement views the nature of our rationalized society as repressive, disempowering, mechanistic, and hostile to our natural humanness. Yet, in spite of this evident disapproval of the bureaucratic nature of the modern rationalized world, self-esteem advocates wholly endorse the capitalistic order. In fact, as with defenses of the Drug Court movement, one of the most common arguments offered for supporting self-esteem legislation is that it is cost-effective. It is a preventative "vaccine" that will keep individuals from committing crimes, doing drugs, going to prison, getting pregnant as teenagers, being dishonest in their businesses, and dropping out of school. Hence government expenditures directed toward these problems (after the fact) could be avoided by initially building people's self-esteem.

Consider, for example, this claim by one self-esteem advocate:

If we can figure out ways of identifying the principles of self-esteem and then promoting them in every way in incorporating them into the way government works . . . we would reduce our public costs for all these problems like welfare and educational failure which reduce our tax base and so forth.[207]

Similarly, a proposal for national self-esteem legislation states that "Congress should implement cost effective measures which are preventive in nature and offer the nation the probability of significant cost savings relative to program costs and long term savings."[208] The California task force report envisions a future California where high self-esteem is an integral part of business life. In such a scenario, "the workplace environment and training programs nurture self-esteem. This has resulted in higher productivity and markedly reduced absenteeism. Californians are actively developing their self-esteem and increasing their productivity."[209]

Perhaps the most pronounced argument for self-esteem's capitalistic efficacy was articulated by Jackie Miller:

> One thing that we want to stress here is that this is not just a nice thing to do, this whole self-esteem movement. It is not just a do-good kind of thing only. I mean there are strong economic implications here. It is an incredible way to save enormous amounts of money.[210]

Thus we see both a call for a gentler and kinder world and an affirmation of the social system that brought about the disenchanting effects of rationalization. Again, the utilitarian and emotivist arguments are complementary rather than contradictory. The following statement by Leroy Foster reveals the saliency with which the two motifs work together: "In the 1990's and into the 21st century higher levels of self-esteem will not be a luxury but an *economic* and *social* necessity for *effectiveness* and *fulfillment* in a multicultural global *marketplace* and global *village*" (emphasis added).[211] Notice the utilitarian/emotivist rhythm with which Foster presents his argument. Self-esteem is both effective and fulfilling, and it is necessary for the village and the marketplace. Therefore the "bottom line" of the "state of esteem" is that it allows us to feel good about ourselves and is, at the same time, cost-effective. James Hillman put it most succinctly when he said, "I believe we now have two ideologies that run the country. One is economics, and the other is therapy."[212]

Summary

The predominance of self-esteem, again, is most pronounced in the area of American education, where it emerged as a result of an evolutionary process begun by educational reformers in the common-school era. In the mid-nineteenth century, Horace Mann and others crusaded for the establishment of a nonsectarian common school that would neutralize the more rigid dogmas of specific Protestant religious beliefs. The effort was the beginning of a process whereby traditional religious legitimations for academic instruction in America's schools were undermined and ultimately replaced with substantively different impulses. During the second half of the nineteenth century, defenses for the purpose of education were based more on the ideals of civic republicanism than on religion, though a mixture of ideological systems undergirded educational efforts in this period. These changes set the stage for the child-centered educational philosophies that emerged in the twentieth century.

Dewey's experiential pragmatism in the Progressive Era and the values clarification movement in the cosmopolitan era represent the natural predecessors to the conspicuously therapeutic tendencies of the 1990s. The heavy emphases on emotions and on the elevation of the self are the dominant features of contemporary values education. Though some policy initiatives seem to challenge this pedagogical emphasis, they have not deterred the expanded legal applicability of the self-esteem theme in public education and other arenas of the modern state. Interestingly, though the movement's supporters defend "feeling good about the self" as a remedy to the difficulties of life in a highly rationalized world, they also fully employ utilitarian rationales to advance the movement, a conflation of the emotive with the utilitarian first evident in the Deweyian philosophies at the turn of the century.

Therefore, as with civil and criminal law, the legitimacy of this arena of the American state rests firmly on a therapeutic orientation, both with respect to the validity component of the legitimation formula—as evident in the substance of the relevant state codes and regulations, which make valid the application of therapeutic themes in the classrooms of America's schools—and in the way these laws are defended or justified. In the next chapter, we focus more exclusively on the justificatory dimension of the legitimation equation in congressional debates over welfare legislation. As with education, state-sponsored welfare has expanded exponentially during the twentieth century, a development given rather extensive scholarly attention. The relevant question to this study, however, is: To which themes have legislators appealed in justifying the state's expanding role in providing for the welfare of its citizens?

6

Welfare Policy

The American welfare state is increasingly made up of a workforce of those trained in the therapeutic approach. In his important work on this topic, *The Rise of the Therapeutic State*, Andrew Polsky documents the ways in which Americans have historically responded to those in need of some kind of welfare: from the charitable efforts of nineteenth-century philanthropists to the therapeutic efforts of state-sponsored case workers in the latter part of the twentieth century. As was the case in education, non-state-sponsored religious efforts preceded, and for the most part made unnecessary, government involvement in caring for the "marginalized." This, of course, would change over time, as the state assumed a more expanded role in the social welfare of its less fortunate citizens.

Though Polsky recognizes the intersection between practice and ideology and notes how state workers actually looked for a discipline in the sciences to provide a philosophical basis for the state's intervening efforts, his understanding of the therapeutic approach is really limited to the specific efforts of state-employed case workers. That state welfare agencies are populated by social workers, psychologists, and family counselors trained in the therapeutic approach certainly offers support to the thesis that the therapeutic ethos is institutionalizing itself into the processes of the modern state.

However, there is more to the impact of the therapeutic culture on U.S. welfare practices than the aggregate infiltration of therapeutically trained practitioners. Another important way to look at the welfare state, particularly given this study's concern with the matter of legitimation, is to focus on the area of welfare policy, namely, what types of welfare policies have been initiated over time and how, from the perspective of the lawmakers, they have been justified.

The welfare state has become a huge part of the U.S. state apparatus, costing billions of dollars annually and constituting a major percentage of the gross national product (GNP). There are a number of angles one could take in seeking to measure the influence of the therapeutic approach on this mammoth enterprise. State action toward the American child represents an important and relatively manageable dimension of state welfare activity that usefully lends itself to historical analysis. By observing the important legislative efforts directed toward the welfare of children over time, this chapter considers the different types of legitimating language members of Congress have used to justify their efforts.

Congress and the Well-Being of Children

Using the *Congressional Record* as a data source, I make comparisons here among the ways in which members of Congress have discussed and justified governmental action toward children from the beginning of the century through the first session of the 104th Congress. The analysis focuses on congressional statements and debates from five different time periods: (1) discussion concerning the institution of child labor laws and the establishment of the Children's Bureau in the Fifty-ninth, Sixtieth, and Sixty-second Congresses (1906–1912); (2) debates surrounding the Sheppard-Towner Act, legislation aimed at reducing infant mortality rates, in the Sixty-seventh Congress (1921–1922); (3) congressional dialogue regarding Social Security Aid to Dependent Children and Emergency Maternity and Infant Care (EMIC)—aid to children of mothers employed in the industries supporting the efforts of World War II—in the Seventy-sixth and Seventy-eighth Congresses (1939–1940 and 1943–1944); (4) statements regarding Operation Good Start and Head Start, legislative initiatives aimed at assisting in the early development of underprivileged and emotionally disturbed children, in the Eighty-ninth and Ninety-first Congresses (1965–1966 and 1969–1970); and (5) congressional discussion of several child abuse bills and of Head Start during the 100th and 101st Congresses (1987–1990).[1] I also briefly consider debates over welfare in the 104th Congress (1994–1995) in an effort to assess whether recent welfare reform efforts constitute a change from the major trends documented in the five historical periods.

In analyzing legislative debate over these various initiatives, I give particular attention to the reasons offered by Congress for supporting the given bills. In other words, considered here are the ways in which members legitimated the state's growing role in the lives of America's children. In some of the Congresses, there was notable opposition to the various bills. Because this study focuses not just on the substance of the initiatives but also on the justificatory sources of legitimation to which politicians appealed, oppositional arguments to the various bills are relevant to and therefore also considered in the analysis. Both types of justification—those for and those against the legislative measures—provide clues as to the salience of changing cultural sources of legitimation.

Child Labor Laws and the Children's Bureau (1906–1912)

With the strong support of President Theodore Roosevelt, the well-being of children became a major focus of governmental concern in the first decade of the twentieth century. In response to growing public concerns about the horrific conditions of children laboring in coal mines and other industries, the federal government took a number of actions to secure their well-being. In 1905, for example, the National Child Labor Committee was established for the purpose of fostering state and local child labor legislation. A year later, President Roosevelt asked the Bureau of Labor to investigate the conditions of women and child wage earners in the United States. In December 1906, with the support of President Roosevelt and the National Child Labor Committee, the first federal legislation was introduced to regulate child labor in the United States. Identical bills were introduced in both houses; in the Senate, by Senator Albert J. Beveridge of Indiana; and in the House, by Congressman Herbert Parsons of New York. Though both bills would eventually die in committees during the Fifty-ninth Congress, within a decade a child labor law passed Congress in the form of the Owen-Keating Bill of 1916, which set the minimum age for employment at fourteen years.

Also during the first decade of the century, the White House held its first Conference on the Care of Dependent Children, where it recommended the establishment of a Children's Bureau. After the conference, President Roosevelt publicly endorsed the idea of the Children's Bureau, explaining that its purpose was to "report upon all matters pertaining to the welfare of children and child life."[2] Legislation was introduced in Congress to establish the Roosevelt-recommended Children's Bureau. As with child labor laws, it was some time before Congress considered this matter in a serious fashion; in fact, it was not until 1912 that the

Children's Bureau was established in the Department of Commerce and Labor.

Of primary importance to this analysis is not the history of the legislation per se but the dialogue surrounding the child welfare bills. The discussions of child labor laws and the establishment of the Children's Bureau in the Fifty-ninth, Sixtieth, and Sixty-second Congresses reveal federal legislators' first attempts to justify major federal action directed exclusively toward the well-being of children.

Traditional Sources of Legitimacy

Like the early efforts to legitimate public education in America, initial calls for congressional action toward child welfare often drew on religious symbols for justifying governmental efforts. For example, the deplorable conditions of child labor were repeatedly referred to as "evil." The following is just one of many statements offered by members of Congress in the first decade of the twentieth century that painted child labor practices as an evil to be opposed: "Therefore, Mr. President, I have offered as an amendment to the District of Columbia child labor bill, the bill which I offered early in the session, to provide a national method for stopping this distinctly national evil." [3]

That the notion of evil was understood in a traditional religious sense is evident from the common practice among members to refer to passages of Scripture in statements of support for or opposition to the bills. Senator William Borah, for example, in attempting to quell the vociferous criticism of the legislation, chided his opponents' supposed corner on wisdom by referring to a passage from the Old Testament Book of Job: "I believe it was Job, or some one to Job, who said: 'Hast thou restrained all wisdom unto thyself?' " [4]

On several occasions, senators defended the child labor legislation through reference to a New Testament passage in the Gospel of Matthew: "Even so it is not the will of your Father which is in heaven, that one of these little ones should perish" (18:14, KJV). Congressman Herbert Parsons, for example, one of the original sponsors of the child labor law, used the passage in his defense of the Children's Bureau:

> Our doctrine . . . is that if possible "not one of these little ones should perish." In the name of the thousands of infants who perish daily for lack of parental knowledge . . . and of the children stultified by work, I ask

that this bill be enacted into law, so that the American people, for reasons selfish as well as humane, can do their full part toward guarding the interests of the child.[5]

Senator Albert Beveridge also appealed to religious symbols in his defense of the child labor bill. He did so by painting the legislation as a religious cause, whose passage depended on the prayers of its faithful supporters: "I thank God, there are some mill owners in the South who would rather have less money and more conscience, who employ children only because their competitors do, and who pray for the passage of this bill."[6]

Senator Beveridge identified by name many industries that employed children for long hours in unsafe working environments. For example, he spoke at length about a North Carolina cotton mill where children between seven and twelve years of age worked for eleven-hour days in dangerous conditions. North Carolina senator Lee Overman took issue with Senator Beveridge:

> I have never seen or heard of any such conditions. I think it is one of the best conducted mills in the country. I know they have one of the most beautiful school buildings and a fine school there carried on by the factory. The superintendent is an elder in the Presbyterian Church, and one of the best men I think I have ever known in my life, who has been very careful with the children.[7]

Interestingly, Senator Overman defended the mill by noting the superintendent's status in a religious denomination. The context suggests that knowledge of such information was given to provide evidence of the superintendent's veracity and of his factory's inculpability.

The invocation of religiously grounded verbiage by members of Congress in order to appeal to the moral codes and symbols that prevailed in the culture was also evident in Senator Jacob Gallinger's explanation for the original funding of the Roosevelt-initiated federal inspection of the conditions of America's children. He made it clear that members of Congress were very conscious of religion's authority in American culture and fully anticipated the reprisal of the American people were Congress not to heed this social reality: "If we had not appropriated it [the funding for the inspection], it would have been said that we were unresponsive to the benevolent and Christian demands of the people of the country."[8]

In fact, the perceived potency of the religious appeals that were offered in support of the child labor measures frustrated some members of Congress who were opposed to the bills. Senator Weldon Heyburn, for example, declared caustically, "If you introduced a measure here, 'Resolved, That the Congress of the United States is in favor of the eternal salvation of mankind' it would doubtless be passed because people would not dare to vote against it."[9] Members of Congress who opposed these measures were, however, just as likely to invoke traditional religious language to support their position as were the bills' advocates. Senator Heyburn, for example, recommended that proponents of the legislation "pray and repent," that they might see their misguided ways.[10]

It was often argued, too, that these measures toward children infringed on the "sacredness" of the family home, an institution imbued with religious significance and into which, it was believed, the government had no right to intrude. "How would the Senator from Montana," asked Senator Overman, "have liked for a Government agent to have gone down into his father's humble home, or his grandfather's in the days of the Revolution, investigating the condition of the sacred home?"[11]

Because supporters of these initiatives believed that the congressional action would result in the improved "moral" welfare of the children, some senators argued in rebuttal that the poor—for whom most of the legislation was directed—were among the most religiously moral people in the country. Consider, for example, these arguments offered by Senator Heyburn:

> The church membership of this country, made up of honest, God-fearing mothers and fathers, is comprised largely of the parents of these poor children about which we are showing so much concern. . . . Wealth does not breed morality. It more often tempts away from the path of morality. Some are moral because they are poor. Mighty few are moral because they are rich. . . . I reassert that the great bulk of the Christian population in this country who go to their churches and take their families with them are from the poor. The Christian religion, except for that class, would be a social parade on Easter day.[12]

Senator Heyburn attempted to defuse the notion that the legislation had a legitimate moral or religious aim by arguing that those who would benefit from the bills were already the most religious people in the country. Thus religious symbols were invoked, in often imaginative ways, either to oppose or to support these early efforts to protect America's children.

As discussed in the early chapters of this book, traditional religion was not the only ideological system to which Americans historically appealed for legitimating governmental policy. Also significant to the American experience were the foundational ideas of "nature" and natural law. Like theistic religion, natural law was a source of moral authority understood to exist outside the individual and to dictate the direction of human thoughts and actions. Senator Heyburn made reference to nature's authority when he argued against the state's greater role in the raising of children:

> The jurisdiction established over the children of mankind in the beginning of the human race has worked out very well. It is in accord with the rules of nature. It is based not upon duty but upon the human instinct that establishes the principle upon which all duties rest. The mother needs no admonition to care for the child, nor does the father. The exceptions to that rule are such as those to the rule against the taking of human life.[13]

Elsewhere, Heyburn appealed again to the authority of "nature and nature's God" when he argued that the government should leave the children to the natural order rather than intervene by plucking them out of life's trials. He believed that it was preferable for children to be "out in the storm of life, learning how to meet the trials and the tribulations," and that they should not be taken "from the natural condition in which the great God had placed them and transferred to one where some salaried person trained them according to the salary he received."[14]

That these justificatory symbols embodied more than the rhetorical devices used to debate a narrow range of welfare law is evident in Senator Beveridge's passionate defense of the bill:

> Why was it that this Republic was established? What does the flag stand for? Mr. President, what do all these things mean? They mean that the people shall be free to correct human abuses. They mean that men and women and children shall day by day grow stronger and nobler.... If they do not mean these things, Mr. President then our institutions, this Republic, our flag, have no meaning and no reason for existence.... I pray God, the passion of my life a Nation of strong, pure human beings; a Nation of wholesome homes, true to the holiest ideals of man; a Nation whose power is glorified by its justice.... Mr. President, it is to make this Nation still surer of this holy destiny that I have presented this bill to stop the murder of American children and the ruin of future American citizens.[15]

Beveridge appealed to these loftier ideals not only to support his proposed bill but to give meaning to America, to its laws and its governing institutions. The ruling order, as such, was viewed as legitimate inasmuch as its laws corresponded to these ideals. If it did not, the state had "no meaning . . . no reason for existence." The legitimating principles appealed to during this period were the traditional cultural systems of natural law, Protestant religion, and civic republicanism. These were invoked to provide legitimacy to the proposed pieces of legislation and, even more profoundly, as reflected in Beveridge's statement, to give meaning to America and to the American state.

Public Understanding of the Self

Because these bills were intended to affect certain individuals— namely, children—it was important for members of Congress to discuss the nature of the persons who were ostensibly in need of government action. How members discussed children in this period is interesting, not only in the terms they did use to describe the child but also in the words they did not use. Absent from all descriptions is any reference to the child's emotions or feelings. Senator Borah, for example, argued in favor of establishing the Children's Bureau when he claimed that the children "must be mentally and morally and physically equipped to discharge the duties of citizenship." [16] He believed the functions of the Bureau would contribute toward this end. Similarly, Senator Beveridge, in deriding the evils of the New England industries that employed many young immigrant children, argued the following:

> These people who come here make in the course of one generation admirable citizens if their *bodies* are not broken and their *souls* are not crushed and their *minds* are not stunted in the meantime. And when you do that to any children, whether they are Americans or "foreigners," you have spoiled citizenship and ruined human life. (emphasis added) [17]

According to both Borah and Beveridge, Congress sought to protect the child's soul, mind, and body. It was these elements that constituted personhood. There is no mention of emotions. This is also true of Senator George Perkins's observation of child labor, which he described as "deleterious and . . . debasing to the moral, spiritual, and physical welfare of mankind." [18]

Thus Congress saw itself as offering protection for the child. The child it sought to protect was made up of the important faculties of intellect, spirituality, and physical strength. To enter into the life of the child was to enter into a nurturance and/or protection of these dimensions. From a contemporary viewpoint, what strikes one as curious about this understanding of the individual is not only the absence of reference to emotions but also the inclusion of reference to morality or spirituality. It seems strange, from the perspective of the modern orthodoxy of a strict separation between church and state, that the government should have any concern for a child's soul, in this sense.

That the soul was understood in a religious context is underscored in a speech by Teddy Roosevelt, entered into the *Congressional Record* in February 1909. Here he argued that one purpose of the Children's Bureau was the establishment of foster homes. According to Roosevelt, religion was one thing government personnel should keep in mind when selecting appropriate foster homes: "Such homes should be selected by a most careful process of investigation, carried on by skilled agents, through personal investigation and with due regard to the religious faith of the child." [19] It was in this context (in the very next line, to be precise) that Roosevelt, like the senators quoted above, spoke of the "careful consideration" that must be taken for the "physical, mental, moral, and spiritual training and development of each child." [20]

Again, moral and spiritual training were regarded as important, whereas emotional development was not. If anything, discourse surrounding these pieces of legislation was deliberately anti-emotive.

The Anti-Emotive Defense

Because these bills had to do with the defense of innocent and abused children, proponents apparently opened themselves to the criticism that such legislation was simply a product of sympathy (as if this were somehow an insubstantial basis for supporting the initiatives). In response to these criticisms, however, proponents did not defend the importance of sentiment or emotive compassion but sought to shift their arguments to a different basis of reasoning altogether.

Senator Albert Beveridge, for example, argued eloquently against the notion that foreign immigrant children were somehow less deserving of sympathy than "true" Americans. Yet he was sure to point out that sympathy was not all that motivated him: "But that does not decrease my sympathy, if I was taking this up as a matter of sympathy, which I am not. I am interested in this matter not only from the point of view of sympathy for these children, but for the future of this Republic." [21] Thus the future of the Republic, not sympathy, was the senator's chief concern. A similar sheepishness about sentimentality is evident in Senator Overman's defense of child labor laws. In the course of his arguments he identified a number of individuals, including President Roosevelt and William Jennings Bryan, who supported the bill and then proclaimed to his opponents, "So it is not merely the work of 'sentimentalists,' or of men who have given their lives to learning that I look for comfort and support." [22] Somehow, sentimentality did not carry enough weight to provide for the bill's legitimacy.

Senator William Chilton highlighted the low justificatory status of "feelings" when he explained his reasons for opposing the establishment of the Children's Bureau, an enterprise he was initially inclined to support: "I am forced to vote against my feelings and support my ideas of the pledges made by my party and the oath which I have taken as a Member of this body." [23] Sentiment, sympathy, and emotions were not bases enough to justify supporting the legislation. At least rhetorically, "ideas" superseded "feelings" in this case.

The Sheppard-Towner Act (1921)

After the Children's Bureau was established in 1912, congressional debate over its role and its level of funding continued. One of the first major programs developed by the Children's Bureau, and managed under its auspices, was the Sheppard-Towner Act. First introduced to Congress in 1919, it was heatedly debated, passed through Congress, and became statutory law in 1921. The Sheppard-Towner Act, named after its sponsors, Senator Morris Sheppard of Texas and Representative Horace Mann Towner of Iowa, provided federal grants-in-aid to the states for the promotion of maternal and infant health and welfare. The program remained in effect through 1929, during which time the federal government spent approximately $7 million to fund the act.

Debate over the measure during the Sixty-seventh Congress provides us with an interesting and lively discussion regarding the legitimacy of the federal government's expanding role in the lives of America's children. Much of the debate centered on the question of whether this act represented America's movement toward a socialist or Bolshevik governing system. As such, proponents were forced into a position of having to articulate a legitimate rationale for the bill's passage and for the expansion of state activity. It should also be noted that the women's movement provided a strong base of support for the bill. Correspondingly, the role of women in political engagement was also an issue of some concern. Here, too, members appealed to prevailing ideological systems when asserting their support for or opposition to such engagement. Interest was intense, and members were actively engaged in the legislative process. As one member observed during the time, "No measure has arisen during my membership here that has provided so much interest and discussion." [24]

The Continuing Potency of Traditional Sources of Legitimation

As with the debates over child labor laws and the Children's Bureau of the previous two decades, discussion of the Sheppard-Towner Act regularly included religious language and symbolism, along with appeals to nature and responsibility to the civic order. Senator Sheppard, for example, in his defense of the measure, described concern for children as "one of the most sacred responsibilities of humanity." [25] Identifying the many children who, without the legislation, would continue to be subjected to poor health and improper treatment, he pronounced, "Someone must answer to the Almighty." [26] Moreover, he declared that "if I could have my way, I would have the Federal Government, in cooperation with the States, take whatever steps might be necessary to make certain the proper care of mother and of child in the supreme and holy crisis of maternity." [27] According to Sheppard, not only was it a holy crisis but it was one that, if neglected, would undermine the Republic: "Every little life that perishes through lack of knowledge or neglect or finds a precarious survival within a feeble and defective body is an accusation of the Republic and an indictment of the flag." [28]

Others were more explicit in appealing to a Protestant worldview. Congressman Daniel Reed of New York, for example, very creatively ascribed religious significance to the Sheppard-Towner Act as he quoted and interpreted poetry that cloaked the care of infants in sacred garb:

> I saw the college and the church that stood
> For all things sane and good;
> I saw God's helpers in the shop and slum

> Blazing a path for health and hope to come;
> And true religion from the grave of creeds
> Springing to meet man's needs. . . .
> And I saw, too, that old, old sight and best—
> Pure mothers with dear babies at the breast.
> These things I saw.
> (How God must love his earth!)

He then interpreted the poem he had just read and offered his endorsement of the legislative measure:

> It is God's helpers in the shop and slum and the mothers of this country who are blazing a path for health and hope to come. It is true religion springing to meet man's need and finding through this legislation an agency for a higher order of service to the women and children of this Republic. I am glad of this opportunity to support this splendid measure.[29]

Perhaps the most explicit effort to justify the legislation according to the mandates of a Protestant worldview was Congressman James Buchanan's long-winded dissertation, which drew heavily on biblical imagery to legitimate the bill:

> As far back as tradition goes or history can reach the mother and her child stand as the magnetic symbols of love and beauty. No epic is more striking or sweeter than the story of the perilous birth and rescue of the mighty leader and lawgiver of Israel, as told in the Book of Exodus in the Old Testament Scriptures. I think the mother of Moses and Pharaoh's daughter must have been the first association to realize the practical value of our modern conception of care and mercy as proposed by this humane legislation.[30]

According to Buchanan, then, Moses' adoption was essentially the historical antecedent to the Sheppard-Towner bill. Moving to the New Testament, Congressman Buchanan next described the slaughter of children ordered by King Herod, an allusion that was perhaps intended to put the bill's opponents in dubious company:

> The King of Egypt and Herod the King of Judea are forever odious as the chief actors in that drama of atrocious cruelty, so vindictively staged to destroy the lives of children, and to support and advance the reckless partisan purposes of that dark day. Truly, "without controversy great is the mystery of godliness."[31]

No doubt, this was an interesting weaving together of political and biblical languages, and it may well have been the first time Herod was accused of political partisanship. Buchanan concluded by asserting that to oppose the measure was to remain in a state of "well-nigh unpardonable sin." [32] Confident in the remaining cultural salience of a religiously informed view of the world, the congressman predicted correctly that the legislation would become law and the program would be funded:

> The overwhelming demand and the self-evident necessity for the most adequate and efficient service leave no righteous ground for opposition to this most benevolent measure. It is bound to become the law, and it is certain to be cherished everywhere and for all times as most humane and Christian.[33]

Members also at times appealed to the authority of nature or the natural order, in conjunction with religion, in their discussions of the bill. Congressman Caleb Layton, for example, opposed the bill because he believed it would "destroy the finest thing in the human heart, that sweet, natural instinct, the God-given instinct of personal love and care for the little one which every normal father and mother entertains." [34] In an interesting mixture of appeals to theism and natural law, Layton argued:

> Seriously, is there not some virtue, some real reason in nature's law—the survival of the fittest? In fact, is not this law imperative, inescapable, beneficent, and founded in the highest of Divine wisdom—the law of evolution—the survival of the fittest being a necessary condition precedent to the working of the law? [35]

Standing historically in a post–Scopes Trial era, it is difficult to understand how Darwinian evolution could be understood as a gift of divine wisdom. Nonetheless, the congressman's argument illustrates how symbols from both cultural systems were employed for legitimating a certain political position.

The Sacred Home

As with congressional debates about child-related legislation in the earliest years of the twentieth century, discussion of the Sheppard-Towner bill often focused on whether the act would infringe on the "sacred" institution of the American family. Sometimes general societal agreement about the sacredness of the home was appealed to in order to support the measure. From this perspective, it was argued that the legislation would strengthen the life of the family. Congressman William Graham of Illinois was one who took this position:

> I believe in the sanctity of the home, and so long as I have a tongue to speak or a hand to strike with I shall defend it. The home is the basis of our established society. In no degree is the sanctity of the home invaded by this act.[36]

More often, though, it was the opponents of the bill who spoke of the sanctity of the home, as a place where the government had no business expanding its domain. Senator James Reed of Missouri, for example, argued that "official meddling can not take the place of mother love. Mother love! The golden cord that stretches from the throne of God, uniting all animate creation to divinity." According to Reed, the love between mother and child was "the one great universal passion—the sinless passion of sacrifice. Incomparable in its sublimity, interference is sacrilege, regulation is mockery."[37] He feared that the bill was "calculated to send governmental agents into the homes of the people to interfere in the most private and sacred relations of life."[38] Senator Reed also drew on biblical imagery in his defense of the sacred home and his opposition to the legislation:

> Ever since Eve first hugged Cain to her breast women have known how to feed a baby, what to feed a baby, and when to feed a baby. The mother of to-day has sense enough to know in general what her baby needs. . . . It is now proposed to turn the control of the mother of the land over to a few single ladies holding Government jobs at Washington.[39]

Congressman Layton opposed the bill based on similar reasoning:

> I am opposed to this bill because its proponents, with the cold impious hand of officialdom, would invade the home, the one place on earth where one expects to breathe a little air of heaven, the one place in which no foreign foot should tread without the permission and the desire of those who live and reign there. The home belongs to the father and the mother. It is their place of seclusion, their place of worship.[40]

Layton went on to lament the whole idea of a government taxing its people "in order to have their most intimate and sacred domestic concerns made a matter of governmental espionage and governmental interference."[41]

Congressman Thomas Sisson of Mississippi was yet another who depicted the family home not only as a sacred place but as an institution that helped to sustain the Republic: "As certain as God's sun shines in the universe and gives life and light to us all, just so certain the home presided over by a good mother is life in society. It is the sun, it is the life of this Republic."[42]

Thus some members of Congress opposed the legislation because it represented the government's continued expansion into the private lives of American citizens and feared that the bill's passage would be a step closer to socialism. To make the expansion of government into the home a truly reprehensible act, the home was necessarily imbued with sanctified meaning. In other words, what legitimated opposition to an extended role of government into private home life was the rhetorical dressing of the home as a holy or sanctified institution.

The Essence of Personhood

As occurred in previous congressional discussions about children, debates surrounding the Sheppard-Towner bill addressed the matter of what constituted the individual self and, in so doing, invoked the traditional themes of civic republicanism and Christian theism. Congressman William Upshaw, for example, offered the following statement:

> God help my Nation, your Nation, to do its best to help these little "immortelles" of time and eternity to come into their glorious birthright of American opportunity under the best possible conditions—conditions that will make for that *physical* strength and that *mental* and *moral* health that will guarantee the greatest security of the Republic and the highest happiness of the people. (emphasis added)[43]

As before, the individual self was defined by his or her physical, mental, and moral capacities.

Also as before, emotions were not even mentioned, much less understood to be at the center of a person's identity. This is evident, for example, in Congressman Israel Foster's assertion that "every American has the right to be born of sound mind and sound body."[44] What is interesting about this statement is not only the repeated claim that one's intellect and physical strength constitute one's personhood but the emphasis that this person also has certain individual rights. "Rights talk," as Mary Ann Glendon might call it, was not glaringly evident in earlier congressional discussions of child welfare legislation, but there were traces of it in discussions surrounding the Sheppard-Towner bill.

Senator Sheppard, for example, argued that the "first obligation of society is to the unborn child. The most fundamental right of every human being is to a normal birth."[45]

If the individual was understood to have certain rights, he or she was also expected to perform certain duties. Individual rights were not the whole of the story. Consider Congressman Bill Lowrey's understanding of the individual's importance in the life of the Republic:

> Democracy depends for its value, for its very life, upon the fiber, the capacity, the virtue, the merit of the individual. . . . If the individual can not be trusted to form the opinion of the locality he inhabits on wholesome lines, and thus lead it to effective action for protection of all men, women and children, then democracy is a failure, and it must disappear from the earth which it encumbers.[46]

The individual was to act on wholesome lines for the protection of all. Hence the individual, though free, was constrained by certain impositions. Such a view was also expressed by Congressman Layton:

> The finest of all principles taught us by our forefathers and given unto us as their most precious heritage was that principle which endeavored to make every individual citizen self-dependent, and to fill him with a sense of his own individual responsibility; to make every man self-initiative and independent; to inculcate in him the duty to govern, not to be governed.[47]

Thus, though the individual self was understood as central to the American experience, his or her freedoms and rights were not the end of the story. The independent self also had certain duties and responsibilities to perform.

In sum, the individual was conceived of as a person with a mind, soul, and body, who had certain individual rights. Yet these rights were constrained by the externally imposed ideals of duty—duties that served to form a virtuous, rather than an unencumbered, self, to borrow Michael Sandel's apt phrase put forth in his 1982 work *Liberalism and the Limits of Justice*. Absent again in these ruminations about the individual self is any reference to feelings or emotions. To the contrary, emotivity or sentiment remained a matter members of Congress dealt with rather gingerly.

Efficacy over Sentimentality

As with discussions regarding the institution of child labor laws and the establishment of the Children's Bureau, proponents of the Sheppard-

Towner Bill were vulnerable to the criticism that the measure was exclusively a piece of "sentimental" legislation. As occurred in the previous legislative period, proponents of the measure tried to shift their defense to a different tactical base. Congressman Reed of New York, for example, argued that the bill was important not because of sentiment but because of efficacy:

> It has been shown that 23,000 mothers die during childbirth in the United States in a year. This awful toll is an economic question, my friends, as well as a sentimental one. It is not necessary, however, to decide this question on the basis of sentiment. It is an economic as well as a sentimental and humanitarian social problem . . . they say that 250,000 babies lose their lives through neglect during a year. You say I am appealing to sentiment. My friends, it can be reduced to an economic basis. It has been demonstrated beyond doubt that it costs only $5 to save a baby, but costs $50 to bury it. . . . Take your pencils and multiply 250,000 by $50 and you will have $12,500,000 a year loss to the United States.[48]

Apparent in Congressman Reed's reasoning is the belief that economic efficacy carried greater persuasive power than did sentimental appeals.

Congressman William Bankhead similarly defended the measure by shifting the argument to a matter of practicality over sentimentality:

> Are those behind this bill merely seeking to put a mere sentiment on the statute books of the country, or does the evidence disclose that we are confronted with a practical proposition involving not only sentiment but also a vital economic situation in the proposed measure?[49]

Bankhead went on to answer his own question: "I say to you it is not only a sentimental but it is a practical proposition of the profoundest significance that should challenge the attention of the Congress of the United States."[50]

Interestingly, in the Sheppard-Towner debates, unlike in the previous congressional discussions, members on several occasions offered a tentative defense of the sentiment motive. Senator William Kenyon, for example, rhetorically posed the following questions: "Will the bill do the work? Will it save any babies? Is it a feasible project? Is it a silly proposition? Is it sentimental and hysterical for the Senate of the United States to be concerning itself about such a measure as this?"[51] In response to his own mockingly critical challenges to the measure, Kenyon answered with a tepid defense of sentimentality: "It may be sentimental legislation—yes; maybe it is. It is a good thing to have some sentiment once in a while in legislation."[52]

In a similarly reticent tone, Congressman Graham offered the following defense of sentimentalism:

> Finally, the charge is made that this bill rests on sentiment only. I think I have demonstrated that it rests upon a sound and substantial foundation other than sentiment. If I were to say, however, that in its consideration I have divested myself of all sentiment, I should not speak the full truth.[53]

Even Congressman Buchanan, who offered the extended theological treatise for the Sheppard-Towner bill reviewed earlier, conceded, "The theme of mother and child is so sanctified and full of tenderness that it is difficult to stifle emotion and to treat it with dispassionate reserve." Thus, in this second period of congressional history, traditional philosophical justifications were joined with appeals to economic rationality and with slightly less defensive appeals to sentiment.

Social Security and Emergency Wartime Aid to Children (1939–1945)

In the late 1930s and early 1940s, Congress considered two important pieces of child welfare legislation: (1) Social Security Aid to Dependent Children, one dimension of the massive network of New Deal welfare programs initiated in the 1930s, and (2) Emergency Maternity and Infant Care (EMIC), a program to finance day care for children of working mothers during World War II. The former, Aid to Dependent Children (ADC), had its origins in the Mothers' Aid programs of the early twentieth century, which were reportedly not very effective and which varied in funding levels among states and among counties within states. In 1935, aid to mothers and infants was incorporated into Title IV of the Social Security Act. Four years later, Congress sought to extend Social Security aid to children to match the level of federal aid provided for the needy aged and blind. It also raised the age limit for federal contributions of aid to dependent school-attending children from sixteen to eighteen years.

Every ten years since Theodore Roosevelt's 1909 Conference on the Care of Dependent Children, the White House held a conference to examine the welfare of America's children. When the 1939 conference convened, the country was turning its attention from the difficulties of the Great Depression to the trials of World War II. The wartime problems considered at the conference would generate the establishment of EMIC, a program whose purpose was to provide for the health and nutritional needs of infants whose mothers were employed in war-related occupations. This became the largest medical assistance program in the United States at the time. Appropriations for the program were first approved by Congress in 1943, at a cost of $1,200,000 to the federal government.

Discussions concerning both ADC and EMIC were clearly colored by America's involvement in World War II. Still, the broader justificatory themes evident during this period reflect an interesting bridge between the arguments offered in the first quarter of the century and those offered in the later decades of the twentieth century.

Children and the War

Though this analysis focuses on the larger, guiding themes of the state's legitimating philosophies, it is difficult to ignore how the pressing needs of the war provided an urgent, and largely undisputed, justification for state action toward children during the 1940s. Particularly with respect to discussions surrounding EMIC, justifications for government action were based in large measure on the fact that the country was at war. Consider, for example, Senator Robert Taft's plea for federal aid to children of working mothers and enlisted fathers:

> The justification for the expenditure of Federal money under that program arises from the fact that the Federal Government is asking the mothers to go into factories, and some care must be taken of their children while the mothers are away from their homes. That is the justification for the expenditure of Federal money, an expenditure which certainly will not continue after the war.[54]

Senator Elbert Thomas offered a similar rationale and noted the implausibility of any possible objections to the measure:

> I agree that mothers should not be in industry. I agree with all my heart and soul that they should not be in industry, and I wish they did not have to be in industry; but they are in industry, and children are being neglected as a result. Because children are being neglected and mothers are not being

taken care of, the Government has stepped in to try to do some good. No one objects to that.[55]

Because the government had asked fathers to go overseas in combat, and because it had asked mothers to support this effort through work in the factories, it saw child-care assistance as, in Congressman Clyde Doyle's words, "its bounden duty."[56]

Parenthetically, Aid to Dependent Children also had its origins in military conflict. The first benefits offered to "widows and orphans" in the earlier Mothers' Aid programs were to those whose husbands and fathers were involved in some form of military conflict. Though concerns about the war played a large part in justifications for the extension of state aid to children during this time period, the larger legitimating themes evident earlier, along with new ones that would become more pronounced later in the century, were also present.

The Evolution from Traditional Forms of Legitimation

Still evident in debates surrounding these measures are references to some of the traditional themes identified in the previous two periods of congressional history. However, the traditional legitimations were coupled with or qualified by new ideas during the World War II period. For example, Congressman Walter Brehm argued in support of extended child welfare programs with the following statement.

> Every child has the inalienable right to be born free from disease, free from deformity, and of pure blood. Every child has the inalienable right to be loved, to have individuality respected, to be trained wisely in body, mind, and soul. In a word, to be brought up in the fear and admiration of the Lord.[57]

Notice that though Brehm invoked religious terminology, he also talked about the need to respect individuality and the "rights" of the child. Unlike former statements, which appealed exclusively to external authorities for legitimation, this argument includes more individualistically based justifications.

A similar conflation of new and old themes is evident in President Franklin D. Roosevelt's statements about child welfare. These were inserted into the *Congressional Record* by Congressman Charles H. Leavy in 1940. The entry was taken from a speech offered by Roosevelt after the White House's children's conference:

And I think that religion, religion especially, helps children to appreciate life in its wholeness, to develop a deep sense of the sacredness of the human personality. In view of the estimate that perhaps one-half of the children of America are having no regular religious instruction, it seems to me important to consider how provision can best be made for some kind of religious training. We can do it, because in this way we are capable of keeping in mind both the wisdom of maintaining the separation of church and state and, at the same time, giving weight to the great importance of religion in personal and social living.[58]

Though subtle, there is an important shift in emphasis here. Displaying a cognizance of religion's less esteemed role in society, Roosevelt referred to the separation of church and state and to the low number of children involved in religious education. More important, however, is the way in which Roosevelt described religion in a functional sense: it provided assistance to the child in personal and social living, and it gave the child a sense of the sacredness of the human personality. Before, the religious ideals themselves constituted the sacred. Here religion provides the individual personality with a sacred quality. As such, religion is recognized for its utility rather than for its inherent value.

In another speech, also inserted into the *Congressional Record,* Roosevelt claimed further that religion gave the child a sense of security and happiness:

We are concerned about the children who are outside the reach of religious influences, and are denied help in attaining faith in an ordered universe and in the fatherhood of God. We are concerned about the future of our democracy when children cannot make the assumptions that mean security and happiness.[59]

Again, religion was regarded as important enough to be discussed in the context of public policy for children but was understood to serve a functional purpose. It gave the child the assumptions that resulted in security and happiness.

The sense in which personal happiness was given greater weight than purely religious mandates is even more pronounced in an article entered into the *Congressional Record* by Senator Edward Robertson in 1945. The selection quoted by Robertson, which included a scriptural reference about children, was revised to place happiness as the essential telos:

In all reverence, I would repeat the words of Holy Writ—"Suffer little children to come unto you," and then rephrase them—"Help us to bring into our hospitals the little children who suffer that we may lead them from the valley of the shadow of despair to the hills of health, of hope, and of happiness."[60]

The end became happiness, rather than company with the God of Christian theism.

The Happy Home

The emphasis on personal happiness was most evident in descriptions about the home. As in previous congressional discussions about children, much importance was placed on the preservation of the family home. In the late 1930s and early 1940s, however, what was once the "sacred" home became the "happy" home. Members sought to justify state involvement in the lives of children on the argument that children were entitled to a happy home. Congressman Everett Dirksen, for example, argued in 1939 that "the finest kind of preparation [children] can have is the preparation that comes from the contentment and felicity that go with a very happy home."[61] Similarly, in defense of the EMIC, Congressman Doyle argued, "It will create happier home conditions and surroundings for workers winning the war."[62] Conspicuously absent from these discussions of the happy home are the sanctified and sacred qualities offered in the debates of the first two periods of congressional history considered here.

The preferred term was *happy*—the happy home made a happy child. President Roosevelt, reflecting what seemed to be the general sentiment among politicians, asserted, "We make the assumption that a happy child should live in a home where he will find warmth and food and affection."[63] It is not that happiness was devoid of any religious meaning; Roosevelt himself spoke about both the importance of the child's "moral and spiritual development" and his or her need for "security and happiness."[64] However, the happiness theme was not always connected to religious ideals—in fact, during this period of congressional history, most often it was not. Usually happiness alone justified state action. It should also be noted that whereas the image of the sacred home was usually used to oppose child welfare legislation, that of the happy home was most often used to justify it.

The Happy Child

Just as a happy environment was the favored condition of the home, the happy child was the ideal state described for the individual child. Congressman Thomas Lane, for example, called for the extension of federal aid to dependent children "so that all of the children, in every State, may have a fair chance to grow up into healthy, happy, and dependable Americans." [65] Similarly, a group of six congresswomen supported wartime aid to children with the following statement:

> Women cannot do their best work in their war jobs, or are prevented from making a contribution altogether, if they are constantly worried and insecure about the care of their children. We know of no better way to secure their services than in making adequate provisions for safeguarding the health and happiness of their children. [66]

Roosevelt likewise spoke of the essentials of what constituted a "happy childhood" and claimed that the purpose of the White House conference on children was to "review the objectives and methods affecting the safety, well-being, and happiness of the younger generation." [67]

How does the idea of the happy child relate to the descriptions of personhood identified in previous political discussions regarding child welfare legislation? In the 1930s and 1940s, mention was still made of the basic dimensions of personhood identified in previous periods. For example, Congressman Jerry Voorhis supported legislation by arguing:

> We must build that foundation today and every day of their formative period of growth. That foundation must be as strong physically, mentally, and morally as it is within our power to make it. This is as much our responsibility and duty for the future as anything we can do. [68]

Thus, the child's makeup was still seen to be comprised of the physical, mental, and moral components. This was also evident in Congressman Brehm's stated belief that the child must be "trained wisely in body, mind and soul." [69] So there were, at the least, vestiges of the previous, more traditionally informed ideals of personhood. These could coexist with the ideals of happiness. But, as we shall see, so could newer understandings of the self.

The New Deal's New Self

Where previous understandings of personhood spoke almost exclusively of the child's mind, body, and soul, discussion of aid in the 1940s added new dimensions. In addition to intellectual, physical, and moral development there was attention given to the importance of emotional or self-appreciative development. Consider, for example, this excerpt from one of Roosevelt's speeches:

> In family life the child should first learn confidence in his own powers, respect for the feelings and the rights of others, the feeling of security and mutual good will and faith in God. Here he should find a common bond between the interests of the individual and the interests of the group.[70]

The child was to recognize his or her own powers and be cognizant of feelings. Recall that previous references to the self made no mention of feelings. Though offered in conjunction with references to more traditional codes and symbols (i.e., faith in God), the child's feeling of security (or happiness) was worthy of discussion—indeed, of legislative action.

Congresswoman Caroline O'Day supported aid to dependent children along the same lines:

> Aid to dependent children helps to foster an attitude of *self-respect,* rather than supine acceptance of dependency. It will reduce the burdens of public relief and assistance that the Federal, State, and local governments will otherwise be called upon to bear in coming years. . . . On every count it is better economy now and it is a better investment for the future. This investment in the homes and the health, in the *self-confidence* and the *self-respect* of dependent children has a dollars and cents value. (emphasis added)[71]

Thus aid was seen to help foster a child's view of himself or herself. The language implies that the government somehow saw a role for itself in helping the child feel good about himself or herself. Recall Congressman Brehm's belief, stated on the House floor in 1943, that "every child has the inalienable right to be loved, to have individuality respected."[72]

An important shift was taking place here. The central theme of happiness provided a basis whereby the traditional forms of legitimation, common in previous discussions about the well-being of children, could coexist with newer ideas of good feelings toward the self. The idea of happiness was broad enough to include both ideals. On the one hand, religious morality and civic duty were understood to result in family and individual happiness. On the other hand, happiness referred to individuals feeling good about themselves. And the latter was not necessarily dependent on the moral and civic reference points of the former. Evident in comments during this period were both types of understanding, and in many cases, they were mixed together. As such, this period represented a transition wherein the older moral codes and symbols were joined with a greater acceptance of emotive or sentimental ideals.

The Continued Salience of Efficacy

A theme that continued from the 1920s into the World War II period was the utilitarian argument about the long-term efficacy of early child care. Note in the O'Day quote above that state fostering of self-respect would "reduce the burdens of public relief and assistance." It was "on every count," according to the congresswoman, "better economy now and . . . a better investment for the future." Similarly, Congressman Doyle argued that the legislation "would save money—it will conserve character—help prevent child delinquency, and therefore numerically reduce the number of crime cases."[73] Likewise, President Roosevelt argued that "the money and hard work that go into these public and private enterprises are again repaid many times."[74] Thus the bills were defended on the grounds that they would have a long-term monetary payoff, that they were economically viable measures.

In sum, present in congressional debates surrounding the establishment and funding of the ADC and EMIC programs of the late 1930s and 1940s were the continuation of features of traditional legitimating themes as well as the introduction of the new ideas of self-respect and the importance of feelings. The most pronounced rationale for federal action during this period was the state's supposed responsibility for fostering the child's happiness. The notion of happiness represented a transition theme of sorts, encompassing both the new and the old. Moreover, the urgency of the war provided a unique and urgent form of state legitimation during the period, and utilitarian efficacy continued as an articulated reason for the expansion of state programs.

Head Start and Operation Good Start (1965–1970)

The Head Start program was one of the original components of the War on Poverty strategy developed during the Lyndon B. Johnson administration. Initiated in 1964, Head Start continues today as one of the most celebrated of the War on Poverty initiatives. Its purpose was, and is, to help disadvantaged children prepare for kindergarten or first grade. The program, initially run under the auspices of the Office of Economic Opportunity and directed by Sargent Shriver, was intended to help impoverished children with basic medical, dental, and nutritional needs; with basic school readiness; and with, in the words of its director, "the general development of the child psychologically." [75] The parents of the children were also assisted by the specialists in the process. Both professionals and volunteers helped provide the service.

Another piece of legislation introduced during this period was Operation Good Start, a program that would provide for the training of child development specialists to assist emotionally disturbed grammar school children. The bill did not pass Congress in its original form, but the overall spirit of the legislation approximated that of Head Start, with interesting legitimations offered by members. Considered here are discussions of both legislative initiatives during the Eighty-ninth Congress (1965–1966) and congressional remarks about the Head Start program during the Ninety-first Congress (1970), when the program was rediscussed and restructured.

The Transformation of Identity

Perhaps the most striking difference between congressional remarks about the state's responsibility toward children during this time period and those during the first quarter of the century is the rhetorically proposed view of the self. Self-identity was understood in the mid- to late 1960s very much in the sense that a child needed to reach his or her "full potential." It was argued, for example, that the child needed "the opportunity to develop to his full potential," [76] that underprivileged children needed "extra help in order to reach their full potential," [77] and that the "early years are critical if children are to develop to their full potential." [78] But what exactly was meant by reaching one's full potential? For one thing, fullness of potential had something to do with arriving at a certain understanding of the self. Head Start was consistently supported on the basis that it "builds self-esteem," [79] that it "develops self-confidence," [80] and that it addresses problems "arising from loss of self-identity, self-fulfillment." [81]

When one member claimed that "identity and dignity" were important and precious to the needy child, he clearly understood these ideas in the way they are typified by Peter Berger in his discussion of a societal movement from a cultural emphasis on honor to a cultural preference for the idea of dignity.[82] According to Berger, under the aegis of "dignity," one's identity is arrived at through a certain sense of self-understanding. With honor, one's identity is determined by one's association with various societal institutions. A shift toward dignity in this sense is certainly evident in these congressional debates. Legislative initiatives directed toward children were appealed to on the basis not of religious or natural mandates but of individual fulfillment. The self, it seems, became the starting point and the basis for state action. And a major component of this self was the child's feelings.

Recall that in debates about the child labor laws and the Sheppard-Towner bill, members of Congress spoke about the need to assist in the physical, mental, and moral development of the child. It was the child's mind, body, and soul that constituted his or her personhood and that beckoned state protection. In the middle of the century, we found traces of congressional concern with the "emotions" of the child as well. But by the mid-1960s, in discussions of Head Start, emotions were conspicuously more central to the child's identity.

Congressman Andrew Jacobs, Jr., for example, observed in 1965 that "Head Start children were to be prepared physically, mentally, and emotionally to make the most of their first experience with formal schooling." [83] Similarly, Congresswoman Margaret Heckler inserted into the record a praiseworthy article about the Head Start program which argued that "positive attention" paid to the child in the critical early years of development led to "significant improvement in cognitive, physical, and emotional development." [84] These comments interestingly not only included emotions as an important dimension of the child's identity but also excluded the formerly common "moral" or "spiritual" component. In essence, "spiritual" development was replaced with "emotional" development.

Even a representative of the religious community identified "emotions" and excluded "morality" in her laudatory description of the Head Start program. Sister Mary James, S.S.J., testifying before the House

Education and Labor Committee in December 1969, argued that one of the purposes of the Head Start program was to contribute to the "physical, social and emotional growth of these children." Her statement was included in the *Congressional Record* by Congressman John Wydler, who cited it while arguing in support of the Head Start program on the House floor in February 1970.[85] Again, in this example, Head Start was considered viable because it contributed to a child's emotional growth.

The Centrality of Emotions

The centrality of emotions, however, was not only evident in the transformation of the tripartite description of the child's personhood. Indeed, overall emotions played an important part in congressional discussions about both pieces of legislation. This was certainly the case in discussions about Operation Good Start. In justifying the need for this bill, Congressman Sam Gibbons observed that, according to one estimation, "there are over 500,000 emotionally disturbed youngsters in the United States."[86] He argued further that "about 1 of every 10 youngsters of school age is emotionally disturbed."[87] Gibbons cited yet another study to validate the existence of emotional disturbance problems among children: "According to the District of Columbia Association for Mental Health, 7,282 schoolchildren were singled out by their teachers last year for psychological study by the school system's pupil appraisal service. About 1,200 were diagnosed as having severe emotional problems."[88] And this, according to some, did not identify all of the emotionally disturbed children. Quoting Dr. Murray Grant, City Health Director of Washington, D.C., Gibbons argued that psychological testing by itself would not reveal all emotional disturbance problems.[89]

Taken by this evidence, Gibbons introduced legislation to help identify and cure emotionally disturbed children—namely, Operation Good Start. Congressman Arnold Olsen of Montana, a supporter of the bill made the following argument in its favor, echoing themes regarding the pathologization of crime that were considered in Chapter 4:

> This bill . . . Operation Good Start provides for financial assistance for the training of child development specialists who will deal with children in the lower ranks of the lower grades of grammar school who are emotionally disturbed. The ranks of the underworld are swelled yearly by children

who grow up emotionally disturbed. If emotionally disturbed children are helped early enough in life, they may have a chance at decent, fruitful lives. The Warren Commission Report shows that if there had been sufficient help available to Lee Oswald when he was growing up in New York City, our beloved President Kennedy would be alive today.[90]

Arguably, emotions could not but be central to a program initiated to treat emotionally disturbed children. In this case, the very existence of the legislation spoke to the greater recognition of the place of emotions in the life of the child. But even in Head Start, the most important legislative action directed toward children during the mid- to late 1960s, emotions played an important role. This was perhaps best typified in the argument advanced that "Head Start's greatest accomplishment is that everyone connected with the program had good feelings."[91] Consider further the following congressional plea regarding the need for Head Start:

> This legislation is offered in recognition of the fact that there are approximately 13.3 million American children between the ages of 1 and 17 whose mothers work outside the home. Many receive little or no attention to their educational and emotional development needs and this is most often true for the 3 million such children from disadvantaged homes.[92]

State action was thus defended on the basis that the emotional needs of children were not being met.

Similarly, in a report introduced by Congressman Wydler, it was argued that Head Start helped students reach their full potential, something that involved more than just reading, writing, and arithmetic:

> The chief objective of all major approaches to the education of young children is to help a child strengthen his strengths so that he may become a more fulfilled human being. A person able to deal with colors, letters and numbers, but knowing nothing of human skills such as feeling, initiative, independence, sharing . . . would not add much to the world.[93]

Among other things, then, Head Start involved training the child in the human skill of feeling.

The elevated status of feelings was also evident in references to the home. Recall that in the first two time periods of congressional history examined herein, the home was largely referred to as a sacred institution. During the World War II period, the term most often associated with the home was *happiness*. A report offered by Congressman Wydler in 1970 would suggest that defenses of the Head Start program preferred to understand the family institution as the "feeling" home. According to this report, the "homes of children who 'make it' seem to be characterized by a certain emotional climate," where the mother is "emotionally secure" and has "a good deal of self-esteem." [94] Moreover, the parent in such a home "feels that he has some control over his own life and his own destiny, rather than believing himself to be a victim of chance, fate and circumstance." [95] Correspondingly, an early child development program such as Head Start was supported on the basis that it "changes the intellectual and educational climate of the home, develops feelings of self-esteem and control." In short, it provided the "type of environment which should lead to higher motivation, self-esteem and achievement." [96]

Feelings were also seen as central to the task of community problem solving. One dimension of the Comprehensive Head Start Child Development Act of 1970 was a multiservice neighborhood center where individual, family, or group problems could be "dealt with creatively." It was conceived of as a meeting place where people could "air their feelings and . . . tackle neighborhood and community problems together." [97] Thus, in many senses, emotions became the modus operandi for life in general. They were to be employed not only for understanding oneself but also for fostering a certain home environment and for communicating with the larger community.

The Role of the Psychologist

It is probably not surprising to the reader at this point to learn that the majority of professionals employed in Head Start typically received some type of psychologically or therapeutically based training. In keeping with Polsky's findings regarding changes in social welfare practices, psychologists and other therapeutic practitioners played an increasingly significant role in the state's attempt to assist children, as is evidenced in the proposal for Operation Good Start and in the operations of Head Start.

Supporters of Operation Good Start wanted $516,750,000 in federal support for fifty-five thousand child development specialists trained in "personality theory, management of individuals in groups, the school as a social system, abnormal psychology, child growth and development, counseling with parents." [98] Likewise, the team of Head Start workers was typically comprised of "teachers, parents, medical, psychological and social workers."[99] Congressional discussion of one Head Start program reported the following: "In addition to academic preparation, the children were given medical and psychological attention ... through school social workers and psychologists."[100] Congressman James Mackay presented a similar report about the personnel involved in setting up Head Start programs:

> The finest instructors in the fields of child growth and development, child guidance, health education, nutrition, sociology, and psychology, offered a concentrated but comprehensive program for the development of the project and setting up of child development centers.[101]

In another report, a child with a speech impediment was considered fortunate because "Head Start secured a psychologist for him to investigate the roots of his stammer."[102]

Psychologists not only were employed in the operation of Head Start programs but were referred to as experts who could legitimate the need for certain state action. Consider this argument offered by Congressman William Steiger of Wisconsin:

> Child psychologists and others who have studied the nature of human development, maintain that there is simply not enough known about how children grow and learn to predict what effects child development programs will have on them. We have created a National Institute for Early Childhood Development, in our bill, to help us gain a better understanding of early childhood development and the effect organized programs have on this process.[103]

In other words, the expertise of child psychologists was offered as a justification for the establishment of a new national institute.

Utilitarian Arguments

Evident in defenses of the War on Poverty initiatives, as in the justifications of the child welfare programs of the past, is the utilitarian argument. Unlike defenses of the Sheppard-Towner Act in 1921, however, the emotivist (or sentimentalist as it was regarded in 1921) appeal in the later initiatives was not superseded by the utilitarian argument. In the child welfare debates of the Johnson era, it appears that the emotivist and utilitarian arguments were on the same plane; that they were equally palatable ways of arguing for a bill's acceptability.

The continuing salience of the utilitarian principle was evidenced when supporters of Operation Good Start were asked to justify the cost of the program: "The money will be spent on the prevention of problems with the usual ratio of 1 ounce of prevention equaling 16 of cure." [104] Similarly, Congressman James Cleveland defended Head Start on the grounds that "the program represents a significant step toward attacking poverty at its roots, rather than dealing with its later symptoms, often at enormous expense." [105] Spending federal dollars to address the emotional problems of children was likewise defended on the basis that it would prevent crime in the future, at a great savings to the state: "The Federal Bureau of Investigation tells us that the cost of crime in the United States is $26 billion a year and is increasing at a rapid rate. Even a small savings—and I believe the savings will be large—in this area alone will more than pay for this program." [106]

In sum, these proposals, first introduced in the mid-1960s, reveal a conspicuously more therapeutic orientation toward the child. The apparent focal point of congressional concern was on the self, a clear shift from the previously authoritative institutions of family and religion. And central to the self during this period were emotions. Feelings not only were central to a person's identity but were the means by which individuals were to relate to one another. Also emerging in this period was the increasing authority of the therapeutic practitioners, the professionals with the necessary expertise to help children reach their full potential and grow in self-esteem. And though the utilitarian rhetoric appears to have remained, no longer was the language of emotivism or sentimentality subservient to it.

Head Start and Child Abuse Bills (1985–1990)

Because Head Start remained an important and very popular program in addressing the needs of children during the late 1980s, congressional discussions concerning the appropriations for and expansions of Head Start are considered again in this section. Also analyzed are congressional discussions about various pieces of child abuse legislation, specifically the Child Abuse Prevention, Treatment, and Adoption Reform Act—one of the most important pieces of child legislation discussed in the 100th Congress. The act, which first passed through Congress in 1974, was expanded and refunded during the late 1980s. Consideration of both of these measures reveals that the legitimating languages that emerged in the 1960s continue to characterize how members talk about the state's role toward children in this later part of the twentieth century.

The Esteemed Self

As in the Johnson era, evident during the late 1980s is an exalted view of the self, in the sense that legislators deemed it necessary that the child's self-esteem be nurtured and built up. Recall that in earlier periods, external authorities were appealed to for legitimation of state intervention. In the late 1980s, as in the late 1960s, the source of legitimation began with the self. In fact, high self-esteem became a telos in its own right. Success of a program was, at least in part, based on the extent to which a certain level of good feelings toward and about the self was achieved.

Consider, for example, Congressman William Goodling's argument in favor of the child abuse bill:

> These children are our future. Unless they are helped, unless the abuse and neglect is stopped, they will be ill prepared to meet the daily challenges of living. Their self-esteem will be low; they will be at great risk of educational failure; they might become runaways; and they will probably grow up to be adults who abuse their children.[107]

As depicted by Goodling, self-esteem was a lamentable consequence of abusive parental behavior. It was not argued that child abuse was wrong and immoral or that children subjected to it were being dealt with unjustly. Rather, injury to children was challenged on the basis that abuse hurt the child's self-esteem. It is likely, of course, that supporters of the measure would have agreed that child abuse was morally wrong, unjust, and the like, but this was not the language they chose to use.

Instead, legislators focused on the self. A low view of the self resulted *from* an abusive past. Likewise, it was believed that a low view of the self resulted *in* certain socially undesirable behaviors. Consider this statement by Senator John Chafee: "A major cause of the high rates of teen pregnancy is low self-esteem and the perception of poor and troubled teens that their 'life options' are limited."[108] Self-esteem, then, was considered as both a cause and an effect. Child abuse resulted in a low self-esteem, which, in turn, caused someone to be abusive. This was certainly the view portrayed by Congressman Dennis Hertel of Michigan:

What type of parent abuses his or her offspring? While child abuse runs across all social, ethnic, and socioeconomic boundaries, those who abuse their children often were abused by their parents when they were children, have low self-esteem, feel worthless and inadequate . . . lack knowledge of the states of child development and therefore hold unrealistic expectations of their children.[109]

A Lexis search of the term *self-esteem* in the *Congressional Record* reveals that use of the phrase has steadily increased in recent years. Lexis allows one to go back only as far as 1985; more interesting would be a comparison with earlier periods. Still, even the increase in recent years is revealing. (See Table 6.1.)

Given this preference for the place of self-esteem, it is not surprising that congressional efforts would be oriented toward helping children grow in their regard for themselves. The legitimacy of the programs was determined on the basis of whether they helped children toward this end. Congressman John Miller of Washington, for example, simply

TABLE 6.1
Congressional Record *Citations of* Self-Esteem

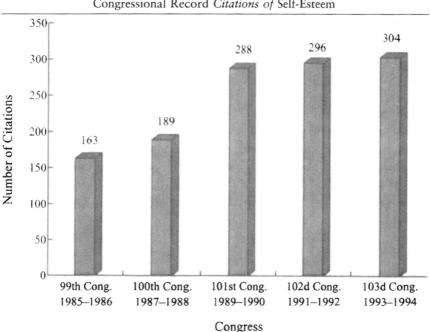

stated, "Head Start builds self-esteem." [110] Also arguing in favor of Head Start, Congressman Dale Kildee of Michigan proposed:

> If a child is helped to understand his or her dignity, that child is more likely to respect the dignity and worth of others, and all society is made safer. For many children, Head Start is the first step in their journey toward this understanding and toward self-respect. We have to put more children on that path. Head Start is currently serving only 16 percent of eligible children. Over 2 1/2 million remain in need. [111]

Because high self-esteem would lead to, among other things, a safer society, and because more than two million children were in need of higher self-esteem, the continuation and expansion of Head Start was arguably justified. This was the reasoning offered by Senator Chafee for his introduction of a related piece of legislation. "So I created," he said, "a demonstration grant program to provide these young people with activities and counseling that will increase their sense of well-being, their sense of self-esteem." [112]

Another measure initiated as a part of Head Start was a program called "Telephone Friends." Through this effort, lonely elderly men and women were introduced to needy young children. They became phone partners, of sorts. According to Congressman Ben Erdreich, this program was a "truly gratifying endeavor" because it "enhanced the lives of all those who participated in it" and improved "self-worth and self-esteem for both seniors and children alike." [113]

The Emotivist Self

As we saw emerging in the 1960s, emotions came to be understood as a major component of the self that was to be esteemed. By the end of the 1980s, Head Start, for example, was defended on the basis that it provided children and their families with "physical, psychological and emotional support." [114] Evident here again is the evolution from the early tripartite self (physical, mental, and spiritual) to the new tripartite self (physical, mental, and emotional). Again, the new and important component was the feeling or emotivist part of the self. Emphasis on this dimension of the self is apparent in Congressman Esteban Torres's belief that Head Start provided schoolchildren "with a comprehensive program to meet their emotional, social, health, nutritional, and psychological needs." [115]

Senator Paul Simon saw great merit in Head Start because it offered help to children who may have been "physically battered" but more commonly were "emotionally deprived."[116] Congressman Charles Rangel argued in support of H.R. 1900 (the Child Abuse Prevention, Treatment, and Adoption Reform Act) on the basis that children "have suffered emotionally from foster care."[117] It was also argued that abused children "feel alone and have limited skills in playing and communication."[118] Correspondingly, members defended H.R. 1900 on the basis that it helped children to succeed "not only intellectually but also emotionally."[119] Elsewhere it was suggested that the best way to build a child's self-esteem was to provide a "range of nonacademic opportunities for service and for feeling good."[120] Congressman Major Owens observed that the children in counseling groups met to, among other things, "discuss their feelings."[121] With the elevation of the emotivist self, it is not surprising that therapeutic forms of intervention became more predominant in state actions directed toward the well-being of children.

The Validity of State Therapeutic Intervention

That Congress justified legislative initiatives on the grounds that they fostered self-esteem points to the larger sense in which the state's role toward children was viewed as most appropriate when some form of therapeutic assistance was provided. It is striking how consistently legislative efforts toward children were defended on the basis that they would provide some form of therapeutic help to children in need.

Congressman William Goodling, for example, supported the passage of H.R. 1900 on the basis that it would provide "assistance to families in stress."[122] What kind of assistance? "The . . . program provides assistance such as individual, group, and family counseling to individuals who adopt special needs kids."[123] Congressman James Jeffords argued in defense of the same measure by claiming that services included "individual, group, and family counseling, assistance to adoptive parent organizations and support groups for adoptive parents, adopted children, and siblings of adopted children."[124] Congressman Owens argued in support of an amendment to the measure that provided "sensitivity training to a greater range of professionals who come into contact with incidents of family violence."[125]

Without therapy, children would remain in the vicious cycle of abuse, it was argued. Again, programs were justified on the basis that they would conquer the pattern of abuse through therapy:

> Apparently it is common for abused children to blame themselves for the pain they have suffered. Other children who aren't fortunate enough to receive therapy go on to become abusers of others as well as themselves and possibly turn to crime. Programs such as those in H.R. 1900 represent some of the best investments in the future of this country that we can possibly make.[126]

Providing a specific example of how counseling worked in this regard, Congressman Owens spoke of a boy named Mario who was positively affected by the program: "Mario, who adopted some abusive habits, is now learning in the counseling that he can deal with anger by taking a walk with a toy, taking a bubble bath or just sitting alone for a while."[127] Giving a clue as to what else occurred in these counseling groups, Owens reported, "In the counseling group, children meet to discuss their feelings, learn that the violence at home is not their fault and develop skills for dealing with anger and for surviving in abusive families. Above all, they learn to love themselves."[128]

Perhaps the most remarkable example of therapy supported by the American state under the auspices of this legislation is the federally funded program Parents Anonymous (PA). Along with the rest of the child abuse legislative package, PA was first established in 1974 and was considered for refunding during the 100th Congress. Senator Alan Cranston from California, one of the original sponsors of the measure, argued the following for continuing it:

> As you may know, I was the original author of a provision in the 1974 Child Abuse Prevention and Treatment Act to authorize funding under the demonstration project authority for self-help organizations. I am particularly proud that this provision helped provide support to Parents Anonymous, which began in my home State of California and has spread throughout the United States to become the Nation's largest child abuse prevention and treatment program, consisting of over 1,500 community-based, volunteer, professionally facilitated, self-help groups. Parents Anonymous is based on the concept that abusive parents, working together, can learn to deal with their frustrations and eliminate the abuse of children. This organization has helped thousands of parents and families to overcome their problems. Indeed, the vitality and strength of this organization and its philosophy of self-help has been truly rewarding to witness.[129]

As with the Drug Court programs investigated in Chapter 4, this program interpreted the actions of child-abusing parents as a kind of behavior that required treatment. Based on the self-help model of AA, the program provided a forum where parents with the "sickness" of child abuse could get help. Not surprisingly, the help they sometimes needed was assistance in attaining a higher view of the self. Congressman Owen quoted an expert as saying that the most helpful thing the state could do for children was, in the context of counseling, to help their parents: "Then they [the parents] can relax, be their age and do the most difficult thing—like themselves exactly how they are." [130]

Utilitarianism

Once again, defenses of the Head Start and child abuse prevention programs were not without utilitarian arguments. In the late 1980s, as in previous periods, the utilitarian argument remained in usage. Congressman Kildee argued, for example, that Head Start was a "very wise investment, not only in terms of developmental gains for children but also in savings to taxpayers." [131] Similarly, Congressman Hayes believed that Head Start's early investment in children was "cost effective" and that it was in our "Nation's best interests to spend more today on addressing and preventing this problem [of rising school-dropout rates]." [132] The most explicit argument for the efficacy of Head Start was offered in a report cited by Senator Paul Simon:

> Experts know that preventive steps in the early years can change a child's life, and also save society money in the long run. For every dollar spent on first-rate preschool programs like Head Start, studies show that we can save $4.75 later in the cost of remedial education, welfare, and crime. [133]

Therapeutic Practitioners

In discussions of child abuse and Head Start legislation during the late 1980s, the apparent importance of psychologists, psychiatrists, and other therapeutic practitioners increased. Indeed, Senator Edward Kennedy in March of 1988 offered tribute to Dr. Reginald S. Louri, the child psychiatrist who "was deeply involved in planning the very successful Head Start program." [134] Tribute was also paid to Dr. Edward F. Zigler, a child psychologist and one of the founders of Head Start. [135]

The involvement of Zigler and Louri in Head Start did not represent isolated cases. According to Congressman Stephen Solarz of New York, "There are psychologists . . . that work in every Head Start program." [136]

Thus the new forms of legitimation that emerged in the 1960s became more prominent in the late 1980s. The previously understood self, constituted by the three parts of mind, body, and soul, was transformed into a self constituted by mind, body, and emotions. State policies directed toward this emotive self were legitimated on the basis that they encouraged a higher, more esteemed, view of the self. Correspondingly, state programs directed toward children were more conspicuously therapeutic, employing the self-help models of AA and other counseling forms. Evident since the congressional discussions around the Sheppard-Towner bill of 1921, the utilitarian argument continued as a viable language of legitimation. Moreover, the therapeutic practitioners, whose emerging authority first became apparent in the 1960s, continued during this period of congressional history.

Welfare Reform: Rejection or Extension of Therapeutic Welfare?

We must ask whether the reform efforts in the 104th Congress somehow challenged what has been documented in this chapter. Before addressing this matter more directly, however, it is important to reassert a point made in Chapter 2; namely, that the main focus of this study is on what David Beetham calls "justification"—that component of the legitimation equation which represents the reigning codes of moral understanding that undergird particular programs and policies. Thus, when speaking of therapeutic legitimation, I do not mean government-sponsored therapy programs alone. Yet the existence of these is certainly emblematic of the presence of therapeutic justifications, and examinations of them often tell us much about the therapeutic sources of legitimation that uphold them. Moreover, they represent the institutional manifestation of Beetham's second component of legitimation, "validity."

That more therapeutically oriented programs such as Head Start were opposed in the 104th Congress, then, does tell us something about the current salience, or lack thereof, of therapeutic justifications. In other words, the boundaries between Beetham's notions of validity and justification are not always as clearly delineated in empirical realities as they are in theoretical conceptualizations. Any success in limiting programs such as Head Start, even apart from the political debates about the program, would certainly say something about the extent to which the therapeutic ethos has or has not impacted the state.

Generally speaking, however, challenges to the welfare system in the 104th Congress were not antitherapeutic. The welfare state and the therapeutic state, as conceived in this project, are clearly two different things. Unlike Head Start and Parents Anonymous, most welfare state programs are neutral with respect to the therapeutic model. One would be hard-pressed, for example, to describe the WIC (Women, Infants, and Children) welfare program as therapeutic, although it is a program that invites any number of possible justifications. What this chapter mainly has considered is how the evolving child welfare programs of the state have been defended or opposed according to reigning cultural codes of moral understanding. When examining recent efforts to "end welfare as we know it," then, the important point of consideration is the kind of language politicians use in either defending or opposing reform efforts.

In this regard, though there has been discussion of resurrecting such classical ideas as shame and of encouraging personal responsibility and traditional family values,[137] much of the political debate over welfare reform in the 104th Congress pivoted around explicitly therapeutic and utilitarian ideas. Both sides agreed that the current welfare system is inefficient and ineffective, that it is simply "not working"—a theme, of course, that has been present in congressional discussions about welfare for some time. Each side also tried to depict itself as compassionate and as the promoters of self-esteem while portraying the other side as mean-spirited and uncaring. Democrat congresswoman Eva Clayton, for example, agreed that both Republicans and Democrats want change but insisted that the Republican notions of change were "mean and cruel and will cause misery."[138] Similarly, Democrat congressman James Clyburn called the Republican welfare reform effort "draconian" and a "mean-spirited attack on welfare."[139]

Interestingly, and perhaps counterintuitively, Republican defenses of welfare reform used the same type of language. Republican congressman Sam Johnson of Texas, for example, accused Democrats of being the cruel party with respect to the welfare issue.

> This week another historic debate is going to begin; another 40-year-old broken welfare program will end. Today the Republicans are going to

bring forward a welfare bill that promotes freedom, rewards determination, and establishes self-esteem. Today mean-spirited Democrats, uncaring Democrats, will try to stop reform, cruel Democrats now defending a system that promoted dependency, rewarded complacency, and established self-defeat.[140]

Here, as elsewhere, self-esteem was a major theme in discussions about welfare policy. Republicans consistently denounced previous welfare programs because, as they claimed, the programs undermined self-esteem. Consider, for example, Republican Congressman Curt Weldon's personal "feeling[s]" on the matter:

> We spent $6 trillion on poverty programs that in inner city areas and in areas where I taught school and grew up actually created disincentives for people and actually took away self-pride, self-initiative and took away the ability of people who were poor to feel good about who they are.[141]

Republican congresswoman Linda Smith of Washington spoke against previous welfare policy by telling the story of a young girl, Sally, who got pregnant when she was fifteen and became, as Smith claimed, "trapped on welfare." The congresswoman spoke of the current welfare system as an "unfeeling system," desperately in need of reform. Moreover, she claimed that the present system made Sally and girls like her "lose all their self-esteem."[142] Republican congresswoman Jennifer Dunn of Washington similarly argued that the current system "pulls people down and robs them of their self-esteem." The Republican bill, according to Dunn, would, in contrast, provide "the hope of work and the promise of self-respect. We want to give people self-respect. We want to restore their self-esteem through the dignity of holding a job."[143] Also supporting the Republican initiative, Congressman Howard McKeon argued that the welfare reform bill would encourage work, which in turn "provides a sense of being" and "increases self-esteem."[144] Republican congressman Todd Tiarht likewise supported the bill's advocacy of work with the argument that it contributed toward self-esteem: "You cannot have self-esteem without accomplishment. You cannot have accomplishment without work."[145]

Therapeutic themes were also evident in Republican Congresswoman Marge Roukema's defense of reform efforts. According to Roukema, the American people "worry that we are wasting billions upon billions in hard-earned taxpayer dollars to support a system that promotes unhealthy, unproductive, dysfunctional families that sentence children to a lifetime of economic, social, and emotional deprivation."[146]

Democrats, like Republicans, appealed to a therapeutic code of moral understanding in their opposition to Republican welfare reform efforts. In addition to denouncing the mean-spirited efforts of Republicans, Democrats rhetorically portrayed themselves as the sentimental protectors of policies that promoted self-esteem and individual well-being. Eni Faleomavaega, the House delegate from American Samoa, for example, urged members not to "gag programs that we know make a difference, in motivation, in personal self-esteem, in positive reinforcement and outlook on life."[147] Likewise, Democrat congressman Tom Foglietta of Pennsylvania argued against rescission of the federal School Lunch Program on the grounds that states and localities would fail to offer viable alternatives. As an example of what might occur, he spoke of a local alternative to the federal School Lunch Program established in Pennsylvania. In the new program less fortunate children came to a "sharing table" that consisted of "the scraps, the half sandwiches and the unfinished cokes that were left by the more affluent students." Such a program, according to Foglietta, is "dehumanizing" and "destructive to any kind of self-esteem and pride."[148] The day before, Foglietta had described the same "sharing table" program and had posed the same questions with respect to it: "Could you think of anything more dehumanizing? Could you think of anything more destructive of self-esteem, of self-pride, of self-worth than that kind of a program?"[149]

The Republican welfare reform bill would also reduce funding of the popular Head Start program, considered in the previous two sections of this chapter. Reviewing the success of the program, Senator Daniel Akaka stated, "Project Head Start has consistently received praise for its work. Since its inception in 1965, the program has helped 14 million underprivileged children prepare for school. And this year, Head Start will serve approximately 740,000 kids, roughly a third of all poor children aged 3 to 4."[150] Consistent with previous arguments in favor of Head Start, Akaka defended the program by asserting that "Head Start has had a positive impact on children's motivation, self-esteem, socialization, and social maturity."[151]

Other Great Society welfare programs were defended with similar terms. Democrat congressman William Luther of Minnesota, for example, spoke out against Republican efforts to kill the Summer Youth Jobs

Program arguing that doing so would take away an important program for at-risk youth:

> Let's be honest with ourselves—many at-risk young people simply don't have what most of us had in our own lives—a requirement to get up in the morning, a person to show them how to work, or someone to appreciate their accomplishments and build their self-confidence and self-esteem.[152]

Congressman Cleo Fields also opposed cutting funding of the Summer Youth Jobs Program, based on his own personal experience with the program:

> I know what it felt like to have a summer job during the summertime. I mean it gave me self-esteem. It gave me pride. It gave me dignity. I was getting up and I was going to work. I went to work, Monday through Friday. And I made a salary. I got a check with my name on it. And I was able to buy my school clothes, and I was able to help my mother pay her rent. And that made me feel good.[153]

Even Democrats favoring reform, in the form of government-sponsored work programs and otherwise, relied on self-esteem as a theme to legitimate these new initiatives. Congresswoman Sheila Jackson-Lee, for example, proposed several amendments for job training because, as she claimed, "a job . . . will give you a sense of independence, self-esteem and self-worth."[154] Similarly, Senator Harry Reid of Nevada offered the positive example of a Nevada-based welfare-to-work program and defended it on the grounds that "providing individuals with work greatly enhances their self-esteem, their sense of responsibility and citizenship."[155] In addition to devaluing self-esteem, the absence of work was seen to affect other psychological issues: "Without full employment we are . . . exposing many families to social, psychological, and physiological costs, including disruption of family life, loss of individual dignity and self-respect, and the aggravation of physical and psychological illnesses."[156]

Thus both Democrats and Republicans appealed to therapeutic themes, most prominently to the notion of self-esteem, in either their opposition to or support of welfare reform efforts. And once again, as we saw in the areas of tort law, criminal justice, and education, appeals to the therapeutic ethos were joined with appeals to a utilitarian concern with what works. It is therefore erroneous to consider efforts to "end welfare as we know it" antitherapeutic. Though the welfare state has been attacked in this instance—with reduction of spending in some areas—arguments in the 104th Congress for either continuing or cutting programs rested on therapeutic legitimations. Regardless of whether programs were cut or sustained, debates over the measures were sprinkled with therapeutic justifications, just as arguments for and against child labor laws at the beginning of the century were sprinkled with appeals to religious ideals. At the same time that welfare programs have expanded, justifications for them have changed. From a Habermasian perspective, the need for an acceptable form of legitimation is particularly acute in such a climate. In the contemporary context, utilitarian and therapeutic ideals are offering themselves as the most pronounced bases of legitimation for the state's evolving welfare programs.

Before turning to an analysis of another arena of state activity—the rhetoric of electoral politics—I briefly consider another forum of the U.S. Congress, one located in the committee room rather than on the House or Senate floor. The following excursus evaluates the content of one of the most viewed and analyzed hearings in congressional history.

Excursus

The Clarence Thomas and Anita Hill Hearings

The most visible public focus on congressional discourse in recent memory fell on the much-heralded Clarence Thomas-Anita Hill hearings before the Senate Judiciary Committee in 1991. The hearings, which raised the matter of sexual harassment to the forefront of public consciousness, have been much analyzed and discussed since they transpired.[1] Though the event has been reconsidered through a number of different prisms (e.g., racial and gender inequality, political and ideological conflict) and by a number of different disciplines (e.g., psychology, literature, and political science)—not to mention the volumes of editorial material offered by political pundits—what is missing from these analyses is any consideration of the pervasiveness with which the therapeutic ethos infused the hearings.

It is well known that the so-called Thomas-Hill hearings came about as a result of allegations of sexual harassment made by Anita Hill of Clarence Thomas. Thomas had been nominated by President George Bush in 1991 to fill the position of retiring Judge Thurgood Marshall on the U.S. Supreme Court. Hill, who had worked for Judge Thomas at the Department of Education and at the EEOC (Equal Employment Opportunity Commission) from 1981 to 1983, alleged that Thomas had sexually harassed her during her tenure of employment in these governmental agencies. Thomas, who had already completed five days of questioning before the Senate Judiciary Committee, was considered likely to be confirmed by the U.S. Senate before information about these allegations was leaked to the press. A storm of controversy followed the leak, which culminated in the Senate agreeing to an extension of the hearings before the Judiciary Committee. In addition to the principal witnesses, others supporting both Anita Hill and Clarence Thomas were brought before the committee in an effort to ascertain the credibility of the allegations. The extended hearings lasted for a total of three days.

The highly publicized nature of the hearings make this an interesting case study for considering the extent to which the therapeutic has influenced political deliberations.

The Foundational Self

As discussed in Chapter 1, the therapeutic ethos, in contrast to traditional codes of moral understanding, makes the individual the ultimate unit of analysis. Such concepts as self-esteem, self-actualization, and self-fulfillment are central features of the therapeutic worldview. Discourse throughout the Thomas-Hill hearings reflected the extent to which individuals have embraced a belief in the primacy of self. A pronounced endorsement of the doctrine of the preeminent individual was advanced by Senator Joseph Biden when he defended his reasons for maintaining Professor Hill's anonymity:

> I don't know how we can call ourselves civil libertarians, I don't know how we can call ourselves people interested in the individual, if, in the name of a larger cause to justify the ends, we make a judgment for an individual that that individual chooses and has a right not to make.[2]

Although what Senator Biden meant by this comment is not completely clear, it is evident that somehow he intended to advocate the rights and choices of the individual over some "larger cause" beyond that individual. Yet, as Mary Ann Glendon has pointed out, "no one can be an absolutist for all our . . . rights, because taking any one of them as far as it can go soon brings it into conflict with others."[3] This certainly seems to be what happened in this case. Eventually Judge Thomas's rights came into conflict with Professor Hill's, and vice versa.

The point is not that either of these individuals was not justified in the arguments he or she set forth but rather that the flavor of their arguments centered on their individual interests and desires. Certainly, individual rights may have been violated in this case. Yet, from the outset neither participant was willing to consider the possibility of a middle ground, of some mutual misunderstanding. Instead, both spoke from extreme and polarized positions and did so by speaking of their own personal rights and self-interests. Consider Clarence Thomas's justification for his indignation with the proceedings:

> You spent the entire day destroying what it has taken me 43 years to build
> and providing a forum for that. . . . This leaked on me and it is drowning
> my life, my career and my integrity, and you can't give it back to me, and
> this Committee can't give it back to me, and this Senate can't give it back
> to me. You have robbed me of something that can never be restored.[4]

Here "the self," rather than God or a community or even logical reasoning, was appealed to as the basis for claiming an injustice.

Similarly, Professor Hill justified her reticence to come forward earlier
about Judge Thomas's behavior by citing concern over her career. She
explained, for example, that she did not say anything earlier because she
"did not want to invoke any kind of retaliation against [her] professionally"; she "did not feel that it was necessary to cut off all ties or burn all
bridges."[5] In her words: "I hoped to maintain a professional relationship, for a variety of reasons. One was a sense that I could not afford to
antagonize a person in such a high position."[6] In short, she did not talk
because she "was afraid of damage to [her] professional life."[7]

John Carr, a supporting witness and friend of Anita Hill, concurred
with her "reasoning" as it concerned the importance of protecting her
career opportunities. Empathizing with Hill, Carr stated:

> As a young professional at my career, I am concerned that I will be on
> good terms with the people who have a say or an impact or are in a
> position to judge my career, and I would be extremely, extremely hesitant
> to say anything to offend or cut them off, for fear that in the future they
> might adversely impact my career.[8]

Thus it was acceptable for Anita Hill to maintain her professional
relationship with Clarence Thomas in spite of the alleged improprieties,
because "to categorically cut off that relationship would have been
detrimental to her career going forward."[9]

Both players in this drama appealed to their positions through references to the self, both portraying themselves as victims. Though "vic-
timspeak" was an evident and interesting component of the hearings,
what was even more interesting was the basis on which claims to injustice or to victimhood were made. The emotivist ethic was a pronounced
feature of these hearings and served as the basis whereby one could
make a claim of injustice.

The Ethic of Emotivity

Anyone who followed the hearings could not but notice the persistent expressions of emotion evident throughout the proceedings. Both Thomas and Hill repeatedly referred to how the occurrence and the accusations had hurt them. Consider Thomas's opening statement, in which he claimed to have been "shocked, surprised, hurt and enormously saddened" and to "have suffered immensely." [10] Connecting the assault on his emotions to the notion of justice, Thomas claimed, "I have never, in all my life, felt such hurt, such pain, such agony. My family and I have been done a grave and irreparable injustice." [11] Thus the basis for his claim to injustice appears to be the fact that his feelings were hurt. A simple exegesis of this statement reveals that Thomas was arguing not about the truthfulness of the claims but about the extent to which the claims hurt him. He certainly claimed that the accusations were unfounded, yet in the context of talking about justice, he appealed to his feelings.

Thomas continued to express his personal hurt throughout the hearing. For example, in discussing his first knowledge of the accusations, Thomas claimed, "I was stunned. I was hurt. I was confused. I was pained. . . . All I can tell you [is] it was painful." [12] Again, in responding to questions from Senator Orrin Hatch, Thomas said:

> Senator, as I have said before, this whole affair has been anguish for me. I feel as though I have been abused in this process, as I said last night, and I continue to feel that way. I feel as though something has been lodged against me and painted on me and it will leave an indelible mark on me.[13]

Anita Hill's appeal to emotions in her opening statement was equally thick. Hill claimed that Judge Thomas's overtures made her "very uncomfortable." [14] Additionally, the sexual advances "troubled" her, causing her "to feel severe stress on the job." [15] This seems to have been the foundation for her claim against Thomas. The questioning by the senators in response to her statement also reflected this emphasis. Consider, for example, this exchange with Senator Patrick Leahy:

> *Senator Leahy:* You said that when you talked with Ms. Hoerchner [a friend from Yale Law School], you were very concerned, and upset and that's why you did. Describe to us, how you felt when this happened?

> *Ms. Hill:* Well, I was really upset. I felt like my job could be taken away or at least threatened . . . but it was also just unpleasant and something that I didn't want to have to deal with.[16]

Because of the preeminence of "feelings" as a measure of the importance of this issue, the senator considered it necessary to get both a past and a present perspective on Professor Hill's emotions:

> *Senator Leahy:* Now, when you think back on this, you described how you felt at the time, how do you feel about it today?
>
> *Ms. Hill:* Well, I am a little farther removed from it in time, but even today I still feel hurt and maybe today I feel more angry and disgusted. I don't feel quite as threatened. The situation, I am removed from it. My career is on solid ground and so the threat is not there. But the anger and hurt is there.[17]

Continuing later with the same general line of questioning, Senator Leahy pressed Professor Hill even further on her feelings. In fact, at one point he even explicitly instructed her not to consider the objective legal definition of harassment but to focus on her feelings:

> *Senator Leahy:* Now without saying whether you felt that fulfilled a specific statutory definition of harassment, tell us in your own words, Professor Hill, after one of those conversations, how did you feel?
>
> *Ms. Hill:* I was embarrassed. . . . It was—just the nature of the conversation was very offensive and disgusting, and degrading.
>
> *Senator Leahy:* Without going into a statutory description of what is or is not sexual harassment, how did you feel after—and I quote from your statement, "on several occasions Thomas told me graphically of his own sexual prowess." How did you feel then?
>
> *Ms. Hill:* That was really embarrassing. . . . I felt, I just, it was just, I mean it is hard for me to describe. It just made me feel very bad about the whole situation.[18]

And, just in case the point was not clear enough, Senator Leahy concluded his inquiry by asking the same questions one more time:

> *Senator Leahy:* How did you feel the time that you had those conversations?
>
> *Ms. Hill:* During the time that I had those conversations I was very depressed. I was embarrassed by the type and content of the conversations. . . .

Senator Leahy: Now that was years ago. As you recount them today, how
   do your feel today?
Ms. Hill: Today I feel more angry about the situation. . . . It is still embarrassing . . . but I am angrier about it and I think that it needs to be
   addressed by this committee.[19]

The way in which feelings represented the basis for an authoritative
moral claim was also evidenced in the comments of Angela Wright,
a thirty-seven-year-old reporter for the *Charlotte Observer,* living in
Charlotte, North Carolina. Like Anita Hill, Wright claimed to have
received unwelcome advances from Clarence Thomas while working for
him in a previous job. The alleged acts of Thomas in this account were
similar to those purported by Anita Hill. What differed was Wright's
response to them. According to Wright, Thomas's advances were "an-
noying and obnoxious," but she "never did feel threatened or intimi-
dated" by them.[20] Unlike Anita Hill, who was "really very troubled"
and "distressed" by Clarence Thomas's behavior, Angela Wright was
not really bothered by it; it didn't make her "feel bad." In fact, when
interviewed by the staff of the Judiciary Committee, she admitted that
Thomas's behavior toward her "fit the legal definition of sexual harassment."[21] Yet, from her perspective, harassment is really based on a
feeling: "Harassment to me dictates some—I mean indicates some feeling that there is some threat. No, I never did feel threatened or intimi-
dated."[22] She subsequently did not appear as a witness before the committee, although her interview with Senate staffers was submitted to the
record.

In a fitting conclusion to the Judiciary Committee's final questioning
of Judge Thomas, Senator Biden summed up the committee's position on
the matter of feelings:

But Judge, everybody says, "We know how you feel." No one can know
how you feel. That always excites me, when I hear people tell me how it
feels.
   "Oh, you lost your family, I know how it feels."
   "Oh, you lost this. I know how it feels."
   "You went through that, and they ruined your reputation by it. I know
how it feels."
   No one knows how it feels, but I hope we stop this stuff. The press did
nothing wrong; it is not their fault. It is the nature of what happens here
when something goes public. This is not a right and wrong, and the

presumption is with you. . . . So, Judge I don't know exactly how you feel, but you have clearly demonstrated how you feel, and some of us, not all of us here, have an inkling how you feel.[23]

Senator Biden essentially affirmed that the issue of central concern was not a matter of "right and wrong," i.e., whether it was wrong that the press reported the alleged harassment charges. What was of primary importance was how a person felt. Injustice was based on the extent to which a person's feelings were hurt, not on whether a particular action was morally right or morally wrong.

Biden's comments also make clear that one should broach an interpretation of another's feelings with the utmost caution. Yet it appears from other discussions that not everyone is required to avoid such presumptuousness. Some have been qualified—indeed, credentialed—to interpret other's feelings.

The Therapeutic Experts

Throughout the hearings, reference was made to the new experts of the therapeutic culture: the psychologists and psychiatrists. And the language of the experts was used in the Senate's futile attempt to determine the truth. Such psychological terms as *fantasy, repression, self-blame,* and *depression* were repeatedly invoked by the various actors in the drama. It was commonplace for all involved to turn rhetorically to the "experts," as if they possessed a superior insight into the motivations and actions of the participants in this political spectacle.

Anita Hill, for example, responded in an interesting manner to Senator Alan Simpson's incredulity that she would stay in contact with a man who had sexually harassed her. Not only did she refer to the therapeutic experts as the ones who would know why she did what she did, but she distanced herself from responsibility for her action, as if it were some disease that happened to her: "It takes an expert in psychology to explain how that can happen, but it can happen, because it happened to me."[24] Again, in this context, what happened to her was that she continued to associate in a friendly manner with a man who had allegedly sexually harassed her. Senator Biden joined in her deference to the "experts" on this matter when he stated, "It is every single psychiatrist and psychologist who considers himself an expert in the field who will point out that the nature of [your] response is not at all atypical."[25]

Likewise, Judge Thomas, in responding to questions from Senator Howell Heflin about Anita Hill's possible motivations for making a false claim, on several occasions acknowledged his inability to make such an assessment because he was not "a psychologist or psychiatrist."[26] The various senators also referred to professional psychologists and psychiatrists as the "experts" in our modern therapeutic culture. For example, in an entertaining exchange between Senator Biden and John Doggett (a witness who testified that Professor Hill had unjustly accused him of "leading her on"), an effort was made to discredit the witness by questioning his therapeutic credentials:

> *Senator Biden:* . . . Are you a psychiatrist?
> *Mr. Doggett:* Senator, I am trying to follow your question, but I may have to ask you to restate it.
> *Senator Biden:* My question is are you a psychiatrist?
> *Mr. Doggett:* Absolutely not.
> *Senator Biden:* Well, how from that kind of an exchange can you draw the conclusion that she obviously has a serious problem?[27]

Several moments later, Doggett was describing his observations of Anita Hill at different social events and deemed it necessary to qualify his limited ability to perceive things correctly: "I observed from a distance—and I am not a psychiatrist, I am not an expert, just a man."[28] Interestingly, Professor Hill majored in psychology while at the University of Oklahoma. As a result, her "expertise" was solicited on occasion to interpret her own behavior. For example, Senator Leahy questioned Hill regarding contradictions in her testimony about how many people she had confided the alleged harassment to. In explaining the discrepancy, Professor Hill invoked a psychological term: "I am really finding that I repressed a lot of things that happened during that time, and I am recalling more, in more detail."[29] Picking up on this comment, Senator Biden asked (or rather, stated) the following: "Now, let me ask you this. . . . You indicated, and it is totally understandable, that you repressed a lot. Again, with every expert over the years with whom I have spoken about this subject . . . [they hold] that there is repression, the person represses thinking about it."[30] Professor Hill agreed with Senator Biden's analysis.

In an exchange with Senator Heflin, Professor Hill was even asked to use her knowledge of psychology to explain the meaning of the term *fantasy:* "Well, the issue of fantasy has arisen. . . . Have you studied in your psychology studies . . . the question of fantasies?"[31] Several moments later, Heflin also asked Hill to interpret Judge Thomas's allegedly forward behavior from a psychological perspective: "As a psychology major, what elements of human nature seem to go into that type of a situation?"[32] Professor Hill responded, "Well I can't say exactly. I can say that I felt that he was using his power and authority over me."[33]

The press also deferred to the "experts" in their coverage of the event. Consider, for example, the following headline from a *Washington Post* article published during the hearings: "Who's Telling the Truth? Experts Say Answer May Never Be Known." We learn who these experts are when the article states that "it is quite likely that without the benefit of further . . . psychiatric insights, the Senate Judiciary Committee will never learn who is telling the truth."[34] And in a *Washington Post* editorial, Charles Krauthammer, who has had some psychiatric experience, posited his own diagnosis: "During my three years as resident psychiatrist at a Boston hospital, I treated many psychotic and delusional patients. I may be rusty, but Anita Hill showed me no signs of delusion."[35]

Thus we see clearly that the therapeutic ethos triumphed in the Thomas-Hill hearings. The victimized self served as the foundation for making decisions and taking particular action; emotivism predominated as a legitimate basis for witnesses to cry out against personal injustices; and the experts were appealed to as the only ones who really knew what happened. This was certainly an unusual—indeed, unprecedented—occurrence in the U.S. Congress. The review in Chapter 6 of congressional discussions surrounding child welfare policy suggests that this type of language is not atypical for today but is a marked departure from former languages of legitimation in Congress.

Turning now to another realm of the modern American state, we consider whether such an evolution has also taken place in the area of electoral politics.

7

Political Rhetoric

Chapter 6 and the Excursus on the Thomas-Hill hearings focused on discussions and policy initiatives in the legislative branch of the U.S. government. This chapter concerns itself instead with the rhetorical content of important national-level debates, primarily presidential. The political rhetoric of the Clinton presidency is prototypically therapeutic in style. The extent to which President Bill Clinton's oratory reflects a therapeutic approach in justifications for and positions on policy matters invites us to investigate the possibility that an important transformation has come to pass in this area of American political life; that is, does a historical comparative study of national political discourse reveal a profound alteration in the substance of political debate, with the therapeutic orientation representing the novel rhetorical style for the late twentieth century? Analysis of national-level debates between contenders of the two major political parties serves the purpose of placing contemporary oratorical approaches in a larger historical context. Before turning to an analysis of the debates, let us consider just how pronounced therapeutic rhetoric is in the Clinton presidency.

The Therapeutic President

From a number of vantage points, President Bill Clinton appears to draw heavily on a therapeutic view of the world in his approach to political life. Both as a candidate and as president, Clinton has regularly empathized with the "pain" and "feelings" of American citizens and has habitually employed emotivist language when justifying particular policy proposals or positions. So prominent and distinct is this type of language that Clinton was regularly parodied in his first years of office by *Saturday Night Live*'s Phil ("I feel your pain") Hartman and in the *New Republic*'s emotivist "Flapjack" file. Indeed, Clinton frequently asserts his empathetic caring and ability to relate to the pain of Americans.

Consider, for example, the following interchange in New York between Clinton and Bob Rafsky, a member of the AIDS activist group ACT UP, during the 1992 presidential campaign:

> *Rafsky:* This is the center of the AIDS epidemic, what are you going to do? Are you going to start a war on AIDS? Are you going to just go on and ignore it? . . . We're dying in this state. What are you going to do about AIDS?
> *Clinton:* Can we talk now?
> *Rafsky:* Go ahead and talk.
> *Clinton:* Most places where I go, nobody wants us to talk. They want us to listen to them. I'm listening. You can talk. I know how it hurts. I've got friends who've died of AIDS.

Later in the exchange, Clinton identified further with the emotional anguish of those suffering from AIDS and those fighting for its cure:

> I feel your pain, I feel your pain. . . . I understand that you're hurting, but you won't stop hurting by trying to hurt other people. That is what I try to tell all you folks. You're not going to stop hurting by trying to hurt other people.[1]

The president seemed to implore all Americans to assume such a caring stance when, in his first inaugural address in January 1993, he beckoned the country to "feel the pain" and "see the promise of America."

Further evidence of the president's kinship with the therapeutic approach came immediately after he assumed office, when Clinton summoned his cabinet to Camp David for the weekend. Using professional "facilitators," the group "shared" intimate aspects of their lives in an effort to build "trust" and "caring relationships," an activity referred to as "human resource development."[2] During the session, President Clinton disclosed the trauma he experienced as a child when he was taunted by other children for being overweight. "Don't try to make this sound weird," one participant told a *Washington Post* reporter after the encounter. "It was actually great. It was just people talking about themselves."[3]

The Politics of Feeling

Another way in which a therapeutic perspective seems to inform Clinton's approach to the presidency is the extent to which decisions about certain policy positions or nominations are justified by his feelings. He continually employs the phrase "I feel good about . . ." to defend his stance on certain issues.[4] Discussing his first months in office, for example, Clinton stated, "I think we're getting good results. We've been here three months, we've passed a number of bills, and I feel good about it."[5] Likewise, in commenting on his first one hundred days in office, he claimed to "feel basically quite good about what's happened."[6] Regarding Russia's position toward developments in Bosnia, Clinton held, "So, I feel pretty good about that."[7] Responding to questions about his decision to not push for a middle-class tax cut, he concluded that "I think we're going to do quite well, and I feel good about it."[8] In July 1994, after having to back down on one of his main proposals during a Group of Seven (G-7) meeting and with a negative market reaction to his statements, Clinton held, "So I still felt very good about this G-7 summit."[9]

Clinton uses the same diction in determining and justifying his support for certain nominations or political candidates. For example, in April 1993, when it was announced that Supreme Court Justice Byron White would retire, Clinton indicated that what he was looking for in a new justice was "someone with a big heart."[10] Such a qualification arguably departs from a legal-rational perspective, which would be more likely to highlight a nominee's legal knowledge, skills, and expertise. When Clinton did decide on a nominee for his first Supreme Court appointment, it was reportedly based in large measure on personal chemistry. He stated that he "felt very strongly" about Ruth Bader Ginsburg and believed that her "incredible inner strength and character" would "help to create a good atmosphere at the Court."[11] Subsequently, Ginsburg got the nomination and ultimately the job, as the nation's second female Supreme Court justice.

When the opportunity for a second Supreme Court appointment arose, Clinton claimed that he was "going to attempt to do what I did last time, even against all the pressure of time deadlines, and that's to make a really good decision that I feel good about."[12] Clinton was involved on a highly personal level in selecting his appointees, and the barometer for determining potential nominees seemed to be the degree in which Clinton himself had an emotionally positive response to the person. Editorialist Richard Cohen noted this feature of the Clinton presidency: "The president's need to 'feel good' about this or that makes his presidency extremely self-referential and sometimes injects a disproportionate personal element into policy-making considerations."[13]

Clinton has unashamedly defended himself against the criticism that his appointments are too personal and self-referential. Consider the following explanation for his approach to selecting cabinet members:

> I did micromanage the cabinet appointments. I spent more time on the Cabinet appointments than anybody in history had, and I plead guilty to that. I personally interviewed them all. But they're in my Cabinet, and I spent a lot of time talking about what we wanted the mission of the department to be. I plead guilty to that, because I want people who'd be more or less in synch with me.[14]

Failed nominees and candidates have also been beneficiaries of President Clinton's empathy and personal concern. After Lani Guinier's nomination as head of the Justice Department's Civil Rights Division was withdrawn, for example, Clinton said his regard for her "love" was unchanged.[15] Likewise, in an endorsement of Los Angeles's Democrat mayoral candidate Mike Woo, the president stated the following:

> I feel a personal affinity for him because he supported me early in the race for President before the New Hampshire primary.... It is 100 percent positive feeling. I have nothing against his opponent. I just care a lot about this community. I care a lot about this State. I want to do everything I can to make it work. I think this will help. And I think the decision was an appropriate one and one I feel very comfortable with.[16]

When asked about Woo's Republican opponent and the eventual victor in the mayoral race, Richard Riordan, Clinton made it clear that his support for Woo was not because of bad feelings for Riordan: "There's nothing negative here in my feelings about Dick Riordan."[17]

The Politics of Meaning

Recall, too, first lady Hillary Rodham Clinton's discussion of alienation and the problem of meaning noted in Chapter 2. In the same 1993 speech in Austin, Texas, the answer she proposed for addressing these problems was what she called the "politics of meaning," which involves, among other things, redefining "who we are as human beings in this postmodern age." But what exactly is meant by the "politics of meaning"? What is the proposed answer to meaninglessness that is asserted here?

Though the specifics of the proposal are not particularly lucid, one thing is apparent: it derives from a therapeutic ideological system. Hillary Clinton's ideas were adopted from the writings of Michael Lerner, editor and publisher of *Tikkun* magazine, a progressive New York–based bimonthly periodical. Lerner received his doctorate in psychology at Berkeley and helped found the Institute for Labor and Mental Health in 1977, where he worked as a psychotherapist examining "the psychodynamics of the working class."[18] Acknowledging her intellectual indebtedness to his writings, Hillary Clinton reportedly asked Lerner, who has been described as the "guru" of the White House, "Am I your mouthpiece or what?"[19] Lerner says that he first had contact with the Clintons in 1988, when the then governor of Arkansas wrote to Lerner telling him that his "politics of meaning" had helped to clarify his thinking.

Like Hillary Clinton, Lerner speaks of the problem of meaninglessness, of poignant alienation, and of the negative effects of impersonal bureaucratization. His policy recommendations for addressing these problems include having the Department of Labor initiate an annual national "Occupational Stress Day," dedicated to educating the public and the government about the stress that people face at work. He also believes the Labor Department should insist that businesses offer Occupational Stress Groups (OSGs), in which workers can learn how to recognize stress more fully at the workplace. Furthermore, he recommends the Labor Department mandate that every employer allow workers to elect an Occupational Safety and Health Committee (OSHC) empowered to increase workers' mental health and opportunities to actualize their skills and talents.[20] To establish and facilitate the functioning of these policies, Lerner proposes that the government "create a program to train a corps of union personnel, worker representatives, and psychotherapists in the relevant skills to assist developing a new spirit of cooperation, mutual caring, and dedication to work."[21] Hence evident within Lerner's proposition are recommendations for the institutionalization of therapeutic forms and ideas.

President Clinton has also joined in the discussion of the politics of meaning. Consider, for example, this exchange with reporters in May 1993:

> *Reporter:* Mr. President, in your New York speech this past week at Cooper Union, you spoke of a crisis of belief and hope, and earlier Mrs. Clinton in a speech talked about a crisis of meaning. How do you see these crises manifesting themselves, what are the causes of them, and how severe do you see this?

> *Clinton:* Well, I think they manifested themselves in people's honest feel-
> ings that things are not going very well in this country and that they
> haven't gone very well in a long time, in the alienation people feel
> from the political process, and in the alienation they often feel from
> one another in the same neighborhoods and communities.[22]

The therapeutic answer, then, stems from a therapeutic problem. People
feel alienated, and the solution to this problematic condition is therapeutic remedies in the form of political policy solutions or, at least, rhetorical affirmations.

The Social Construction of the Therapeutic Presidency

A number of journalists have noted President Clinton's therapeutic
proclivities. Joe Klein, writing in the *New Republic,* for example, observed that during the 1992 campaign, Clinton, unlike many other
politicians past and present, was willing to listen to people:

> His empathy struck a chord. His appeal wasn't charisma, it was therapy.
> He promised a twelve-step presidency. This is the aspect of Clintonism
> easiest to mock . . . but it does raise some rather troubling questions. At a
> time when the traditional American desire for "self-improvement" has
> been supplanted by a futile quest for "self-esteem," what constitutes lead-
> ership? Is it overweening empathy, the president as national group "facili-
> tator"? Or is something more rigorous required?[23]

Though it seems that Clinton's therapeutic style is unique to his own
personality, culturally astute and historically informed reporters have
observed that the Clintons' penchant for therapeutic rhetoric is the
consequence of a larger cultural phenomenon. Peter Berger observed
that if Freud had not existed he would have been invented, and one
could say the same about Bill Clinton. He is a president who, in many
ways, is right for his times. His use of therapeutic language says as much,
if not more, about the culture as it does about Clinton's personality. The
therapeutic nature of his presidency is a reflection of the pervasiveness
of the therapeutic ethos within the larger culture.

This is basically what Tom McNichol was saying when, in the *Washington Post,* he observed that "Bill Clinton is the first chief executive
whose values were shaped by the therapeutic movement that has come
to dominate the way Americans think about themselves, not to mention

the day-time talk shows."[24] In other words, Clinton is a product of the dominance of a therapeutic impulse in the larger culture. His use of therapeutic language is itself evidence of the process whereby a cultural orientation is externalizing itself into the political processes of the United States government. The citizenry responded to a candidate who espoused the sentiments that they held (and hold) most dear. As McNichol observed further, Clinton's activities suggest that "the self-help concepts cluttering the nation's bookshelves for more than a decade . . . are now promising to clutter our national politics."[25]

If such externalization is indeed taking place, then we should observe a couple things about the political process. First, there should be some evidence that other candidates are compelled, in some measure, to appeal to this value system of the American citizenry. Second, we should observe a historical transformation in the types of legitimating appeals that presidential candidates have used in their attempts to connect with the values of the American people.

Political Oratory

Recall the proposition developed in the first two chapters of this study, that the state's adoption of a therapeutic source of legitimation is realized through the dialectical relationship between prevailing cultural values or cultural consciousness and the institutions of the modern American state. The dialogue between the two actors in this drama (culture and the state) is perhaps most directly observable in the realm of electoral politics. Political campaigns provide the citizenry with an opportunity to select a candidate who best reflects its values and view of the world. In this respect, candidates represent symbols of collective national life. A candidate's success is based in no small measure on his or her ability to appeal to the sentiments that prevail in a particular culture at a particular time in history.[26]

From the perspective of classical rhetoric, debates are the prototype for assessing the extent to which a candidate is able to demonstrate his or her leadership qualities; appeal to the interests, concerns, and values of the audience; and present logically persuasive arguments in defense of certain policy positions. As rhetorical theorist Edward Hinck explains, an important "function of the debates, then, is to give the audience an opportunity to evaluate the candidates for their ability to represent national values." [27] For this reason, a number of rhetoric and communications theorists have studied America's presidential debates. The debates have been analyzed from a variety of different perspectives, including for their educational value and influence on the outcomes of elections; the importance of the rules and formats of the debates, that is, the time limits, panels of questioners, and so forth; the significance of television's role and the portrayal of image; and the rhetorical styles employed by the various candidates. [28]

Though some communications scholars assessing these widely viewed events consider the importance of the candidates' abilities to appeal to the values of the citizenry, analysis of changing American values as reflected in the debates is largely missing. Rarely noted is the substantive difference between, for example, the moral appeals made by Abraham Lincoln and those made by Ronald Reagan or the extent to which these differences mirror the changing consciousness in American culture.

Aristotelian Rhetoric

A heuristic framework derived from classical rhetoric provides a useful starting point for analyzing America's presidential debates. It was Aristotle who identified the three important modes of persuasion that occur in rhetorical discussion: *ethos,* the credibility or character of the speaker; *logos,* the logical plausibility of the speaker's argument; and *pathos,* the speaker's appeal to the emotional sentiments of the audience. [29] Aristotle also identified three particular forms of oratory: deliberative oratory (political), judicial or forensic oratory (legal), and epideictic or demonstrative oratory (ceremonial or eulogistic). One can infer from Aristotle's typologies that though each type of oratory employs all three modes of persuasion to some degree, the ethical proof is most prominent in the political, the logical is most prominent in the legal, and the emotional is most prominent in the ceremonial. [30]

In Aristotle's *Rhetoric,* each of these forms of oratory also corresponds with different references in time. For example, political oratory corresponds with the future—that is, a politician puts forth his or her vision about the way things should be. Legal oratory corresponds with the past—that is, the courtroom lawyer discusses what someone did or did not do in the past. Ceremonial rhetoric corresponds with the present—that is, a person is praised or blamed in his or her present state of existence.[31] The rhetorical types hence can be summarized as follows:

Kind of Speech	Mode of Persuasion	Time
Political	Ethos	Future
Legal	Logos	Past
Ceremonial	Pathos	Present

A movement toward a more therapeutic orientation in political discourse, however, might make these categories problematic. Indeed, the emotional appeal (pathos) is clearly most akin to the therapeutic mentality, though even in Aristotle's analysis, emotions were informed by certain notions of virtue. Explanations of pathos in Aristotle's writings are often reflective more of moral affections than of emotions and are, at times, specifically referred to in this way.[32] In any respect, traditional legal and political discourse, in Aristotle's typological framework, necessarily involved the portrayal of ethical character and the appeal to logical reasoning. Actions of the past and visions for the future were directly relevant to the salience and palatability of a speech's persuasive power.

In the contemporary context, then, a shift toward a heavier reliance on emotional appeals not only represents a shift away from greater concern with the past and with the future but indicates a fundamental transformation in the nature of political rhetoric. Political rhetoric with a more accented preference for the emotional would, according to classical representations of public speech types, more closely resemble ceremonial than political speaking.

A historical consideration of America's debates, however, reveals that the typologies of classical rhetoric more accurately depicted the nature of political oratory in the United States in the past than they do today. Moreover, evidence of changing sources of legitimation reveals that the prevailing cultural sentiments of American society have changed—a transformation that would explain the possible inapplicability of a classical rhetorical framework to contemporary political oratory. Using four political debates—between Lincoln and Douglas (1858), Kennedy and Nixon (1960), Reagan and Mondale (1984), and Clinton, Bush, and Perot (1992)—I seek to assess the extent to which the sources of legitimation to which candidates appeal have changed over time.

The Lincoln-Douglas Debates

Though the Kennedy-Nixon debates in 1960 were actually the first presidential debates where candidates from the two major parties faced each other in person for the sake of political deliberation, the Lincoln-Douglas debates rest in American folklore as the first time that two likely contenders for the presidency stood on a platform and faced each other in a debate format. For most of America's political history, face-to-face debates between presidential contenders (and for that matter, between contenders for other national offices) were regarded as a violation of protocol and an affront to political propriety. More common were the campaigning efforts of surrogates, who typically stumped on behalf of their party's nominees.

The famous 1858 Lincoln-Douglas debates, though a contest for a Illinois Senate seat, were, by nineteenth-century standards, very unusual. As a *New York Evening Post* correspondent reported in 1858, "The present political canvass in Illinois is a singular one, and I think, without a parallel in the history of electioneering campaigns in this country."[33] Though Stephen Douglas ultimately won the Illinois Senate seat, the contests addressed the important and divisive national issue of slavery and provided Abraham Lincoln with the national exposure he needed to win the presidency two years later, when he again faced Douglas in a campaign for national office.

The 1858 debates, however, hurt Douglas's chances for the presidency because of the arguments he advanced in support of the doctrine of popular sovereignty—a position favorable neither to Northern abolitionists nor to proslavery Southerners. In fact, Douglas's alienation from Southern Democrats resulted in the nomination of two Democrat candidates for the 1860 presidential race; Northern Democrats supported Douglas while Southern Democrats supported John Breckinridge, a split that helped Lincoln to secure the presidency. The 1858 Senate debates, then, were directly relevant to the outcome of the 1860 presidential elections. Prior to 1960, the Lincoln-Douglas debates came the closest to being a presidential debate between two major party candidates, and they are often considered in the literature as the historical antecedents to the modern presidential debates.[34] Because of this, and the fact that the debates provide a useful historical comparison, I include them in the present analysis.

Though there are similarities between the 1858 debates and the modern-day presidential debates, in terms of the presence of two candidates from the major parties facing each other on the platform, the discussion of national issues, and the focus of widespread national attention on the contests, there are also some major differences. The most obvious, of course, is technology. Every presidential debate since, and including, the Kennedy-Nixon debates has been televised. While the Lincoln-Douglas debates had huge audiences (with as many as fifteen thousand in attendance at some of the debates) and were printed for an even wider circulation in the major newspapers of the day, there is still no comparison to the audiences reached through live national television coverage.

Moreover, there were significant differences in terms of format. The Lincoln-Douglas debates lasted three hours. In each of the seven debates, the first candidate was allowed an hour to open the debate. The second would speak for an hour and a half. Then the first candidate would be given an additional half hour to respond. The structure of the time was such that it allowed for the advancement of complex, syllogistic arguments. Also, because there were no moderators in these debates Lincoln and Douglas could respond directly and often somewhat caustically to each other's accusations and arguments.

The Centrality of Logos

The long and often complex arguments advanced by both Abraham Lincoln and Stephen Douglas during the debates clearly reveal an emphasis on the place of reason. They spoke to audiences that were apparently able and willing to listen to long arguments that built on previous points and that presupposed a familiarity with other speeches and government documents. On several occasions, Stephen Douglas reminded audience participants to restrain their enthusiasm and applause and to listen to the logic of his arguments. For example, in Ottawa, the first of the seven debates, Douglas opened, "I desire to address myself to your judgment, your understanding, and your consciences, and not to your passions or your enthusiasm." [35] In Quincy, the sixth debate, Douglas pleaded with the crowd in a similar way: "I desire to be heard rather than to be applauded. I wish to address myself to your reason, your judgment, your sense of justice, and not to your passion."

Douglas wanted to be judged not on passion or sentiment but on the reasonableness of his principles. As he stated, "I wish to be judged by my principles, by those great public measures and constitutional princi-

ples upon which the peace, the happiness and the perpetuity of this
republic now rest." Douglas's position in this regard calls to mind
the antisentimentalist assertions of the early defenders of child welfare
legislation, considered in Chapter 6. Recall that supporters of child
welfare legislation in the first part of the twentieth century were careful
to point out that their support was not based solely on sentiment.
Instead, the stronger appeal then as in the Lincoln-Douglas debates, was
to logic. Consider the following statement, offered by Lincoln in the
Galesburg debate:

> Judge Douglas declares that if any community want slavery they have a
> right to have it. He can say that logically, if he says that there is no wrong
> in slavery; but if you admit that there is a wrong in it, he cannot logically
> say that anybody has a right to do wrong. He insists that, upon the score
> of equality, the owners of slaves and owners of property—of horses and
> every other sort of property—should be alike and hold them alike in a
> new territory. That is perfectly logical, if the two species of property are
> alike and are equally founded in right. But if you admit that one of them
> is wrong, you cannot institute any equality between right and wrong. And
> from this difference of sentiment—the belief on the part of one that the
> institution is wrong, and a policy springing from the belief which looks to
> the arrest of the enlargement of that wrong; and this other sentiment, that
> it is no wrong, and a policy sprung from that sentiment which will tolerate
> no idea of preventing that wrong from growing larger, and looks to there
> never being an end of it through all the existence of things,—arises the
> real difference between Judge Douglas and his friends, on the one hand,
> and the Republicans on the other. Now, I confess myself as belonging to
> that class in the country who contemplate slavery as a moral, social and
> political evil, having due regard for its actual existence amongst us and the
> difficulties of getting rid of it in any satisfactory way, and to all the
> constitutional obligations which have been thrown about it; but, neverthe-
> less, desire a policy that looks to the prevention of it as a wrong, and
> looks hopefully to the time when as a wrong it may come to an end.

The contemporary appetite for sound-bite-long appeals would have
no patience for such a musing argument (and this excerpt represents
approximately two or three minutes of a ninety-minute-long statement).
Evident in this remark is not only Lincoln's penchant for discourse based
on logic but a heavy concern with right and wrong. Lincoln, particularly
in the final debate, spoke at length about "right" and "wrong." To him,
this differentiation was a central matter for determining appropriate

state action. Important to this analysis, however, is understanding what provided the basis for determining what was right and what was wrong. It becomes clear in the Lincoln-Douglas debates that traditional sources of legitimation informed understandings of right and wrong.

"A House Divided"

Both Lincoln and Douglas supported their positions on the basis of traditional religious ideals and symbols. This was certainly the case, though not exclusively so, with the slavery issue—the major topic of concern in the debates. Consider, for example, Lincoln's famous biblical metaphor "A house divided against itself cannot stand." There was much discussion in the debates about this metaphor. Lincoln reviewed the basic argument, which he originally offered in a Springfield speech prior to the debates, in the Alton debate.

> A house divided against itself cannot stand. I believe this government cannot endure permanently half slave and half free. I do not expect the house to fall—but I do expect it will cease to be divided. It will become all one thing, or all the other. Either the opponents of slavery will arrest the further spread of it, and place it where the public mind shall rest in the belief that it is in the course of ultimate extinction, or its advocates will push it forward till it shall become alike lawful in all the states—old as well as new, North as well as South.

Douglas criticized Lincoln's use of the metaphor, to which Lincoln offered the following retort during the Ottawa debate:

> He has read from my speech in Springfield, in which I say that "a house divided against itself cannot stand." Does the Judge say it can stand? [Laughter.] I don't know whether he does or not. The Judge does not seem to be attending to me just now, but I would like to know if it is his opinion that a house divided against itself can stand. If he does, then there is a question of veracity, not between him and me, but between the Judge and an authority of a somewhat higher character. [Laughter and applause.]
>
> Now, my friends, I ask your attention to this matter for the purpose of saying something seriously. I know that the Judge may readily enough agree with me that the maxim which was put forth by the Savior is true, but he may allege that I misapply it.

Lincoln justified use of the metaphor by appealing to the philosophical system from which it was derived, namely, the traditional Christian religious ethic. Douglas responded to Lincoln's challenge regarding the legitimacy of the appeal, but he did so on the basis that Lincoln himself suggested, that is, on the applicability of the passage, not on the veracity of the quote or its source.

In the Galesburg debate, Douglas cleverly applied the metaphor to Lincoln's own party, in which there was also division over the slavery issue:

> If it be true, as I have shown it is, that the whole Republican party in the northern part of the state stands committed to the doctrine of no more slave states, and that this same doctrine is repudiated by the Republicans in the other part of the state, I wonder whether Mr. Lincoln and his party do not present the case which he cited from the Scriptures, of a house divided against itself which cannot stand.[36]

Douglas also tried to show how Lincoln's use of the metaphor was a misapplication when he argued that the framers of the Constitution established a government that contained both free and slave states from its outset:

> Is this sectional warfare to be waged between Northern states and Southern states until they all shall become uniform in their local and domestic institutions merely because Mr. Lincoln says that a house divided against itself cannot stand, and pretends that this scriptural quotation, this language of our Lord and Master, is applicable to the American Union and the American Constitution? Washington and his compeers in the convention that framed the Constitution, made this government divided into free and slave states. It was composed then of thirteen sovereign and independent states, each having sovereign authority over its local and domestic institutions, and all bound together by the federal Constitution. Mr. Lincoln likens that bond of the federal Constitution joining free and slave states together to a house divided against itself. And says that it is contrary to the law of God and cannot stand? When did he learn, and by what authority does he proclaim that this government is contrary to the law of God and cannot stand. It has stood thus divided into free and slave states from its organization up to this day.

In both instances, Douglas took issue with Lincoln not for using the metaphor or for taking it from a religious source but for misapplying it. The problem was one of application. According to Douglas, if Lincoln was to be consistent, he needed to offer a reason for the differences within his own party and the existence of both free and slave states since the nation's origin.

Proslavery Legitimations

That Douglas's contention with the "house divided" metaphor was not a difficulty with its source is underscored by the fact that Douglas himself drew heavily on religious imagery to support his own positions. He claimed, for example, that principle compelled him and his party to "always do right, and trust the consequences to God and the people." [37] Likewise, he claimed that his resistance to the urgings of President James Buchanan to change his position on the Kansas-Missouri Compromise while in the Senate was based on the belief that he "was accountable to Illinois, as [his] constituency, and to God, but not to the President or to any other power on earth." Consider the following resolve, offered by Douglas during the Freeport debate.

> I have stood by my principles in fair weather and in foul, in the sunshine and in the rain. I have defended the great principles of self-government here among you when Northern sentiment ran in a torrent against me. And I have defended that same great principle when Southern sentiment came down like an avalanche upon me. I was not afraid of any test they put to me. I knew I was right—I knew my principles were sound—I knew that the people would see in the end that I had done right, and I knew that the God of Heaven would smile upon me if I was faithful in the performance of my duty.

Similarly, in the Jonesboro debate, Douglas sought further to provide religious legitimacy to his position regarding slavery when he claimed, "I do not believe that the Almighty made the negro capable of self-government." In the same speech, he argued that the founders were surely directed by divine guidance when they chose not to put "their negroes on equality with themselves." Instead of establishing such equality, claimed Douglas, the founders "with uplifted eyes to Heaven . . . implored the Divine blessing upon them . . . never dreaming that they were violating divine law by still holding the negroes in bondage and depriving them equality."

Douglas also questioned just how Christian Lincoln's antislavery sentiments were, arguing that the Republican candidate's policies would starve the slaves to the point of extinction. During the Quincy debate, for example, Douglas argued that Lincoln's support for the prohibition of slavery in the new U.S. territories would "smother slavery out" and that, subsequently, slavery would be eliminated "only by extinguishing the Negro race, for his policy would drive them to starvation." Douglas then added sardonically, "This is the humane and Christian remedy that he proposes for the great crime of slavery." In the final debate in Alton, Douglas took issue with Lincoln in a similar fashion when he argued that Lincoln's policies would "extinguish slavery by . . . starving [slaves] out of existence as you smoke a fox out of his hole." What was so appalling to Douglas about this position was the fact that Lincoln erroneously justified his actions according to religious precepts: "And he intends to do that in the name of humanity and Christianity. . . . Mr. Lincoln makes out that line of policy, and appeals to the moral sense of justice, and the Christian feeling of the community to sustain him."

Douglas's comments highlight the fact that there was some general "Christian feeling" within the culture to which the candidates could appeal. His point of contention was not that appealing to such a sentiment was wrong or that the sentiment itself was wrong but that Lincoln was somehow acting disingenuously or, at least, ignorantly by aligning his positions with that sentiment. Lincoln did align himself with this religious ethos, in the same way that Douglas did, indicating the extent to which a religious ethos prevailed within the culture and provided a basis for the legitimation of state policies.

Abolitionist Legitimations

Lincoln often argued in favor of the eventual abolition of slavery by citing the Declaration of Independence, which guaranteed the equality of and freedom for all men. As Douglas himself observed:

> Mr. Lincoln, following the example and lead of all the little Abolition orators, who go around and lecture in the basements of schools and churches, reads from the Declaration of Independence, that all men were created equal, and then asks how can you deprive a negro of that equality which God and the Declaration of Independence awards to him. He and they maintain that negro equality is guaranteed by the laws of God, and that it is asserted in the Declaration of Independence.

Douglas took issue with this argument, calling it a "monstrous heresy." He reminded the audience that Thomas Jefferson, the author of the document, was the owner of many slaves and remained so until his death: "Did he intend to say in the Declaration that his negro slaves, which he held and treated as property, were created his equals by Divine law, and that he was violating the law of God every day of his life by holding them as slaves?"

Lincoln responded to this question by once again appealing to a religious ethos, and his retort suggests that Jefferson himself was haunted by the prevailing power of the same:

> And I will remind Judge Douglas and this audience, that while Mr. Jefferson was the owner of slaves, as undoubtedly he was, in speaking upon this very subject, he used the strong language that "he trembled for his country when he remembered that God was just"; and I will offer the highest premium in my power to Judge Douglas if he will show that he, in all his life, ever uttered a sentiment at all akin to that of Jefferson.

Lincoln also appealed to religious ideals when he likened Douglas's opposition to antislavery arguments to Satan warring against the Bible. Moreover, he mocked Douglas's commitment to the legal authority of the Dred Scott decision by arguing that Douglas's deference approximated that of submission to a religious declaration: "He [Douglas] did not commit himself on account of the merit or demerit of the decision, but it is a 'Thus saith the Lord.' The next decision, as much as this, will be a 'Thus saith the Lord.' "

Vision for America

The slavery issue was not the only topic for which appeals to traditional sources of legitimation were made. Douglas, for example, invoked moral language in reference to Illinois's state debt. Statements about America's identity and destiny likewise prompted the evocation of traditional religious symbols. Indeed, when offering definitions of America and declarations about its future, both candidates drew heavily on religious images to give legitimacy to their respective visions. Stephen Douglas, for example, declared that during the whole period of America's existence, "Divine Providence has smiled upon us, and showered upon our nation richer and more abundant blessings than have ever been conferred upon any other."

In the first debate at Ottawa, Douglas similarly spoke of America's divine and manifest destiny when he stated, "We have crossed the Allegheny mountains and filled up the whole North West, turning the prairie into a garden, and building up churches and schools, thus spreading civilization and Christianity where before there was nothing but savage-barbarism." Because of America's divine mission, Douglas believed that the country would increase in territory, power, and strength and would be a guide for freedom throughout the civilized world.

Lincoln also spoke of America's future with reference to providence, when he predicted that slavery would ultimately become extinct: "I do not suppose that in the most peaceful way ultimate extinction would occur in less than a hundred years at the least; but that it will occur in the best way for both races in God's own good time, I have no doubt." Such specific discussions about the future reveal that the Lincoln-Douglas debates corresponded to the reference in time that Aristotle deemed most characteristic of political oratory. Not only was the future discussed, but the vision of the future was constructed on a religiously informed view of the world.

Such justifications for America's identity and for state policies during this period were not unique to the Lincoln-Douglas debates. In the Pryne-Bromlow debates of the same year, the contestants A. Pryne and W. G. Bromlow reportedly argued about the legitimacy of slavery through a chapter-and-verse exegesis of relevant scriptural passages.[38] Not surprisingly, such reference to traditional religious sources of legitimation would become less explicit over time, as we see in turning to more recent presidential debates.

The Kennedy-Nixon Debates

The 1960 Kennedy-Nixon debates are famous for being the first event of its kind that was televised to a national audience. There were four one-hour debates in all, one on each of the following dates: September 26, October 7, October 13, and October 21. The audience for the debates was enormous, with more than seventy million viewers for the first debate and more than fifty million viewers for each of the next three.

Much has been written about how the debates benefited the young Democrat senator from Massachusetts, who, through a skillful use of the medium of television, assuaged concerns about his inexperience and inspired supporters with his wit, vigor, and infectious energy. The debates covered a wider range of issues than was covered in the Lincoln-Douglas debates, though U.S. policy regarding communism—in particular, the handling of conflict with Communist China over control of the

Chinese coastal islands of Matsu and Quemoy—dominated much of the discussion. What is of interest for this analysis, however, is how the rhetorical styles of the two candidates appealed to certain types of legitimating philosophies.

The Residual Influence of Traditional Forms of Legitimation

Although the candidates in the 1960 debates made references to such American ideals as democracy, freedom, equality of opportunity, and independence, etc., these symbols were not conspicuously associated with religious ideals. Yet there was still a sense in which religion was relevant to democratic principles, if only a residual one. It also seems as if the candidates believed it necessary to represent and associate themselves with these cultural sentiments. Consider, for example, this statement offered by Richard Nixon in the last of the four debates:

> What will determine whether Senator Kennedy or I, if I am elected, was a great president? It will not be our ambition that will determine it, because greatness is not something that is written on a campaign poster. It will be determined to the extent that we represent the deepest ideals, the highest feelings and faith of the American people.[39]

There is certainly a recognition here that the success of the candidates depended on the extent to which they were able to tap into and represent the faith values of the American citizenry. However, there is a qualitative difference between "the deepest ideals, highest feelings and faith of the American people" and the more explicitly religious notion of the "Christian feelings of the community" proposed in the Lincoln-Douglas debates. The descriptions of American cultural sentiment do not necessarily contradict each other, but one is more clearly identified than the other with a particular religious perspective.

Thus discussion of issues in the Kennedy-Nixon debates was not as closely linked to traditional systems of moral understanding as it was in the Lincoln-Douglas debates. Consider, for example, discussions of communism, the most prominent topic in the debates. Both candidates opposed the spread of communism on moral grounds. John F. Kennedy, for example, argued against communism in the context of a discussion of moral leadership:

> There is a very strong moral basis for this concept of equality of opportunity. . . . We sit on a conspicuous stage. We are a goldfish bowl before the

world. We have to practice what we preach. We set a very high standard for ourselves. The communists do not. They set a low standard of materialism. We preach in the Declaration of Independence and in the Constitution, in the statement of our greatest leaders, we preach very high standards; and if we're not going to be charged before the world with hypocrisy we have to meet those standards. I believe the president of the United States should indicate it.... Unless the president speaks, then of course the country doesn't speak, and Franklin Roosevelt said: "The presidency of the United States is above all a place of moral leadership."

Similarly, Nixon invoked religion as an ideological basis for opposition to communism. "Also as far as religion is concerned, I have seen Communism abroad. I see what it does. Communism is the enemy of all religions; and we who do believe in God must join together." In another debate he offered a similar argument: "This is primarily an ideological battle—a battle for the minds and hearts and the souls of men. We must not meet the Communists purely in the field of gross atheistic materialism. We must stand for our ideals."

However, that an important shift had occurred in terms of the substance of the value systems to which the candidates appealed was revealed—perhaps only subtly so—in another discussion of communism by Nixon:

And you cannot fight a victory for Communism or a strategy of victory for Communism with the strategy simply of holding the line. And so I say that we believe that our policies of military strength, of economic strength, of diplomatic firmness first will keep the peace and keep it without surrender. We also believe that in the great field of ideals that we can lead America to the victory for freedom—victory in the newly developing countries, victory also in the captive countries—provided we have faith in ourselves and faith in our principles.

What is striking about the "faith" that Nixon discussed is its object. The object of faith, according to this statement, had shifted from an external basis of authority to "ourselves" and "our principles," a possible foreshadowing of the kind of self-referential political dialogue typical today. The introduction of "ourselves" as an object of allegiance suggests that the substance of "our principles" may have undergone an important transformation.

The most explicit linkage between religion and certain policy positions occurred in references to communism. Consider Nixon's closing remarks in the fourth debate: "And so I say in conclusion, keep America's faith strong. See that the young people of America, particularly, have faith in the ideals of freedom and faith in God, which distinguishes us from the atheistic materialists who oppose us." On issues other than communism, however, candidates were less explicit about associating their positions with a religious worldview, though other genres of argument used in these debates were similar to those used in the Lincoln-Douglas debates.

A Rendezvous with Destiny

As in the Lincoln-Douglas debates, both candidates in the 1960 presidential debates spoke of America's destiny. But whereas in the former debates this destiny was associated closely with the spread of "civilization and Christianity," in the latter it was less discernibly related to a religious mission. Kennedy spoke of America's destiny in relationship to the concept of freedom in his closing remarks in the last debate:

> I believe in 1960 and sixty-one and two and three we have a rendezvous with destiny. And I believe it incumbent upon us to be the defenders of the United States and the defenders of Freedom, and to do that, we must give this country leadership and we must get America moving again.

Freedom here stands on its own, as a symbol not directly related to a particular moral code. Kennedy made reference to some external source that gave meaning to the idea of freedom. His statements at best assume a certain common understanding of the principle and at worst represent a rhetorical invocation of hollowed-out symbols.

Nixon spoke of America's destiny in a similar way: "We must have a great goal. And that is: not just to keep freedom for ourselves but to extend it to all the world, to extend it to all the world because that is America's destiny." But what is meant by freedom? A number of recent works suggest that a public understanding of American freedom has changed over time, and that the codes of moral understanding available to Americans are in no small measure related to this shift.[40] Yet the vestiges of a common understanding of freedom and the sources that gave it meaning perhaps remained strong enough within the culture that people understood what it meant in this context.

However, it may be that freedom, standing alone without a philosophical legitimation, was in the tenuous position of becoming an empty symbol. Recall in the discussion of state legitimation in Chapter 2 that the state necessarily draws on some form of legitimation to justify itself to society. The association of America's destiny with the ideal of freedom, but without explaining the meaning of freedom, may represent a situation where older codes of moral understanding were fading but the resonance of related symbols still carried a residual level of cultural capital. This may have been what was happening when Nixon and Kennedy discussed America's destiny in relation to freedom.

Right and Wrong

Such a situation, in which traditional codes were deteriorating but still had some resonance with the American people, may likewise provide an explanation for the ways in which the 1960 presidential candidates discussed notions of right and wrong. As with the issue of America's destiny, there are qualitative differences between how Lincoln and Douglas discussed right and wrong and how Nixon and Kennedy did so. To begin with, there is certainly less evidence of Aristotelian logos in the 1960 debates. Gone were the complex syllogisms and sophisticated moral reasonings of the 1858 debates. Gone, too, was the more explicit integration of notions of right and wrong with traditional ideological systems.

However, the idea of right and wrong was discussed—or perhaps more accurately, the idea of *right* was discussed. For example, Nixon suggested that the candidates should be judged not on the number and cost of programs they proposed but on whether the right things were being done. Nixon stated in the first debate that "it isn't a question of how much the federal government spends; it isn't a question of which government does the most. It's a question of which administration does the right thing." Likewise, in discussing America's status abroad, Nixon claimed that "in this whole matter of prestige, in the final analysis, it's whether you stand for what's right."

Again absent from this notion of right is any justification explicitly derived from a particular external system of moral understanding. Lincoln talked continually about right and wrong in the 1858 debates, but he did so according to a certain religious worldview: slavery was wrong because all men were created equal in the eyes of God. Nixon, in contrast, invoked the idea of a moral right without directly linking it with a religious ethos—or for that matter, with any system of moral understanding—as had been done in previous political oratory.

In fact, in one discussion in which Nixon spoke of America setting the "right example," the Republican candidate pointed out the irrelevance of religion to a presidential race—ironically, a statement he offered immediately after justifying opposition to communism with a religious inference. In response to a reporter who asked about a public statement of support offered by a member of the Ku Klux Klan who was ostensibly motivated by religious ideas, Nixon declared:

> The worst thing that I can think can happen in this campaign would be for it to be decided on religious issues. I obviously repudiate the Klan; I repudiate anybody who uses the religious issue; I will not tolerate it. I have ordered all of my people to have nothing to do with it and I say— say to this great audience, whoever may be listening, remember, if you believe in America, if you want America to set the right example to the world, that we cannot have religious or racial prejudice. We cannot have it in our hearts. But we certainly cannot have it in a presidential campaign.

Interestingly, Kennedy gave a famous speech earlier in the campaign to a group of Protestant ministers in Houston, Texas, in which he also spoke of the irrelevance of religious belief to the presidency and of the importance of belief in America. The perspectives of both candidates indicate the extent to which Protestant religion no longer existed as a homogeneous philosophical system that provided any kind of wide-scale basis for moral understandings within American culture. The statements also reflect the extent to which religion was increasingly becoming understood as a private matter that had little relevance to matters of public policy.

The Question of Character

If Aristotelian logos disappeared from the Kennedy-Nixon debates, ethos did not. In a certain sense, it was even more important in this election than in the Lincoln-Douglas confrontation, because John F. Kennedy's age and experience raised questions about his qualifications for office. Yet both candidates affirmed rhetorically what Aristotle saw as central to good political oratory, namely, what he called *ethos*, "good moral character."[41] As noted earlier, Kennedy discussed moral leadership when he cited Franklin Roosevelt: "The presidency of the United States is above all a place of moral leadership." Likewise, Nixon spoke to the issue of character in the third televised debate when he praised President Dwight Eisenhower as possessing greater moral character than President Harry Truman:

> Senator Kennedy and I have felt Mr. Truman's ire; and consequently, I think he can speak with some feeling on this subject. I just do want to say one thing, however. We all have tempers; I have one; I'm sure Senator Kennedy has one. But when a man's president of the United States, or a former president, he has an obligation not to lose his temper in public. One thing I've noted as I've traveled around the country is the tremendous number of children who come out to see the presidential candidates. I see mothers holding their babies up, so that they can see a man who might be president of the United States. I know Senator Kennedy sees them, too. It makes you realize that whoever is president is going to be a man that all the children of America will look up to or will look down to. And I can only say that I'm very proud that President Eisenhower restored dignity and decency and, frankly, good language to the conduct of the presidency of the United States. And I only hope that, should I win this election, that I could approach President Eisenhower in maintaining the dignity of the office; in seeing to it that whenever any mother or father talks to his child, he can look at the man in the White House and, whatever he may think of his policies, he will say: "Well, there is a man who maintains the kind of standards personally that I would want my child to follow."

Whether either Kennedy or Nixon lived up to the type of character qualities espoused in the debates is, of course, another matter; but that good character was an ideal to be publicly upheld went unquestioned.

In sum, then, rhetoric in the Kennedy-Nixon debates was less closely aligned to traditional codes of moral understanding than was the oratory in the Lincoln-Douglas debates. Instead, references were made to certain symbols without a clear identification of their philosophical sources. Still, some references were made to religion, particularly in legitimating opposition to communism. As such, it appears that both Kennedy and Nixon appealed to the vestiges of older moral orders that were increasingly less pervasive in American culture but whose symbols resonated enough to provide a certain, albeit perhaps limited, level of legitimation for the candidate's suitability to hold America's highest office.

The Reagan-Mondale Debates

The length of the 1984 Reagan-Mondale debates was even less than the four hours of total debate time in the 1960 debates, which, in turn, were significantly shorter than the twenty-one hours of debate in 1858. The 1984 debates between incumbent president Ronald Reagan and former vice president Walter Mondale lasted only three hours and ten minutes in all: a one hundred-minute session on October 7 and a ninety-minute session on October 21, or only ten minutes more than the time it took for only one of the seven Lincoln-Douglas debates. Certainly, these structural differences significantly mitigated the possibility of the type of refined and eloquent oratory evident in the Lincoln-Douglas debates and were in keeping with the sound-bite quality of political rhetoric to which Americans were becoming accustomed.

An analysis of these debates reveals some of the same patterns that arose during the 1960 debates in terms of the ways in which candidates appealed to certain sources of legitimation. There was, however, the additional feature of identifiable and prominent leanings toward pathos, an emphasis that foreshadowed the preeminence of the therapeutic impulse in contemporary political rhetoric. This is not to say that appeals to traditional codes of moral understanding were absent from the content of the debates; indeed not. However, a close look at discussions of religion in the 1984 debates reveals its increasing marginality as a basis for making certain policy decisions, even with a candidate who had publicly aligned himself with the "traditional values" of religious conservatives. Instead, when pressed on important issues, both candidates employed some of the same type of rhetoric evident in the Clinton administration that was reviewed at the start of this chapter.

Traditional Religion's Legitimacy

Ronald Reagan was the celebrated candidate of religious conservatives because of his public alignment with what came to be called the New Religious Right and with the issues important to this movement, such as prayer in school and a "pro-life" stance on abortion. His association with this movement became an issue in the campaign and was a point of discussion in the debates.

When asked in the debates by journalist Fred Barnes whether he considered himself a born-again Christian and whether his religious beliefs affected his role as president, Reagan's answer was interesting. On the one hand, he acknowledged that he resorted to prayer, that he was raised by his mother to have "the firmest possible belief and faith in God," and that, as Lincoln once claimed, he would be the "most stupid man in the world" if he did not "turn to someone who was stronger and greater than all others."[42] On the other hand, he also indicated, in words similar to those used by Nixon in 1960, that religion should not be a part of the presidential campaign:

> At the same time, however, I have not believed that prayer should be introduced into an election or be a part of a political campaign or religion a part of that campaign. As a matter of fact, I think religion became a part of this campaign when Mr. Mondale's running mate said I was not a good Christian.

Such a response was in keeping with the publicly popular view that one's religion was valid in the private sphere but irrelevant to public policy.

Mondale was even more explicit in his denunciation of religion's place in the world of government, though he expressed admiration for Reagan's faith and provided information that was to give evidence of his own "deep religious faith." Moreover, according to Mondale, faith "instructs us about the moral life we should lead." Still, there was a sense in which this moral life did not include political life: "What bothers me is the growing tendency to try to use one's own personal interpretation of faith politically, to question others' faith, and to try to use the instrumentalities of government to impose those views on others. All history tells us that that is a mistake."

While Reagan and Mondale stepped away from religious legitimations to support policy positions, Reagan, in particular, utilized religious symbols in certain instances. For example, President Reagan is famous for his description of the former Soviet Union as an "evil empire." Questioned about this during the debates, Reagan somewhat defensively asserted, "I believe that many of the things they have done are evil in any concept of morality that we have." Though he stood up to his use of the term *evil*, he was careful to acknowledge the existence of a plurality of moralities in American culture. In the Kennedy-Nixon debates, when both candidates spoke of the "atheistic materialists who oppose us," they exhibited markedly less defensiveness about vilifying the former Soviet Union in this way; and there was less criticism from the media for demonizing the Soviet Union in this manner.

Candidates also appealed to religious symbols in the discussion of abortion. Although Reagan shifted the abortion debate to a constitutional rather than a moral context as is discussed later in this section, he did acknowledge in the discussion that the taking of a human life is a "sin" and that "our Judeo-Christian tradition" informs us regarding the right to take a human life in self-defense, thus justifying abortion in cases where the mother's life is in danger.

Finally, religious matters were also broached when Reagan was asked about public statements regarding the imminence of a biblical Armageddon. Again stepping away from the topic as a matter that in any way informed his policy decisions, the president asserted that references to Armageddon stemmed from private philosophical discussions with "others interested in the same thing."

Thus, though symbols from a religious system of moral understanding formed part of the rhetorical content of the 1984 debates, they were appealed to only in a somewhat superficial and reluctant manner. The religiously informed moral musings that characterized the Lincoln-Douglas debates were clearly absent. Appeals to religious concepts were more symbolic than complexly integrated with a position on or justification for a certain policy. In this respect, the Reagan-Mondale debates were much like the Kennedy-Nixon debates. Appeals were made to certain moral principles, but without definition, elaboration, or embellishment.

The Emergence of Pathos

In the Reagan-Mondale debates, however, pathos assumed a more predominant role than it had in either of the two previously considered political debates. Indeed, one of the strengths of the "Great Communicator's" presidency was the popularly held view that Reagan made people feel good. Mondale conceded this point to Reagan in the debates: "I'm going to give the president some credit. I think the president has done some things to raise the sense of spirit, morale, good feeling in this country, and he's entitled to credit for that."

Reagan himself referred to the revival of spirit in the country in a discussion about the economic recovery. Interestingly, though, in acknowledging "the revival of patriotism and optimism, the new spirit that we're finding all over America," the president spoke of the need for a continuation of the recovery, so that those hit by the recession and those who "didn't even feel the pain of the recession" might equally reap its benefits. So Clinton was not the first presidential candidate to identify with the pain felt by American citizens, nor was he the first to justify certain positions on the basis of feelings.

Consider, for example, the issue of abortion. When Reagan was asked about the controversial issue in the context of certain religious beliefs, he offered the following response: "But with regard to abortion—and I have a feeling that there's been some reference without naming it here in remarks Mr. Mondale tied to injecting religion into government—with me, abortion is not a problem of religion. It's a problem of the Constitution." Thus Reagan begged off from identifying his view of abortion with a religious or moral perspective. Instead, he shifted the discussion to a constitutional issue and concluded his remarks with the rather subjective qualifier that this was how he *felt* about the matter: "So this has been my feeling about abortion. That we have a problem now to determine, and all the evidence so far comes down on the side of the unborn child being a living human being."

In response to a follow-up question from Diane Sawyer, Reagan went even further in disassociating his position on the abortion issue from religious faith when he indicated that the church to which he belonged did not encourage a certain view on the matter:

> As I say, I feel that we have a problem here to resolve, and no one's approached it from that matter [whether the unborn child is a human life]. It does not happen that the church that I belong to had that as part of its dogma; I know that some churches do.

When the same question was put to Mondale, he identified the abortion issue as a highly personal and moral issue but made no attempt to support his position from a religious point of view. Like Reagan, he leaned to the realm of feelings,[43] though without first shifting the discussion to a matter of constitutionality:

> This is one of the most emotional and difficult issues that could possibly be debated. . . . Is it really the view of the American people, however you feel on the question of abortion, that government ought to be reaching into your living rooms and making choices like this? . . . I think these questions are inherently personal and moral, and every individual instance is different. . . . In America on basic moral questions we have always let the people decide in their own personal lives. We haven't felt so insecure that we've reached for the club of the state to have our point of view.

In his response, then, Mondale appealed to emotions in several respects: he identified the issue as an emotional one, he acknowledged that individuals have different feelings about the matter, and finally he suggested that the country as a whole can feel so "insecure" about a point of view that it reaches for the state to enforce it. One wonders whether Lincoln realized his position on slavery was one of national emotional insecurity. But one need not wonder whether Lincoln would employ such emotivist language to support his position, because the record indicates that he clearly did not.

Abortion was not the only issue to which such appeals to emotions were made. Reagan began a defense of his record on the environment in a similar way: "I feel as strongly as anyone about the preservation of the environment. . . ." Similarly, Mondale argued for action regarding the debt by appealing to emotions: "Would fathers and mothers feel proud of themselves if they loaded their children with debts like this nation has now, over a trillion dollars on the shoulders of our children?" Recall that Stephen Douglas, in contrast, argued against debt on moral grounds.

The Question of Leadership

The rhetorical content of the 1984 debates, then, reveals both an alignment, albeit superficial, with a transcendent religious worldview and a slightly discernible bent toward more therapeutic language. And though Aristotelian ethos still carried weight, there was a certain sense in which pathos began to challenge it as the central mode of persuasion in this realm of political oratory. This tendency was evident in discussions of the topic most closely associated with the notion of ethos, namely, the concept of moral leadership. Both candidates spoke of leadership in terms of doing what was morally right. As in the Kennedy-Nixon debates, however, this view of right was not conspicuously associated with traditional moral codes and symbols.

Mondale stated that "I've fought for a fair nation and despite the politics of it, I stand where I stand, and I think I'm right." Speaking specifically about American foreign policy in Latin America, he called into question Reagan's ability to lead and uphold a level of moral authority:

That's why I object to the covert action in Nicaragua. That's a classic example of a strategy that's embarrassed us, strengthened our opposition and undermined the moral authority of our people and our country in the region. Strength requires knowledge, command. We've seen in the Nicaraguan example a policy that has actually hurt us, strengthened our opposition and undermined the moral authority of our country in that region.

Reagan also spoke of leadership as a moral enterprise. He claimed, for example, that in his presidency, to avoid being guided by political considerations, he had instructed his cabinet not to discuss the political ramifications that surrounded various issues: "I don't want to hear them. I want to hear only arguments as to whether it is good or bad for the people. Is it morally right? And on that basis and that basis alone we make a decision on every issue."

In the same discussion, however, President Reagan introduced a rather subjective and self-referential philosophy for leadership:

> Now, leadership. First of all, I think that you have to have some principles you believe in. And mine, I happen to believe in the people and that the people are supposed to be dominant in our society, that they, not government, are to have control of their own affairs to the greatest extent possible with an orderly society.

To discuss the foundations for his philosophy of leadership, Reagan began with principles that he thought one should have and that he happened to believe in. This certainly reflects a more tentative and less resolute idea of the basis for right and wrong than was reflected in Lincoln's rhetoric.

Thus views of moral leadership and ideas of right and wrong approximated the type of discussion on the same topics that characterized in the Kennedy-Nixon debate. As in the 1960 debates, moral leadership and ideas of right were asserted without reference to a philosophical basis for these views. In the 1984 debates, however, particularly with Reagan, therapeutic rhetoric was offered concomitantly with symbolic gestures toward such principles as moral leadership.

Consider, for example, Reagan's closing remarks in the second debate, when he, like Kennedy, invoked Franklin Roosevelt's "rendezvous with destiny" phrase. Kennedy's use of the phrase was associated with the undefined principle of freedom and was a departure from the more religiously derived idea of "manifest destiny" discussed in the Lincoln-Douglas debates. Reagan's use of Roosevelt's phrase was likewise connected to the idea of freedom, but it was offered in the context of a rambling anecdote about driving along the California coast; viewing the beauty of the ocean, sun, and mountains; and thinking about what people will think of us one hundred years from now. This example of Reagan's "It's morning in America" rhetoric, then, did not directly draw on a philosophical system to substantiate the candidate's view of America's future nor was there even a concrete vision about what destiny might hold. This vision might be described as self-referentially poetic, rather than as principled or even philosophical. But it helped to shape the auditors' emotional response to the candidate in a favorable way.

Consider, too, one of the most remembered moments in the 1984 debates, when Reagan defused a question about his age and its influence on his ability to lead: "I want you to know that also I will not make age an issue of this campaign. I am not going to exploit for political purposes my opponent's youth and inexperience." He neutralized the issue not by defending his character and leadership qualities but through a humorous and well-received one-liner.

In sum, the 1984 debates were somewhat complex. Traditional religion—even religion's role in government and electoral politics—was clearly a part of the discussion. The responses of the candidates, however, reveal an absence of justifications for policy positions on the basis of religiously informed moral reasoning. As in the Kennedy-Nixon debates, principles of freedom and of right and wrong were addressed, but without an identification with any kind of philosophical system that gave definition to these ideas. Even Reagan, who was publicly aligned with the Religious Right, was reticent to defend positions on the basis of the traditions represented in that movement.

Unlike the Kennedy-Nixon debates, however, the 1984 debates contain traces of therapeutically derived justifications; and as was evident in the Thomas-Hill hearings, both sides of the cultural divide used this language. The rhetorical content of the 1984 debates suggests that Reagan was the more skillful of the two candidates at appealing to and shaping the emotional sentiments of his audience. If this was part of Reagan's public appeal and ability to win the presidency in 1984, it was even more the case for the 1992 presidential candidate who was most in tune with the therapeutic culture.

The Clinton-Bush-Perot Debates

The 1992 presidential debates were the first of the presidential debates examined here in which therapeutic symbols and codes provided the dominant form of legitimation. The 1992 debates stood in contrast to the Kennedy-Nixon debates, in which references to such principles as freedom, equality, and moral leadership were advanced without strong ties to a religious code of moral understanding, and to the Reagan-Mondale debates, in which superficial references to religious symbols were joined with traces of more therapeutic language.

Not surprisingly, of the three candidates Bill Clinton was the most comfortable with the new modus operandi. If Clinton were the only candidate compelled to address Americans in this way, however, then the theory that the candidates were socially driven to appeal to the therapeutic ethos because of its salience in the larger cultural landscape would be called into question. An analysis of these debates reveals that each of the candidates attempted to employ therapeutic defenses for his candidacy and his position on various policy matters. Clinton, however, was clearly the most adept at communicating in this manner.

The Triumph of Pathos

The 1992 debates were the first presidential debates in which Aristotelian pathos superseded Aristotelian ethos in importance. Clinton in particular was able to shift the discussion away from the character issue and argue instead that the candidate most suited for office was the candidate who cared most for the people. When asked specifically about the issue of experience, for example, Clinton answered, "Experience is important, yes. I've gotten a lot of experience in dealing with ordinary people over the last year, month. I've touched more people's lives and seen more heartbreak and hope, more pain and promise than anybody else who's run for president this year."[44] With this assertion, he made the standard for qualification for office the degree to which a candidate empathized with the pain of the American people. Such a standard is novel in the sense that it cannot be measured or quantified in some kind of objective way, and it obviously departs from previous standards, which placed greater emphasis on such things as expertise, years in office, and moral character. Clinton's effectiveness here in eliminating ethos as a viable criterion for evaluating a candidate became apparent in the second debate when a questioner pleaded with the candidates to stop talking about the character issue: "Can we focus on the issues and not the personalities and the mud?"

One of the character issues that Clinton's opponents tried to raise throughout the campaign regarded his draft record and his participation in demonstrations against the Vietnam War while he was a Rhodes Scholar at Oxford. President George Bush made reference to this issue during the debates but, interestingly, did so by appealing to his feelings:

> My argument with Governor Clinton—you can call it mud wrestling, but I think it's fair to put in focus—is I am deeply troubled by someone who demonstrates and organizes demonstrations in a foreign land when his country's at war. Probably a lot of kids here disagree with me. But that's what I feel. That's what I feel passionately about. I'm thinking of Ross Perot's running mate sitting in the jail [in Vietnam]. How would he feel about it? But maybe that's generational. I don't know.

Bush raised the issue of Clinton's demonstrations in Europe, but he did so without appealing to a cultural ethos that might give meaning to such ideals as honor, national loyalty, or courage. Instead, he asserted that this was a matter about which he *felt* very strongly and even conceded that others might feel differently. He claimed to be deeply troubled by it, not because it was wrong but because it was something he felt passionately about. He even suggested that Ross Perot's running mate, Admiral James Stockdale, might not feel very good about it.

Clinton, for his part, defended himself against this accusation by likewise appealing to feelings: "I was opposed to the war. I couldn't help that. I felt very strongly about it, and I didn't want to go at the time." Clinton's response is somewhat reminiscent of Martin Luther's famous statement "Here I stand, I can do no other." Recall, too, Mondale's statement of resolve offered in the 1984 debates: "I stand where I stand, and I think I'm right." These are all statements of resolve: but whereas Luther's was an appeal to conscience and to what he understood to be transcendent mandates, and whereas Mondale's was to what he *thought* was right, Clinton's appeal was to his feelings.

The Therapeutic Compulsion

Perhaps the most striking thing about the 1992 debates was the extent to which Bush and Perot likewise employed a therapeutic mode of discourse. One would not consider either George Bush or Ross Perot the most likely personality to be inclined toward this style of discourse. Nevertheless, on a number of occasions both resorted to therapeutic language. Consider, for example, Bush's response to a question about the AIDS epidemic:

> I think that we're showing the proper compassion and concern. So I can't tell you where it's coming from, but I am very much concerned about AIDS and I believe that we've got the best researchers in the world out there at NIH [National Institutes of Health] working the problem. We're funding them—I wish there was more money—but we're funding them far more than any time in the past, and we're going to keep on doing that. . . . Mary Fisher . . . electrified the Republican convention by talking about the compassion and the concern that we feel. It was a beautiful moment. . . . So I think the appeal is yes, we care.

Then, as if, for a moment, to express what he really thought about the matter of AIDS, the president slipped into a seemingly "uncaring" posture:

> And the other thing is part of AIDS—it's one of the few diseases where behavior matters. And I once called on somebody, "Well, change your behavior. Is the behavior you're using prone to cause AIDS? Change the behavior." Next thing I know, one of these ACT-UP groups is out saying, "Bush ought to change his behavior." You can't talk about it rationally. The extremes are hurting the AIDS cause. To go into a Catholic mass in a beautiful cathedral in New York under the cause of helping in AIDS and start throwing condoms around in the mass, I'm sorry, I think it sets back the cause.

But, as if correcting himself, he moved back into a more empathetic mode:

> We cannot move to the extreme. We've got to care. We've got to continue everything we can at the federal and the local level. Barbara I think is doing a superb job in destroying the myth about AIDS. And all of us are in this fight together, all of us care. Do not go to the extreme.

Ross Perot likewise defended his views with therapeutic rationales. Consider his pontification about racial divisiveness: "But let me just say to all of America: if you hate people, I don't want your vote. That's how strongly I feel about it." Once again, racial division was decried not on a moral basis but on the basis that Perot felt strongly about it. Speaking to the same issue, Perot encouraged Americans to "love one another"; and in his closing remarks, he told Americans that he was running for president because, as he put it, "I love you." Responding to a question about America's posture toward developments in Bosnia, Perot asserted the following: "Certainly we care about the people, we care about the children, we care about the tragedy." The statement, however, was offered in the context of arguing for European, rather than United States, responsibility for the region.

Perot also expressed strong feelings toward those who volunteered themselves for military service. In discussing this affection, he unveiled the archetype of therapeutic discourse.

> There's another group that I feel very close to, and these are the men and women who fought on the battlefield, the children—the families—of the ones who died and the people who left parts of their bodies over there. I'd never ask you to do anything for me, but I owe you this, and I'm doing it for you. And I can't tell you what it means to me at these rallies when I see you and you come up and the look in your eyes—and I know how you feel and you know how I feel.

Here is a complete conversation, even without words, conducted only on the basis of feelings.

All three candidates used therapeutic language when discussing children and the American family. Bush stated that when first lady Barbara Bush "holds an AIDS baby, she's showing a certain compassion for the family; when she reads to children, the same thing." He affirmed her public demonstration of empathy. Clinton defined the family as, in part, a place where children "know they're the most important people in the world"; and Ross Perot, drawing heavily, though perhaps unwittingly, on developmental psychology, claimed, "A little child before they're 18 months learns to think well of himself or herself—or poorly. They develop a positive or negative self-image."

The Talk Show Debate

The language employed by the candidates was not the only thing in these debates to resemble the therapeutic model. Indeed, the very structure of the second debate, which was held in Richmond, Virginia, on October 15, 1992, more closely resembled a daytime television talk show than it did a typical presidential debate. A moderator, who assumed the role of a Phil Donahue or an Oprah Winfrey, roamed the studio with a microphone, taking questions from the audience. This was the first time in the history of the presidential debates that citizens other than national journalism personalities were allowed to ask questions of the candidates directly. The questions themselves were thick on the emotive and typical of the type of discourse in the daytime talk shows. Consider, for example, this interchange between an audience member and the candidates:

> *Questioner:* Forgive the notes here, but I'm shy on camera. The focus of my work as a domestic mediator is meeting the needs of the children that I work with, by way of their parents, and not the wants of their parents. And I ask the three of you, how can we, as symbolically the children of the future president, expect the two of you, the three of you to meet our needs, the need in housing and in crime and you name it, as opposed to the wants of your political spin doctors and your political parties?
>
> *Moderator:* So your question is?
>
> *Questioner:* Can we focus on the issues and not the personalities and the mud? I think there's a need, if we could take a poll here with the folks from Gallup perhaps, I think there's a real need here to focus at this point on the needs.
>
> *Clinton:* I agree with him.
>
> *Bush:* Let's do it.
>
> *Moderator:* President Bush?
>
> *Bush:* Let's do it. Let's talk about programs for children.
>
> *Questioner:* Could we cross our hearts? It sounds silly here, but could we make a commitment? You know, we're not under oath at this point, but could you make a commitment to the citizens of the United States to meet our needs, and we have many, and not yours again? I repeat that. It's a real need, I think, that we all have.
>
> *Bush:* I think it depends how you define it. I mean, I think in general let's talk about these issues, let's talk about the programs. But in the presidency, a lot goes into it. Caring goes into it. That's not particularly specific. Strength goes into it. That's not particularly specific. Standing up against aggression. That's not specific in terms of a program. This is what a president has to do. So in principle, though, I'll take your point and think we ought to discuss child care or whatever else it is.

It seems that the questioner was not deeply interested in the specific issues or in knowing what the candidates thought about them. Instead, he seemed more concerned with having the candidates "cross their hearts" and swear to show compassion for the "real needs" of the people. Bush's attempt to empathize by inserting the phrase that "caring goes into" the presidency had the appearance of being wholly disingenuous.

Bush's inability to empathize with the audience in this fashion was even more pronounced in another exchange during the Richmond debate. The following question was first asked by a member of the audience, and it led to contrasting responses from the candidates:

> *Questioner:* How has the national debt personally affected each of your lives? And if it hasn't, how can you honestly find a cure for the economic problems of the common people if you have no experience in what's ailing them?

After Ross Perot offered a brief response, the question was put to President Bush:

> *Bush:* Well, I think the national debt affects everybody.
> *Moderator:* You personally.
> *Bush:* Obviously it has a lot to do with interest rates—
> *Moderator:* She's saying, "you personally." You, on a personal basis. How has it affected you? Has it affected you personally?
> *Bush:* I'm sure it has. I love my grandchildren—
> *Moderator:* How?
> *Bush:* I want to think that they're going to be able to afford an education. I think that that's an important part of being a parent. If the question—maybe I—get it wrong. Are you suggesting that if somebody has means that the national debt doesn't affect them?
> *Questioner:* What I'm saying is—
> *Bush:* I'm not sure I get—help me with the question and I'll try to answer it.
> *Questioner:* Well, I've had friends that have been laid off from jobs.
> *Bush:* Yeah.
> *Questioner:* I know people who cannot afford to pay the mortgage on their homes, their car payment. I have personal problems with the national debt. But how has it affected you, and if you have no experience in it, how can you help us, if you don't know what we're feeling?
> *Moderator:* I think she means more the recession—the economic problems today the country faces rather than the deficit.
> *Bush:* Well, listen, you ought to be in the White House for a day and hear what I hear and see what I see and read the mail I read and touch

the people that I touch from time to time. I was in the Lomax AME Church. It's a black church just outside of Washington, D.C. And I read the bulletin about teenage pregnancies, about the difficulties that families are having to make ends meet. I talk to parents. I mean, you've got to care. Everybody cares if people aren't doing well. But I don't think it's fair to say, you haven't had cancer. Therefore, you don't know what it's like. I don't think it's fair to say, you know, whatever it is, that if you haven't been hit by it personally. But everybody's affected by the debt because of the tremendous interest that goes into paying on that debt everything's more expensive. Everything comes out of your pocket and my pocket. So it's that. But I think in terms of the recession, of course you feel it when you're president of the United States. And that's why I'm trying to do something about it by stimulating the export, [in]vesting more, better education systems. Thank you. I'm glad you clarified it.

The questioner was not interested in President Bush's policy position regarding the national debt or his proposals for reducing the deficit. Her concern was not really even with the recession and any ideas the president might have for resolving it. What she was really concerned about was Bush's personal experience with the economic woes faced by Americans. If he did not have personal experience of economic hardship, then how could he know what she was "feeling"? In essence, then, what the questioner was looking for was a therapeutic response. Bush first tried to address the question at face value according to the literal words that the questioner used. After the moderator clarified what the audience participant was really asking, Bush feebly attempted a empathetic response but failed to connect with the questioner.

Clinton, in contrast, handled the question with great ease when it was directed to him. He took several strides into the audience and directly engaged the questioner:

Clinton: Tell me how it's affected you again.
Questioner: Um—
Clinton: You know people who've lost their jobs and lost their homes?
Questioner: Well, yeah, uh-huh.
Clinton: Well, I've been governor of a small state for 12 years. I'll tell you how it's affected me. Every year Congress and the president sign laws that make us do more things and gives us less money to do it with. I see people in my state, middle-class people—their taxes have gone up in Washington and their services have gone down while the

wealthy have gotten tax cuts. I have seen what's happened in this last four years when—in my state, when people lose their jobs there's a good chance I'll know them by their names. When a factory closes, I know the people who ran it. When the businesses go bankrupt, I know them. And I've been out here for 13 months meeting in meetings just like this ever since October, with people like you all over America, people that have lost their jobs, lost their livelihood, lost their health insurance. . . .

Clinton responded empathetically by discussing how the country's economic woes had directly affected him and those with whom he had personal contact. In word and in style, he connected with the questioner. He showed that he cared.

Clinton's ability in this regard was really no surprise. It was the Clinton campaign that recommended the Richmond debate format, a setup that closely resembled the electronic town-meeting format Clinton had been conducting throughout the campaign. In fact, at the end of the Richmond debate the candidate took credit for the format and expressed his appreciation to the audience for making it a "positive experience":

Thank you, Carole, and thank you ladies and gentlemen. Since I suggested this format I hope it's been good for all of you. I really tried to be faithful to your request that we answer the questions specifically and pointedly. I thought I owed that to you and I respect you for being here and for the impact you've had on making this a more positive experience.

The Therapeutic Candidate

Clearly, Clinton was the most comfortable of the candidates with the second debate, as was reflected in his empathetic response to the woman who asked about the debt. Another interesting feature about this response was the emphasis he placed on his own experience. Here, as in many situations throughout the 1992 debates, Clinton's response was conspicuously self-referential. His asserted superiority as a candidate was based on his subjective experience "in dealing with ordinary people." In other words, he did not defend positions by appealing to a standard outside himself but instead began with his personal experience.

This was certainly the case when he discussed drug policy, specifically the proposal to legalize drugs. Consider his reason for opposing the legalization of drugs in the first debate:

> Like Mr. Perot, I have held crack babies in my arms. But I know more about this, I think, than anybody else up here because I have a brother who's a recovering drug addict. I'm very proud of him. But I can tell you this. If drugs were legal, I don't think he'd be alive today. I am adamantly opposed to legalizing drugs. He is alive today because of the criminal justice system.

Clinton justified his stance and declared his superiority on this matter according to his personal experience and the visceral nature of his response to his brother's drug problem. He did not appeal to a philosophical or moral foundation to oppose the legalization of drugs. Not surprisingly, he went on to advocate a drug policy that included a strong emphasis on the type of therapeutic treatment programs discussed in Chapter 4.

Clinton also appealed to personal experience in responding to a question about racial division in the United States:

> I grew up in the segregated South, thankfully raised by a grandfather with almost no formal education but with a heart of gold who taught me early that all people were equal in the eyes of God. I saw the winds of hatred divide people and keep the people of my state poorer than they would have been, spiritually and economically. And I've done everything I could in my public life to overcome racial divisions.

In this case, even though Clinton's grandfather expressed ideas about race in language reminiscent of Lincoln's, the Democrat candidate again began with himself, with his personal experience. What if he did not have a grandfather who taught him these things? Or what of a person who did not have such a personal experience? What would enjoin him or her to agree with Clinton on the problem of racial inequality? The point is that the candidate justified his position by looking within, rather than by appealing to some external authority.

By operating within the genre of pathos, Clinton was effective at connecting with his future constituency. The following is typical of Clinton's rhetorical ability to highlight personal contact and emotional concern with Americans:

> Most of all, I'd like to thank all of you who have touched me in some way over this last year, all the thousands of whom I've seen. . . . I'd like to thank all the folks around America that no one ever knows about—the woman that was holding the AIDS baby she adopted in Cedar Rapids, Iowa, who asked me to do something more for adoption; the woman who

stopped along the road in Wisconsin and wept because her husband had lost his job after 27 years; all the people who are having a tough time and the people who are winning but who know how desperately we need to change.

The Triumph of Therapeutic Discourse

Change did occur. Bill Clinton was elected president in 1992 and re-elected in 1996, victories that were related in no small measure to his ability to connect with the prevailing cultural values of the American people. The therapeutic rhetoric employed by Clinton and the other candidates in the 1992 debates points to a fundamental change in the nature of political discourse, one evident elsewhere in contemporary electoral politics.

Consider, for example, rhetoric from the conventions of the two major political parties in 1992. One account of the Democratic National Convention observed that if Clinton were to win, he would "be the first post-therapy President ever to inhabit the White House."[45] The article, titled "I'm in Therapy, You're in Therapy: A Much-Analyzed Candidate Offers a Twelve-Step Plan to Democrats Anonymous," reported that both the Clintons and the Gores had been involved in counseling: the former, to work through marital problems and issues related to Roger Clinton's drug addiction and a stepfather's alcoholism, and the latter, to work through difficulties surrounding their son's car accident-related injuries. Both Clinton and his running mate, Al Gore, talked publicly about these matters.

Clinton's proclivity toward "sprinkl[ing] his interviews with the trendy language of codependency" set the tone for a convention that in some ways took on the atmosphere of a twelve-step group meeting. Pilar Perez, a Jerry Brown delegate from California, for example, observed that "everyone in the state's delegation was comparing the convention to group therapy."[46] Indeed, traces of the various features of America's increasingly therapeutic culture—the elevation of the self as a source of moral authority, the greater emphasis on emotions for understanding oneself and one's relations with others, the victim mind-set, and the self-referential practice of "sharing" or displaying one's internal workings as though the public were a personal self-help group—were evident in a number of the speeches given at the Democratic convention. Al Gore, for example, shared his feelings about his son's accident during his acceptance speech: "I want to tell you this straight from my heart: that experience changed me forever." [47] Likewise, Jesse Jackson identified with the felt pain of Americans: "Across the globe, we feel the pain that comes with new birth. Here in our country pain abounds." [48] New York mayor David Dinkins, in his welcoming address, observed that by walking the streets of New York, one can "feel the pain of an entire nation." [49]

Identifying specifically with the pain of single-parent children, Clinton offered these empathetic words:

> And I want to say to every child in America tonight who's out there trying to grow up without a father or a mother, I know how you feel. You're special, too. You matter to America. And don't you ever let anybody tell you you can't become whatever you want to be. And if other politicians make you feel like you're not a part of their family, come on and be part of ours. [50]

But Clinton and the Democrats were not the only politicians employing the sentimental and emotive language of therapy. Recall Bush's attempt in New Hampshire to reassure voters that he was in touch with their felt needs: "Message, I care." [51] Even the fire-breathing Pat Buchanan, in his vitriolic convention speech, tried to connect with those hurt by hard times: "We need to reconnect with them. We need to let them know we know how bad they're hurting. They don't expect miracles, but they need to know we care." [52]

Two years later, Republicans even more explicitly employed therapeutic language after their 1994 takeover of Congress. In one of his first acts as newly elected Speaker of the House, Newt Gingrich brought in a "corporate psychotherapist" to consult Republicans on how to "forcefully articulate the Republicans' social agenda without appearing insensitive." Advice offered by Morris Schectman, who specializes in helping organizations "change their culture," included warnings to Republicans that changes in welfare policy could cause some of their constituencies to "enter a kind of grieving period." [53]

Gingrich's use of the therapeutic model may surprise some. Arguably, the rhetoric that emanated from the leadership of the 1994 Republican revolution was not generally regarded as therapeutic. The introduction of a school prayer amendment and measures to limit abortion, as well as a public alignment with such groups as the Christian Coalition, would suggest that Republicans were substantively appealing to some of the traditional sources of state justification reviewed in Chapter 2. With some, to be sure, this was the case. But, as we saw with tort reform efforts in Chapter 3 and "tough on crime" initiatives in Chapter 4, the guiding thrust of the "Contract with America" agenda was not "pro-foundational." In other words, the defining feature of the movement was not an effort to reclaim former sources of state legitimation; at the heart of the Republican agenda, rather, was a conspicuous utilitarianism.

Garry Wills, for one, notes the irony of Gingrich's appeals to tradition when juxtaposed to his overriding commitment to technological progress and his denouncement of societal efforts that "enforce behavioral codes." As Wills explains, "There is a cultural dissonance between Newt the visionary futurist and Newt the conservative politician."[54] Yet the dissonance helps explain how Gingrich could, on the one hand, appeal to the image of George Washington praying at Valley Forge and, on the other hand, employ a psychotherapist to help get the Republican message out. The defining force of his philosophy is progressive pragmatism rather than the substantive claims of foundational sources of legitimation. If the Contract with America effort was not pro-foundational, it was certainly not antitherapeutic. Therapeutic programs that are perceived to oppose progress may be criticized, but inasmuch as the therapeutic model serves the ends of progress, it, like historical anecdotes steeped in tradition, is employed.

The triumph of therapeutic rhetoric in American politics may have reached its climax in the 1996 political conventions of both parties. From Elizabeth Dole's "Oprah-esque" tribute to her husband at the Republican convention in San Diego to Al Gore's emotive story about his sister's death from lung cancer at the Democratic convention in Chicago, sentiment far and away prevailed over sustained discussion about policy, not to mention reasoned defenses for those policies. Interestingly, after the Democratic convention journalists challenged the "authenticity" of Gore's visceral abhorrence of tobacco, pointing to his support of tobacco production for years after the untimely death of his sister—support that reportedly involved continuing to grow tobacco on his family's farm and receiving over $16,000 in campaign contributions from tobacco companies. Gore took cover from these charges by appealing, once again, to a therapeutically inspired defense. It was, as he explained, "emotional numbness" that prevented him from "integrating into all aspects of [his] life the implications of what that tragedy really meant." [55] He embellished on the topic further by discussing the importance of integrating emotions into policy more generally: "I really do believe that in our politics and in our personal lives, we are seeing an effort to integrate our emotional lives and our intellectual lives in a more balanced fashion." Then, as if to argue in support of the thesis being advanced in the present study, he stated, "We are in the midst of a profound shift in the way we approach issues. . . . People are becoming more willing to give some respect to the importance of the way people feel and to try to balance emotions and logic in a more artful way." [56]

Evidence of this shift was pronounced at both political conventions in 1996, where pathos was the operative rhetorical style. Whether it was Nancy Reagan, Christopher Reeves, police officers shot in the line of duty, Secretary of Commerce Ron Brown's widow, a Pennsylvania rape victim, military heroes, or gun-control activists Jim and Sarah Brady, both parties employed nonpoliticos to make sentimental appeals in a style that was undeniably epideictic, to use Aristotle's term. That is, the conventions were clearly ceremonial or eulogistic in form. Indeed, the tone of many of the speeches (and of the accompanying videos), from politicians and nonpoliticians alike resembled what one might expect to find at a funeral. And if the tearful faces in the audience, caught by the panning television cameras during the convention speeches, are any indication, Americans welcomed and fully embraced this communication style.

Even beyond the conventions, therapeutic themes heavily colored the 1996 presidential campaign. Like Bush and Perot in 1992, Senator Robert Dole was less successful than Clinton in employing the therapeutic style, though he gave it a valiant effort. As one journalist observed during the campaign:

> Dole has struggled for months to fuse his cool, conservative prescriptions for America . . . with a warm, caring image of himself as someone who has known poverty and pain and can empathize with . . . the electorate. To conjure up a more humane persona the 72–year-old Kansan . . . has emoted regularly in public. . . . Yet the "I care" persona has often fallen flat on the campaign trail. It came across as anomalous for a deal-making career politician, like wearing Birkenstocks with a blue suit. [57]

As in 1992, the 1996 debates reflected therapeutic proclivities both in format and in style. The daytime talk show format introduced in 1992 returned in 1996, and in both debates, candidates again appeared determined to connect emotionally with voters.

Summary

In contemporary political rhetoric, pathos has emerged as the dominant form of persuasion. Absent in all the debates since 1960 has been the logical discourse strongly represented in the Lincoln-Douglas debates. Moreover, advanced in 1992, for the first time in the history of presidential debates, was the notion that character had no relevance to a candidate's suitability for office.

For this reason, Aristotle's typological characterization of different types of oratory is, by contemporary standards, inapplicable. Both political and legal rhetoric now more closely resemble what Aristotle would have typified as ceremonial rhetoric. And not only the predominant modes of persuasion but also the references to time have moved in the direction of the ceremonial. The preoccupation with the present—concomitant with instinctive disregard for the past and less defined visions for the future—also indicates the extent to which political and legal rhetoric have changed.

It must be reiterated that this type of rhetoric is not simply a product of the individual styles of politicians but is determined by the sentiments of the citizenry. Candidates may say, "I feel," when they really mean, "I think" or "I believe." One could argue, in such instances, that they are not really navigating their lives according to the dictates of their emotions. But if they are compelled to use a certain type of language in order to make ideas palatable to a particular audience, even when it goes against their cognitive inclinations, this all the more affirms the notion that the culture is placing certain social pressures on the politician.

The candidates are thus symbols of collective national life. The very process whereby candidates who reflect the predominant cultural values are able to get elected is an example of the dialectical process being investigated in this project. The substantive transformation in the nature of political rhetoric, as revealed through an analysis of the presidential debates, indicates that the source of legitimation to which contemporary politicians appeal is the therapeutic ethos.

8

The Therapeutic State

In the previous five chapters, we found that the therapeutic cultural ethos has penetrated a number of realms of the American state. From the presence of psychological experts testifying on behalf of emotionally injured victims in civil case law, to the therapeutic treatment of "client/patient" offenders in the criminal justice system, to the feeling, self-esteeming emphasis in contemporary education, to the sentimentalized congressional arguments for state protection of the emotional well-being of children, to the use of therapeutic language in presidential rhetoric, the various features of the therapeutic ethos as depicted in Chapter 1 are clearly evident in major institutions of the American state.

Though fairly exhaustive, even these examples do not represent the extent of the infusion. Similar developments can be found in other state institutions, including the state's military apparatus, where today's soldiers are granted greater autonomy than in the past and where social control through "persuasion" rather than through "coercion" has become the contemporary modus operandi. The sharp decline in court martials per total number of soldiers is just one example of this softer form of social control in the U.S. military.[1] Expansion of mental health and self-help group programs in military hospitals, increased treatment efforts to stem the reported growth in domestic violence among military families, experimentation with and treatment of ADD-diagnosed military children and their parents by army psychiatrists, and the growing presence of military psychologists to help soldiers work through stress and other war-related psychological difficulties are other indicators of the influence of the therapeutic impulse in the U.S. military.[2]

Ellen Herman, in her 1995 analysis of the political and social influence of psychology, expressed her belief that the military was the place where psychology's impact on public policy first emerged. Herman argues, for example, that "psychology's political progress was founded, first and foremost, on the ever-present militarism of the war and postwar years."[3] Though there is some question as to whether the emergence of the American therapeutic state did begin in the military, that the therapeutic impulse has impacted on the military is convincingly demonstrated in Herman's work. She documents, for example, the movement from the "propaganda" efforts of World War I to the military use of "psychological warfare" in World War II. On the conviction that "emotional appeals worked more effectively than rational ones," World War II military agencies such as the Psychological Warfare Division (PWD) and the Foreign Moral Analysis Division (FMAD) engaged in efforts to understand and influence enemy morale; for instance, through analyses of psychological and social tensions in Japanese society, through psychological interpretations of the German anti-Semitic personality, and by disseminating psychologically demoralizing messages into enemy territory with artillery-fired paper leaflets.[4] The last of these practice continued through the Vietnam War. So important were psychological weapons in the war effort that Dwight D. Eisenhower once wrote, "Without a doubt, psychological warfare has proved its right to a place of dignity in our military arsenal."[5]

After the war, according to Herman, the same psychological practices "migrated across the Atlantic and were quickly applied to domestic developments."[6] One example is the growth in national mental health services that followed passage of the 1946 National Mental Health Act (NMHA). The NMHA laid the foundation for the establishment of the National Institute of Mental Health (NIMH). Funding for the NIMH grew rapidly after its founding. In 1950, the first official year of the NIMH, the agency's budget was $8.7 million. In 1960, only ten years later, the NIMH budget was over $100 million, and by 1967, it was $315 million.[7] The growth of federal involvement in this area was justified on the grounds that "mental health was necessary to the efficacy of . . . national security, domestic tranquillity, and economic competitiveness."[8]

Recent national efforts for greater state involvement in the area of health care have likewise included a sizable expansion in provisions for mental health. Tipper Gore, in her advocacy of mental health provisions in the failed Clinton health care plan, argued that 28 percent of all Americans suffer from mental problems (including alcohol and drug addictions) and that 50 million Americans are mentally ill, including 14 million children.[9] And though major national health care reform has yet to make its way through Congress, individual state-sponsored insurance programs have expanded coverage (and premiums) for counseling and other mental health matters. In 1993, for example, Blue Cross and Blue Shield of Virginia, in compliance with state regulations, substantially increased mental health coverage for its state college-based programs.[10] The demand for these types of health services, moreover, seems to be increasing. Robert Gallagher, director of the University of Pittsburgh's counseling center and observer of university counseling services nation-wide, notes that "despite tightened belts in academia, there's been a gradual increase in patient demand . . . and the number of sessions per counseled student is increasing."[11]

Preventive efforts in other state-sponsored health insurance programs also reflect the influence of the therapeutic perspective. Consider, for example, the Wellness Planner, put out by Health Net, California's health care plan. Here state-employed beneficiaries are encouraged to pursue health in six different areas of Wellness: physical, emotional, occupational, intellectual, social, and spiritual. With regard to the emotional, state employees are encouraged to "express yourself . . . devote some attention to your emotional Wellness . . . work on diffusing tension or stress through exercise, meditation, relaxation or laughter . . . work on positively communicating with your family or coworkers so they will know how you feel." One of the "goal ideas" for the section on "Intellectual Wellness" is to "practice active listening: giving eye contact, positive body language—to really *hear* others this month." Finally, in the section on spirituality, beneficiaries of Health Net are encouraged to "find a way to nurture your spirit each day. Meditate, practice relaxation, say affirmations, perform yoga—or simply take time alone to reflect."[12]

Thus the impact of therapeutic concepts is not limited to isolated institutions within the state. In fact, the state's adoption of a therapeutic perspective is really a comprehensive, though relatively recent, phenomenon. A consistent theme within each of the case studies considered in Chapters 3–7 is the concomitant presence of utilitarian and therapeutic rationales for justifying state programs, a feature of the therapeutic state that may have some bearing on the larger issue of a societal shift from modernism to postmodernism.

Therapeutic Utilitarianism

In Chapters 1 and 2, I spoke of the therapeutic proposition as, in part, a response to the effects of industrial rationalization on modern society. The therapeutic perspective responds by offering itself as a soft remedy to the harshness of life in a highly rationalized society. The question of whether this development represents a departure from instrumental rationalism or is a further extension of the same process is a subset of the larger intellectual debate over whether postmodernism is a departure from or an extension of modernism. Answering the former question is certainly relevant to the larger discussion about the modernity/postmodernity distinction.

Evidence considered in Chapters 3–7 suggests that therapeutic forms of legitimation, though prominent, are often conflated with utilitarian forms of legitimation (a type of justification that is emblematic of instrumental rationalism). In the area of civil case law, economists have joined psychologists in developing an "objective" system to determine the monetary value of the "loss of enjoyment of life" in personal injury cases, and recent tort reform efforts were largely fueled by the utilitarian concern with regulating and limiting the rising costs of civil litigation. In criminal law, the Drug Court movement is defended on the basis that it reduces recidivism rates and costs the criminal justice system less. Self-esteem programs in education and elsewhere are justified on the basis that they are efficacious. Congressional arguments for child welfare programs, though increasingly defended by sentimental appeals, even in the contemporary context have not shaken loose from reliance on utilitarian justifications. And the presence of Ross Perot (the managerial candidate) and Bill Clinton (the therapeutic candidate) on the same debate stage provides a metaphor for the interesting conflation between therapeutic and utilitarian forms of legitimation.

In some cases, the two prominent languages of legitimation conflict with each other. In the case of the Drug Courts, our analysis of the various studies on the court treatment programs revealed that the utilitarian defense sometimes challenged the therapeutic or treatment approach to program evaluation. In several instances, a therapeutic basis of evaluation clearly superseded a utilitarian one, though statements about the Drug Court's efficacy were never abandoned. Here the utilitarian argument seemed to serve as a cosmetic rather than a determinative basis for defending the program.

Similarly, self-esteem programs in the schools and other places are often defended on the basis that they work, that they are effective in reducing crime, drug use, teen pregnancies, and the like. In fact, movement advocates point to a scientific assessment of self-esteem's influence on a host of social ills. In this collection of case studies, one will recall, no correlation is found between self-esteem and these various behaviors. But these findings have been disregarded, on the basis that though initial empirical evidence may not substantiate a causal relationship, such a relation still exists because "our intuition tells us so." Again, though empirical, scientific, modern methods are appealed to, they are seen as helpful only inasmuch as they support a more subjective, intuitive, therapeutic defense.

In the case of national tort reform and state workers' compensation reform, however, the driving force against the recovery of awards for emotional and other intangible injuries was economics. Likewise, in debates over welfare and criminal justice reform, the major reasons offered for revamping or eliminating programs were that they were too costly and ineffective. And much of the drive behind reform efforts in education is based on utilitarian concerns about the efficacy of America's educational system. In these instances, then, the utilitarian challenged the therapeutic orientation. Generally speaking, however, the two languages have coexisted, at times working in tandem and at others in conflict. Even when, on the surface, the two orientations appeared to be in conflict, closer examination revealed a more complementary coexistence (e.g., in political discussions about tort reform considered at the end of Chapter 3).

Whether conflictual or complementary, the therapeutic and the utilitarian were the two languages available for justifying state laws, policies, and programs. It would be a mistake, then, to see the movement to "end welfare as we know it," to get "tough on crime," or to reform civil litigation as "pro-foundational" in the sense that what was behind the initiative was a concern with returning to the traditional sources of legitimation that once gave meaning to the American civil order. Certainly, in some instances, the motivation behind reform may stem from regret over America's departure from traditional codes of moral understanding. But even these positions, when translated into the nomenclature of contemporary political discourse, gravitate toward the prevailing utilitarian and therapeutic languages.

The coexistence of these two languages is, in certain respects, counterintuitive. One symbolizes the "bottom line" impersonality of a highly rationalized modern world, the very orientation that in the Weberian sense, was believed to have undermined the former sources of legitimation and to have contributed toward the problem of alienation and disenchantment. The other is the "soft and sensitive" orientation, often promoted on the grounds that it remedies the harshness of life in a mechanistic, bureaucratic, impersonal world. How is it that these seemingly contradictory modes of discourse actually complement, or at least coexist, with each other?

One reason is that both speak to the perceived limitlessness and plasticity of our world. According to a utilitarian perspective, industry, technology, advances in communication and transportation, and the like enable us to control and re-create our natural world. Similarly, with the tools of the therapeutic perspective, we can control and re-create our inner psyches. In both instances, the respective orientation provides us with the equipment to create and re-create ourselves. There are no limits to what we can make of our inner and outer worlds. Both universes are mutable and open to our creative imaginations.

In a certain sense, then, therapeutic utilitarianism represents a component of what one might call "postmodern nihilism," inasmuch as nihilism signifies the belief that there is no ultimate metaphysical meaning to life and celebrates the departure from older, more traditional moral orders. Recall Friedrich Nietzsche's redefinition of truth, from that which could be sought and known to truth as a "mobile army of metaphors." Therapeutic language allows us to understand ourselves through self-creation rather than through the pursuit of truth. It gives us new metaphors and new words to describe and reinterpret ourselves. As such, one's understanding of oneself is not limited by references to things outside of the self. It is largely self-created and mutable to new creations. Again, there are no limits.

Richard Rorty, drawing a parallel between Freud and Nietzsche, recognizes the extent to which the language of therapy, unlike the languages of traditional moral orders, better serves this end (or perhaps I should say, this process) of self-creation. According to Rorty, concepts such as "obsessional" and "paranoid" are much more open to individual application and nuance, to individual contingencies, than are "the names of virtue and vices which we inherit from the Greeks and the Christians."[13] This kind of nihilism, though, is postmodern and post-Nietzschean in the sense that it is nihilism with a happy face on it. It is not the depressive nihilism that groans about the oppressive, binding influence of older moral orders; nor is it the morosely combative nihilism that says, "We believe in nothing." Rather, it is the more sanguine nihilism that says, "We believe in anything."

So, although the therapeutic and utilitarian ideals on the surface appear contradictory, in actuality they jointly endorse the belief in human limitlessness and represent the major languages of legitimation used by the state to justify itself in the contemporary context.

A Postmodern State?

What does the state's employment of both utilitarian and therapeutic languages say about the larger intellectual debate regarding whether we live in a "high modern" (to borrow Anthony Giddens's term) or in a postmodern era? How is it that culture would speak of the therapeutic as an answer to the harshness of a mechanistic technological society but that, in the context of political languages of legitimation, therapeutically oriented programs are justified on the basis of their instrumental efficacy?

One way of understanding this would be to argue that while the contemporary therapeutic culture may be postmodern in the sense that changes within it represent a fundamental and profound break from the previous epistemic order, the state and other societal institutions in the public realm are still fundamentally modern or high modern. They still essentially function within the structural parameters established by the processes of modernity.

The impact of psychology on culture is certainly pronounced. Its incompatibility with previous codes of moral understanding, which were, as Hannah Arendt notes, all derived from outside the "range of human deeds," highlights the significance of the shift. Within the therapeutic culture, cues are taken instead from the emotivist determinations of the self. Consider the portrayal of the utilitarian and expressive forms of individualism depicted in *Habits of the Heart*, by Robert Bellah and his colleagues. Both forms of language, shown to be dominant in American culture, are ultimately self-referential. The utilitarian language employed by Brian Palmer and others interviewed in *Habits of the Heart* is, in the final analysis, reflexively subjective. It is not that life works because of external life principles. Even the idea of "it works" is determined by the subjective determinations of the self. Thus the *individualistic utilitarianism* of the culture may not be the same as the *structural utilitarianism* of the state. Subjective determinations of what "works for me" are not measured against tests of program efficacy, budgetary constraints, cost-effective guidelines, and the like. This is not to deny the endemic quality of individual pragmatism in American culture. It is to suggest, however, that such pragmatism is qualitatively distinct from structural utilitarianism. For the latter, there still exist certain empirical measurements upon which the ideas of success and efficacy are ostensibly determined. The culture, in contrast, is not so restrained by these requirements. Individual determinations of what constitutes success and what works for the individual are more relative.

Given the continued importance of structural utilitarianism at the level of the state, it would seem that this public institution is still significantly modern and that the conflation of utilitarian and therapeutic rationales for state action represents high modernity rather than postmodernity. That is, within the functions of the state, the therapeutic ethos has joined with, rather than supplanted, the clearly modern notions of empirical verifiability, cost-effectiveness, and the like. But will this hold? The aesthetic use of utilitarianism in the examples of the Drug Court and the self-esteem movement seems to indicate that utilitarianism may eventually serve only an ironic, rather than a determinative, purpose. Moreover, in some instances we found that the therapeutic impulse is beginning to effect structural change, in addition to changes in the substance of discourse. Consider both the changes in the fundamental process of adjudication effected by the Drug Court movement and the substantively altered formats of political conventions and presidential debates. These particular developments suggest that the fuller realization of a *post*modern state may be forthcoming.

However, these examples seem to be the exceptions rather than the rule. More commonly, utilitarian arguments are used not in an ironic way but because they represent the most convincing means of substantiating a state initiative or program. Comparatively, then, it may be most appropriate to characterize the culture as postmodern and the state as high modern or hypermodern, because of the unyielding stronghold of the modern and the less self-referential notion of efficacy within the latter.

Such a distinction may also help explain why Bill Clinton, though effective as a candidate through use of therapeutic rhetoric, has sometimes struggled to generate the same level of enthusiasm for his presidency. As a candidate, expressions of empathy, particularly when juxtaposed to the less therapeutically inclined candidates of George Bush and Ross Perot in 1992 and Bob Dole in 1996, were enough to demonstrate caring and concern and to elicit support. But within the actual functionings of the American political system, the officeholder must effectively deliver to make the system work. Empathetic rhetoric alone will not suffice.

Interestingly, Clinton's approval ratings as president improved markedly during the 1996 campaign season and in moments during his presidency that invited his characteristically eulogistic style. For example, the aftermath of the Oklahoma City bombing in May 1995 welcomed his therapeutic style. As William Schnieder, writing in the *Washington Post,* observed:

> It took a tragedy to remind Americans of what they like about Bill Clinton. Remember all those jokes about how Clinton "feels your pain"? Well, we were all feeling pain after the Oklahoma City bombing. The president expressed the country's pain eloquently at the memorial service. Clinton showed empathy and compassion — exactly what he does best.[14]

Clinton's sometimes lower approval ratings may have something to do with his inability — or overability — to appease both sides in America's culture wars. Clinton has been relentlessly criticized for his penchant for ingratiating himself with whatever interest group he happens to be relating to, irrespective of conflicts in ideology. Such a practice represents not only typical political posturing but a bit of a tone deafness to the deeply rooted nature of the American culture wars. Underestimating the strength of the culture wars led, for example, to the unanticipated public controversy over the issue of gays in the military at the beginning of the Clinton presidency.

The deeply embedded nature of the culture wars also raises questions about the modern/postmodern condition of the culture and the state. In his work on the subject, *Culture Wars,* James Hunter depicts the contemporary cultural environment as one characterized by intense conflict between the orthodox — those whose worldviews derive from the standards of certain transcendent, unchanging truths — and the progressives, whose worldviews keep pace with the changing currents of culture. Given the continued engagement of the orthodox (and their ostensible commitment to older moral orders), how, one might ask, can it be argued that contemporary culture is, indeed, a fundamentally new epistemic order? The ongoing intensity of the culture wars says something about the continued (residual though it may be) importance of traditional moral codes and symbols. In light of this, the therapeutic ethos is perhaps best understood as an increasingly dominant impulse within a complex and sometimes conflictual cultural system where older moral orders still carry some cultural capital.

However, even within the orthodox camp of the culture wars, the influence of the therapeutic ethos is pronounced. Hunter found this in his discussions with the culturally orthodox over the heatedly contested abortion issue, documented in *Before the Shooting Begins*. Likewise, in an analysis of the 1992 presidential campaign, where cultural skirmishes over family and other divisive issues flourished, I found the presence of therapeutic rationales on each side of the cultural divide.[15] Recall, too, how both sides of the Thomas-Hill conflict, a very visible skirmish in the larger culture wars, invoked therapeutic language. Moreover, several studies of conservative evangelicals, a core constituency of the orthodox side of the American culture wars, reveal the substantial influence of the therapeutic perspective.[16] Orthodox adoption of therapeutic language and practices portends the ultimate undermining of its claim to traditional codes of moral understanding.

The subjective, self-referential emotivism of the therapeutic orientation is, at its core, incompatible with the supposedly unchanging standards and doctrines of "reason" and "revelation." Though the orthodox align themselves with a worldview derived from these traditional cultural systems, they do so using the language of a therapeutic system of moral understanding. Perhaps unwittingly, then, the orthodox employ a form of discourse that challenges the very substance of the traditional ideals with which they align themselves. Theoretically and practically, the therapeutic perspective is antithetical to an orthodox orientation. It places on a subjective level systems of meaning that once stood over and above the claims of the emotivist self. Thus, though traditional moral codes are still evident in American culture, the dominant impulse of the therapeutic orientation, even among those affiliated with traditional codes of moral understanding, may well signify a shift toward a distinctly postmodern cultural system.

If the therapeutic impulse undermines orthodox tendencies at the cultural level, the utilitarian impulse seems to be orthodoxy's greatest threat at the state level. To be sure, orthodox inclinations are often necessarily translated into therapeutic terms for the sake of political discussions, as evident in some of the examples cited above. But it is utilitarianism that most often provides the acceptable point of entry at the level of the state for those with culturally orthodox leanings. This is particularly the case in the Republican Party, where the tension between cultural conservatives and fiscal libertarians persistently threatens party unity. The Contract with America agenda is just one example of how party unity was sustained by maintaining the focus on economic issues. One indication of the tenuous nature of this alliance was the Republican leadership's decision to put off debate over controversial social issues such as abortion and school prayer until after other elements of the contract were considered.[17] Republicans still ran into difficulties, however, when anti-abortion members threatened to break rank when parts of the welfare reform bill were perceived to encourage abortion among welfare recipients.

Recall, moreover, how reform efforts in the areas of crime, welfare, education, and civil litigation were politically legitimated by economically based arguments. We saw in previous chapters how arguments against therapeutic impulses within the state were rooted not in appeals to traditional sources of legitimation that somehow challenged the philosophical premises of a therapeutic outlook but in utilitarian concerns. For the most part, though, utilitarian impulses coexisted with, rather than challenged, therapeutic impulses and served to justify arguments both supporting and opposing reform.

In any respect, it is likely that the utilitarian orientation is a greater threat than support to orthodox impulses at the state level, because of the very structural nature of the state and its ideal-typical legal-rational orientation. Once again, this appears to set the state apart from the culture. That orthodoxy is undermined primarily by the therapeutic impulse at the cultural level and by utilitarianism at the state level also suggests a distinction between the state and culture concerning the modernism/postmodernism issue, one that again characterizes the state as high modern and the culture as postmodern.

To summarize, the coexistence of both legitimating languages in each of the areas of the state investigated herein would lead one to conclude that the continued salience of *structural utilitarianism* at the state level is evidence that the contemporary political order is merely an extension of modernity, rather than a distinctly "postmodern" epoch of its own. At the cultural level, though, the dominance of the therapeutic ethos along with *individual utilitarianism* is qualitatively different and less beholden to the externally derived parameters of scientific empiricism.

Understanding the substantive nature of the postmodern or high modern state is important not only for theoretical, conceptual purposes but also for understanding how, given its therapeutic-utilitarian nature, the state will, in turn, act back on culture.

An Assessment of the Continuing Dialogue

Recall that the relationship between the state and culture, as depicted here, is a dialectical process. Just as the culture influences the state, so the state influences the culture. The main purpose of this project has been to investigate the possibility of a comprehensive infusion of a therapeutic ethos into the functionings of the modern state—that is, to explore culture's influence on the state. Evidence considered in Chapters 3–7 demonstrates that such a conflation has indeed transpired. But given the emergence of the therapeutic state, what is and will be its subsequent influence back on culture? How, for example, does the state application of power, based on a therapeutic form of legitimation, effect culture? The manifestations of the therapeutic state's influence on culture have yet to be fully realized. Evidence considered here, however, provides hints about what the nature and likely effect of state action will be, based on this source of legitimation.

What does it mean for the state that it has adopted the therapeutic ethos as a new source of legitimation? One might reasonably propose that it matters very little. Therapeutic language and programs, on the surface, appear fairly innocuous, and in many cases, as their advocates often argue, they are efficacious. Many of the programs, based as they are on therapeutic modes of dialogue, are personal, humane, and sensitive to the individual needs of citizens benefiting from them. Is this not a welcome development? Given the nature of the modern state, however, it may not be so easy to dismiss the state's adoption of the therapeutic ethos as a benign, linguistically neutral development.

For one thing, as considered in Chapter 2, the state continues to expand itself into an increasing number of areas of societal life. In Gianfranco Poggi's terms, the state continues to advance over the state/society line: "State policy continues to impinge widely (and indeed increasingly) on the life circumstances of the citizenry."[18] According to Poggi and to economists Harold Vatter and John Walker, state expansion is a defining feature of the modern state, even in spite of the espoused intentions of politicians to slow its growth. According to Poggi, "The dynamic of the expansion and diversification of state activity expresses the push of interest lodged inside the state itself." [19] It is the very nature of the modern state.

A therapeutic basis of legitimation provides the state with the tools to continue this advance still further into the personal lives of citizens. The therapeutic orientation is concerned not only with behavior but with the internal workings of individuals—with their intentions, family relationships, motives, and so forth. How innocuous, then, is an expanding state that carries with it a therapeutic form of legitimation? Is it simply putting a happy face, as in Maryland's self-esteem efforts among state employees, on its otherwise unchanging programs? Or is there something more going on here? Therapeutic codes and symbols provide the state with the tools whereby it can continue to expand into new frontiers. This, in essence, is what William Connolly means when, in his discussion of state legitimation, he observes, "The current proclivity to characterize behavior once thought to be eccentric as mental illness in need of medical care presents merely one sign of the penetration of public-private bureaucracies into the inner citadels of private life." [20] In other words, therapeutic ideals provide the means whereby the state can expand itself still further into the private lives of its citizens.

Following Habermas, we know that language, not to mention state programs, is not neutral. Both carry with them certain understandings of the world and particular definitions of reality. We also know, following Poggi, that the state is, at its very core, coercive. [21] Political power is rooted in its ultimate authority to impose itself (with violence, if necessary) over against the will of the citizens within its domain. How, then, does the therapeutic perspective, as a new language of legitimation, serve to justify the expansion of the coercive state? Evidence presented in Chapters 3–7 of this project at least implicitly answers this question. Let me highlight a few of these previously reviewed examples, as well as some additional ones, to illustrate this point.

Therapeutic Coercion

In many states, a DWI (driving while intoxicated) offender is required to undergo alcoholism treatment, and often the condition for keeping his or her license or avoiding a jail sentence is to stay alcohol-free. [22] Many of the compulsory treatment programs, based as they are on the AA model, essentially insist that violators admit that they are alcoholics. Those refusing to accept such a pathological interpretation of their behavior can run into problems.

Consider, for example, a New Jersey woman who, nearly two years after being arrested for a drunk driving offense, was ordered to report to a county center for testing. After paying a fifty-dollar fee and taking a one hundred-question test, she was told she was an alcoholic and must report to eighteen weeks of counseling, which would cost her twenty dollars per session. She reportedly balked at participating in the program, claiming that she was not an alcoholic and that she had already paid the court-ordered penalties for her drunk driving offense. At the time, the woman was more than eight months pregnant and had not had anything to drink during her pregnancy. She never denied having been under the influence of alcohol on the night of her arrest, but she claimed that even during this time in her life, it was a rare occasion that she would drink more than a couple of glasses of beer or wine. As a result of her refusal to accept her pathological identity and corresponding treatment, the state reportedly revoked her driver's license indefinitely and considered whether to arrest her for violating a state mandate.[23]

Recall, too, Melton Roach, Jr.'s situation as a participant in one of Northern Virginia's therapeutic community prison programs. Though he was a model prisoner in many respects, staffers did not view him as ready for release because he suppressed his feelings and needed to learn to care for himself before thinking about caring for others. Likewise, Arnie Hall, at the maximum-security correction facility near Austin, Texas, failed his treatment program because he cut off his feelings and did not come to understand how his parents' treatment of him as a child helped explain his criminal activity. In both instances, the conditions for success and possible release were based in part on the participants' willingness to adopt a particular view of the world, of themselves, and of their relationships with others.

Outside the walls of state correctional facilities, a popular form of therapeutic social control is the compulsory use of "sensitivity training." This method of therapeutic "normalization," which has become an increasingly popular tool used by the state, has gained public attention through several highly publicized campus controversies, where students insensitive to certain race, gender, and sexual orientation issues have been penalized with assignments to take sensitivity training. In 1992, for example, all 150 lawmakers in the New York State Assembly were required to attend a one-day sensitivity training seminar to discuss sexual harassment.[24] Similarly, after police conflicts with homosexuals and Latinos in Washington, D.C., the entire District of Columbia police force was required to attend a department-wide multicultural sensitivity training program.[25]

In Connecticut, employers with fifty or more employees are required by a 1992 state law to enroll their managers in sensitivity training on company time. The main purpose of the training is to make managers sensitive to sexual harassment issues. Some participants observe, however, that the substance of instruction in the sessions encourages an ideological adoption of a victim mind-set. Christina Hoff Sommers, who has participated in sensitivity training sessions as a professor at Clark University, notes, for example, how trainers "take the most thin-skinned, chronically offended person in a group as the norm," giving the facilitators grounds for redefining as insensitive previously accepted behavior.[26] Lynn Chu, a member of a federal grant panel that examined sensitivity training proposals, observes that in some of the programs that she reviewed, women who did not perceive themselves as harassed were urged to "recognize their error as victims of internalized sexism." According to Chu, some of the programs "verge on indoctrination."[27]

That these sensitivity training programs can be coercive was made particularly evident in a Federal Aviation Association-sponsored seminar for air traffic controllers. According to the Federal Aviation Association (FAA), the seminars were started for the purpose of increasing racial awareness and for enlightening people "to the differences between male and female."[28] The two- to three-day workshops included, among other things, lectures, role-playing, and "experimental exercises" aimed at practically demonstrating instances of discrimination. Douglas Hartman, an air traffic controller who participated in a June 1992 training program, claimed that though the seminars were not technically required, it was generally believed that refusing to participate could mitigate one's career opportunities. "It's a matter of semantics," Hartman said. "It was mandatorily voluntary."[29] In these seminars, organizers not only propagated the victim ideology of the therapeutic ethos but self-consciously denigrated traditional systems of moral understanding. According to Hartman, "organizers condemned the Bible as sexist and religion . . . as a device of the power structure designed to keep people, particularly women, in their place."[30]

Controllers claimed the seminars went too far when "experimental exercises" included a session in which male participants were forced into a room of female colleagues who then prodded the men through a gauntlet of hands. The females reportedly touched and fondled the men's "legs, buttocks and genitalia" and made sexually demeaning comments. The experiment, which lasted for several minutes, was apparently an effort to help the men realize what female navy officers felt when they were harassed by navy aviators in the 1991 Tailhook Convention scandal. Female controllers participating in the seminar were also pressured into publicly recalling disturbing past personal experiences.[31]

After the seminar, Douglas Hartman brought a $300,000 suit against the FAA for "sexual harassment." When the seminars became public as a result of this case, the FAA reportedly stopped the program and broke contract with the consulting firm that was conducting them. It also agreed to compensate for the "psychological" injuries that participants incurred through participating in the exercises. One controller, for example, was compensated $75,000 for emotional damages as a consequence of the training seminars. These remedies came, however, only after the negative revelations of the Hartman case. Prior to this, the "mandatorily voluntary" seminars had been going on for more than five years.[32] (It is interesting to note that even the protests against the program were totally in keeping with the therapeutic orientation. Objections were based on the same cultural disposition as were the seminars.)

Though the above are certainly the exceptional examples of forced compliance with state mandates, many of the programs reviewed in Chapters 3–7 are also coercive, though perhaps less conspicuously so. Consider, for example, the Drug Courts. Here participants waive basic constitutional rights and are placed under the authoritative control of therapeutic practitioners. In this case, the court becomes directly involved in areas of the offender's life previously left outside the purview of the court. Judges and counselors get involved in the client's family, work, and social life. In most cases, moreover, the time a client is involved in the criminal justice program is extended as a consequence. Indeed, offenders often spend more time in jail than they would have if they had pled guilty to the drug charge. As Judge Stanley Goldstein tells offenders in his Drug Court:

> If you play games with me you're going to do more time in jail than if you
> never came in here in the first place. . . . You could have gone to trial and

got convicted and still do less time than you're going to do here if you keep fooling around with me. The only way you can beat me is to finish this program and graduate.[33]

Compliance with the program and acceptance of its perspective are essential prerequisites to getting out of court-sponsored treatment. Indeed, what treatment providers often look for is the adoption of a particular worldview.

For example, in a meeting between probation officer Deborah Swanson and Oakland, California, Drug Court judge Jeffrey Tauber, prior to a session of Oakland's Drug Court, Swanson commended to the judge the progress of one client who was, as she claimed, almost ready to advance to phase 3 of the treatment program. The only thing keeping the client from advancing to the final stage of treatment was that he had not had a single clean drug test. One might argue that his continued drug use should preclude him from continuing in the program, much less from graduating to the next level of treatment. Yet his was an apparently positive case because he was complying with the treatment program. He was, as Swanson claimed, "buying into the treatment." In the end, it was recommended that he be put in detox and reappear in court three weeks later.[34] The important point illustrated here is that success is evaluated in large measure by whether or not clients adopt a particular perspective.

Such a view was certainly apparent in the approaches of two counselors in the Dade County, Florida, Drug Court. According to Artie Anderson and Luis Altamirano in Dade County's treatment facility, it was important that offenders begin to see their drug use as an addiction or disease problem. Those not willing to see it as such were considered to be in denial. Apparently, this was a big problem among Hispanic clients, of whom there are many in the Dade County area. According to Altamirano, the less acculturated Latino clients are to American societal life, the more resistant they are to accepting an addiction or disease understanding of their behavior. As he explains, "Their denial is bigger." And this is because they have not had as much education about the "facts" of drug addiction as a disease. Through therapy and education, however, even those from Hispanic backgrounds come to accept this pathological interpretation of their behavior. This is the ideal, according to Anderson: "What we would like to do is have people get over their denial and say, 'Hi, I'm Joe, I'm an addict. I'm in treatment to help myself.' "[35]

State insistence on adopting components of the therapeutic worldview can be more subtle in other situations. Consider, for example, the expansion of civil cases involving emotional damage claims. One may not necessarily be inclined to argue a case on the basis of mental, psychic, or emotional damages, but because it is an increasingly accepted and efficacious way of securing monetary compensation, one is often compelled to employ this form of defense. In Chapter 3, we saw that plaintiffs who called on the expertise of psychologists or psychiatrists to aid in their cases were more likely to win. These developments doubtless make plaintiffs and their lawyers more inclined to draw on experts from therapeutic vocations and to employ therapeutically based legal strategies. Moreover, they represent avenues whereby the state becomes involved not only in the evaluation of behavior but in an assessment of the internal processes of individual psyches. Therapeutic experts testify as to the inner cognitive and emotional processes of the individual. Therapeutic codes and symbols therefore provide the state with the tools whereby it can continue to expand into new, formerly private areas of societal life.

It is also hard to deny the coercive nature of an educational system that would refuse school admission to a student because of his unwillingness to take Ritalin. In certain respects, the popular use of Prozac and Ritalin cannot but remind one of the fictional predictions of widespread drug pacifications in such futuristic novels as Aldous Huxley's *Brave New World* and Walker Percy's *Thanatos Syndrome*. That these psychopharmacological remedies parallel Huxley's "soma" is underscored by the popular perception that pervasive use of these drugs is an innocuous—indeed, welcome—phenomenon. That is, rather than Big Brother forcing something on us, Americans generally welcome these pharmaceutical remedies to perceived ailments.

Legitimation Reconsidered

Thus, although often subtly, the state employs a therapeutic form of legitimation to control socially those within its domain. In the contemporary situation, it does this by invoking the language of the therapeutic perspective, a form of language in keeping with evident tendencies in American culture. To send someone to counseling, to treatment, or to a sensitivity training seminar; to talk about self-esteem and one's emotional well-being; to appeal to the expert knowledge of psychologists; and to speak of one's victimized position in a business situation are all acceptable strategies because they are consistent with visible cultural impulses. Hence such apparently coercive measures are largely accepted by American citizens and are not seen to be coercive per se. As Lois McNay explains:

> Individuals are controlled through the power of the norm and this power is effective because it is relatively invisible. In modern society, the behavior of individuals is regulated not through overt repression but through a set of standards and values associated with normality which are set into play by a network of ostensibly beneficent and scientific forms of knowledge.[36]

In other words, the ideals of a "scientifically" based, therapeutic understanding of the world are so embedded in American culture that overt coercion is rarely necessary. Instead, most citizens naturally comply with programs and policies based on therapeutic rationales, because they are so "obviously" plausible. The basic nature of the coercive and expanding state, then, has not changed. What has changed is the source of legitimation by which the state justifies its continued expansion—an expansion that, through use of therapeutic symbols, can move into realms of societal life once left untouched by the state.

The application of a therapeutic form of legitimation represents an extension of psychologically based governmental power in the way in which Michel Foucault understands it in his work. Foucault traces the changes in the penal system from state concern with the behavior of citizens to state concern with the internal workings of citizens—with their intentions and motives, with their souls. He also observes that psychology provided the knowledge base for the new form of state authority.

What we have found here reveals a more widespread use of this base of knowledge-power. Whereas, in Foucault, the power of psychological knowledge was exercised within the enclosed walls of the prison, here we find that the universal acceptance of and access to therapeutic knowledge justifies a broader and more diffuse application of its premises for the purposes of state power. No longer is the expert authority of the therapeutic practitioner confined to the institutional parameters of the prison or the mental hospital. Instead, the popular acceptance of a therapeutic worldview allows this knowledge-power to be exercised in a number of different public and private forums. In the courtroom, in the classroom, in political debates, in congressional hearings and floor deliberations, this source of knowledge is used to legitimate state action.

The need for precluding public exposure to the (sometimes egregious) exercise of power based on this knowledge system is less necessary because of the higher value of cultural capital ascribed to it. Still, in some instances, the exercise of authority based on therapeutic justifications is still hidden from larger public observation. When the state spends a certain percentage of crime-related funds on drug and alcohol treatment and addiction prevention, do most people know the substance of this treatment? When an ADD-diagnosed child is encouraged to go into counseling, do parents know what is discussed in these sessions? Indeed, the medically and legally sanctioned principle of client confidentiality often protects counselors and the programs they run from public scrutiny.

In many cases, "treatment" and "counseling" are catchall terms that rarely elicit questioning. The DWI offender is said to be in AA, the drug offender in treatment, the problematic child in counseling. It is commonly believed that such involvements will be beneficial, or at least not detrimental. In terms of public discussion, however, the substance of what transpires in these sessions is not exposed, except in such sensationalized cases as the FAA-sponsored sensitivity seminars. Critical inquiry into the content of the various counseling proceedings is rarely pursued. Consider, for example, the state regulations for school counselors considered in Chapter 5. That counselors are necessary and that a certain number of counselors should be available to a certain number of students is accepted—indeed, required—by the various states. In terms of what the counselors do when they meet with the students, however, there is less explicit guidance or knowledge. Counselors are instructed to be concerned with the typical therapeutic ideals, such as self-esteem and the emotional and mental well-being of the child; but how counselors actually instruct children within the parameters of these ideals is not generally known or asked about.

When I asked Judge Gerald Bakarich of the emerging Sacramento, California, Drug Court what would happen in the treatment program where he will be sending clients, he did not know. Still, he pointed to the reports from other courts about treatment's efficacy and asserted that the treatment facility which the court planned to use was a good one. In discussing the viability of the treatment approach to other crimes, he referred to Western Corrections—a program that offers education and treatment to offenders of a variety of small crimes, and which Bakarich often used while presiding over another court. Again, when asked about the content of the treatment to which clients were exposed, the judge was strangely unfamiliar.[37]

In light of discussions with these counselors and observations of the treatment process, it is clear that the therapeutic model is not always a neutral one. The claim of a Los Angeles Drug Court counselor that only over time will clients begin to identify and talk about their abusive pasts, that many at first do not open up about past abuse or even realize that they were abused, is revealing.[38] It bespeaks an assumption that many of the Drug Court clients were abused and that many are initially in denial. The counselors are, in fact, looking for the admission of past abuse, just as educators are looking for children with ADD. Offenders wishing to please counselors (who are their ticket to getting out of the program) will certainly be inclined to tell counselors what they want to hear.

Thus the therapeutic experts still maintain a certain monopoly on the exercise of power based on this source of knowledge because of their credentials and ostensible qualifications to interpret and understand human behavior. And the therapeutic ideals of confidentiality and ano-nymity often make it difficult to raise to the level of public scrutiny the nature of instruction that transpires within the various counseling situations. Though there is still some sense in which the expertise of therapeutic practitioners is exercised within closed systems, this is less the case than is depicted in Foucault's assessment of the institutional application of psychologically based knowledge-power. In the contem-porary American context, the popular therapeutic ethos is more diffusely understood and employed, which makes it all the more plausible as a basis of legitimation.

The Problem of Consent

The question remains of whether this new form of legitimation will ultimately be effective in engendering confidence among American citi-zens on a long-term basis. That is, does the therapeutic system of moral understanding bring about consent, the third component of legitimacy in David Beetham's formula? Or is it only a temporary and inadequate remedy to a continuing crisis of legitimacy in the American state?

Though the issue of consent is not the focus of this book, the question of whether the therapeutic state engenders the confidence of the citizens is highly significant for determining whether the therapeutic state will be a lasting phenomenon. In light of his discussion of the disenchanting effects of rationalization, Weber would likely argue that it cannot last; that for a new source of legitimation to sustain the social order as traditional ideological systems once did, it must answer the questions that a theodicy provides. To be sure, the subjective, self-referential nature of the therapeutic model does not provide ultimate explanations for death and suffering in the way that cultural manifestations of Protestant religion once did. The defining characteristics of the therapeutic code of moral understanding, it might be argued further, are incapable of providing the moral foundation for civil society. The therapeutic emphasis on the victimized and emotive concerns of the self are tendentiously anticommunal. How, one might ask, can such an orientation effectively provide the basis for a new form of civil solidarity?

This is an important question, and one perhaps best left to the political philosopher. I suggest, however, that a source of legitimation need not necessarily be a solidarity-building force on the cultural level for it to be the basis on which the state justifies its laws and, ultimately, its authority. Irrespective of its substantive qualities, the therapeutic cultural orientation is what presently exists at the cultural level. It rests in the institutionalized background of the collective consciousness. Limited criticism notwithstanding, the widely diffused symbols of the therapeutic orientation increasingly represent the moral reference points to which individuals appeal in order to navigate their way through social life. The subjective orientation of the therapeutic disposition in effect mitigates the importance of it being both a lasting and unifying force on the cultural level and a basis of authority on the state level. In a therapeutically defined moral universe such logical consistency is not required.

Regardless of whether the therapeutic state will qualitatively replace the previous pillars of the American Republic, its institutionalization into the state in the present context provides the individual the possibility of experiencing a unifying cosmology. The president invokes the same symbols and uses the same type of language that our children experience in the schools, that we see on television talk shows, that we read in our self-help manuals, and that we hear in our consultations with counselors and even clergy. The therapeutic orientation provides an antidote to the cognitive difficulties that modern individuals have, for a long time, experienced while living in a world with highly bifurcated public and private spheres. Therefore this orientation cuts not only across the orthodox/progressive divide, as mentioned earlier, but across the private/public divide as well. It also transcends sectarian, gender, and ethnic differences. Somewhat paradoxically, then, an anticommunal ethos is the most universal moral common denominator available to individuals living in the post- or high modern world. Its institutionalization into the state extends the parameters of this "therapeutic canopy" still further.

Still, if this orientation ultimately does not serve as a cohesive force on the cultural level, won't this fact eventually become apparent and make its legitimating force less plausible? Habermas writes that a state program or procedure can "legitimize only indirectly, through references to authorities which, for their part, must be recognized."[39] He is referring here to the idea that not only is the legal-rational functioning of the state on its own an insufficient basis of legitimation, but the philosophical system appealed to by the state must be recognized as authoritarian. As Habermas explains further:

> If binding decisions are legitimate, that is, if they can be made independently of the concrete exercise of force and of the manifest threat of sanctions, and can be regularly implemented even against the interests of those affected, then they must be considered as the fulfillment of recognized norms. This unconstrained normative validity is based on the supposition that the norm could, if necessary, be justified and defended against critique. And this supposition is itself not automatic. It is the consequence of an interpretation which admits of consensus and which has a justificatory function, in other words, of a world-view which legitimizes authority.[40]

Is the therapeutic ideological system recognized in this way? Can it defend itself against critique and make state decisions and actions binding independent of "the concrete exercise of force"?

John Scharr, in his work on legitimacy, would say that it cannot; that the now-implausible philosophical systems that have been undermined over time have not been sufficiently replaced by current cultural tendencies. As he explains, "The work of dissolution is almost complete, and modern man now appears ready to attempt a life built upon no other ideal than happiness, comfort and self-expression."[41] Scharr argues that this cultural orientation cannot sustain civil life in the way that the older sources of legitimation did. It is so qualitatively different that it "places the question of authority and legitimacy on a wholly new footing," one that cannot sustain the weight of the state's justificatory needs.[42] According to Scharr, then, Weber's prediction is already manifesting itself.

If the therapeutic ethos is failing in this way, then why and how can it remain a plausible source of state legitimation? Scharr's conceptual distinction between acquiescence and consensus may be useful for addressing this question.[43] As Scharr conceives it, acquiescence can occur without there really being consent. One may acquiesce to the state's authority not because one believes the state to be legitimate, based on a strongly agreed-upon code of moral understanding, but out of "interest or necessity." Consensus, by contrast, refers to the binding and generally accepted influence of a moral order that possesses "unconstrained normative validity," in the way Habermas refers to it. The latter elicits consent on a much deeper and more widespread level.

Which best characterizes the therapeutic basis of legitimation in the American state: acquiescence or consensus? Consider contemporary policy proposals for addressing crime in the United States. Here one finds not only the growing application of treatment and education approaches but a concomitant and harsher tough-on-crime, "three strikes and you're out" attitude. The presence of both tendencies may suggest that state authority is ultimately accepted not because of the universal and unquestioned salience of a therapeutic form of legitimation but because the state is, at its core, coercive. Understood in this way, the therapeutic system of moral understanding is not one that "can be made independently of the concrete exercise of force." Rather, it is the soft front or veneer of a state system whose authority rests ultimately in its power to enforce its authority physically. It is a smiley face with a wink.

If this is true, state adoption of the therapeutic consciousness represents a thinly veiled, and perhaps temporary, basis of state legitimation. The fact that it may be temporary does not mean that it is not, at the present moment, effectively serving its legitimating purpose. The general popularity of the therapeutic ethos in the culture and the substantial adoption of it by the state, as shown in this study, suggest that the therapeutic code of moral understanding is presently more than just a thin veil. In many instances, acceptance of it is more than mere acquiescence.

But how long consent will be characterized by consensus rather than acquiescence remains a question that only time will answer. In the meantime, one must ask: How will a therapeutically legitimated political order change the very nature of the state? Émile Durkheim once envisioned a central function of the modern state to be the protection of individual liberties. This was certainly a central feature of the American political experiment. In keeping with this legacy, the therapeutic state does promise a liberation of sorts. But will it protect the liberty of the individual in the way Durkheim argued it should in the modern context? Or will the consequences of the therapeutic state be something quite distinct from the maintenance of liberty?

The Paradox of Unintended Consequences

Just as the Protestant forebears to capitalism's triumph, as depicted in Weber's *Protestant Ethic,* did not intend that their particular religious orientation would result in the kind of capitalistic system that it produced, so, it seems, the practitioners of the therapeutic orientation do not see the institutional applications of the therapeutic model as coercive or in any way a violation of individual liberties. The various judges, probation officers, social workers, treatment providers, and educators that I talked with, observed, and read about in most cases appear to have a genuine concern for people and an earnest desire to offer help and assistance. They generally evidenced an atypical regard for, and commitment to, helping their fellow citizens and, in many cases, gave sacrificially of themselves toward this end.

Based on the belief systems that they hold, these individuals are doing the most they can to help people. When Judge Goldstein says he views the clients/offenders who come into his courtroom as children whom he desperately wants to see succeed, he views his program as something that liberates people, that gets them off the cycle of destructive drug use. Assemblyman John Vasconcellos believes that humans are naturally inclined to live "constructive, responsible lives"; on this understanding, the best thing that a parent or teacher can do for a child is to build the child's self-esteem and foster his or her natural inclination toward good. Based on a similar perspective, members of the U.S. Congress believe that Head Start and Parents Anonymous are the types of programs that will genuinely help America's families. Advocates of various sensitivity training seminars sincerely believe that these programs will build greater tolerance and understanding among individuals from different groups.

The state is, in many instances, trying to offer a soft touch to the harshness of life in a highly rationalized society. Educators who eliminate grades and encourage self-esteem are seeking to assuage the stress of an overcompetitive environment. Drug Court programs offer defendants a cooperative rather than an adversarial climate for handling their offense, where the judge, instead of punishing, wants to help. Treatment providers celebrate the possibility of retrieving for the offender a clean criminal record, so he or she will not be forgotten by a system that discriminates against people with such backgrounds. Welfare programs seek to build the emotional well-being and self-esteem of children so that they might break out of the cycle of poverty. Politicians offer a politics of meaning to address the problem of individual alienation in modern life. And so the story goes. The various programs and policies aver a liberation of sorts.

Though it is not the purpose of this project to judge the efficacy or the soundness of these various programs, it is difficult to argue with the stories of individuals who have undeniably been helped by them. The testimonies of individuals who, through participation in the Drug Courts, have gotten off drugs and have been able to secure jobs, without the very real problem of a criminal record, are certainly persuasive. So, too, are the stories of children who, with the assistance of Head Start, have been rescued from the problems of illiteracy, gang involvement, and drug use. Liberation, then, has been realized, at least in some cases.

Still, the larger sociohistorical perspective on the matter reveals that these programs and policies do not recover the same kind of human touch and social concern that existed prior to the onset of industrialism. Without historical context, what often goes unnoticed is that the therapeutic form of humanitarianism is a completely new form. The mystical and spiritual elements of life that many in the contemporary context wish to resurrect were previously rooted not in the self but in external systems of moral understanding. In each of the areas of the state, we traced the process whereby the forces of modern rationalism undermined classical and traditional religious understandings of the world. The religious ideals of suffering and death that made personal injury law obsolete, the religiously based purpose for education evident in early American statutes and in the instructional content of the *New England Primer* and the *McGuffey Readers,* the philanthropic efforts toward the poor among early American pietists in the area of social welfare, and the invocation of providence by politicians in early American public discourse are all examples of the manner in which society sought to touch, educate, and provide for its people.

Because of the effects of modernization, however, any effort to return to religiously based approaches is wholly implausible. Thus restoring some type of caring touch in the high modern or postmodern context must be based on something else—something that has universal appeal, is cross-cultural, and is nonreligious in a sectarian sense. The therapeutic ethos fits these requirements. What goes unnoticed is that therapeutic tools, like the religiously based tools and ideas that preceded them, are not neutral. They carry with them certain understandings of the individual, society, and the world.[44] And as discussed above, these tools ostensibly offer the individual the liberating prospect of being able to re-create himself or herself.

But is liberation really the effect of a state committed to therapeutic utilitarianism? Just as the cultural orientation that resulted in modern capitalism, according to Weber, had disenchanting and unintended consequences, so, it seems, the institutional effects of a therapeutic source of legitimation may also eventuate in consequences unintended by its advocates. What promises the advancement of freedom may also result in unintended restrictions on individual liberty. Weber's modern iron cage may become the postmodern padded cage. Foucault may have been the first to identify the infringements on freedom that institutionalized psychology visits upon the individual. In *Madness and Civilization*, Foucault argued that the modern normalizing and medicalizing processes, based as they are on an ostensibly objective basis of knowledge, in effect alienate and deprive fundamental liberties to the one labeled as mad. The result of the labeling process is that the one categorized as mad loses his or her voice.

These are the main polemical issues with which both Andrew Polsky and Thomas Szasz were concerned in their respective works on social welfare and insanity-based criminal defenses. According to Polsky, therapeutic practitioners in the state social services use a psychoanalytic disciplinary approach to "normalize" marginal citizens, subsequently violating their freedoms. Likewise, the libertarian Szasz views the use of psychiatry within certain dimensions of the criminal justice system as an egregious violation of liberty.

Does state appropriation of the therapeutic ethos represent a challenge to individual liberties? It may be too early to tell. Still, some developments suggest that, at the least, it might. Recall the moment in the film *One Flew Over the Cuckoo's Nest* when McMurphy, while in the pool of the treatment facility in which he was detained, told the attendant that he had only so many days left in his sentence. The attendant informed McMurphy that his tenure at the facility was indefinite; it was the treatment personnel, rather than court or law enforcement personnel, who would determine when he was ready to be released. Here the power to determine the length of one's sentence, not to mention the health of one's mental condition, was left in the hands of the therapeutic practitioners. In a similar, though less glaring, way, Drug Court participants are held under the authority of the court for an undetermined period of time. If they leave town or miss counseling or court appointments, the judge puts out a bench warrant for their arrest. Questions about liberty also arise when one is told by the state that one must take a certain therapeutic drug to attend public school, attend a sensitivity training seminar to stay in school or to keep a certain job, adopt a particular understanding of oneself and of one's relationships to get out of prison, pay higher health insurance premiums to cover state-required mental health costs, and the like.

This is not to suggest that previous moral orders did not violate individual liberties. The religious justifications for slavery and civil rights violations certainly provide examples of the way in which they did. But these older meaning systems also provided the cultural basis for protesting against—and in some cases triumphing over—violations of liberty and justice. Therapeutic knowledge, like religion, is not neutral but provides a source of power whereby individuals can be controlled. Increasingly, the answer to a legal infraction or a breach in social protocol is counseling, treatment, or sensitivity training. And because of the cultural salience of therapeutic knowledge, these forms of social control are largely accepted. But does the therapeutic system of meaning contain within it the moral grounds for opposing these taken-for-granted practices if somehow they were to seriously inhibit freedom?

The extent to which the liberty promised by the therapeutic system of moral understanding is realized will certainly play a part in determining the nature of consent. But even if consent is not characterized by consensus, this is not to say that citizens will not have to acquiesce to state authority that is therapeutically justified. The history of other state systems reveals that this has happened before. Again, it is too early to tell what effects the American therapeutic state will ultimately have on culture. It is, however, safe to conclude that the state has adopted elements of the therapeutic impulse as a new form of legitimation, the application of which portends a transformation in the very nature of the state and in the way state authority is exercised over the citizens within its domain.

Appendix 1

TABLE A.1

Federal Social Welfare Expenditures, 1960–1990
(in billions of dollars)

	1960	1970	1980	1990
Social Insurance	14	45	191	419
Public Aid	2	10	49	93
Veterans	5	9	21	31
Health and Medical		16	69	188
Education	1	6	13	18
Housing	0.2	1	6	17

SOURCE: *Statistical Abstract of the United States 1993*, Table 578, p. 368; and *Historical Statistics, Colonial Times to 1970*, Series H 32–47, p. 341. "Health and Medical" includes medical services provided within social insurance, public aid, veterans, vocational rehabilitation, and antipoverty programs. In 1960, this category did not exist.

Appendix 2

TABLE A.2
Percent Voting in Presidential Elections

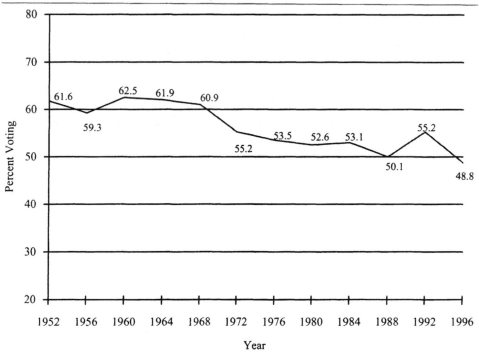

SOURCE: Based on *Statistical Abstract of the United States 1992,*Table 455, p. 284; and *Congressional Quarterly Weekly Report,* 9 November 1996, p. 3194.

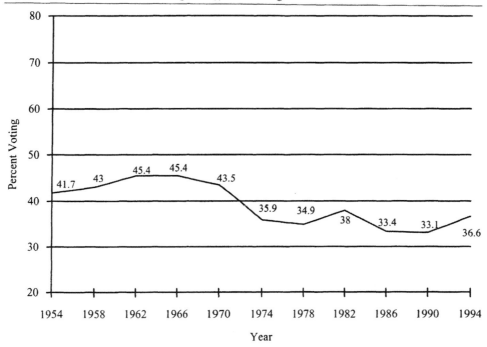

Percent Voting in Off-Year Congressional Elections

SOURCE: Based on *Statistical Abstract of the United States 1993*, Table 455, p. 284; and *America Votes 21: A Handbook of Contemporary American Election Statistics,* comp. and ed. Richard M. Scammon and Alice V. McGillivray (Washington, D.C.: Elections Research Center, Congressional Quarterly, 1995).

Appendix 3

TABLE A.3
Trust in Government

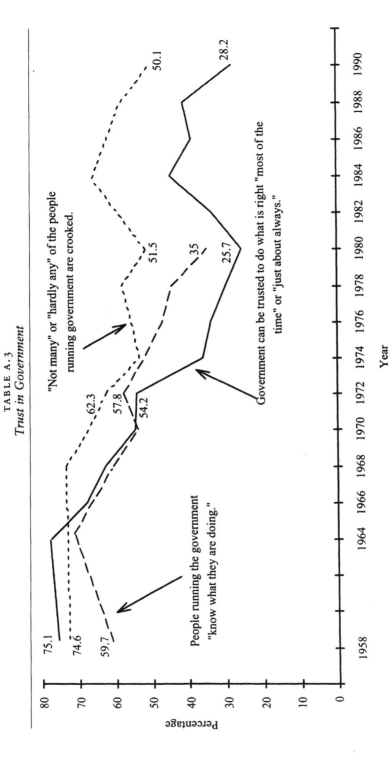

Year

SOURCE: Center for Political Studies, University of Michigan, American National Election Studies, 1952–1990 Cumulative Data File, distributed by Inter-University Consortium for Political and Social Research, Ann Arbor, Michigan. The questions represented in this table were not asked in 1960 and 1962.

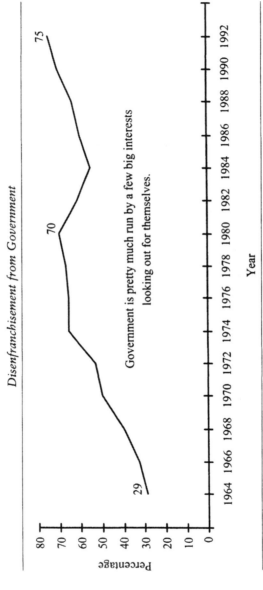

Disenfranchisement from Government

Government is pretty much run by a few big interests looking out for themselves.

Percentage

Year

1964 1966 1968 1970 1972 1974 1976 1978 1980 1982 1984 1986 1988 1990 1992

SOURCE: Center for Political Studies, University of Michigan, American National Election Studies, 1952–1990 Cumulative Data File and 1992 NES results, distributed by Inter-University Consortium for Political and Social Research, Ann Arbor, Michigan.

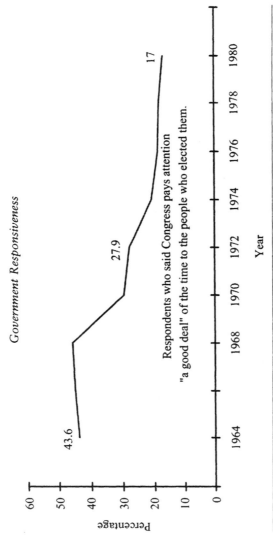

Government Responsiveness

Percentage

60 50 40 30 20 10 0

1964   1968   1970   1972   1974   1976   1978   1980

Year

43.6

27.9

17

Respondents who said Congress pays attention
"a good deal" of the time to the people who elected them.

SOURCE: Center for Political Studies, University of Michigan, American National Election Studies, 1952–1990 Cumulative Data File, distributed by Inter-University Consortium for Political and Social Research, Ann Arbor, Michigan. This question was not asked by the NES in 1966.

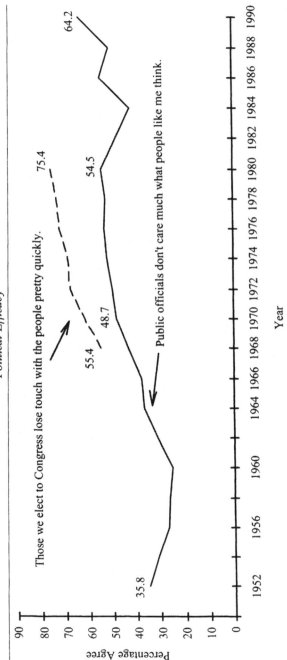

Political Efficacy

Those we elect to Congress lose touch with the people pretty quickly.

75.4

55.4

48.7

35.8

64.2

54.5

Public officials don't care much what people like me think.

Year

1952 1956 1960 1964 1966 1968 1970 1972 1974 1976 1978 1980 1982 1984 1986 1988 1990

Percentage Agree

90 80 70 60 50 40 30 20 10 0

SOURCE: Center for Political Studies, University of Michigan, American National Election Studies, 1952–1990 Cumulative Data File, distributed by Inter-University Consortium for Political and Social Research, Ann Arbor, Michigan. Question about public officials not caring what "people like me think" was not asked by the NES in 1954, 1958, and 1962.

Appendix 4

TABLE A.4
Confidence in Government

Government entity	Percent with "some" or "very little" confidence
Federal Government	69%
State Government	62%
The Presidency	62%
Congress	75%

SOURCE: *The State of Disunion* survey (Charlottesville, Va.: The Post-Modernity Project, University of Virginia, 1996). Table indicates the percentages of those surveyed.

Objections to Politics and Government

Objection	Percent agreeing or mostly agreeing with stated objection
Elected officials don't care what people like me think.	69%
Our system is good, but the people running it are incompetent.	66%
Leaders are more concerned with managing their images than with solving our nation's problems.	78%
Government is run by a few big interests looking out for themselves.	81%
Political events these days seem more like theater or entertainment than like something to be taken seriously.	80%
Our country is run by a close network of special interests, public officials, and the media.	81%
The federal government controls too much of our daily lives.	63%
People like me don't have any say in what the government does.	60%
Politicians are more interested in winning elections than in doing what is right.	79%

SOURCE: *The State of Disunion* survey (Charlottesville, Va.: The Post-Modernity Project, University of Virginia, 1996). Table indicates the percentage of those surveyed who chose "agree" or "mostly agree" in response to each of the above statements.

Appendix 5

TABLE A.5
State Self-Esteem Legislation

State	Date	Code	Area	Statutory language
Alaska	1993	AS 47.18.100	Social Services	(a) Projects funded under AS 47.18.100 shall be designed with a holistic approach that recognizes the interconnectedness of adolescent parenthood and a broad array of related circumstances, such as low self-esteem, domestic violence, substance abuse . . .
	1994	AS 47.21.010	Social Services	(b) Adventure-based education is a short-term, intensive training program designed to remedy failure patterns and encourage development of self-esteem, self-confidence, and social awareness
California	1994	Cal Well & Inst Code 727.1	Corrections	SEC. 2.(a) It is the intention of the Legislature by this section of this act to reduce the recidivism rate of juvenile offenders by increasing their self-esteem and encouraging them to become involved in interpersonal relationships, through the use of trained volunteers who provide them with individualized attention and direction.
	1994	Cal Ed Code 58901	Education	(h) The Legislature intends to foster, by the Demonstration of Restructuring in Public Education, improved education for California's pupils by assisting educators to do all of the following: (1) Foster self-esteem and a sense of belonging. . . .
Colorado	1994	CRS 8–12–102	Labor	Work is an integral factor in providing a sense of purpose, direction, and self-esteem necessary to the overall physical and mental health of an individual.
Florida	1993	Fla. Stat. 228.501	Education	The Department of Education shall revise curriculum frameworks, as appropriate, to include building self-esteem and enhancing decision making skills. Each such revised framework shall be approved . . . by the State Board of Education.
Georgia	1994	OCGA 20–2–143	Education	Such standards shall include instruction relating to the handling of peer pressure, promotion of high self-esteem, local community values, and abstinence from sexual activity as an effective method of prevention of pregnancy, sexually transmitted disease, and AIDS.
	1994	OCGA 20–2–1031	Education	These partnerships further promote better student achievement, higher self-esteem, closer community ties to the public schools. . . .
Hawaii	1993	HRS 226–3	Economic Development	Society's role is to encourage conditions within which individuals and groups can approach their desired levels of self-reliance and self-determination. This enables people to gain confidence and self-esteem; citizens contribute more when they possess such qualities . . .

TABLE A.5 (continued)

State	Date	Code	Area	Statutory language
Illinois	1993	HRS 321–241.5	Health	The department of health, in cooperation with the department of education, may establish a statewide teenage health program designed to enhance self-esteem...
	1994	105 ILCS 5/27-32.2	Education	The curriculum shall emphasize methods for increasing the life-coping skills, self-esteem and parenting skills of adolescents and teenagers.... The State Board of Education shall distribute the curriculum format and instructional materials therefore to all school districts...
	1994	730 ILCS 5/3–9–1	Corrections	c) The Dept. of Corrections shall develop and establish a suicide reduction program in all institutions or facilities housing persons committed to the Juvenile Division. The program shall be designed to increase the life coping skills and self-esteem of juvenile offenders...
Iowa	1993	IC 279.50	Education	Each school board shall provide instruction in human growth and development including instruction regarding human sexuality, self-esteem, stress management, interpersonal relationships, domestic abuse, and AIDS as required in section 256.11, in grades one through twelve.
Kansas	1994	Kan. ALS 265	Labor	. . . [11] understanding employer requirements and expectations, telephone canvassing for job leads, proper dress and conduct on the job and ways to enhance self-esteem, self-image and confidence.
Louisiana	1993	La.R.S.17:3951	Education	A. (1) The legislature hereby recognizes that healthy self-esteem and a sense of personal and social responsibility is a crucial factor in the lives of all persons and often is at the core of the quality of their lives. (2) The legislature further recognizes that the root cause of many of our major social problems, including, but not limited to, crimes of violence, chronic alcoholism and drug abuse, spousal and child abuse, teenage pregnancy, poverty and chronic welfare dependency, and homelessness, are due to lack of healthy self-esteem and sense of personal and social responsibility. (3) The legislature further recognizes that low self-esteem has wide-ranging, negative influences on individual human behavior, the costs of which both in human and societal terms are manifested in a number of ways, many of which convert into significant expenditure of state monies. B. The legislature declares, therefore, that it is the purpose of this Chapter to create the Louisiana Commission on Promoting Esteem in order to develop a statewide, comprehensive, coordinated plan to significantly increase and promote healthy self-esteem and a sense of personal and social responsibility among the citizens of our state...
	1994	La.ALS 47	Education	Any public elementary or secondary school in Louisiana may offer instruction in violence prevention, self-esteem, and peer mediation. The curriculum for such instruction shall be developed and approved by the State Board of Secondary Education.

State	Year	Citation	Category	
Maine	1993	20-A M.R.S.	Education	F. The school has a climate which promotes individual self-esteem, high expectations for achievement and a positive attitude toward learning.
Massachusetts	1994	MAL ch. 69:1	Education	It is therefore the intent of this title to ensure: (1) that each public school classroom provides the conditions for all pupils to engage fully in learning as an inherently meaningful and enjoyable activity without threats to their sense of security or self-esteem.
Minnesota	1994	Minn. ALS 636	Corrections	(A) The initiative programs shall contain programs designed to promote the inmate's self-esteem, self-discipline, and economic self-sufficiency by providing structured training and education with respect to basic life skills, including, . . . (2) wilderness camping experiences that ensure that youth begin to build self-esteem about themselves.
Missouri	1993	191.598 R.S.Mo.	Health and Welfare	. . . (b) Emotional health topics including; a. Preventing depression and suicide; b. Managing stress; c. Self esteem . . .
Montana	1993	Mont. Code Anno. 27–1–202	Civil Liability	. . . issue on mental and emotional distress when jury was properly instructed on proximate cause and damages were related to a franchisor's unreasonable failure to evaluate relocation of franchise, causing franchisees' sense of loss and devastation, loss of self-esteem, and feeling of shame . . .
New Jersey	1993	N.J. Stat. 18A:35–4.15	Education	The Legislature finds and declares that: a. chess increases strategic thinking skills, stimulates intellectual creativity, and improves problem-solving ability while raising self-esteem.
New York	1994	NY CLS Family Ct Act 141	Juvenile Delinquency	Mental Health Services (MHS) psychologist recommended appellant be placed in structured environment where his behavior could be monitored and he could receive counseling to help him acquire self-esteem and self-control. . . . Psychologist and certified social worker testified that placement away from home would damage appellant's self-esteem . . .
North Carolina	1993	N.C. Gen. Stat. 148–1	Corrections	Whereas, self-esteem and self-discipline are key elements in helping inmates develop employable skills and positive work habits; and Whereas, other states have had highly successful programs utilizing the Napoleon Hill Foundation's PMA Science of Success course, which focuses on the development of self-esteem, self-discipline, and other principles of successful living; Now, therefore, The General Assembly of North Carolina enacts: Section 1. The Division of Prisons of the Department of Corrections shall undertake a pilot program to determine whether an inmate study course based on developing positive mental attitudes through self-esteem and self-discipline will affect the incidence of institutional disciplinary infractions and recidivism. The pilot program shall be set up at a minimum of six sites statewide.

TABLE A.5 (continued)

State	Date	Code	Area	Statutory language
	1993	N.C. Gen. Stat. 115C–238.14	Education	(7) Programs shall provide each student a school-based adult advocate to foster self-esteem, protect learning options, ensure that students needs are being met, and ensure that students are being treated equitably.
Ohio	1994	ORC Ann. 2951–02	Corrections	. . probation conditions; need for court-appointed counsel relates directly to underlying crimes, and acceptance of responsibility for full consequences by repayment enhances probationer's self-esteem in community and contributes to his rehabilitation.
Oregon	1993	ORS 336.455	Education	(j) Assist students in the development and practice of effective communication skills, the development of self-esteem and the ability to resist peer pressure.
	1993	ORS 421.500	Corrections	(3) The absence of a program that instills discipline, enhances self-esteem and promotes alternatives to criminal behavior has a major impact on overcrowding of prisons and criminal recidivism in this state.
Pennsylvania	1994	62 P.S. 2172	Social Services	(1) The family is the basic institution in society in which our children's sense of self-esteem and positive self-image are developed and nurtured. These feelings and values are essential to a healthy, productive and independent life during childhood.
Rhode Island	1993	R.I. Gen. Laws 23–13–20	Health	. . that the complex social problems of teenage pregnancy be addressed by the thoughtful orchestration of community institutions and interest groups to support a sound school program designed both to enhance the personal competence and self-esteem of youth, and improve parent skills in providing explicit sexuality education in the home.
South Carolina	1993	S.C. ALS 344	Health	. . principles of sharing ordinary places, developing meaningful relationships, learning things that are useful, making choices, as well as promoting an individual's self-esteem.
Tennessee	1994	Tenn. Code Ann. 4–3–2626	Youth Development	An entity may contract with the department to operate more than one (1) program. Each such model program shall serve not more than twenty-five (25) adolescents and shall strive to improve self-esteem . . .
Texas	1994	Tex. Educ. Code 21.929	Education	(c) Programs for parents of children enrolled in school must include training parents in helping their children develop: (1) self-esteem . . .
Utah	1994	Utah Code Ann. 53A–15–204	Education	(1) There is appropriated for fiscal year 1993–94 $60,000 to be used for a pilot program designed to increase the self-esteem and the physical, intellectual, and life skills of students with disabilities through a holistic integrated arts program.
	1994	Utah Code Ann. 53A–15–601	Education	. . Fund to the State Board of Education for fiscal year 1993–94 $100,000 to be used for a gang prevention and intervention program designed to help at-risk students stay in school and enhance self-esteem and intellectual life skills.

Virginia	1994	Va. Code Ann. 22.1–253.13:1	Education	These objectives shall include, but not be limited to, basic skills of communication, computation and critical reasoning including problem solving and decision making, and the development of personal qualities such as self-esteem. . . . School boards shall implement these objectives . . .
Washington	1994	Rev. Code Wash. 43.270.020	Education	Activities which may be funded through this program include those which: (1) Prevent substance abuse through educational and self-esteem efforts . . .
	1994	Rev. Code Wash. 43.310	Corrections	Cultural Awareness retreats shall include but are not limited to the following programs: (1) To develop positive attitudes and self-esteem.
West Virginia	1994	W.Va. Code 18–8A–1	Education	. . . programs and materials must be made available to homeless and at risk children to assure opportunities for an equal education. Programs shall include . . . self esteem enhancement, behavior modification and other programs relating to student development.
Wisconsin	1993	Wis. Stat. 115.362	Education	. . . for grades kindergarten to 12. 4. Provide instruction to pupils in communication, problem solving and decision making, dealing effectively with peer pressure, critical thinking, stress reduction, self improvement and self-esteem.

Federal Self-Esteem Regulations

Agency/Regulation	Date	Program	Regulatory language
HHS 59 FR 37342	1994	Administration for Native Americans: Availability of Financial Assistance	Establishing programs which involve extended families or tribal societies in activities that strengthen cultural identity and promote community development or self-esteem.
USDA 59 FR 26783	1994	Battery Creek High School Recreational RC&D Project	The Battery Creek High School has an enrollment of 1,200 students of which 61.5% are minority. Improved recreational facilities will enable students to practice and compete with other schools which will increase self-esteem, reduce dropout rate . . . .
Dept. of Education 55 FR 29649	1990	Indian Nations at Risk Task Force: Invitation for Submission of Papers on Indian Education Issues	Examine strategies to enhance the development of positive self-esteem through exposure to culturally congruent curriculum and instructional methods and rigorous academic coursework.
Dept. of Education 57 FR 52682	1992	Special Projects and Demonstrations for Providing Vocational Rehabilitation Services to Individuals with Severe Handicaps	. . . among relevant agencies, such as rehabilitation service providers, law enforcement agencies, and drug treatment programs in the formulation, implementation, and evaluation of rehabilitation programming; (d) training in social effectiveness, decisionmaking skills, self-esteem, and assertiveness . . .
Dept. of Education 57 FR 49274	1992	Deaf Students Education Services	Compounding the manifest educational considerations, the communication nature of the disability is inherently isolating, with considerable effect on the interaction with peers and teachers that make up the educational process. This interaction, for the purpose of transmitting knowledge and developing the child's self-esteem and identity, is dependent upon direct communication.
United States Information Agency 57 FR 34338	1992	Group Projects for International Visitor Grantees	Additionally, emphasis will be placed on the non-monetary benefits which these individuals realize through their volunteer efforts such as enhanced self-esteem and greater social awareness.
Dept. of Education 57 FR 31614	1992	Research in Education of Individuals with Disabilities Program	The keys to change are programs, parents, and education or rehabilitation professionals that emphasize independence more than the performance of basic social and vocational skills. The development of individuality, self-esteem, goal oriented behavior, assertive behavior, and decision making ability are also critical outcomes.

Agency	Year	Title	Excerpt
Dept. of Education 49 FR 18607	1984	Correctional Education Policy Statement	. . . job skills aggravate a released offender's difficulties in securing employment, thus, influencing the return to crime. However, with the tools for survival—basic education and a marketable job skill, coupled with the rise in self-esteem which is the inevitable result of achievement—a released inmate's chances for rehabilitation are considerably increased.
HHS 49 FR 49727	1984	Announcement of Availability of Grants for Research on Adolescent Family Life	4. What is the impact, both positive and negative, of pregnancy and childbearing, on the adolescent's sense of self-esteem? Is there a developmental progression, i.e. higher self-esteem during pregnancy, lower self-esteem as the infant becomes more demanding? Proposals addressing these questions should be mindful of existing research that suggests that certain aspects of the adolescent's psychological development, i.e. low self-esteem, and poor interpersonal and familial relations, may have led to the adolescent pregnancy.
Dept. of Education 50 FR 46810	1985	National Institute of Handicapped Research; Funding Priorities, FY 1986	Low self-esteem, lack of social skills, and disorganization are characteristics often found in children with severe learning disabilities. Disruptive and other behaviors associated with these characteristics frequently lead to family dysfunction, and thus inadequate care for the learning. . . .
EPA 50 FR 47142	1985	National Primary Drinking Water Regulations; Fluoride	An independent panel, convened at EPA's request to study the question of psychological and behavioral effects, concluded that persons with dental fluorosis could be at risk of "behavior problems" as a result of an "impaired self-image" or "loss of self-esteem."
Commerce (NOAA) 51 FR 32334	1986	Northern Anchovy Fishery: Notice of final harvest quotas	These proposals will involve those recipients who are able to work in work activities. They will increase the self-esteem and employability of many recipients and will promote self-support through jobs in the regular economy.

Federal Self-Esteem Regulations (continued)

Agency/Regulation	Date	Program	Regulatory language
HHS 51 FR 34712	1986	Announcement of availability of funds and request for applications under the Office of Human Development Services' Coordinated Discretionary Fund's Program.	Among Indian students participating in public school systems, feelings of isolation and low self-esteem are promoted by their minority status and the absence of culture-sensitive services which deal with Indians as members of a special group with an honored heritage. Evidence of insensitivity to Indianness in school curricula is frequent, and failure to "connect" with Indian children and youth is a common occurrence.
Dept. of Education 53 FR 32092	1988	Office of Elementary and Secondary Education; Intent to Repay to the New Jersey State Department of Education Funds Recovered as a Result of Final Audit Determinations	. . . $42,210 of the grantback will be used to purchase 20 computers, and the remaining $27,725 will be used to pay for teachers' salaries and benefits. Students will participate in motivational activities to improve attendance and strengthen self-esteem. The program will be provided for eight weeks in September and October 1988. The computers that will be purchased with grantback funds will also be used by eligible students in PSD's regular school year . . .
Dept. of Education 57 FR 20162	1992	Cooperative Demonstration Program (Correctional Education)	Seven commenters offered recommendations regarding specific curriculum components, program structure, and staffing. The curriculum components that commenters felt should be specifically addressed include high school equivalency preparation, self-esteem, ethics, social skills, life skills preventative programs, decision-making skills, prevocational and career assessment, and non-traditional vocational training for female offenders.

Notes

NOTES TO CHAPTER 1

1. Peter Berger, "Toward a Sociological Understanding of Psychoanalysis," *Social Research*, 32 (1965), 27.

2. Martin L. Gross, *The Psychological Society* (New York: Random House, 1978).

3. Charles Sykes, *A Nation of Victims: The Decay of the American Character* (New York: St. Martin's Press, 1992).

4. Philip Rieff, *The Triumph of the Therapeutic* (Chicago: University of Chicago Press, 1966).

5. Christopher Lasch, *The Culture of Narcissism* (New York: W. W. Norton & Co., 1978).

6. Bernie Zilbergeld, *The Shrinking of America* (Boston: Little, Brown & Co., 1983).

7. Robert Bellah et al., *Habits of the Heart: Individualism and Commitment in American Life* (Berkeley: University of California Press, 1985).

8. Richard Sennett, *The Fall of Public Man: On the Social Psychology of Capitalism* (New York: Vintage Books, 1976).

9. James Collier, *The Rise of Selfishness in America* (Oxford: Oxford University Press, 1991).

10. Daniel Bell, *The Cultural Contradictions of Capitalism* (New York: Basic Books, 1976), p. xxi.

11. Alasdair MacIntyre, *After Virtue: A Study in Moral Theory* (Notre Dame, Ind.: University of Notre Dame Press, 1984), p. 24.

12. John Stedman Rice very cogently advances this distinction in *A Disease of One's Own: Psychotherapy, Addiction, and the Emergence of Co-Dependency* (New Brunswick, N.J.: Transaction Publishers, 1996).

13. Bell, *Cultural Contradictions of Capitalism*, p. 72.

14. "Discourse on Inequality," in *Rousseau's Political Writings*, ed. Alan Ritter (New York: W.W. Norton & Co., 1988), pp. 26–29.

15. Carl Rogers, *On Becoming a Person* (Boston: Houghton Mifflin Co., 1961), pp. 91.

16. From telephone conversation with Anna Lisa Damley, in the research

department of *Self* magazine, on October 14, 1994. The total circulation for *Self* in June 1994 was 1,250,102—724,626 by subscribers and 532,476 off newsstands.

17. *Books in Print: 1993–94* (New York: R. R. Bowker Co.) was updated to the computer listing of *Books in Print* on October 11, 1994.

18. *Books in Print: An Author-Title-Series Index to the Publishers' Trade List Annual,* 1978 and 1950, ed. B. A. Uhlendorf (New York: R. R. Bowker Co.).

19. These terms are offered by Charles Sykes, Kenneth Gergen, Michael Sandel, Alasdair MacIntyre, and Daniel Bell, respectively.

20. Rieff, *Triumph of the Therapeutic,* p. 5.

21. Sennett, *Fall of Public Man,* p. 22.

22. Bell, *Cultural Contradictions of Capitalism,* p. 72.

23. Jean Bethke Elshtain, *Meditations on Modern Political Thought* (New York: Praeger Publishers, 1986), p. 92. Also see James Davison Hunter's *Before the Shooting Begins: Searching for Democracy in America's Culture Wars* (New York: Free Press, 1993), where he finds sentimental or emotivist discourse to be a dominant element of public debates over the controversial abortion issue.

24. Edwin Schur, *The Awareness Trap: Self-Absorption instead of Social Change* (New York: Quadrangle/ The New York Times Book Co., 1976), p. 17.

25. As cited in ibid., p. 18.

26. See Berger's excursus in Peter Berger, Brigitte Berger, and Hansfried Keller, *The Homeless Mind* (New York: Vintage Books, 1974), pp. 83–96; and Lionel Trilling, *Sincerity and Authenticity* (Cambridge, Mass.: Harvard University Press, 1972).

27. MacIntyre, *After Virtue,* p. 22.

28. Rieff, *Triumph of the Therapeutic,* p. 255.

29. Ibid., p. 249.

30. Zilbergeld, *Shrinking of America,* p. 32.

31. Ellen Herman, *The Romance of American Psychology: Political Culture in the Age of Experts* (Berkeley: University of California Press, 1995), p. 3.

32. Ibid.

33. Ibid.

34. Zilbergeld, *Shrinking of America,* p. 33. Also consider John Rice's discussion of the "therapeutic foundation" in "A Disease of One's Own: Psychotherapy, Addiction, and the Emergence of 'Co-Dependency' " (Ph.D. diss., University of Virginia, Charlottesville, May 1992), pp. 27–31 .

35. James Davison Hunter, "The Modern Malaise," in *Making Sense of Modern Times,* ed. James Davison Hunter and Stephen C. Ainlay (New York: Routledge & Kegan Paul, 1986), p. 92.

36. Only computer science and biology edged out psychology, but not by very much. See Herman, *Romance of American Psychology,* p. 3.

37. Ibid., pp. 2–3.

38. Os Guinness, "America's Last Men and Their Magnificent Talking Cure" (unpublished paper, Burke, Virginia, 1991), p. 7.

39. Hunter, "Modern Malaise," p. 88.

40. From telephone conversation with Jennifer Ogdon, in the circulation department of *Psychology Today,* on February 28, 1995. Of the 325,000 copies sold each month, 63.5 percent are from subscriptions, and 36.5 percent are from single-copy sales.

41. Zilbergeld, *Shrinking of America,* p. 32.

42. Christopher Lasch, *Haven in a Heartless World* (New York: Basic Books, 1977), p. 100.

43. Rieff, *Triumph of the Therapeutic,* p. 3.

44. MacIntyre, *After Virtue,* p. 13.

45. Lasch, *Haven in a Heartless World,* p. 98. Also, Charles Sykes quips, "In place of evil therapeutic society has substituted 'illness' " (*Nation of Victims,* p. 13).

46. Stanton Peele, *Diseasing of America: Addiction Treatment Out of Control* (Toronto: Lexington Books, 1989), p. 46.

47. Cited in Herbert Fingarette, *Heavy Drinking: The Myth of Alcoholism as a Disease* (Berkeley: University of California Press, 1988), p. 13.

48. Ibid., p. 18.

49. The disease view of alcoholism can actually be traced back to Benjamin Rush, a physician and signer of the Declaration of Independence, who in 1785 advanced the notion that excessive drinking was an illness. However, Rush's views were not given scientific validation until the late 1940s when the Yale Center of Alcohol Studies endorsed the disease view of alcoholism. Elvin Jellineck, the most well known member of the center, produced two seminal articles that ostensibly offered empirical support for this view. In the 1940s members of the Yale Center joined with prominent members of AA to create the National Council of Alcoholics (NCA), which publicly and aggressively advanced the notion that alcoholism is a disease that must be treated.

50. John Rice, in *A Disease of One's Own,* makes the important observation that since the mid-1980s, the disease view has become the predominant understanding of codependent group participants. Rice also observes how many of the behaviors of those functioning within the relational universe of alcoholics have been reinterpreted in pathological terms. For example, such diagnostic labels as "the Hero," "the Enabler," "the Mascot," "the Lost Child," "the Martyr," and "the Scapegoat" are syndrome labels, used to describe the symptomatic responses of individuals to an alcoholic friend or family member. John Bradshaw and others essentially view these responses as pathologies.

51. Ibid., pp. 24–25.

52. Sykes, *Nation of Victims,* p. 9.

53. *Diagnostic and Statistical Manual of Mental Disorders, Third Edition, Revised* (DSM III-R) (Washington, D.C.: American Psychiatric Association, 1987), p. xviii. DSM IV, the most recent edition was published in 1994.

54. David Allen Larson, "Mental Impairments and the Rehabilitation Act of 1973," *Louisiana Law Review* (1988): 849.

55. DSM III-R, p. 321.

56. Ibid., pp. 330–31.

57. Ibid., pp. 349–54.

58. In DSM III-R, for example, "Developmental Arithmetic Disorder" can be detected when one's "arithmetic skills, as measured by a standardized, individually administered test, are markedly below the expected level, given the person's schooling and intellectual capacity." Similarly, "Developmental Expressive Writing Disorder" is detectable when one's writing skills are below par. In the same vein are "Developmental Reading Disorder," "Development Expressive Language Disorder," and "Developmental Receptive Language Disorder" (pp. 42–43).

59. Claudia Willis, "Life in Overdrive," *Time,* 18 July 1994, p. 43.

60. Ibid.

61. Ibid. These are taken from the DSM III-R description of ADD.

62. Geoffrey Cowley, "The Culture of Prozac," *Newsweek,* 7 February 1994, p. 41, and David J. Rothman, "Shiny Happy People," *New Republic,* 14 February 1994, p. 34.

63. Robert Wright, "The Coverage of Happiness," *New Republic,* 14 March 1994, pp. 24–29.

64. Peele, *Diseasing of America,* p. 25.

65. Sykes, *Nation of Victims,* p. 14.

66. Larson, "Mental Impairments," p. 48.

67. Gross, *Psychological Society,* p. 5.

68. Elshtain, *Meditations,* pp. 92–93.

69. Peele, *Diseasing of America,* p. 54.

70. Fingarette, *Heavy Drinking,* p. 15.

71. The *Wall Street Journal* recently reported, for example, that "America is engulfed by a wave of disorder-seeking and blame-shifting. . . . It is somebody else's or some other thing's fault when individuals are messed up" ("A Therapeutic State?" *Wall Street Journal,* 3 January 1994, sec. A, 6:1).

72. Sykes, *Nation of Victims,* p. 137, quoting Stan Katz and Aimee Liu, *The Codependency Conspiracy.*

73. Ibid., p. 141, quoting Melody Beattie, *Codependent No More.*

74. Ibid., p. 125.

75. See, for example, "Religious Right and Clinton," *Christian Century,* 13–20 July 1994, p. 675.

76. Kevin Sack, "Victims All: 'It's Not Me That's Guilty. My Addiction Just Took Over,' " *New York Times*, 6 December 1992, sec. 4, 4:4.

77. *School District of Philadelphia v. Friedman*, no. 2073 C.D., 7 April 1986, Pennsylvania Commonwealth Court.

78. Larson, "Mental Impairments," p. 857.

79. Sykes, *Nation of Victims*, p. 127.

80. Ibid., p. 128.

81. The man's name is Moosa Hanoukai. See "At the Bar," *New York Times*, 20 May 1994, sec. B, p. 20.

82. Robert Hughes, *Culture of Complaint* (Oxford: Oxford University Press, 1993), p. 9.

83. Berger, "Toward a Sociological Understanding," p. 38.

84. See Berger, Berger, and Kellner, *Homeless Mind*, 1974, p. 63f.

85. Berger, "Toward a Sociological Understanding," p. 39.

86. See James Davison Hunter, *American Evangelicalism* (New Brunswick, N.J.: Rutgers University Press, 1983); Berger, Berger, and Kellner, *Homeless Mind*, pp. 63–82; and Robert Bellah, *The Broken Covenant: American Civil Religion in Time of Trial*, pp. 87–111.

87. See James Davison Hunter, *Culture Wars: The Struggle to Define America* (New York: Basic Books, 1991).

88. For considerations of the effects of instrumental rationality on modern life, see Jacques Ellul, *Technological Society* (New York: Vintage Books, 1964); Berger, Berger, and Kellner, *Homeless Mind*; and Bell, *Cultural Contradictions of Capitalism*. For a specific discussion about the way in which instrumental rationalism has undermined traditional sources of legitimation, see John H. Scharr, "Legitimacy in the Modern State," in *Legitimacy and the State*, ed. William Connolly (Oxford: Basil Blackwell Publisher, 1984).

89. Rieff, *Triumph of the Therapeutic*, p. 61.

NOTES TO CHAPTER 2

1. *Congressional Record*, 104th Cong., 1st sess., 21 March 1995, 52: H 3359.

2. Lack of conceptual clarity about the Weberian concept of legitimation has generally centered on two basic issues: one concerns his definition of legitimacy; the second, the evolutionary use of Weber's typology, i.e., the conventional argument that political orders have historically evolved from charismatic to traditional to legal-rational forms of legitimation. Regarding the definitional problem, Weber asserts that an important element of legitimacy is "the belief in legitimacy" (in *Economy and Society*, ed. Guenther Roth and Claus Wittich [Berkeley: University of California Press, 1978], 1:213). Even more explicitly:

"Today the most common form of legitimacy is the belief in legality" (*Economy and Society,* 1:37). Richard Merelman and S. M. Lipset are among those who have followed Weber in this way, defining legitimacy essentially as a matter of what people believe about the state's credibility. S. M. Lipset, for example, states, "Legitimacy involves the capacity of a political system to engender and maintain the belief that existing political institutions are the most appropriate or proper ones for the society" (*Political Man: The Social Bases of Politics* [New York: Anchor Books, 1960], p. 86). Similarly, Richard M. Merelman defines political legitimacy as "the quality of 'oughtness' that is *perceived* by the public to inhere in a political regime. That government is legitimate which is *viewed* as morally proper for a society" (emphasis added). Merelman states further that legitimacy is "a quality attributed to a regime by a population. That quality is the outcome of the government's capacity to engender legitimacy" ("Learning and Legitimacy," *American Political Science Review* 60 [1966]: 548). John Scharr, David Beetham, and Alan Hyde, by contrast, take issue with Weber on this point, arguing that such a formulation unnecessarily narrows the concept of legitimacy and limits its analytical utility. Understanding legitimacy in this way theoretically confines the researcher to investigations into what people believe about the legitimacy of the state and effectively eliminates from the legitimation equation analyses of the substantive content of the distinct moral systems appealed to by the state in particular historical contexts. As David Beetham points out, "A given power relationship is not legitimate because people believe in its legitimacy, but because it can be justified in terms of their beliefs" (*The Legitimation of Power* [Atlantic Highlands, N.J.: Humanities Press International, 1991], p. 11). The theoretical focus of this project follows the latter group of scholars, holding that legitimacy does not have to do simply with what people believe about the legitimacy of the state—that this represents only one component of a larger phenomenon.

3. Weber wrote, "Today the most common form of legitimacy is the belief in legality, the compliance with enactments which are formally correct and have been made in the accustomed manner" (*Economy and Society,* 1:37). John Scharr summarizes this conventional evolutionary model credited to Weber: "Since Weber, we have been busy putting the phenomena into one or another of his three boxes and charting the progress by which charismatic authority becomes routinized into traditional authority, which, under the impact of science and secularism, gives way in turn to rational-legal authority" ("Legitimacy and the Modern State," in *Legitimacy and the State,* ed. William Connolly [Oxford: Basil Blackwell Publisher, 1984], pp. 104–5).

4. This is the position to which Niklas Luhmann holds. As he writes, "The law of a society is positivized when the legitimacy of pure legality is recognized, that is, when law is respected because it is made by responsible decision in

accordance with definite rules" (from "Soziologie des politischen Systems," in Soziologische Aufklärung [1970] p. 167, cited in Jürgen Habermas, *Legitimation Crisis* [Boston: Beacon Press, 1973], p. 98).

5. See also Alan Hyde, "The Concept of Legitimation in the Sociology of Law," *Wisconsin Law Review* (1983): 379–426.

6. Habermas, *Legitimation Crisis*, p. 101.

7. Ibid., p. 241. This substantive emphasis in Habermas's work has led some interpreters to conclude that, ultimately, his concept of legitimation is rooted in culture. Consider, for example, the following interpretive paraphrase of Habermas's legitimation theory by Robert Wuthnow: "In other words the state's right to make binding decisions—tantamount to exercising coercive power—rooted in its ability to prevent social disintegration. But understandings of disintegration are dependent on collective values. Therefore, the state's legitimacy depends ultimately on culture" (in Robert Wuthnow et al., "The Critical Theory of Jürgen Habermas," *Cultural Analysis: The Work of Peter L. Berger, Mary Douglas, Michel Foucault and Jürgen Habermas* [New York: Routledge & Kegan Paul, 1984], p. 218).

8. S. M. Lipset, for example, like Habermas, holds that the efficacy of a legal-rational system is not all that sustains legitimacy. He likewise believes in the necessity of some type of moral or philosophical underpinning to the political order and thus conceives of legitimacy as dependent on the value systems that prevail within a given culture. "While effectiveness is primarily an instrumental dimension," Lipset explains, "legitimacy is more affective and evaluative. Groups will regard a political system as legitimate or illegitimate according to the way in which its values fit in with their primary values" (*Political Man*, pp. 86–87). For Lipset, as for Habermas, legitimacy contains a moral quality. Somehow the instrumental efficacy of a system is not enough to constitute an independent type of legitimation. Also emphasizing the normative dimension of legitimacy, Alan Hyde has argued, "In determining which standards of conduct are obligatory, people seem to care a great deal more about the substance or content of the standards than they do about a legal source or pedigree. Indeed, they may evaluate the legitimacy of the source by their approval of the substantive norm" ("Concept of Legitimation," p. 411). Without specifying a departure from Weber's formula, others have likewise favored the moral or symbolic qualities of legitimation. This is clearly the focus in C. Wright Mills and Hans Gerth's discussion of the term: "The symbols which thus justify a social structure or an institutional order are called symbols of 'legitimation,' or 'master symbols,' or 'symbols of justification.' . . . In discussing political symbols, our chief concern is with those which sanction political authority. The party politician will, in one way or the other, use the master symbols of the political order, and will also develop special rhetorics: both the content and the delivery of his speech will

become stereotyped around those modes that are felt to be effectively persuasive appeals" (*Character and Social Structure: The Psychology of Social Institutions* [London: Routledge & Kegan Paul, 1954], pp. 276, 284).

9. Beetham, *Legitimation of Power*, p. 17. Such a conceptual model reframes the evolutionary process. Within the conventional Weberian formula, the evolution proceeds from charismatic to traditional to legal-rational. Within Beetham's framework, because the three elements of legitimation—validity, justification, and consent—exist in every political order, documentation of a historical change can focus instead on the types of *justifications* that are drawn on to support the *validity* of a given state system. Thus Beetham provides the heuristic framework for a more distinctly cultural interpretation of state legitimation. It allows the researcher to analyze the varying sources of justification offered in different social and historical contexts, a dimension of the legitimation question that has been woefully neglected in the relevant literature.

10. See Peter Berger and Thomas Luckmann, *The Social Construction of Reality* (New York: Anchor Books, 1966); and Peter Berger, *The Sacred Canopy: Elements of a Sociological Theory of Religion* (Garden City, N.Y.: Doubleday & Co., 1967), pp. 1–28.

11. The reader should note that in blending these two variant theoretical constructs as I do, the analysis remains on the broader level of the state and the culture, thus emphasizing the Durkheimian notion of the collective qualities of consciousness rather than the more phenomenological concern with the subjective ruminations of the individual. Though individual consciousness and individual quests for meaning are certainly related to changing cultural codes of moral understanding, the primary units of analysis for this study are the culture and the state. Focusing the analysis in this way is an effort to achieve what Robert Wuthnow argues has often not been attained within "neoclassical" approaches to cultural analysis, namely, the relating of "cultural systems to large scale institutions." See Robert Wuthnow, *Meaning and the Moral Order: Explorations in Cultural Analysis* (Berkeley and Los Angeles: University of California Press, 1987), p. 49.

12. Peter Berger, "Toward a Sociological Understanding of Psychoanalysis," *Social Research*, 32 (1965): 26–41.

13. This reconceptualization, inspired by David Beetham's work, not only challenges the basic evolutionary process of state authority credited to Weber but departs from more materialist explanations of the development of the modern state, e.g., the works of Michael Mann and Theda Skocpol. This is not to say that it offers an ideological, as opposed to a materialist, explanation for the emergence of the state; indeed not. Legitimation is not synonymous with causation. Legitimation may be a part of the cause, just as it is certainly a part of the state's continuance. Even within a strict Marxist understanding of political institutions, ideologies, though they may be "false," are employed to justify a

state's actions. Thus, though structural reasons may be central to understanding the emergence and maintenance of the state, the need for certain legitimations to justify the authority of these structures to society remains. Beetham's explanation considers the significance of culture in this way and thus departs from those theoretical assessments of the state that ignore it. Furthermore, Beetham's work calls into question the theories of legitimacy, based upon the developmental models of psychology, which hold that societies mature through certain stages. According to this approach, each stage of development requires a particular type of state legitimation. Once material and belonging needs have been satisfied, then society moves on to higher, more value-oriented needs, and so on. The problem with this "postmaterialist" view is that societal values have been a continual feature of state legitimation. What has changed is not a focus on values but in the source of values. An example of the postmaterialist approach would be Ronald Inglehart's *The Silent Revolution: Changing Values and Political Styles among Western Publics* (Princeton, N.J.: Princeton University Press, 1977).

14. I should add the caveat that this reclassification of legitimacy from the Weberian formula is less pronounced than it may at first appear. This is due in part to the sometimes vague and multifaceted nature of Weber's use of the terms *legitimacy* and *rationalization,* and to the varying ways in which they have been interpreted by Weber scholars. Weber himself depicts the process of rationalization as a shift from value-oriented rationality to instrumental rationality. His legal-rational type of domination is the institutional manifestation of the latter. According to Weber, the cultural pervasiveness of instrumental rationality undermined traditional cosmologies as plausible sources of collective meaning. And though he considers other ideological systems, such as science, to be inadequate to the task of replacing traditional value systems, he does not, as some contend, explicitly deny the continuing, albeit less salient, presence of substantive or value-oriented forms of rationality in the modern legal system. Reinhard Bendix and Wolfgang Schluchter are among those who propose that Weber did not argue for the ultimate and exclusive triumph of legal-rationality in the modern context but rather anticipated a continuous struggle between substantive rationality and formal legal rationality in the political sphere. Both Schluchter and Bendix speak of the countervailing tendencies of formal and substantive rationality. As Reinhard Bendix explains, "In Weber's view the conflict between formal and substantive justice has no ultimate solution. No degree of formalization can entirely eradicate beliefs in the legitimacy of the legal order that transcend the actual law and its instrumental values, and no concern with substantive justice can entirely subvert the orientation of the legal profession toward the formal properties of the law" (*Max Weber: An Intellectual Portrait,* 2d ed. [Berkeley: University of California Press, 1977], p. 438). See also Wolfgang Schluchter, *The Rise of Western Rationalism: Max Weber's Developmental History* (Berkeley:

University of California Press, 1981), pp. 107f. According to this view of Weber, then, the substantive or justificatory element of the legitimation equation is to a certain degree sustained.

15. Beetham, *Legitimation of Power*, p. 125.

16. John Scharr's work on legitimacy would be an example of an approach that highlights the causal significance of the traditional sources of state legitimation that have been eroded by the processes of modernization. More typical, however, are the less explicitly cultural explanations for the present legitimation "crisis." Habermas, for example, emphasizes the precarious position of the state in a late capitalist order. The demands of the economy on the slate to protect free enterprise, on the one hand, and the expectations of society for the state to compensate for the negative effects of capitalism, on the other hand, necessarily put it in a tenuous position. Similarly, Alan Wolfe (*The Limits of Legitimacy: Political Contradictions of Contemporary Capitalism* [New York: Free Press, 1977]) sees the problem of legitimation as stemming from the state's response to the countering demands of liberalism (capitalist accumulation) and democracy (equal participation). That the state experiences pressures as a consequence of these processes is certainly plausible, but a justificatory function is still necessary for the state to explain its actions in attempting to resolve or live with these pressures. And the availability of certain systems of meaning plays an important part in the state's ability to justify its actions to society, something Habermas also recognizes as important.

17. Habermas, *Legitimation Crisis*, p. 36.

18. Hannah Arendt, "What Was Authority?" in *Authority,* ed. Carl J. Friedrich (Cambridge, Mass.: Harvard University Press, 1958), p. 83.

19. Louis Hartz, *The Liberal Tradition in America: An Interpretation of American Political Thought since the Revolution* (New York: Harcourt, Brace & Company, 1955); Daniel Boorstin, *The Genius of American Politics* (Chicago: University of Chicago Press, 1955).

20. Wood, however, agrees that by the time of the Constitution, republicanism had given way to Lockean liberalism. Gordon Wood, *The Creation of the American Republic: 1776–1778* (Chapel Hill: University of North Carolina Press, 1969); Bernard Bailyn, *The Ideological Origins of the American Revolution* (Cambridge, Mass.: Harvard University Press, 1967).

21. Joyce Appleby, "Republicanism and Ideology," *American Quarterly* 37 (fall 1985): 461–73. John Diggins, *The Lost Soul of American Politics: Virtue, Self-Interest, and the Foundations of Liberalism* (New York: Basic Books, 1984).

22. J. P. A. Pocock, *Virtue, Commerce, and History* (Cambridge: Cambridge University Press, 1985). For earlier discussions by Pocock of republicanism in America, see J. P. A. Pocock, *The Machiavellian Moment: Florentine Political Thought and the Atlantic Republican Tradition* (Princeton, N.J.: Princeton University Press, 1975).

23. This is the basic conclusion of the following works: Adam Seligman, *The Idea of Civil Society* (New York: Free Press, 1992); James Kloppenberg, "The Virtues of Liberalism: Christianity, Republicanism, and Ethics in Early American Political Discourse," *Journal of American History* 74,1 (June 1987): 9–33; Charles Ward Sheldon, *The Political Philosophy of Thomas Jefferson* (Baltimore: Johns Hopkins University Press, 1991). Also, Bruce Ackerman in *We the People* (Cambridge, Mass.: Harvard University Press, 1991) challenges what he believes is the faulty dichotomy between liberalism and republicanism and instead argues for a dualism that incorporates both; see esp. pp. 16–33.

24. Consider, for example, Seligman, *Idea of Civil Society*; Robert Bellah, et al., *Habits of the Heart: Individualism and Commitment in American Life* (Berkeley: University of California Press, 1985), pp. 28f.; Robert Bellah and Phillip Hammond, *Varieties of Civil Religion* (New York: Harper & Row, 1980), pp. 3–22; and Robert Bellah, *The Broken Covenant* (New York: Seabury Press, 1975), pp. 1–35.

25. Arendt, "What Was Authority?" p. 98.

26. Ibid., p. 109. Sheldon also argues that a problem with modern interpretations of the influence of republicanism on early American political thought is the uncareful mixing of Machiavellianism with classical republicanism. Sheldon sees an important and qualitative difference between the two and takes issue with Pocock, who, as Sheldon claims, is less discerning: "This casual mixing of Machiavelli, considered the first great modern theorist for his pessimism over human nature and his reliance on ruthless, deceitful power politics, with the optimism and ethical ideals of Plato and Aristotle, calls into question the value of much of Pocock's paradigm" (*Political Philosophy of Thomas Jefferson*, p. 165).

27. Kloppenberg, "Virtues of Liberalism," p. 14.

28. Cited in Wood, *Creation of the American Republic*, pp. 48–49.

29. Ibid.

30. Ibid., p. 50.

31. Jefferson and Monroe, for example, both accumulated sizable personal debts due, in part, to the time and energies they gave to public service away from their private agricultural enterprises. For example, when both Monroe and Jefferson served as foreign ministers, though they were provided a decent salary for that time, they did not have many other benefits financed for them—e.g., travel expenses, board, etc., which they had to pay for personally. Moreover, Monroe, who was the first president to occupy the White House after it was partially destroyed by the British in 1814, furnished the presidential mansion with his own furnishings.

32. James Madison, speech at the Virginia ratifying convention, 20 June 1788, in *The Writings of James Madison*, vol. 5: *1787–1790*, ed., Gaillard Hunt (New York: G. P. Putnam's Sons, 1904), p. 223.

33. Kloppenberg, "Virtues of Liberalism," p. 16.

34. Cicero, quoted in Seligman, *Idea of Civil Society*, pp. 17–18.

35. Ibid., p. 18.

36. Weber also speaks of the evolutionary process through which the notion of natural law traveled: "We encountered the *lex naturae* earlier as an essentially Stoic creation which was taken over by Christianity for the purpose of constructing a bridge between its own ethics and the norms of the world. It was the law legitimated by God's will for all men of this world of sin and violence and thus stood in contrast to those of God's commands which were revealed directly to the faithful and were evident only to the elect." Speaking further of a less religiously based understanding of natural law, Weber continues, "Natural law has thus been the collective term for those norms which owe their legitimacy not to their origin from a legitimate lawgiver, but to their immanent and teleological qualities. It is the specific and only consistent type of legitimacy of a legal order which can remain once religious revelation and the authoritarian sacredness of a tradition and its bearers have lost their force" (*Economy and Society*, 2:866–67).

37. Seligman., *Idea of a Civil Society*, p. 22.

38. John Locke, *Two Treatises*, bk. 7, sec. 135, quoted by Seligman, *Idea of a Civil Society*, p. 24.

39. Seligman, *Idea of a Civil Society*, p. 36.

40. Robert Bellah, for example, argues that "it was the more modest and conciliatory thought of Hobbes's follower and critic John Locke that had most influence in America" (*Broken Covenant*, p. 25).

41. In a letter from Thomas Jefferson to Thomas Law, 13 June 1814, "The Moral Instinct," in *The Complete Jefferson*, assembled and arranged by Saul K. Padover (New York: Duell, Sloan & Pearce, 1943), pp. 1032–33.

42. Berger, *Sacred Canopy*, p. 32.

43. Ernst Cassirer, *The Myth of the State* (New Haven, Conn.: Yale University Press, 1979), p. 135.

44. Bellah and Hammond, *Varieties of Civil Religion*, p. 5.

45. Wood, *Creation of the American Republic*, p. 118.

46. John Adams, 11 October 1789, cited in John R. Howe, Jr., *The Changing Political Thought of John Adams* (Princeton, N.J.: Princeton University Press, 1966), p. 185.

47. George Washington, "Farewell Address," 19 September 1796, in *The Writings of George Washington from the Original Manuscript Sources, 1745–1799*, vol. 35, *March 30, 1796–July 31, 1797*, ed. John C. Fitzpatrick (Washington, D.C.: U.S. Government Printing Office, 1940), p. 229.

48. Alexis de Tocqueville, *Democracy in America*, 2 vols. (New York: Alfred A. Knopf, 1945), 1:311.

49. Ibid., 1:315.

50. Ibid., 1:316.

51. Seligman, *Idea of Civil Society,* p. 84.

52. Ibid., p. 6 Also speaking to the fragile and contingent nature of this early American political alliance, Bellah understands Lockean liberalism to have been "related to Calvinist theology and classical philosophy in curious patterns of attraction and repulsion" (*Broken Covenant,* p. 25).

53. It is this condition that Habermas was referring to when he observed, "Religion, having retreated into the regions of subjective belief, can no longer satisfy neglected communicative needs, even in conjunction with the secular components of bourgeois ideology" (*Legitimation Crisis,* p. 77). This is also one of the main points of Stephen Carter's *The Culture of Disbelief* (New York: Basic Books, 1993).

54. Mary Ann Glendon, *Rights Talk: The Impoverishment of Public Discourse* (New York: Basic Books, 1991). A 1989 study conducted by the People for the American Way came to the same conclusion, that is, that young Americans emphasize liberty with little regard for ideas of duty and responsibility: "Young people have learned only half of America's story. Consistent with the priority they place on personal happiness, young people reveal notions of America's unique character that emphasize freedom and license almost to the complete exclusion of service or participation. Although they clearly appreciate the democratic freedoms that, in their view, make theirs the best country in the world to live in, they fail to perceive a need to reciprocate by exercising the duties and responsibilities of good citizenship" (People for the American Way, *Democracy's Next Generation* [Washington, D.C.: People for the American Way, 1989], p. 27).

55. Beetham, *Legitimation of Power,* p. 18.

56. Schaar, "Legitimacy in the Modern State," p. 106. See also Bellah, *Broken Covenant,* who likewise holds: "Our ties to tradition, whatever religious or ethnic group we come from, have been enormously eroded in the last century by the advance of modernization" (p. 143).

57. Habermas, *Legitimation Crisis,* p. 71.

58. Ed Crane of the Cato Institute, for example, laments that at the end of the Reagan era, the government was consuming a larger share of the gross national product (GNP) than it was at the end of Carter's presidency, and that during Reagan's two terms, "some 159,000 bureaucrats" were added to the federal payroll (cited by E. J. Dionne in *Why Americans Hate Politics* [New York: Simon & Schuster, 1991], p. 260). Similarly, David Frum asserts that "despite all the caterwauling about Reagan's supposedly savage budget cuts, not one major spending program . . . was eliminated during his Presidency." "That is why," according to Frum, "Federal spending (adjusted for inflation) rose by 50 per cent over the eight Reagan years" (cited by Ed Rubenstein in "How Quickly We Forget," *National Review,* 1 August 1994, p. 17). It is not surpris-

ing, then, that Bertrand Badie and Pierre Birnbaum take notice of the comparative expansion of the American state in the early 1980s in their *The Sociology of the State,* trans. Arthur Goldhammer (Chicago: University of Chicago Press, 1983) pp. 136–37.

59. This is what Harold G. Vatter and John F. Walker argue in *The Inevitability of Government Growth* (New York: Columbia University Press, 1990). They claim that "history is going to make it happen" (p. 213). Similarly, Gianfranco Poggi (who, like Vatter and Walker, points to the salience of Wagner's law—named after the German economist Adolf Wagner, who in 1883 first asserted that government spending rises faster than the national economy) believes that the very tendencies characteristic of the modern state compel it toward "expansion and differentiation," that these tendencies are "built into the state itself." This, according to Poggi, helps explain why Reagan's effort to slow the process of growth failed. See Gianfranco Poggi, *The State: Its Nature, Development and Prospects* (Cambridge: Polity Press, 1990), Chap. 7. Alan Wolfe also asserts that the expansion of the state is concomitant with an inability to bring about any real change: "The activity of the state has increased to the point where it has become a major producer and certainly the major consumer, but often forgotten is that the growth in the potential power of the state is matched by a decline in the options that the state has at its command. For this reason the increased activity of the state reflects, not an expansion of alternatives, but the exhaustion of them" (*Limits of Legitimacy,* p. 258).

60. *Statistical Abstract of the United States* (Washington, D.C.: Government Printing Office, 1993), p. 328, Table 508, and p. 331, Table 513.

61. Ibid., p. 343, Table 531; and *Historical Statistics: Colonial Times to 1970,* Series Y 272–89 (Washington, D.C.: Government Printing Office), p. 1100.

62. *Statistical Abstract of the United States* (Washington, D.C.: Government Printing Office, 1994), nos. 493 and 494, p. 319; and *Historical Statistics,* Series Y 272–89, p. 1100.

63. *Statistical Abstract of the United States,* 1993, p. 349, Table 542.

64. Lawrence Friedman, *Total Justice* (New York: Russell Sage Foundation, 1985), p. 31.

65. *Statistical Abstract of the United States,* 1993, p. 330, Table 512.

66. Ibid., p. 384, Table 609.

67. Ibid., p. 330, Table 512.

68. Ibid., p. 328, Table 509.

69. Theodore Caplow, *American Social Trends* (New York: Harcourt Brace Jovanovich, 1991), p. 108.

70. Ibid., p. 107.

71. Daniel Yankelovich, cited by S. M. Lipset and William Schneider in *The Confidence Gap: Business, Labor, and Government* (New York: Free Press,

1983), p. 15. Also consider E. J. Dionne's *Why Americans Hate Politics,* for a recent assessment of public frustration with contemporary politics in America.

72. Yankelovich, cited by Lipset and Schneider, *Confidence Gap,* p. 15.

73. The correlation between the so-called Perot factor, and the pronounced levels of government disapproval in recent years suggests that the higher participation rate is more indicative of voter alienation than it is of a resurgence of positive interest among the electorate in the political process. As Ruy A. Teixeira explains, Perot appealed to a "vein of discontent about government that the other two candidates did not and could not fully engage" ("Turnout in the 1992 Election," *Brookings Review* 11 (spring 1993): 47).

74. According to Ruy A. Teixeira, author of *The Disappearing American Voter* (Washington, D.C.: The Brookings Institute, 1992), the 55 percent turnout rate in 1992 is still twenty-five percentage points below the average among other industrialized democracies. "If it were not for Switzerland, [America] would be in the cellar of the international rankings" ("Turnout in the 1992 Election," p. 47).

75. Unfortunately, the NES stopped asking this question after 1980.

76. *Statistical Abstract of the United States, 1993,* p. 207, Table 336.

77. Caplow, *American Social Trends,* p. 115.

NOTES TO CHAPTER 3

1. Lawrence M. Friedman, "Civil Wrongs: Personal Injury Law in the Late 19th Century," *American Bar Foundation Research Journal,* nos. 2–3 (1987): 351. Elsewhere Friedman estimates that nearly 90 percent or more of all litigated tort cases fall under the heading, "personal injury" *Total Justice* [New York: Russell Sage Foundation, 1985], p. 53].

2. Friedman, "Civil Wrongs," p. 351.

3. Ibid., p. 376.

4. J. Rainer Twiford, "Emotional Distress in Tort Law," *Behavioral Sciences and the Law* 3 (spring 1985): 123.

5. Friedman, "Civil Wrongs," p. 375.

6. James Willard Hurst, *Law and Social Order* (Ithaca, N.Y.: Cornell University Press, 1982), p. 197.

7. Twiford, "Emotional Distress," p. 123.

8. Friedman, "Civil Wrongs," p. 355.

9. The Digest System, consisting of 466 volumes, contains abstracts of all reported cases decided in particular time periods. There are twelve sets of volumes in all. The first contains all recorded cases between 1658 and 1896. The next eight sets of volumes were published every ten years, beginning in 1906. Then, in 1976, the publishers began issuing the sets every five years. The most recent set covers all cases through 1991.

10. Consider Morris Cohen, Robert C. Berring, and Kent C. Olson's *How to Find the Law,* 9th ed. (St. Paul: West Publishing Co., 1989), pp. 94–99, for an explanation of the Century and Decennial Digest System. Use of the Decennial Digest as a tool for sociohistorical analysis is limited in that the Digest does not represent all cases (just all published cases, the large majority of which are appellate-level cases) and does not constitute an absolutely unbiased or random selection of cases. Unsettled areas of law typically gain more appellate attention and are subsequently overrepresented in the Digest. Still, previous research has employed past and current volumes of the Decennial Digest to ascertain "general indication[s] of growth" within certain areas of law. See, for example, James May, "Antitrust Practice and Procedure in the Formative Era: The Constitutional and Conceptual Reach of State Antitrust Law, 1880–1918," *University of Pennsylvania Law Review* 135 (March 1987): 503; and Vicki Schultz, "Telling Stories about Women and Work: Judicial Interpretations of Sex Segregation in the Workplace in Title VII Cases Raising the Lack of Interest Argument," *Harvard Law Review* 103 (1990): 1766–67. To show that the general growth of emotional damage claims within personal injury law, as indicated in the Digest at the appellate level, is generally representative of activity in the law at other levels, I consider evidence of developments at the lower court level later in this chapter.

11. Though I make reference here to the number of emotional injury "cases," what is actually represented in the Digest is not an emotional damage case per se (where the only injury was an emotional one) but a case where the issue under question concerned a claim of emotional injury and was identified as such by those assembling the Digest.

12. For a discussion of the difficulty of data collection and analysis of state trial court cases, see Friedman, *Total Justice,* p. 17.

13. As with the Decennial Digest, analysis of jury verdict reports has limitations. Publishers who compile jury verdict reports rely on accessible trial court records and the solicited responses of lawyers from both sides of court contests. Lawyers do not always respond, and court records are not always easy to access. The two sources considered here, however, are regarded among the most thorough and have reportedly assembled a high percentage of the total number of trial court cases in their respective jurisdictions. For use of verdict reporters, see Erik Moller, *Trends in Civil Jury Verdicts since 1985* (Santa Monica, Calif. Rand Institute for Civil Justice, 1996) (this study also used *The New York Jury Verdict Reporter*); and Robert MacCoun, "Inside the Black Box: What Empirical Research Tells Us about Decision Making by Civil Juries," from *Verdict: Assessing the Civil Jury System,* ed. Robert E. Litan (Washington, D.C.: The Brookings Institute, 1993), pp. 137–80. Judyth W. Pendell and John R. Evancho, with Aetna in Hartford, Connecticut, have also done research using *The New York Jury Verdict Reporter,* comp. Moran Publishers, and attest to its high

standards. Russel Moran of Moran Publishers and Mark Harlan of Juris Verdictum Press were both very helpful in allowing me access to their collection of reports. Employing the same methodology I used with the Digests, I simply counted the number of cases involving some type of emotional or psychological damage claim listed each year. For the California cases (Juris Verdictum Press), I counted the cases that were indexed as such in the annual compilation of cases called *O'Brien's Evaluator,* i.e., cases under such headings as "Emotional Distress," "Psychological Problems," "Psychiatric Problems," etc. For the New York cases, Moran sent me all cases involving some type of emotional or psychological injury claim between 1981 and 1994, as well as additional statistical information regarding the total number of personal injury cases for each year, thus providing me with the necessary comparative data for Table 3.4. In each instance, then, the publishers set the criteria for determining which cases should be regarded as emotional/psychological injury cases, thus eliminating any possible bias on my part regarding cases to be included in this category. All information presented in Tables 3.3 and 3.4 is based on these data.

14. *O'Brien's Evaluator* is an annual publication of Juris Verdictum Press that indexes and lists all cases from a single year. The publishers sent me copies of *O'Brien's Evaluator* for the years 1981–1995.

15. In the area of "intentional" infliction of emotional damages, the courts moved more quickly in allowing for the recovery of damages unattached to another tort. In other words, when some injury was the result of intentional efforts to cause emotional distress, the courts would allow for recovery of emotional injury damages alone, with the added restrictions that emotional distress be "severe" and the defendant's conduct be found "willful," "wanton," and "outrageous." The evolution I discuss in this section, by contrast, refers to "negligently" caused injury. Though the story of the evolution in the area of intentional emotional injuries would be interesting, I necessarily limit my investigation to the area of negligently inflicted emotional injuries. I do so for several reasons. First, it is a useful way to limit the scope of a very broad topic. Second, that legal recognition of negligently inflicted emotional injuries was so uniformly resisted by the courts in the earlier decades of this century, and that there is less reluctance today, opens the door for an evaluation of the interesting story this development tells. Finally, that an intentionally inflicted injury of any kind (be it emotional or physical) should be compensated is easier to understand in the context of the traditional sources of legitimation reviewed in Chapter 2. That is, it should not be a surprise that the courts would find someone willfully intending to injure another to be liable for his or her actions. Such judgments make sense in the context of classical and Christian systems of meaning, where "sinful" and hurtful actions against one's neighbor and the community are condemned, whereas negligently inflicted injuries are not so logically defensible within these former codes of moral understanding.

16. *Sloane v. Southern California Railway Co.,* 111 Calif. 668, 44 P 320 (1896).

17. *City of Chicago v. Davies,* 110 Ill. App. 427 (1903).

18. *West Kentucky Coal Co. v. Davis,* 138 Ky. 667, 128 SW 1074 (1910).

19. *Zabron v. Cunard S.S. Co.,* 151 Iowa 345, 131 NW 18 (1911).

20. *White v. Sander,* 47 NW 90, 168 Mass. 296 (1897).

21. Consider, for example, *Molien v. Kaiser Foundation Hosp.,* 27 Calif. 3d 933–36, 616 P2d 813 (1980); *Dillon v. Legg,* 68 Calif. 2d 748–53, 69 Calif. Rptr. 72, 441 P2d 912 (1986); John G. Langhenry, Jr., "Personal Injury Law and Emotional Distress," *Federation of Insurance Counsel Quarterly* (spring 1981): 260; Craig H. Millet and Tina I. Waine, "The California Supreme Court Survey—A Review of Decisions: July–November 1980," *Pepperdine Law Review* (January 1981): 537, 547; and Twiford, "Emotional Distress," p. 122, for discussions of the historical justifications for refusing recovery of emotional damages.

22. *Lynch v. Knight,* 9 HL Cas. 577, 11 Eng. Reprint 854, 8 ERC 382.

23. E.g., *Crenshaw v. O'Connell,* 150 SW2d 489, 235 Mo. App. 1085 (1941); *Gardner v. Cumberland Telephone Co.,* 207 Ky. 249, 268 SW 1108 (1925).

24. *Homans v. Boston Elevated Railway Co.,* 180 Mass. 456, 62 NE 737 (1902).

25. *Hess v. Philadelphia Transportation Co.,* 56 A2d 89, 358 Pa. 144 (1948).

26. *Zelinsky v. Chimics,* 196 Pa. Super. 312, 175 A2d 351 (1961).

27. *Porter v. Delaware, L. & W.R. Co.,* 73 N.J. L 405, 63 A 860 (1906).

28. *Morton v. Stack,* 122 Ohio St. 115, 170 NE 869 (1930).

29. *Deutsch v. Shien,* 597 SW2d 141 (Kentucky 1980). See also, for a discussion of this use of the "impact rule," William L. Prosser, W. Page Keeton, Dan B. Dobbs, Robert E. Keeton, and David G. Owen, *Prosser and Keeton on the Law of Torts,* 5th ed. (St. Paul: West Publishing Co., 1984), sec 54.

30. *Christy Brothers Circus v. Turnage,* 38 Ga. App. 581, 144 SE 680 (1928).

31. *Palsgraf v. Long Island Railroad,* 248 N.Y. 339, 162 NE 99 (1928).

32. *Hoyem v. Manhattan Beach City School District,* 150 Calif. Rptr. 1, 585 P2d 851 (1978).

33. *Keck v. Jackson,* 122 Ariz. 114, 593 P2d 668 (1979).

34. *Vaillancourt v. Medical Center Hospital of Vermont, Inc.,* 425 A2d 92, 139 Vt. 138 (1980).

35. *Padgett v. Colonial Wholesale Distribution Co.,* 232 S.C. 593, 103 SE2d 265 (1958).

36. *Woodell v. Pinehurst Surgical Clinic,* 78 N.C. App. 230, 336 SE2d 716 (1985). This case relied on reasoning offered in a 1938 case where the court held that, "mere hurt or embarrassment are not compensable." *Flake v. Greensboro News Co.,* 212 N.C. 780, 195 S.E. (1938).

37. *Dillon v. Legg,* 68 Calif. 2d 728, 69 Cal. Rptr. 72, 441 P2d 912 (1968).

38. Prosser et al., *Prosser and Keaton on the Law of Torts,* p. 366.

39. 68 Calif. 2d 740–1.

40. Langhenry, "Personal Injury Law," p. 266.

41. Consider, for example, Terry Lantry, "An Expanding Legal Duty: The Recovery of Damages for Mental Anguish by Those Observing Tortious Activity," *American Business Law Journal* 19 (1981): 214–26; and Joseph P. Towey, "Negligent Infliction of Mental Distress: Reaction to Dillon v. Legg in California and Other States," *Hastings Law Journal* 25 (April 1974) 1248–65.

42. *Rodriguez v. State,* 472 P2d 509 (Hawaii 1970).

43. 472 P2d at 520.

44. Terri Krivosha Herring, "Administering the Tort of Negligent Infliction of Mental Distress: A Synthesis," *Cardoza Law Review* 4 (1983): 507

45. *Molien v. Kaiser Foundation Hosp.,* 27 Calif. 3d 933–36, 616 P2d 813 (1980).

46. See *Ochoa v. Superior Court,* 39 Calif. 3d 159, 703 P2d, 26 Calif. Rptr. 661 (1985); *Thing v. La Chusa,* 48 Calif. 3d 644, 771 P2d 814, 257 Calif. Rptr. 865 (1989); and *Huggins v. Longs Drug Stores, Inc.,* 24 Calif. Rptr. 2d 587, 862 P2d 148 (1993). The court has restricted *Molien* by limiting recovery of emotional damages to those who were "direct victims" of a negligent action, as opposed to bystanders—to whom an extended version of the *Dillon* standard is still applicable.

47. Consider, for example, Scott Marrs, "Mind over Body: Trends regarding the Physical Injury Requirement in Negligent Infliction of Emotional Distress and 'Fear of Disease' Cases," *Tort and Insurance Law Journal* 28, 1 (1992): 39; and Langhenry, "Personal Injury Law," p. 271.

48. *Ob-Gyn Associates of Albany v. Littleton,* 386 SE2d 151 (Georgia 1989).

49. *Reilly v. United States,* 547 A2d 894 (Rhode Island 1988).

50. *Campbell v. Animal Quarantine Station,* 63 Hawaii 557, 632 P2d 1066 (1981).

51. 632 P2d at 1069.

52. 632 P2d at 1070.

53. *Potter v. Firestone Tire and Rubber Co.,* 274 Calif. Rptr. 885, 225 Calif. App. 3d 213 (1991).

54. 274 Calif. Rptr. at 891.

55. *Reinhardt Motors, Inc. v. Boston,* 516 So. 2d 509 (Alabama 1986).

56. *Shaw v. Cassar,* 558 FSupp 303 (ED Michigan 1983).

57. *Ferrara v. Bernstein,* no. 42, *New York Law Journal* (11 August 1993): 3, col. 1.

58. *Quill v. Trans World Airlines, Inc.,* 361 NW2d 438 (Minnesota 1985).

59. *Herber v. Johns-Mansville Corp.,* 785 F2d 79 (3d Cir 1986).

60. *Bass v. Nooney Co.*, 646 SW2d 765 (Montana 1983).

61. *Corso v. Crawford Dog and Cat Hospital, Inc.*, 415 N.Y. S2d 182, 97 Misc. 2d 530 (1979). In this case, the owner of the poodle arranged an elaborate funeral service and was disappointed when the casket arrived with the body of a dead cat in it.

62. "Jessie Rogers v. Dr. Eustace Cordin," 05319/87, *The New York Jury Verdict Reporter*, IX/50–6, Verdict: 11 February 1992.

63. "Marilyn Veater v. Dr. Steven Alan Fayer," 011872/89, *The New York Jury Verdict Reporter*, XI/1–2, Verdict: 21 December 1992.

64. "Michael Romei v. Shell Oil Co., Peter Sutherland, and Renata Karlin," 11005/90, *The New York Verdict Reporter*, XII/13–3, Verdict: 7 February 1994. In New York, the zone-of-danger rule is still the reigning standard for recovery of negligently inflicted emotional injuries. In this case, the emotional injury essentially was compensated as an independent tort. Compensation was allowed, however, because it was claimed that the infliction of emotional injury was "intentional." As noted earlier, the court has historically been more open to recovery for the intentional infliction of emotional injuries. Still, this case illustrates the extent to which, even in a case where another type of tort (defamation, libel, or discrimination) was the ostensible basis for the claim, what was really at issue—and what was ultimately compensated—was the emotional injury.

65. To construct Table 3.5, I used a number of legal resources: the Digest System, the American Law Reports, and the Lexis computer system. I also relied on earlier legal studies, including the comment "Negligent Infliction of Mental Distress: A Jurisdictional Survey of Existing Limitations Devices and Proposal Based on an Analysis of Objective v. Subjective Indices of Distress," *Villanova Law Review* 33 (1988): 792–807; and Marrs, "Mind over Body."

66. Rodney A. Smolla, "Let the Author Beware: The Rejuvenation of the American Law of Libel," *University of Pennsylvania Law Review* 132 (1983): 1.

67. Howard P. Schneiderman, "Constitutional Right of Privacy and State Action," *Gonzales Law Review* 6 (1970): 54.

68. *Harris v. Forklift*, 510 U.S. 17, 114 S. Ct. 367 (1993).

69. Smolla, "Let the Author Beware," pp. 19–20.

70. For a discussion of the difference between an orthodox legal and a social scientific approach to the study of law see Friedman, *Total Justice*, pp. 27–29. Here Friedman distinguishes between the different research bents of orthodox legal scholars, who typically view the legal world as "a tough self-contained entity, evolving and unfolding according to its own internal norms and rules," and the social scientists, who understand legal changes as largely "determined by outside social influences." Like Friedman, I obviously lean toward a conception of law that sees society playing "the dominant role in molding law," as opposed to a view that sees the law as essentially autonomous. The more typical tendency among lawyers and legal writers to view law as autonomous makes

legal recognition of the influence of the therapeutic culture all the more intriguing.

71. Twiford, "Emotional Distress," p. 123.

72. Smolla, "Let the Author Beware," p. 1.

73. Stanley Ingber, "Rethinking Intangible Injuries: A Focus on Remedy," *California Law Review* 73 (1985): 773.

74. Comment, "Negligent Infliction of Mental Distress," p. 802.

75. *D'Ambra v. U.S.*, 338 A2d 524 (1975).

76. *Taylor v. Baptist Medical Center*, 400 S2d 369, 374 (Alabama 1981).

77. *Sinn v. Burd*, 486 Pa. 146, 404 A2d 672, 678 (1979).

78. *James v. Lieb*, 375 NW2d 109 (Nebraska 1985).

79. Gary Perrin, *Mental/Emotional Injuries: An Examination of Trial Court Claims, Verdicts, and Effect of the Artificial Legal Standards* (Ann Arbor, Mich.: University Microfilms, 1989).

80. See Stan V. Smith, "Economic Analysis Whose Time Has Come," *The Brief* (summer 1993), 24f. In this article Smith cites Larry Bodine, former editor and publisher of the *ABA Journal*, as stating that the theory of hedonic damages "has moved quietly, case by case, into the mainstream of modern tort law," p. 26.

81. As early as the 1920s, some state courts would, on occasion, allow a psychologist to testify as an expert witness. They did so, however, without directly addressing the larger issue of whether or not psychologists qualify as expert witnesses. Also, in these rare cases limitations were usually placed on the psychologist in terms of what he or she could testify about.

82. *American Law Reports (ALR)*, 1961, p. 922; *People v. Hawthorne* 293 Mich. 15, 291 NW 205 (1940).

83. 78 ALR2d § 2, pp. 920–21.

84. Ibid.

85. *Sandow v. Weyerhaeuser Co.*, 449 P2d 429 (Oregon 1969).

86. *People v. Noble*, 42 Ill. 487, 248 NE2d 96 (1969).

87. Robert E. Schulman, "The Psychologist as an Expert Witness," *Kansas Law Review* 15 (1966): 90.

88. Laws of Florida, chap. 81–235: 490.002.

89. Schulman, "Psychologist as Expert Witness," p. 89.

90. According to Jules L. Greenberg, "The gradual or protracted psychiatric stress cases grew, by judicial interpretation, out of the analogy of psychological injuries to physical ones" ("Causation and Threshold Determinations in Workers' Compensation Psychiatric Stress Claims: Back to the Future," *Western State University Law Review* 22 [1992]: 144. In the important *Baker v. WCAB* case, for example, the court, citing an earlier case, asserted: "We perceive no logical basis for a different requirement for a psychoneurotic injury. To one experiencing it, such an injury is as real and disabling as a physical injury" (*Baker v. WCAB,*

96 Calif. Rptr. 286 [1971]). For the history of emotional distress cases within workers' compensation litigation, see also Joseph Zuber, "The Employment-Related Emotional Distress Morass: Confusing Signals from California's Courts and Legislature," *Pacific Law Journal* 21 (1989): 1035–67. For a discussion of the recent expansion of emotional injuries in workers' compensation cases, see Susan Dentzer, "A Cure for Job Stress," *Newsweek,* 2 June 1986, pp. 46–47.

91. *Albertson's Inc. v. WCAB (Bradley),* 182 Calif. Rptr. 304, 308 (1982).

92. Rahul Jacob, "Stress on the Job? Go to California," *Fortune,* 31 July 1989, p. 22.

93. Californians for Compensation Reform, made up of corporations and insurers, was initiated to lobby California's legislature in order to cut the rising costs of workers' compensation litigation. Among its members were Clorox, General Electric, Marriott, McDonnell Douglas, and Northrop. And although other states have followed California's lead in limiting workers' compensation rewards for psychological distress, it is still believed that "stress will continue to be a major factor in the workplace and stress claims will probably not diminish" (Greenberg, "Causation and Threshold Determinations," p. 130).

94. California Labor Code, sec. 3208.3 (West Supp. 1992).

95. Peter Passell, "Civil Justice System Is Overhaul Target," *New York Times,* 27 January 1995, B7.

96. The only exception was the inclusion of a provision that called for the elimination of "joint and several liability" for noneconomic damages, designed to protect defendants (usually ones with "deep pockets") from having to pay judgments disproportionate to their fault. The provision, however, was only for product liability cases, and it did not limit recovery of emotional damages. It only ensured that a defendant would pay for noneconomic damage awards according to the percentage of fault determined by the court.

97. Senate, Senator Slade Gorton of Washington, *Congressional Record,* 104th Cong., 1st sess., 24 April 1995, 141, S5577.

98. House, Representative Henry Hyde of Illinois, *Congressional Record,* 104th Cong., 1st sess., 9 March 1995, 141, H2936.

99. Senate, Senator Jan Kyl of Arizona, *Congressional Record,* 104th Cong., 1st sess., 1 May 1995, S5876.

100. Ibid.

101. Ibid. p. S5875.

NOTES TO CHAPTER 4

1. Stanton Peele, *Diseasing of America: Addiction Treatment Out of Control* (Toronto: Lexington Books, 1989), pp. 27–28.

2. Claudia Willis, "Life in Overdrive," *Time,* 18 July 1994, p. 43.

3. Federal Bureau of Investigation (FBI), *Uniform Crime Reports for the United States, 1992* (Washington, D.C.: U.S. Department of Justice, Federal Bureau of Investigation, 1992) p. 216.

4. National Institute of Justice, *Searching for Answers: Annual Evaluation Report on Drugs and Crime: 1992* (Washington, D.C.: U.S. Department of Justice, National Institute of Justice, June 1993), p. 58.

5. Ibid.

6. Testimony of Richard H. Girgenti, director of Criminal Justice Services, State of New York, before the House Select Committee on Narcotics Abuse and Control, 28 October 1991, p. 69.

7. Jill Smolowe, Lock 'Em Up and Throw Away the Key, *Time,* 7 February 1994, p. 56.

8. National Institute of Justice, *Searching for Answers,* p. 58.

9. Bureau of Justice Statistics, *A National Report: Drugs, Crime, and the Justice System* (Washington D.C.: U.S. Department of Justice, Bureau of Crime Statistics, December 1992), pp. 2, 3.

10. Ibid., p. 3.

11. National Institute of Justice. *Drug Use Forecasting Research Update: Fourth Quarter, 1990* (Washington, D.C.: National Institute of Justice, 1991).

12. Douglas Lipton, Gregory Falkin, and Harry Wexler, "Correctional Drug Abuse Treatment in the United States: An Overview," in *Drug Abuse Treatment in Prisons and Jails,* ed. Carl G. Leukefeld and Frank M. Tims, National Institute of Drug Abuse (NIDA) Research Monograph 118 (Washington, D.C.: U.S. Department of Health and Human Services, 1992), p. 9.

13. *Strategies for Action: Combating Drug and Alcohol Abuse in Dade County* (a publication of Metropolitan Dade County, Florida), p. 1.

14. National Institute of Justice, *Searching for Answers,* p. 54.

15. Bureau of Justice Statistics, *A National Report,* p. 4.

16. Ibid.

17. Office of National Drug Control Policy, *Understanding Drug Treatment* (Washington, D.C.: Office of National Drug Control Policy, June 1990), p. 2.

18. *Robinson v. California,* 370 US 660 (1962).

19. Andrew Mecca, for example, observes that "there have been a multitude of models in this area [diversion programs], and the most prominent, in terms of funding support and number of clients served, is TASC (Treatment Alternatives to Street Crime)" (cited in "TASC—Treatment Alternatives to Street Crime: Historical Perspective and Future Implications," *Offender Rehabilitation* 2, [spring 1978]: p. 279).

20. DNADA was the predecessor to what is now called the National Institute of Drug Abuse (NIDA).

21. Bureau of Justice Assistance, *Treatment Alternatives to Street Crime:*

TASC Programs (Washington, D.C.: U.S. Department of Justice, Bureau of Justice Assistance, January 1988), p. 5.

22. Ibid., p. 5.

23. General Accounting Office (GAO), *Drug Control Treatment Alternatives Program for Drug Offenders Needs Stronger Emphasis,* report to the chairman, House Select Committee on Narcotics Abuse and Control, 11 February 1993, p. 3.

24. Beth Weinman, "A Coordinated Approach for Drug-Abusing Offenders," in *Drug Abuse Treatment in Prisons and Jails,* ed. Leukefeld and Tims, p. 234.

25. Matthew Cassidy, associate executive director of TASC, testimony presented to the House Select Committee on Narcotics Abuse and Control, 28 October 1991, attachment C.

26. Weinman, "A Coordinated Approach," p. 241.

27. Cassidy testimony, 28 October 1991.

28. Susan Timber, phone conversation with the authors, 7 February 1994.

29. See, for example, the description of the Dade County Drug Court in Michael Isikoff and William Booth's "Miami 'Drug Court' Demonstrates Reno's Unorthodox Approach," *Washington Post,* 20 February 1993, A1.

30. *Miami's Drug Court: A Different Approach,* (Washington, D.C.: U.S. Department of Justice, National Institute of Justice, June 1993), pp. 2–3.

31. Ibid., p. 5.

32. Ibid., p. 7.

33. "Clark County Drug Court," a four-page summary of the Clark County Drug Court sent to author with cover letter from Drug Court judge Jack Lehman, 4 March 1994. Eighth Judicial District Court, Clark County, Nevada, p. 4.

34. For a discussion of nondrug charges included in the Los Angeles Drug Court program, consider Somini Sengupta, "County Drug Shift Weighed," *Los Angeles Times,* 17 May 1993, A1. The Clark County, Nevada, Drug Court, as another example, has expanded to include people with "charges such as burglary or writing bad checks." See "Clark County Drug Court," p. 2. Also see John Goldkamp, *Justice and Treatment Innovation: The Drug Court Movement,* pp. 59–60. Here it is reported that "one of the dramatic discoveries of the First National Drug Court Conference was that in a number of locations the innovative and collaborative methods characterizing the first generation of treatment drug courts were being adapted to other justice system populations." Examples included the treatment of "women offenders" in Kalamazoo, Michigan, "domestic violence" cases in Dade County, and "misdemeanor arrests" in Midtown, Manhattan.

35. Judge Steven Marcus, interview with the author in Marcus's chambers of the Los Angeles Criminal Court Building, 8 August 1994.

36. This changed in Broward County after the passage of legislation in

Florida in April 1993, making it statutory law that a judge can allow for dismissal of a case after successful completion of preadjudicative diversion.

37. See Florida Statute 948.08, passed April 2, 1993. One of the main reasons the courts were given this discretion was the resistance by the state attorney in Broward County, Florida, Michael Satz, to dismissing cases.

38. Tom Sander, "Broward Drug Court Turns Lives Around—As 25 Who Graduated Can Attest," *Sun-Sentinel,* 30 August 1993.

39. National Institute of Justice, *Searching for Answers,* p. 55.

40. Diane Magliola, phone conversation with the authors, 10 February 1994.

41. Jeffrey Tauber, "A Judicial Primer on Drug Courts and Court-Ordered Drug Rehabilitation Programs" (paper presented at the California Continuing Judicial Studies Program in Dana Point, California, 20 August 1993), p. 16.

42. With the Republican takeover of Congress in 1994 the crime bill was revamped, and this money was put in serious jeopardy. In the end, the Drug Courts ended up getting $18 million for the 1996 fiscal year.

43. Columbia Pretrial Services, paper prepared for Center for Substance Abuse Treatment, U.S. Department of Health and Human Services, 30 June 1993, pp. 12–13.

44. Ibid., p. 12.

45. *Miami's Drug Court,* p. 5.

46. Jane Gross, "Probation and Therapy Help Some Drug Users," *New York Times,* 21 June 1991, B, 6:3.

47. Ibid.

48. Tauber, "A Judicial Primer," p. 8.

49. Ibid.

50. *Miami's Drug Court,* p. 9.

51. Patrick May, "Drug Court Specializes in Second Chances," *Miami Herald,* 21 October 1990, 1B.

52. Tom Sander, "Broward County Turns Lives Around," *Sun-Sentinel,* 30 August 1993.

53. *Sun-Sentinel,* 18 November 1992, p. 13.

54. Elizabeth Wiener, "Drug Court Judges Cite Need to Blend Strictness, Compassion," Criminal Justice Newsletter (CJN) *Drug Letter* (January 1994): 5.

55. Ibid., p. 6.

56. "Kalamazoo County Substance Abuse Diversion Program for Female Offenders: Policies and Procedures" (Kalamazoo County program paper, 19 April 1993), p. 12.

57. Ed Finnerty, "Treatment, Not Prison, Goal for Addiction," *Kalamazoo Gazette,* 2 November 1992.

58. Author's field notes, 5 August 1994, Los Angeles Criminal Courtroom.

59. Ibid.

60. "Clark County Drug Court," p. 1.

61. Ibid., p. 2.

62. Allan V. Horwitz, for example defines the act of psychotherapy as follows: "Therapy no longer serves to tie individuals into the community but, instead, is designed to free them from group ties. The goal of psychoanalytic treatment is to allow patients to become autonomous and regulate their lives by norms of their own choosing. To achieve this goal, the individual personality becomes the center of therapeutic concern, and therapeutic techniques turn individuals inward to gain insight into how their past experiences have led to their current problems. . . . Therapy becomes limited to a dialogue between the patient and the therapist, with no participation by outside family or community members. Within this isolated setting, patients communicate their private feelings that they keep hidden from the world" ("Therapy and Social Solidarity," in *Toward a General Theory of Social Control,* ed. Donald Black [New York: Academic Press, 1984], 1:236).

63. Caroline S. Cooper and Joseph A. Trotter, Jr., "Drug Case Management and Treatment Intervention Strategies in the State and Local Courts," part of the Bureau of Justice Assistance/State Justice Institute Management Technical Assistance and Training Project, American University, Washington, D.C., September 1994, p. 51.

64. Ibid., supplement, p. 34.

65. Ibid., p. 63.

66. *Program Workbook,* Impact Drug and Alcohol Treatment Center, in-house workbook given to author during August 1994 visit to the Los Angeles Drug Court. p. 53.

67. Ibid., p. 56.

68. Author's field notes, 5 August 1994, Los Angeles AA meeting.

69. Ibid.

70. Ibid.

71. Ibid.

72. *Program Workbook,* Impact Drug and Alcohol Treatment Center, p. 62.

73. Ibid., p. 70.

74. Ibid., pp. 70, 73, 76.

75. Tauber, "A Judicial Primer," p. 8.

76. Ibid.

77. Ronald Smothers, "Miami Tries Treatment, Not Jail, in Drug Cases," *New York Times,* 19 February 1993, A, 10:5.

78. John Goldkamp and Doris Weiland, *Assessing the Impact of Dade County's Felony Drug Court—Final Report,* National Institute of Justice Research Report, August 1993, pp. 6–7.

79. Gross, "Probation and Therapy," B, 6:3.

80. Ibid.

81. Cited in Michael Moline, "Oakland's Drug Plan Starts Fast, Moves Ahead," *San Francisco Daily Journal,* 14 January 1992, A8.

82. Kathleen Kernicky, "Betting on Pins and Needles," *Sun-Sentinel,* 8 December 1991, IB.

83. Arty Frieberg and Kevin Davis quoting Judge Fogan, "Drug Users Get 2nd Chance in Court but Not at Work," *Sun-Sentinel,* 31 May 1992.

84. "S.T.O.P.: Sanction—Treatment—Opportunity—Progress. An Early Drug Intervention and Case Management Program," Portland, Oregon, Drug Court program paper, (1993), p.4.

85. Goldkamp and Weiland, *Assessing the Impact,* p. 16.

86. Ibid.

87. "S.T.O.P.," p. 14.

88. Cited in Toni Locy, "Court to Seek Treatment for Addicted Defendants," *Boston Globe,* 24 January 1994, p. 14.

89. Tauber, "A Judicial Primer," p. 10.

90. Finnerty, citing Judge Schma, "Treatment, Not Prison."

91. "Drug Court" (unpublished paper on Los Angeles Drug Court), 1993, p. 3.

92. Isikoff and Booth, "Miami 'Drug Court'," A8.

93. Smothers, quoting Timothy Murray of Dade County, "Miami Tries Treatment, Not Jail," A, 10:5.

94. Lehman, "Clark County Drug Court," p. 4.

95. Karen Kaplan, quoting Judge Fogan, "Drug Court Experiment Saves Money, Cuts Crime," *San Francisco Chronicle,* 11 August 1992, A, 4:3.

96. Quoted from a Berrien County, Michigan, Drug Court document "92–93 Goals and Their Current Status" (20 July 1993).

97. Grant proposal, "Mobile Diversionary Drug Treatment Program (MDDT)," submitted by Alabama Department of Corrections in cooperation with the Thirteenth Judicial Circuit, Mobile, Alabama, to Bureau of Justice Assistance Edward Byrne Memorial State and Local Law Enforcement Assistance Program, p. 48.

98. Jeffrey Tauber, "The Importance of Immediate and Intensive Intervention in a Court-Ordered Drug Rehabilitation Program: An Evaluation of the F.I.R.S.T. Diversion Project after Two Years" (paper presented to the President's Commission on Model State Drug Laws, Philadelphia) 10 March 1993, p. 13.

99. Libby Deschenes and Peter Greenwood, *Experimental Evaluations of Drug Court, Maricopa County, Arizona* (Santa Monica, Calif.: Rand Corporation, 1993), appendix 1.

100. W. Clinton Terry, "Broward County Drug Court: A Preliminary Report" (Florida International University, unpublished paper, November 1993), pp. 23–24.

101. Ibid., p. 25.

102. American Bar Association (ABA), *The State of Criminal Justice* (Washington, D.C.: ABA, Section of Criminal Justice, 1993), p. 65.

103. Ibid., p. 69.

104. Ibid., p. 71.

105. Goldkamp and Weiland, *Assessing the Impact,* p. 89.

106. Ibid., appendix B.

107. Ibid., p. 91n.

108. Ibid., p. 67.

109. Ibid., p. 43.

110. Ibid., p. 45.

111. Ibid., p. 47.

112. Ibid., pp. 65–66.

113. Ibid., p. 49.

114. Ibid.

115. ABA, *State of Criminal Justice,* p. 69.

116. Goldkamp and Weiland, *Assessing the Impact,* p. 13.

117. Ibid., p. 52.

118. Terry, "Broward County Drug Court," p. 26.

119. Ibid.

120. "S.T.O.P.," p. 14.

121. Judge Lawrence Terry, phone conversation with the author, 22 March 1994.

122. The surveys were conducted by the U.S. Department of Justice, Bureau of Justice Statistics of State Correctional Facilities, and were obtained for this analysis from the Inter-University Consortium for Political and Social Research in Ann Arbor, Michigan. Paul F. Bergen, the Social Sciences Data Services coordinator at the University of Virginia's Alderman Library, assisted me in securing the data set. Each survey (1974, 1979, 1984, and 1990) was conducted under the direction of the Bureau of Justice Statistics. The 1984 and 1990 surveys were conducted by the U.S. Department of Commerce, Bureau of the Census, under the direction of the Bureau of Justice Statistics, and each surveyed state correctional facilities on a whole range of issues—size, type and number of personnel, programs, etc. The 1990 survey also included data from federal correctional facilities, which I excluded from the analysis in order to make the data as consistent as possible. One will notice, in observing Tables 4.3, 4.4, and 4.5, that Tables 4.3 and 4.5 exclude 1979 data and Table 4.4 excludes 1984 data. This was necessary for two reasons. First, the 1984 survey did not divide up drug, alcohol, and psychological/psychiatric counseling into separate variables; all were included as a single and inseparable variable. Therefore, when dividing up the different types of programs, 1984 could not be included. Second, the way the questions were posed in 1979 did not account for inmates who may

have been in all three types of counseling. In other words, the results of the 1979 survey indicate that inmates involved in more than one type of program may have been counted more than once, thus inflating the total number of inmates involved in counseling or treatment programs. The 1990 survey, by contrast, asks the question in such a way that inmates were not counted more than once, and the 1984 survey counted only the number of inmates in either psychological, drug, or alcohol treatment. Hence even the separated-out responses for 1979 in Table 4.4 are a bit inflated. Nevertheless, the general trend toward greater involvement in counseling programs in America's prisons over the past twenty years is indisputable.

123. U.S. Department of Justice, Bureau of Justice Statistics, "Correctional Populations in the U.S., 1991," August 1993, p. 37.

124. Ibid.

125. U.S. Department of Justice, Bureau of Justice Statistics, 1990, "Correctional Populations in the U.S.," p. 53.

126. U.S. Department of Justice, Bureau of Justice Statistics, "Survey of State Prison Inmates, 1991," March 1993, p. 24.

127. Figures for Table 4.6 were taken from two main sources: (1) Bureau of Justice Statistics, Drugs, Crime, and the Justice System (Washington, D.C.: U.S. Department of Justice, Bureau of Justice Statistics, December 1992), p. 200; and (2) the preliminary findings of surveys conducted by the National Criminal Justice Association, Narcotic and Drug Research, Inc., and National Institute of Corrections, and Abt. Associates, Inc., and reported by Lipton, Falkin, and Wexler in "Correctional Drug Abuse Treatment," pp. 11–12, and by Robert Frohling in "Promising Approaches to Drug Treatment in Correctional Settings," National Conference of State Legislatures Criminal Justice Paper #7, (1989), p. 2.

128. As reported by Harry Wexler, D.S. Lipton, and J. Blackmore in *Cost of Treatment in Reform*, Project REFORM final report (New York: Narcotic and Drug Research, Inc., 1990), and by Lipton, Falkin, and Wexler in "Correctional Drug Abuse Treatment," p. 23.

129. See Donald W. Murray, Jr., "Drug Abuse Treatment Programs in the Federal Bureau of Prisons: Initiatives for the 1990's," in *Drug Abuse Treatment in Prisons and Jails,* ed. Leukefeld and Tims, pp 67–68.

130. David L. Winett, Rod Mullen, Lois L. Lowe, and Elizabeth A. Missakian, "Amity Rightturn: A Demonstration in Drug Abuse Treatment Program for Inmates and Parolees," in *Drug Abuse Treatment in Prisons and Jails,* ed. Leukefeld and Tims, p. 90.

131. See Murray, "Drug Abuse Treatment Programs," p. 62.

132. Robert Peters and Roger May, "Drug Treatment Services in Jail," in *Drug Abuse Treatment in Prisons and Jails,* ed. Leukefeld and Tims, p. 42.

133. NIDA Treatment Research Report, *Drug Abuse Treatment in Prisons*

(Washington, D.C.: U.S. Department of Health and Human Services, 1979), p. 7.

134. Lipton, Falkin, and Wexler, "Correctional Drug Abuse Treatment," p. 13.

135. Ibid., p. 16.

136. Marcia Slacum Greene, "Learning to Turn a Life Away from Crime," *Washington Post,* 12 December 1993, A1.

137. Ibid.

138. Ibid.

139. Richard Woodbury, "Taming the Killers," *Time,* 11 October 1993, pp. 58–59.

140. Linnet Myers, "The Making of a Rapist: A Dark Legacy of Abuse," *Chicago Tribune,* 1 June 1989, 5, 2:2.

141. As reported by Linnet Myers in "Never Again? Most Rapists Can't Stop Themselves: Can Therapy?" *Chicago Tribune,* 1 June 1989, 5, 2:1.

142. Ruth Bonapace, "Storm Clouds Are Building at Prison for Sex Offenders," *New York Times* (N.J. ed.), 25 July 1993, 1:2.

143. Ibid.

144. Lipton, Falkin, and Wexler, "Correctional Drug Abuse Treatment," p. 13.

145. Leukefeld and Tims, eds., *Drug Abuse Treatment in Prisons and Jails,* p. 281.

146. Ibid., p. 280.

147. Judge Ronald Taylor of the Berrien County, Michigan, Drug Court explained to me, in a phone conversation on 31 May 1995, that he and six or seven other Drug Court judges lobbied members of the House of Representatives to sustain federal funding of the Drug Courts. Though initially opposed to the programs, members of Congress were persuaded by the fact that the programs were often "more intrusive" than the normal criminal adjudicative practices.

148. Ibid.

149. Richard Lacayo, "Lock 'em Up," *Time,* 7 February 1994, p. 53.

150. Bureau of Justice Statistics, *A National Report,* p. 183.

151. National Institute of Justice, *Searching for Answers,* p. 100.

152. Judge Thomas Merrigan, Franklin County District Court, Greenfield, Massachusetts, speaking at the 1995 National Symposium on the Implementation and Operation of Drug Courts, Portland, Oregon, 6 December 1995.

NOTES TO CHAPTER 5

1. David Tyack, Thomas James, and Aaron Benavot, *Law and the Shaping of Public Education, 1785–1954* (Madison: University of Wisconsin Press, 1987), p. 4.

2. A good portion of the curricula analyzed in this chapter is from material I collected while working with James Hunter on his Moral Literacy Project, which he graciously allowed me to have access to for this study.

3. Mustafa Kemal Emirbayer, "Moral Education in America, 1830–1990: A Contribution to the Sociology of Moral Education" (Ph.D. diss. Cambridge, Mass.: Harvard University, October 1989 [University Microfilms International, Dissertation Information Service, Ann Arbor, 1990], p. 103).

4. John B. Dillon, *Oddities of Colonial Legislation in America, as Applied to the Public Lands, Primitive Education, Religion, Morals, Indians, etc., etc.* (Indianapolis: Robert Douglas Publishers, 1879), pp. 106–7.

5. Ibid., pp. 111–12.

6. Ibid., p. 114.

7. Ibid., p. 104.

8. Bryce Christenson, "Against the Wall," *Persuasion at Work,* 9, 2 (February 1986): 2.

9. Ibid.

10. Lawrence Cremin, *American Education: The Colonial Experience, 1607–1783* (New York: Harper & Row, 1970), p. 187.

11. Cited by John S. Baker, Jr., "Parent-Centered Education," *Notre Dame Journal of Law, Ethics, and Public Policy* (Summer 1988): 539.

12. Laws of the State of New York, 28th sess. (1805), pp. 515–22, as cited in Robert H. Bremner, ed., *Children and Youth in America: A Documentary History,* vol. 1: 1600–1865, (Cambridge, Mass.: Harvard University Press, 1971), p. 256.

13. Ibid., 1:259–60.

14. For discussions of the *New England Primer,* see Carl Kaestle, "Moral Education and Common Schools in America: A Historian's View," *Journal of Moral Education* 13, 2 (May 1984): 101–2; Emirbayer, pp. 103–4; and Cremin, *American Education,* p. 394.

15. Emirbayer, "Moral Education in America," pp. 109–10.

16. James Davison Hunter, *Culture Wars: The Struggle to Define America* (New York: Basic Books, 1991), p. 69.

17. Kaestle, "Moral Education and Common Schools," p. 63; and Emirbayer, "Moral Education in America," p. 108.

18. Stephen Thernstrom, *Poverty and Progress: Social Mobility in a Nineteenth Century City* (Cambridge, Mass.: Harvard University Press, 1964), p. 11.

19. Emirbayer, "Moral Education in America," p. 111.

20. Kaestle, "Moral Education and Common Schools," p. 69.

21. Emirbayer, "Moral Education in America," p. 118.

22. Perry Miller, *The Life of the Mind in America from the Revolution to the Civil War* (New York: Harcourt, Brace & World, 1965), p. 310.

23. Horace Mann, in the Massachusetts Board of Education's, *Tenth Annual Report* (1847), as cited in Bremner, *Children and Youth,* 1:456.

24. Ibid., 1:466.

25. See Jesse Flanders, Legislative Control of the Elementary Curriculum, (New York: Bureau of Publications, Teachers College, Columbia University, 1925).

26. Ibid., p. 153.

27. Ibid.

28. Ibid., p. 152.

29. John H. Westerhoff, *McGuffey and His Readers: Piety, Morality and Education in Nineteenth-Century America* (Nashville: Abingdon Press, 1978), p. 15.

30. W.H. McGuffey, *The Eclectic First Reader* (Cincinnati: Truman & Smith, 1836; reprint, Mott Media, 1982), pp. 118–20.

31. Tack, James, and Benavot, *Law and the Shaping of Public Education,* pp. 100–102.

32. As Westerhoff notes, "The theistic Calvinist world view so dominant in the first editions had disappeared, and the prominent values of salvation, righteousness, and piety were entirely missing. All that remained were lessons affirming the morality and life-style of the emerging middle class and those cultural beliefs, attitudes, and values that undergird American civil religion" (*McGuffey and His Readers,* p. 15).

33. Flanders, *Legislative Control,* p. 159.

34. Ibid., p. 160.

35. *United States Bureau of Education Bulletin,* 2 (1914): 10.

36. Tack, James, and Benavot, *Law and the Shaping of Public Education,* p. 97.

37. B. G. Northrop, in Bremner, ed., *Children and Youth in America: A Documentary History,* vol. 2: *1866–1932,* p. 1421.

38. Ibid.

39. *United States Bureau of Education Bulletin,* 2 (1914): 105–6.

40. Ibid., p. 105

41. Ibid., p. 106.

42. Seventh Biennial Report of the Superintendent of Public Instruction of the State of Illinois, 1867–68, cited in Grace Abbot, *The Child and the State* (New York: Greenwood Press, 1938), 1:290.

43. *Journal of Proceedings and Addresses of the National Education Association* (1890), as cited in Abbot, *The Child and the State,* 1:312.

44. Oscar Handlin, "John Dewey's Contribution to Education," in *The American Experience in Education,* ed. John Barnard and David Burner (New York: Franklin Watts, 1975), pp. 208–9.

45. John Dewey and Evelyn Dewey, *Schools of Tomorrow* (New York: E.P.

Dutton & Co., 1919), pp. 303–16, reprinted in Bremner, ed., *Children and Youth,* 2:1126.

46. Ibid.

47. John Dewey, "Credo," from selections cited in Neil Gerard McCloskey, *Public Schools and Moral Education: The Influence of Horace Mann, William Torrey Harris, and John Dewey* (New York: Columbia University Press, 1958), p. 232.

48. Robert Church, "Moral Education in the Schools," in *Morality Examined,* ed. Lindley J. Stiles and Bruce D. Johnson (Princeton, N.J.: Princeton Book Company, 1977), p. 72.

49. Dewey and Dewey, *Schools of Tomorrow,* cited in Bremner, ed., *Children and Youth,* 2:1126.

50. Virginia Code (1887), sec. 1497.

51. Virginia Code (1928), sec. 688.

52. Cited in Flanders, *Legislative Control,* p. 161. This statutory language, according to Flanders, goes back as far as 1903. It is likely that it was instituted a number of years earlier.

53. Laws of Florida, chap. 28055: 231.09.

54. Boyd H. Bode, "The New Education Ten Years After," *New Republic* 63 (1930): 63.

55. John Dewey, "The Educational Situation" (1902), pp. 9–13, reprinted in Bremner, ed., *Children and Youth,* 2:1134.

56. Cited in Bremner, ed., *Children and Youth,* 2:1141–42.

57. Ibid., 2:1143.

58. Ibid., 2:1146.

59. Cited in Bremner, ed., *Children and Youth in America: A Documentary History,* vol. 3: *1933–1973,* pp. 1590–92.

60. Ibid., 3:1590.

61. Dewey and Dewey, *Schools of Tomorrow,* cited in Bremner, ed., *Children and Youth,* 2:1129.

62. Ibid., 2:1125.

63. Bode, "The New Education," 63.

64. Kaestle, "Moral Education and Common Schools," p. 107.

65. Robert Michaelsen, *Piety in the Public Schools* (New York: Macmilllan, 1970), p. 257, quoted by Kaestle, "Moral Education and Common Schools," 1984, p. 106.

66. Richard Hersh, John Miller, and Glen Fielding, *Models of Moral Education* (New York: Longman, 1980), p. 34.

67. Dwight D. Eisenhower, quoted by Kaestle, "Moral Education and Common Schools," p. 107.

68. H. Warren Button and Eugene E. Provenzo, *History of Education and Culture in America* (New York: Allyn and Bacon, 1989) p. 313.

69. See *Engel v. Vitale*, 370 U.S. 421 (1962); and *School District of Abington Township, Pa. v. Schemp/Murray v. Curlett*, 374 U.S. 203 (1963).

70. Idaho State Law (1919), sec. 944.

71. Idaho State Law (1963), sec. 33–1224.

72. See M. A. McGheney, "Control of the Curriculum," in *The Courts and Education*, ed. Clifford P. Hooker (Chicago: University of Chicago Press, 1978).

73. Leland W. Howe and Mary Martha Howe, *Personalizing Education* (New York: Hart Publishing Co., Inc., 1975), p. 18.

74. Louis Raths, Merrill Harmin, and Sidney B. Simon, "Selections from *Values and Teaching*," in *Moral Education: It Comes with the Territory*, ed. David Purpel and Kevin Ryan (Berkeley, Calif.: McCutchan Publishing Corporation, 1976), pp. 76–78.

75. Alan L. Lockwood, "A Critical View of Values Clarification," in *Moral Education*, ed. Urpel and Ryan, p. 164.

76. Ibid., p. 160.

77. Howe and Howe, *Personalizing Education*, p. 18.

78. Ibid., p. 19.

79. Maury Smith, *A Practical Guide to Values Clarification* (La Jolla, Calif.: University Associates, 1977), p. 5.

80. See Leonard Lund and Cathleen Wild, *Ten Years After a Nation at Risk* (New York: The Conference Board, 1993), for a discussion of business efforts to revive American education and evaluation of the success of these efforts.

81. An elementary school teacher whom I interviewed in Albuquerque, New Mexico, in November 1994, who was also working on a graduate degree in education, affirmed this observation She both acknowledged and celebrated the reincarnation of values clarification in the form of such ideals as building the self-esteem of children.

82. In a memo sent to parents of students at an elementary school in central Virginia, for example, the school's counselor explains that one reason for the recent rise is that "we are getting better at diagnosing ADD so we are keeping a number of undiagnosed children from slipping through the cracks." Another reason for the large number of cases among American children is that "our founding fathers (and mothers!) were impulsive enough to leave their homelands to come to a land where they knew not the consequences of their choice. We strongly suspect ADD to be largely transmitted genetically from parent to child. In fact, it is rare that practitioners treat a child who does not have a parent who subsequent to the child's evaluation will say, 'He's just like me!' We do seem to be seeing about 5% of our population with what appears to be true ADD and we strongly suspect a genetic link in most families affected" (memo titled "Attention Deficit Disorder," from Lucy Riddick, school counselor, Meriwether Lewis Elementary School, Albemarle County, Virginia, sent to parents in December 1994).

83. Consider, for example, Diane Divoky's "Ritalin: Education's Fix-It Drug," *Phi Delta Kappan* 70, 8 (April 1989): 599–605.

84. Rita Kramer, *Ed School Follies* (New York: Free Press, 1991), p. 209.

85. Ibid., p. 210.

86. Ibid., p. 25.

87. These data are based on the responses I received after contacting, by letter, all fifty state boards of education. In the letter I asked the boards to provide me information regarding state regulations for public school counselors. All "Selected Task Descriptions" listed in Table 5.1 are direct quotes from these regulations.

88. California Task Force to Promote Self-Esteem and Personal Responsibility, The report is titled *Toward a State of Esteem: The Final Report of the California Task Force to Promote Self-esteem and Personal and Social Responsibility* (Sacramento: California Department of Education, 1990).

89. Reported in Beth Ann Krier, "California's Newest Export," *Los Angeles Times*, 5 June 1990, E9.

90. California Task Force to Promote Self-Esteem and Personal Responsibility, in Appendix B of *Appendixes to: Toward a State of Esteem* (Sacramento: California Department of Education, 1990), pp. 6–32. The appendix identifies 177 programs with "a conspicuous self-esteem component" that receive state funding.

91. Ibid.

92. Quoted in George Skelton, "Wilson Does Some Bonding for Self-esteem," *Los Angeles Times*, 24 January 1991.

93. Ellen Herman, "Are Politics and Therapy Compatible?" *Utne Reader* (January/February 1992): 97.

94. Dana Priest, "Md., Va. Focus on Building Citizens' Self-esteem," *Washington Post*, 16 August 1990, MDH 1.

95. Jackie Miller, director of Partnerships for Change, interview with the author, 1 October 1992.

96. "Hey, I'm Terrific," *Newsweek*, 17 February 1992, p. 46.

97. Priest, "Md., Va. Focus on Self-Esteem," MDH 1.

98. Ibid.

99. *A Village of Hope: Moving toward a State of Esteem: Action Update # 2 on Self-esteem Programs and Public Policy* (September 1991–January 1992), from the office of California assemblyman John Vasconcellos.

100. Hugh Dellios, "Joke's on Assembly when Off-Beat Bills Hit Floor for Debate," *Chicago Tribune*, 28 April 1991, p. A.1.

101. From the office of California assemblyman John Vasconcellos, document titled "Self-esteem Movement: Status of (Inter)national Developments" (July 24, 1990).

102. Ibid.

103. Assemblyman John Vasconcellos, interview with the author, Sacramento, California, 10 February 1995.

104. Ibid.

105. "National Economic and Social Esteem: Regenerating a Nation of Excellence" (legislative proposal, May 1992).

106. Jack Kemp, letter to Jackie Miller, 11 May 1992.

107. Colin Powell, letter to James Newman, chairperson of the Los Angeles Task Force to Promote Self-Esteem, 11 July 1991, copy of letter given to author by Miller and Michael in October 1992.

108. Barbara Bush, letter to participants in the Self-esteem in the Workplace Conference, 11 November 1991, copy of letter given to author by Miller and Michael in October 1992.

109. Public Law 103–262, 20 United States Code Service: 3282 (1994), approved 31 May 1994.

110. 20 United States Code Service: 3172 (1994).

111. 20 United States Code Service: 1110c (1994).

112. Department of Health and Human Services (HHS), Program Announcement, "Runaway and Homeless Youth Program," *Federal Register* 59, no. 91 (12 May 1994): 24772.

113. HHS, Notice of Grant Applications, "Adolescent Health Centers for American Indians/Alaska Natives," *Federal Register* 58, no. 98 (24 May 1993): 29831.

114. President, Proclamation, "25th Anniversary of Head Start, Proclamation 6140," *Federal Register* 55 (24 May 1990): 21735. In Chapter 6 we will find this to be an important idea to which members of Congress appeal to in defending the Head Start program.

115. Department of HHS, *Federal Register* 56 (31 July 1991): 36640.

116. HHS, *Federal Register* 58, no. 5 (8 January 1993): 3436.

117. Department of Education, "Research in Educational Individuals with Disabilities Program," *Federal Register* 57 (16 July 1992): 31614.

118. Department of Education, "National Institute on Disability and Rehabilitation Research," *Federal Register* 57 (17 April 1992): 14288.

119. Department of Education, "Bilingual Education: Desegregation Support Program, *Federal Register* 46 (21 July 1981): 37594.

120. California Education Code (1994), sec. 54721.

121. California Education Code (1994), sec. 69630.

122. Iowa Code (1993), sec. 256A.4.

123. Massachusetts Annotated Laws (1994), chap. 69, sec. 1L.

124. Minnesota Statute (1993) 121.882.

125. Tennessee Code Annotated (1994), sec. 49–1–520.

126. District of Columbia Board of Education, Daniel H. Eaton, chair,

"Commission on Values-Centered Goals for the District of Columbia: Final Report" (September 1988), p. iv.

127. *Family Life Education: Curriculum Guidelines*, Virginia Department of Education, Richmond, Virginia, 1983, p. 1.

128. *Toward a State of Esteem*, p. 6.

129. "Character Education and the Teacher," p. 2.

130. Don Dinkmeyer and Don Dinkmeyer, Jr., *Tell Me About DUSO . . .*, pamphlet (Circle Pines, Minn.: American Guidance Service, 1991).

131. "What Is the Community of Caring?" (paper issued by Community of Caring, Washington, D.C.), 1990, p. 1.

132. Larry K. Olson, Richard W. St. Pierre, and Jan M. Ozias, *Being Healthy: Teachers Edition* (Orlando, Fla.: Harcourt Brace Jovanovich, 1990), p. 13.

133. *Thomas Jefferson Center 1989 Annual Report* (Pasadena, Calif.: Thomas Jefferson Center, 1989), p. i.

134. Christine Baroque, quoted in *San Diego Union*, 11 June 1987, p. 1.

135. Linda Meeks and Philip Heit, *Health: Focus on You* (Columbus, Ohio: Charles E. Merrill Publishing Co., 1990), pp. 10–11. Merrill has since been bought out by McGraw-Hill Book Co.

136. Julius B. Richmond, Elenore T. Pounds, and Charles B. Corbin, *Health for Life* (Glenview, Ill.: Scott, Foresman & Co., 1992), p. 18.

137. Frances Schoonmaker Bolin, *Growing Up Caring: Exploring Values and Decision Making* (Lake Forest, Ill.: Glencoe Publishing Co./McGraw-Hill Book Co., 1990), p. 123.

138. *Character Education Curriculum News* 3, 1 (February 1991): 1 (San Antonio, Texas: Character Education Institute).

139. Teen Aid, *Me, My World, My Future* (Spokane, Wash.: Teen Aid), p. 19.

140. Ibid., p. 21.

141. Thomas Jefferson Center, *How to Be Successful in Less Than Ten Minutes a Day* (Pasadena, Calif.: Thomas Jefferson Center), p. 9.

142. Ibid., p. 14

143. CEI, "Character Education and the Teacher," p. 1.

144. Meeks and Heit, *Health: Focus on You*, Grade Seven ed., pp. 43–44.

145. Ibid., p. 44.

146. Toward a State of Esteem, pp. 26, 27.

147. *Family Life Education*, p. 9.

148. Ibid., pp. 19–20.

149. Ibid.

150. CEI, "Character Education and the Teacher," p. 2.

151. Don Dinkmeyer and Don Dinkmeyer, Jr., *DUSO-1: Developing Understanding of Self and Others, Teacher's Guide*, rev. ed. (Circle Pines, Minn.: American Guidance Service, 1982), p. 9.

152. Ibid., p. 10.

153. Ibid., p. 25.

154. *Skills for Adolescence: Middle and Junior High Schools,* rev. and exp. ed. (Granville, Ohio: Quest International, 1988), unit 3, p. 11.

155. Ibid., unit 3, p. 3.

156. Ibid., unit 3, pp. 4, 8.

157. Ibid., unit 3, p. 9.

158. Ibid., unit 3, pp. 11, 12.

159. Ibid., unit 3, p. 18.

160. Meeks and Heit, *Health: Focus on You,* Grade One ed., pp. 14–15.

161. Meeks and Heit, *Health: Focus on You,* Teacher ed., pp. 14–15.

162. Teen Aid, *Me, My World, My Future,* Teacher ed., p. 11.

163. *Toward a State of Esteem,* p. 26.

164. Bolin, *Growing Up Caring,* p. 116.

165. Jerry Adler, "Hey, I'm Terrific," p. 48.

166. Charles Krauthammer, "Education: Doing Bad and Feeling Good," *Time,* February 5, 1990, p. 78.

167. Jerry Adler, "Hey, I'm Terrific," p. 50.

168. Christopher Lasch, "For Shame: Why Americans Should Be Wary of Self-esteem," *New Republic,* 10 August 1992, p. 34.

169. Andy Mecca, quoted in George Skelton, "Wilson Does Some Bonding for Self-Esteem," *Los Angeles Times,* 24 January 1991, A:3.

170. Vasconcellos interview, 10 February 1995.

171. John Leo, "The Trouble with Self-esteem," *U.S. News and World Report,* 2 April 1990, p. 16.

172. See, for example, Heather MacDonald, "Why Johnny Can't Write," *Public Interest* 120 (summer 1995): 3–13; and Thomas Sowell, *Inside American Education: The Decline, the Deception, the Dogmas* (New York: Free Press, 1993).

173. "Congress to Debate School Vouchers," *Christian Century* (19 April 1995): 414.

174. See Lund and Wild, *Ten Years After a Nation at Risk.*

175. See, for example, John Katzman and Steven Hodas, *Class Action: How to Create Accountability, Innovation and Excellence in American Schools* (New York: Villard, 1995); and Al Antoli's "Wired for Success," *Washington Post Education Review,* 6 August 1995, p. 4. Antoli cites James Wilsford, superintendent of the Orangeburg, South Carolina, schools: "The real restructuring in teaching and learning is occurring around technology."

176. Consider, for example, Blyth McVicker Clinchy, "Goals 2000: The Student as Object," *Phi Delta Kappan* (January 1995): 383–92; Nel Noddings, "A Morally Defensible Mission for Schools in the Twenty-first Century," *Phi Delta Kappan* (January 1995): 365–68.

177. In years prior to 1985 the total number of public school students was

higher, but the percentage of those enrolled in public schools as compared to the total number of school-age children was actually lower. In 1980, 40.8 million children, or 86 percent of the school-age population, were enrolled in public schools. In 1970, 45.8 million, or 85 percent of the school-age population, were enrolled in public schools. See the *Digest of Education Statistics* (Washington, D.C.: National Center for Education Statistics, U.S. Department of Education, 1994), pp. 12, 25.

178. Alan Ehrenhalt, "Making the Curriculum Count," *Washington Post*, 6 August 1995, Education Review, p. 5.

179. Melinda Wagner, *God's Schools: Choice and Compromise in American Society* (New Brunswick, N.J.: Rutgers University Press, 1990).

180. Louisiana Commission on Promoting Esteem (COPE), 1993, Louisiana Revised Statutes, 17:3951.

181. *Toward a State of Esteem*, p. 4.

182. Assemblyman John Vasconcellos has produced a workbook titled *Self-esteem in the Workplace: A Key to Business Success* (Sacramento, Calif.: August 1992).

183. *Toward a State of Esteem*, p. 42.

184. Vasconcellos interview, 10 February 1995.

185. Jackie Miller, interview with the author, Washington D.C., 1 October 1992.

186. Andy Michael, interview with the author, Washington, D.C., 1 October 1992.

187. Vasconcellos interview, 10 February 1995.

188. Ibid.

189. Bolin, *Growing Up Caring*, p. 106.

190. *Toward a State of Esteem*, p. 5.

191. Ibid.

192. It was Carl Rogers who, drawing on Rousseau and Locke, offered the unconstrained view of the self. He said at a dinner party in Irvine, California, in 1986, "You know, I've been practicing psychology for more than sixty years, and I have really come to believe that we human beings are innately inclined toward becoming constructive and life-affirming and responsible and trustworthy." See John Vasconcellos, in preface to *Social Importance of Self-esteem*, p. xii.

193. Miller interview, 1 October 1992.

194. *Toward a State of Esteem*, p. 27.

195. Vasconcellos, in preface to *Social Importance of Self-esteem*, p. xix Eds. Andrew Wecca, Neil Smelser, and John Uniconcellos (Berkeley: University of California, 1989).

196. *Toward a State of Esteem*, p. 142.

197. Smelser, in introduction to *Social Importance of Self-esteem*, p. 15.

198. Cited in Lasch, "For Shame," pp. 33–34.

199. Vasconcellos interview, 10 February 1995.

200. Ibid.

201. Ibid.

202. Ibid.

203. Michael interview, 1 October 1992.

204. Leroy Foster, lecture given at the Third Annual Self-esteem Conference in Richmond, Virginia, 31 October 1992.

205. Miller interview, 1 October 1992.

206. CEI, "Character Education and the Teacher," pp. 2, 4.

207. Miller interview, 1 October 1992.

208. "National Economic and Social Esteem" (legislative proposal, May 1992) p. 2.

209. *Toward a State of Esteem*, p. 11.

210. Miller interview, 1 October 1992.

211. Leroy Foster, quoted in handout given during his lecture at the Third Annual Self-esteem Conference in Richmond, Virginia, 31 October 1992.

212. James Hillman, in an interview with Sy Safransky, *Utne Reader* (January-February 1992): 98.

NOTES TO CHAPTER 6

1. To ascertain the most important pieces of child welfare legislation and to get a historically representative sample, I used the index to the *Congressional Record* (hereafter *Cong. Rec.*) and those legislative efforts highlighted in Robert H. Bremner, ed. *Children and Youth in America: A Documentary History*, 3 vols. (Cambridge, Mass.: Harvard University Press, 1971).

2. President Theodore Roosevelt, speech delivered at the White House and placed in *Congr. Rec.*, 60th Cong., 2d sess., 15 February 1909, 43, pt. 3:2363.

3. Senate, Senator Albert J. Beveridge of Indiana, *Cong. Rec.*, 59th Cong., 2d sess., 23 January 1907, 41, pt. 2:1552.

4. Senate, Senator William Borah of Idaho, *Cong. Rec.* 62d Cong., 2d sess., 8 January 1912, 48, pt. 1:705.

5. House, Congressman Herbert Parsons of New York, *Cong. Rec.*, 60th Cong., 1st sess., 29 February 1909, 43, pt. 4:2909.

6. Senate, Senator Beveridge. *Cong. Rec.*, 59th Cong., 2d sess., 28 January 1907, 41, pt. 2:1792.

7. Senate, Senator Lee S. Overman of North Carolina, *Cong. Rec.*, 59th Cong., 2d sess., 19 January 1907, 41, pt. 2:1868.

8. Senate, Senator Jacob H. Galliger of New Hampshire, *Cong. Rec.*, 62d Cong., 2d sess., 30 January 1912, 48, pt. 2:1520.

9. Senate, Senator Weldon R. Heyburn of Idaho, *Cong. Rec.*, 62d Cong., 2d sess., 11 December 1911, 48, pt. 1:189.

10. Senate, Senator Heyburn, *Cong. Rec.*, 62d Cong., 2d sess., 24 January 1912, 48, pt. 2:1249.

11. Senate, Senator Overman, *Cong. Rec.*, 62d Cong., 2d sess., 24 January 1912, 48, pt. 2:1249.

12. Senate, Senator Heyburn, *Cong. Rec.*, 62d Cong., 2d sess., 30 January 1912, 48, pt. 2:1526.

13. Senate, Senator Heyburn, *Cong. Rec.*, 62d Cong., 2d sess., 11 December, 1911, 48, pt. 1:189.

14. Senate, Senator Heyburn, *Cong. Rec.*, 62d Cong., 2d sess., 8 January 1912, 48, pt. 1:705.

15. Senate, Senator Beveridge, *Cong. Rec.*, 59th Cong., 2d sess., 29 January 1907, 41, pt. 2:1883.

16. Senate, Senator Borah, *Cong. Rec.*, 62d Cong., 2d sess., 8 January 1912, 48, pt. 1:704.

17. Senate, Senator Beveridge, *Cong. Rec.*, 59th Cong., 2d sess., 28 January 1907, 41, pt. 2:1795.

18. Senate, Senator George C. Perkins of California, *Cong. Rec.*, 59th Cong., 2d sess., 29 January 1907, 41, pt. 2:1875.

19. Roosevelt speech, p. 2364.

20. Ibid., p. 2363.

21. Senate, Senator Beveridge, *Cong. Rec.*, 59th Cong., 2d sess., 28 January 1907, 41, pt. 2:1796.

22. Senate, Senator Overman, *Cong. Rec.*, 59th Cong., 2d sess., 29 January 1907, 41, pt. 2:1896.

23. Senate, Senator William E. Chilton of West Virginia, *Cong. Rec.*, 62d Cong., 2d sess., 30 January 1907, 48, pt. 2:1528.

24. House, Congressman Walter H. Newton of Minnesota, *Cong. Rec.*, 67th Cong., 1st sess., 19 November 1921, 61, pt. 8:7996.

25. Senate, Senator Morris Sheppard of Texas, *Cong. Rec.*, 67th Cong., 1st sess., 28 June 1921, 61, pt. 3:3144.

26. Ibid. p. 3145.

27. Ibid. p. 3146.

28. Ibid.

29. House, Congressman Daniel A. Reed of New York, *Cong. Rec.*, 67th Cong., 1st sess., 19 November 1921, 61, pt. 8:7994.

30. House, Congressman James A. Buchanan of Texas, *Cong. Rec.*, 67th Cong., 1st sess., 19 November 1921, 61, pt. 8:8005.

31. Ibid.

32. Ibid., pp. 8005–6.

33. Ibid., p. 8007.

34. House, Congressman Caleb R. Layton of Delaware, *Cong. Rec.*, 67th Cong., 1st sess., 1 November 1921, 61, pt. 7:7146.

35. Ibid.

36. House, Congressman William J. Graham of Illinois, *Cong. Rec.*, 67th Cong., 1st sess., 19 November 1921, 61, pt. 8:7992.

37. Senate, Senator James A. Reed of Missouri, *Cong. Rec.*, 67th Cong., 1st sess., 29 June 1921, 61, pt. 9:8759.

38. Ibid.

39. Ibid.

40. House, Congressman Layton, *Cong. Rec.*, 67th Cong., 1st sess., 1 November 1921, 61, pt. 7:7146.

41. Ibid., p. 7148.

42. House, Congressman Thomas U. Sisson of Mississippi, *Cong. Rec.*, 67th Cong., 1st sess., 19 November 1921, 61, pt. 8:7985.

43. House, Congressman William Upshaw of Georgia, *Cong. Rec.*, 67th Cong., 1st sess., 19 November 1921, 61, pt. 8:8000.

44. House, Congressman Israel M. Foster of Ohio, *Cong. Rec.*, 67th Cong., 1st sess., 19 November 1921, 61, pt. 8:7998.

45. Senate, Senator Sheppard, *Cong. Rec.*, 67th Cong., 1st sess., 28 June 1921, 61, pt. 3:3145.

46. House, Congressman Bill G. Lowrey of Mississippi, *Cong. Rec.*, 67th Cong., 1st sess., 19 November 1921, 61, pt. 8:8008.

47. House, Congressman Layton, *Cong. Rec.*, 67th Cong., 1st sess., 1 November 1921, 61, pt. 7:7146.

48. House, Congressman Reed, *Cong. Rec.*, 67th Cong., 1st sess., 19 November 1921, 61, pt. 8:7993.

49. House, Congressman William B. Bankhead of Alabama, *Cong. Rec.*, 67th Cong., 1st sess., 19 November 1921, 61, pt. 8:7992.

50. Ibid., p. 7993.

51. Senate, Senator William S. Kenyon of Iowa, *Cong. Rec.*, 67th Cong., 1st sess., 28 June 1921, 61, pt. 3:3143.

52. Ibid.

53. House, Congressman Graham, *Cong. Rec.*, 67th Cong., 1st sess., 19 November 1921, 61, pt. 8:7992.

54. Senate, Senator Robert A. Taft of Ohio, *Cong. Rec.*, 78th Cong., 1st sess., 30 June 1943, 89, pt. 5:6791.

55. Senate, Senator Elbert D. Thomas of Utah, *Cong. Rec.*, 78th Cong., 1st sess., 30 June 1943, 89, pt. 5:6793–94.

56. House, Congressman Clyde G. Doyle of California, *Cong. Rec.*, 79th Cong., 1st sess., 2 March 1945, 91, pt. 2:943.

57. House, Congressman Walter E. Brehm of Ohio, *Cong. Rec.*, 78th Cong., 1st sess., 26 February 1943, 89, pt. 9:1367.

58. President Franklin D. Roosevelt, speech delivered at the White House and placed in *Cong. Rec.* by Congressman Charles H. Leavy of Washington, 76th Cong., 3d sess., 23 January 1940, 86, pt. 13:A304.

59. President Franklin D. Roosevelt, speech delivered at the White House and inserted in *Cong. Rec.* by Senator Robert Wagner of New York, 76th Cong., 1st sess., 27 April 1939, 84, pt. 12:A1693–94.

60. Senate, Senator Edward V. Robertson of Wyoming, quoting from a radio address titled "Suffer Little Children to Come unto You" that was delivered by George E. Stringfellow on 6 March 1945, *Cong. Rec.*, 79th Cong., 1st sess., 7 March 1945, 91, pt. 10:A1050–51.

61. House, Congressman Everett M. Dirksen of Illinois, *Cong. Rec.*, 76th Cong., 1st sess., 22 March 1939, 84, pt. 3:3128.

62. House, Congressman Doyle, *Cong. Rec.*, 79th Cong., 1st sess., 2 March 1945, 91, pt. 2:943.

63. Roosevelt speech, inserted into *Cong. Rec.* by Senator Wagner, pt. 12:A1693–94.

64. Roosevelt speech, inserted into *Cong. Rec.* by Congressman Leavy, 86, pt. 13:304.

65. House, Congressman Thomas Lane of Massachusetts, *Cong. Rec.*, 79th Cong., 2d sess., 12 April 1946, 29, pt. 3:A2115.

66. House, Congresswoman Mary T. Norton of New Jersey for Congresswomen Mary T. Norton, Edith Nourse Rogers, Frances P. Bolton, Margaret Chase Smith, Winifred C. Stanley, and Clare Boothe Luce, *Cong. Rec.*, 78th Cong., 2d sess., 25 February 1944, 90, pt. 8:A983.

67. Roosevelt speech, inserted into *Cong. Rec.* by Senator Wagner, p. 12:A1693–94.

68. House, Congressman Jerry Voorhis of California, *Cong. Rec.*, 78th Cong., 1st sess., 22 March 1943, 89, pt. 9:2312.

69. House, Congressman Brehm, *Cong. Rec.*, 78th Cong., 1st sess., 26 February 1943, 89, pt. 9:1367.

70. Roosevelt speech, inserted into *Cong. Rec.* by Congressman Leavy, p. 12:A304.

71. House, Congresswoman Caroline O'Day of New York, *Cong. Rec.*, 76th Cong., 1st sess., 22 May 1939, 84, pt. 12:A 2144.

72. House, Congressman Brehm, *Cong. Rec.*, 78th Cong., 1st sess., 26 February 1943, 89, pt. 9:1367.

73. House, Congressman Doyle, *Cong. Rec.*, 79th Cong., 1st sess., 2 March 1945, 91, pt. 2:943.

74. Roosevelt speech, paced in *Cong. Rec.* by Congressman Leavy, pt. 13:A 304.

75. Sargent Shriver, statement before the Senate Committee on Labor and Public Welfare, Subcommittee on Employment, *Hearing on S. 3164: Amend-*

370 | Notes to Chapter 6

ments to the Economic Opportunity Act of 1964, 89th Cong., 2d sess., 1966, p. 44, quoted in Bremner, ed., *Children and Youth in America,* vol. 3: 1933–1973, parts 5–7, p. 1820.

76. House, Congressman Sam Gibbons of Florida citing a 25 January 1966 article from the *Washington Star,* "Chance to Catch Up—Head Start Becomes Key to the Future," by Benjamin Fine, *Cong. Rec.,* 89th Cong., 2d sess., 26 January 1966, pt. A364.

77. House, Congressman Dallenback of Oregon, *Cong. Rec.,* 91st Cong., 2d sess., 9 February 1970, 116, pt. 3:2789.

78. Senate, Senator George Murphy of California, *Cong. Rec.,* 91st Cong., 2d sess., 19 February 1970, 116, pt. 3:4086.

79. House, Congressman Andrew Jacobs, Jr. of Indiana, citing a 15 August 1965 *Indiana Star* article, "Operation Head Start Called Startling Success," *Cong. Rec.,* 89th Cong., 1st sess., 24 August 1965, 111, pt. A4756.

80. House, Congressman Gibbons, citing article, "Catch Up," Fine, pt. A364.

81. House, Congressman Winston L. Prouty of Vermont, *Cong. Rec.,* 91st Cong,. 2d sess., 19 February 1970, 116, pt. 3:4085.

82. See the excursus, in Peter Berger's *The Homeless Mind,* pp. 83–96.

83. House, Congressman Jacobs, *Cong. Rec.,* 89th Cong., 1st sess., 24 August 1965, pt. A4756.

84. House, Congresswoman Margaret M. Heckler of Massachusetts, citing an article, "Day-Care Facilities Urged for Arlington Preschoolers," *Washington Post,* 14 December 1969, *Cong. Rec.,* 91st Cong., 2d sess., 9 February 1970, 116, pt. 3:2809.

85. House, Congressman John W. Wydler of New York, citing the testimony of Sister Mary James, S.S.J., before the House Education and Labor Committee, *Cong. Rec.,* 91st Cong., 2d sess., 9 February 1970, 116, pt. 3:2814.

86. House, Congressman Gibbons, *Cong. Rec.,* 89th Cong., 1st sess., 22 October 1965, 111, pt. 21:28607.

87. Ibid.

88. Ibid.

89. Ibid.

90. House, Congressman Arnold Olsen of Montana, *Cong. Rec.,* 89th Cong., 1st sess., 6 October 1965, 111, pt. 19:26140.

91. House, Congressman Jacobs, quoting a *Washington Post* article, "Is Head Start a Success? Ask Any 5-Year-Old in It," by Eve Edstrom, *Cong. Rec.,* 89th Cong., 2d sess., 7 February 1966, pt. A566.

92. House, Congressman Prouty, *Cong. Rec.,* 91st Cong., 2d sess., 19 February 1970, 116, pt. 3:4085.

93. House, Congressman Wydler, *Cong. Rec.,* 91st Cong., 2d sess., 9 February 1970, 116, pt. 3:2811.

94. Ibid., p. 2813.

95. Ibid.

96. Ibid., p. 2814.

97. House, Congressman John R. Anderson of Illinois, *Cong. Rec.*, 91st Cong., 2d sess., 9 February 1970, 116, pt. 3:2816.

98. House, Congressman Gibbons, *Cong. Rec.*, 89th Cong., 1st sess., 30 September 1965, 111, pt. 19:25737–38.

99. House, Congressman Jacobs, citing *Indiana Star* article, pt. A4756.

100. Ibid.

101. House, Congressman James A. Mackay of Georgia quoting a Mrs. Claude Burgess, "Head Start Can Succeed: The Decatur, Ga., Story," *Cong. Rec.*, 89th Cong., 1st sess., 2 August 1965, 111, pt. 14:18983.

102. House, Congressman Jacobs, quoting an article by Eve Edstrom, "Is Head Start a Success?" pt. A566.

103. House, Congressman Steiger of Wisconsin, *Cong. Rec.*, 91st Cong., 2d sess., 9 February 1970, 116, pt. 3:2818.

104. House, Congressman Gibbons, *Cong. Rec.*, 89th Cong., 1st sess., 30 September 1965, 111, pt. 19:25737.

105. House, Congressman James C. Cleveland of New Hampshire, *Cong. Rec.*, 89th Cong., 1st sess., 9 June 1965, 112, pt. 10:12942.

106. House, Congressman Gibbons, *Cong. Rec.*, 89th Cong., 1st sess., 30 September 1965, 111, pt. 19:25738.

107. House, Congressman William Goodling of Pennsylvania, *Cong. Rec.*, 100th Cong., 2d sess., 14 April 1988, 134, no. 47:E1034.

108. Senate, Senator John Chafee of Rhode Island, *Cong. Rec.*, 100th Cong., 2d sess., 16 June 1988, 134, no. 89:S7966.

109. House, Congressman Dennis Hertel of Michigan, *Cong. Rec.*, 99th Cong., 1st sess., 24 April 1985, 131, no. 49:E1744.

110. House, Congressman John Miller of Washington, *Cong. Rec.*, 101st Cong., 2d sess., 20 February 1990, 136, no. 12:E276.

111. House, Congressman Dale Kildee of Michigan, *Cong. Rec.*, 100th Cong., 1st sess., 10 February 1987, 133, H656.

112. Senate, Senator Chafee, *Cong. Rec.*, 100th Cong., 2d sess., 16 June 1988, 134, no. 89:S7966.

113. House, Congressman Ben Erdreich of Alabama, *Cong. Rec.*, 100th Cong., 2d sess., 2 May 1988, 134, no. 59:E1339. E1333–34.

114. House, Congressman Stephen J. Solarz of New York, *Cong. Rec.*, 101st Cong., 2d sess., 6 June 1990, 136, no. 70:E1799.

115. House, Congressman Esteban Torres of California, *Cong. Rec.*, 101st Cong., 2d sess., 2 May 1990, 136, no. 52:H733.

116. Senate, Senator Paul Simon of Illinois, *Cong. Rec.*, 100th Cong., 2d sess., 27 April 1988, 134, no. 56:S4978.

117. House, Congressman Charles Rangel of New York, *Cong. Rec.*, 100th Cong., 2d sess., 12 April 1988, 134, no. 45:H1443.

118. House, Congressman Major R. Owens of New York inserted into the record 31 May 1987 *New York Times* article, "Group for Children Aims to Break Cycle of Abuse." Quoted is a statement from child advocate Naomi Malone, *Cong. Rec.*, 100th Cong., 1st sess., 8 June 1987, pt. H14900.

119. House, Congressman Kildee, *Cong. Rec.*, 100th Cong., 1st sess., 10 February 1987, 133, H656.

120. Senate, Senator Chafee quoting Wright Edelman of the Children's Defense Fund, *Cong. Rec.*, 100th Cong., 2d sess., 16 June 1988, 134, S7966.

121. House, Congressman Owens, *Cong. Rec.*, 100th Cong., 1st sess., 8 June 1987, 133, H14900.

122. House, Congressman Goodling, *Cong. Rec.*, 100th Cong., 2d sess., 14 April 1988, 134, no. 47:E1034.

123. Ibid.

124. House, Congressman James Jeffords of Vermont, *Cong. Rec.*, 100th Cong., 2d sess., 13 April 1988, 134, no. 46:H1610.

125. House, Congressman Owens, *Cong. Rec.*, 100th Cong., 2d sess., 12 April 1988, 134, no. 45:H1440.

126. House, Congressman Owens, *Cong. Rec.*, 100th Cong., 1st sess., 8 June 1987, 133, H14900.

127. Ibid.

128. Ibid.

129. Senate, Senator Alan Cranston of California, *Cong. Rec.*, 100th Cong., 1st sess., 3 November 1987, 133, S14900.

130. House, Congressman Owen, quoting Ms. Malone, p. H14900.

131. House, Congressman Kildee, *Cong. Rec.*, 100th Cong., 1st sess., 10 February 1987, 133, H656.

132. House, Congressman Hayes, *Cong. Rec.*, 100th Cong., 1st sess., 10 February 1987, 133, H656.

133. Senate, Senator Simon, *Cong. Rec.*, 100th Cong., 2d sess., 27 April 1988, 134, no. 56:S4978.

134. Senate, Senator Edward Kennedy of Massachusetts, *Cong. Rec.*, 100th Cong., 2d sess., 23 March 1988, 134, no. 37:S2854.

135. Senate, Senator Christopher Dodd, *Cong. Rec.*, 101st Cong., 1st sess., 22 June 1989, 135, no. 85:S7225.

136. House, Congressman Solarz, *Cong. Rec.*, 101st Cong., 2d sess., 6 June 1990, 136, no. 70:E1799.

137. See, for example, Jonathan Alter and Pat Wingert, "The Return of Shame," *Newsweek,* 6 February 1995, pp. 21+.

138. House, Congressman Eva Clayton of North Carolina, *Cong. Rec.,* 104th Cong., 1st sess., 22 March 1995, 141, no. 53:H3544.

139. House, Congressman James Clyburn of South Carolina, *Cong. Rec.*, 104th Cong., 1st sess., 22 March 1995, 141, no. 53:H3544.

140. House, Congressman Sam Johnson of Texas, *Cong. Rec.*, 104th Cong., 1st sess., 21 March 1995, 141, no. 52:H3341.

141. House, Congressman Curt Weldon of Pennsylvania, *Cong. Rec.*, 104th Cong., 1st sess., 22 March 1995, 141, no. 53:H3550.

142. House, Congresswoman Linda Smith of Washington, *Cong. Rec.*, 104th Cong., 1st sess., 22 March 1995, 141, no. 53:H3551.

143. House, Congresswoman Jennifer Dunn of Washington, *Cong. Rec.*, 104th Cong., 1st sess., 21 March 1995, 141, no. 52:H3361.

144. House, Congressman Howard McKeon of California, *Cong. Rec.*, 104th Cong., 1st sess., 21 March 1995, 141, no. 52:H3382.

145. House, Congressman Todd Thiarht of Kansas, *Cong. Rec.*, 104th Cong., 1st sess., 24 March 1995, 141, no. 55: H3740.

146. House, Congresswoman Marge Roukema of New Jersey, *Cong. Rec.*, 104th Cong., 1st sess., 21 March 1995, 141, no. 52:H3347.

147. House, Delegate Eni Faleomavaega of American Samoa, *Cong. Rec.*, 104th Cong., 1st sess., 4 April 1995, 141, no. 62:H4173.

148. House, Congressman Thomas Foglietta of Pennsylvania, *Cong. Rec.*, 104th Cong., 1st sess., 24 March 1995, 141, no. 55:H3770.

149. House, Congressman Foglietta, *Cong. Rec.*, 104th Cong., 1st sess., 23 March 1995, 141, no. 54:H3590.

150. House, Senator Daniel Akaka of Hawaii, *Cong. Rec.*, 104th Cong. 1st sess., 22 May 1995, 141, no. 85:S7113.

151. Ibid.

152. House, Congressman William Luther of Minnesota, *Cong. Rec.*, 104th Cong., 1st sess., 16 March 1995, 141, no. 49:H3298.

153. House, Congressman Cleo Fields of Louisiana, *Cong. Rec.,* 104th Cong., 1st sess., 28 March 1995, 141, no. 57:H3872.

154. House, Congresswoman Sheila Jackson-Lee of Texas, *Cong. Rec.*, 104th Cong., 1st sess., 22 March 1995, 141, no. 53:H3554.

155. Senate, Senator Harry Reid of Nevada, *Cong. Rec.*, 104th Cong., 1st sess., 24 March 1995, 141, no. 55:S4568.

156. House, Congressmen Major R. Owens and Bernard Sanders, *Cong. Rec.*, 104th Cong., 1st sess., 2 February 1995, 144, no. 21:E260.

NOTES TO EXCURSUS

1. Consider, for example, Robert Chrisman and Robert L. Allen's *Court of Appeal: The Black Community Speaks Out on the Racial and Sexual Politics of Clarence Thomas v. Anita Hill* (1992); Toni Morrison's edited collection of essays, *Race-ing Justice, En-gendering Power: Essays on Anita Hill, Clarence*

Thomas, and the Construction of Social Reality (1992); Cornel West's *Race Matters*(1993); and David Brock's *The Real Anita Hill: The Untold Story* (1993), to name a few.

2. Senator Joseph Biden of Delaware, in *Nomination of Judge Clarence Thomas to Be Associate Justice of the Supreme Court of the United States: Hearings before the Committee on the Judiciary, United States Senate,* 102d Cong., 1st sess., 11, 12, and 13 October 1991, p. 127. Hereafter cited as Thomas Hearings.

3. Mary Ann Glendon, *Rights Talk: The Impoverishment of Political Discourse* (New York: Free Press, 1991), p. 44.

4. Thomas Hearings, p. 150.

5. Ibid., p. 77.

6. Ibid., p. 97.

7. Ibid., p. 119.

8. Ibid., p. 280.

9. Ibid.

10. Ibid., p. 5.

11. Ibid., p. 7.

12. Ibid., p. 184.

13. Ibid., p. 189.

14. Ibid., p. 35.

15. Ibid., pp. 36–37.

16. Ibid., p. 71.

17. Ibid.

18. Ibid., p. 104.

19. Ibid., p. 107.

20. Ibid., p. 45.

21. Ibid., p. 451.

22. Ibid., p. 450.

23. Ibid., p. 249.

24. Ibid., p. 119.

25. Ibid., p. 126.

26. Ibid., pp. 175–76.

27. Ibid., p. 524.

28. Ibid., p. 527.

29. Ibid., pp. 71–72.

30. Ibid., p. 79.

31. Ibid., p. 82.

32. Ibid., p. 83.

33. Ibid.

34. Barbara Vobejda, "Who's Telling the Truth? Experts Say Answer May Never Be Known," *Washington Post,* 13 October 1991, A31.

35. Charles Krauthammer, "The Case of Hill v. Thomas," *Washington Post,* 18 October 1991, A21.

NOTES TO CHAPTER 7

1. In "The 1992 Campaign," *New York Times,* 28 March 1992, 1:9.

2. Charles Paul Freund, "Getting His Heads Together," *Washington Post,* 7 February 1993, C5. See also Ann Devron, "I'm O.K. if You're O.K. and Hugs All Around," *Washington Post National Weekly Edition,* 15–21 February 1993, pp. 15–21: and Tom McNichol, "The New Co-Dependent Covenant," *Washington Post,* 28 February 1993, C1.

3. Freund, "Getting His Heads Together," C5.

4. Consider, for example, Richard Cohen's "The Personal President," *Washington Post,* 17 June 1993, A23, where Cohen observes that "what is most striking about Clinton's troubles is the centrality of Clinton himself and the phrase that he uses over and over again, 'I feel good about . . . .' "

5. President Bill Clinton, quoted in "Excerpts from Clinton's News Conference in the Rose Garden," *New York Times,* 15 May 1993, 1:8.

6. President Bill Clinton, in an exchange with reporters prior to a meeting with members of the House Ways and Means Committee, 29 April 1993, in *Selected Speeches of President William Jefferson Clinton* (Washington, D.C.: Government Printing Office, 1993), p. 711.

7. President Bill Clinton, exchange with reporters on 28 April 1993 after announcing his nomination for the director of the Office of National Drug Control Policy, in *Selected Speeches of President William Jefferson Clinton* (Washington, D.C.: Government Printing Office, 1993), p. 706.

8. President Bill Clinton, exchange with reporters in Little Rock, Arkansas, "The New Presidency: Excerpts from an Interview with Clinton after the Air Strikes," *New York Times,* 14 January 1993, A10.

9. Reuters/Susan Cornwell, "Clinton Feels Good about Summit despite Setbacks," 8 July 1994, available from clarinews@clarinet.com.

10. President Bill Clinton cited by Jeffrey Rosen in "The Next Justice," *New Republic,* 12 April 1993, p. 21.

11. Exchange with reporters in the Rose Garden, 14 June 1993, in *Selected Speeches of President William Jefferson Clinton* (Washington, D.C.: Government Printing Office, 1993), p. 1078.

12. Gwen Ifill, "Clinton Keeps Watchers Waiting on Selection for Supreme Court," *New York Times,* 13 May 1994, A22.

13. Cohen, "The Personal President," A23.

14. Clinton, exchange with reporters in Little Rock, Arkansas, 14 January 1993, in "The New Presidency," A10.

15. Richard Cohen, writing for the *Washington Post,* questioned the rele-

vance of Clinton's personal feelings to groups such as the Congressional Black Caucus who strongly supported the Guinier nomination ("The Personal President," A23).

16. President Bill Clinton, remarks endorsing Michael Woo for mayor of Los Angeles in Van Nuys, California, 18 May 1993, in *Selected Speeches of President William Jefferson Clinton* (Washington, D.C.: Government Printing Office, 1993), p. 903.

17. Ibid.

18. From Henry Allen, "The Guru of the White House," *Washington Post,* 9 June 1993, D1-2.

19. Ibid.

20. Michael Lerner, "Work: A Politics of Meaning Approach to Policy," *Tikkun,* 8, 3 (May–June 1993): 23f.

21. Ibid., p. 87.

22. President Bill Clinton, quoted in "Excerpts from Clinton's News Conference in the Rose Garden," *New York Times,* 15 May 1993, 1:8.

23. Joe Klein, "The Tribe of Idols," *New Republic,* 29 November 1993, p. 38.

24. McNichol, "New Co-Dependent Covenant," C1.

25. Ibid.

26. This essentially is what Garry Wills finds in his recent book on leadership *Certain Trumpets: The Call of Leaders* (New York: Simon & Schuster, 1994). His basic thesis is that those rising to positions of leadership do so because of their ability to articulate the values of a given culture.

27. Edward Hinck, *Enacting the Presidency: Political Argument, Presidential Debates, and Presidential Character* (London: Praeger Publishers, 1993), p. 7.

28. Consider, for example, Susan Hellweg, Michael Pfau, and Steven Brydon, *Televised Presidential Debates* (1992): Hinck, *Enacting the Presidency* (1993); and Kathleen Hall Jamieson and David Birdsell *Presidential Debates* (1988).

29. Aristotle, *The Rhetoric and the Poetics of Aristotle,* transl. W. Rhys Roberts, Introduction by Edward P. J. Corbett (New York: Modern Library, 1954), bk. 1, chap. 2, pp. 24–25.

30. Edward P. J. Corbett comes to this conclusion in his introduction to the *Rhetoric,* p. xvii.

31. Aristotle, *Rhetoric,* bk. 1, chap. 3, pp. 32–33.

32. In discussing the "emotions" of pity and indignation, for example, Aristotle argues that these feelings are associated with good "moral character" (*Rhetoric,* pp. 116–117).

33. *New York Evening Post,* 21 October 1858, as cited in Kathleen Hall Jamieson and David Birdsell, *Presidential Debates: The Challenge of Creating an Informed Electorate* (Oxford: Oxford University Press, 1988), p. 7.

34. Consider, for example, Sidney Kraus, *The Great Debates: Background—Perspective—Effects* (Bloomington: Indiana University Press, 1962), pp. 56–57; and Jamieson and Birdsell, *Presidential Debates*, pp. 7–10 and 35–83.

35. All citations for the Lincoln-Douglas debates, which from here on will not be footnoted, were taken from Paul M. Angle's printing of the speeches in *The Complete Lincoln-Douglas Debates of 1858* (Chicago: University of Chicago Press, 1991), pp. 102–76, 189–275, and 285–402. There were seven debates in all: the Ottawa debate, the Freeport debate, the Jonesboro debate, the Charleston debate, the Galesburg debate, and the Alton debate. For most quotes, I name the debate where the statement was made.

36. Three weeks earlier, Douglas had offered the same basic point at the Charleston debate: "And here let me recall to Mr. Lincoln the scriptural quotation which he has applied to the federal government, that a house divided against itself cannot stand, and ask him how does he expect this Abolition party to stand when in one-half of the state it advocates a set of principles which it has repudiated in the other half."

37. Angle, ed., *Complete Lincoln-Douglas Debates*, pp. 368–69.

38. Jamieson and Birdsell, *Presidential Debates*, p. 82.

39. All citations from the Kennedy-Nixon debates, which from here on will not be footnoted, were taken from Sidney Kraus's listing of the texts of the debates in *The Great Debates*, pp. 348–430.

40. Consider, for example, Michael J. Sandel, "Freedom of Conscience or Freedom of Choice," in *Articles of Faith, Articles of Peace,* ed. J. D. Hunter and Os Guinness (Washington, D.C.: The Brookings Institute, 1990); and People for the American Way, *Democracy's Next Generation* (Washington D.C.: People for the American Way, 1989).

41. Aristotle, *Rhetoric*, pp. 90–91.

42. All citation from the Reagan-Mondale debates were taken from the day-after transcriptions printed in The *Washington Post,* 8 October 1984, A22–25, and 22 October 1984, A10–12.

43. James Davison Hunter, in his 1993 *Before the Shooting Begins,* likewise finds that both traditionalists and progressives employ emotivist language when discussing the abortion issue.

44. All citations from the Clinton-Bush-Perot debates were taken from the day-after transcriptions printed in the *Washington Post,* 12 October 1992, A16–19; 16 October 1992, A33–36; and 20 October 1992, A22–25.

45. "I'm in Therapy, You're in Therapy: A Much-Analyzed Candidate Offers a Twelve-Step Plan to Democrats Anonymous," *New York Times,* 15 July 1992, A7.

46. Ibid.

47. "Excerpts from Speech by Gore at Convention," *New York Times,* 17 July 1992, A15.

48. "Excerpts from Remarks Delivered by Jackson and Carter at the Convention," *New York Times*, 15 July 1992, A12.

49. Mayor David Dinkins, cited in Robin Toner, "Appeal for Trust," *New York Times*, 14 July 1992, A1.

50. "Transcript of Speech by Clinton Accepting Democratic Nomination," *New York Times*, 17 July 1992, A14.

51. Sidney Blumenthal, "All the President's Wars," *New Yorker*, 28 December 1992–4 January 1993, p. 70.

52. E. J. Dionne, Jr., "Buchanan Heaps Scorn on Democrats," *Washington Post*, 18 August 1992, A18.

53. Serge F. Kovaleski, "Gingrich's Guru: Corporate Psychotherapist Enlisted to Shape Message," *Washington Post*, 8 December 1994, A1 and A9.

54. Garry Wills, "The Visionary," *New York Review of Books* 42 (23 March 1995): 4–8.

55. David Broder and Dan Balz, "Gore Had to Cross 'Numbness' Barrier on Tobacco Issue," *Washington Post*, 30 August 1996, A33, A35.

56. Ibid. See also Bill Turque, "What Mr. Smooth Is Teaching Mr. Stiff," *Newsweek*, 2 September 1996, p. 26. In Turque's report, Gore is reported to have said that his years with Clinton have made him a more empathetic person. "I've learned the value of paying much more careful attention to the ways people feel."

57. Blaine Hardsen, "Reading between the One-Liners: A Rock Stump Speech Starts to Roll," *Washington Post*, 27 March 1996, A15.

NOTES TO CHAPTER 8

1. See Louis Hicks, "From Coercion to Persuasion: Social Control in the United States Army from 1917 to 1989" (master's thesis, University of Virginia, May 1991).

2. See, for example, Eric Schmitt, "Military Struggling to Stem an Increase in Family Violence," *New York Times*, 23 May 1994, A1: and Bruce Bower, "Hyperactivity: The Family Factor," *Science News* 133 (18 June 1994): 399.

3. Ellen Herman, *The Romance of American Psychology: Political Culture in the Age of Experts* (Berkeley: University of California Press, 1995), p. 105.

4. Ibid., pp. 30–42.

5. Dwight D. Eisenhower, letter to PWD brigadier general Robert McClure, cited in ibid., p. 40.

6. Ibid., p. 61.

7. Ibid., p. 248.

8. Ibid., p. 241.

9. "A Therapeutic State?" *Wall Street Journal*, 3 January 1994, A, 6:1.

10. See Virginia Blue Cross and Blue Shield, "Student Health Insurance Policy: University of Virginia and the University's Clinch Valley College," 1993–

1994, form 1B–673D93C (7/93); and a July 1993 memo to University of Virginia students from the Student Council of the University of Virginia, where reference is made to "changes in mental health benefits, consistent with recent state regulations" (Charlottesville, Virginia).

11. Cited in "A Therapeutic State?" p. 6.

12. From Health Net, *Your Six-Month Wellness Planner,*" (1993), brochure sent to California state employees, WEL 7889 6/93.

13. Richard Rorty, *Contingency, Irony and Solidarity* (Cambridge: Cambridge University Press, 1989), p. 32.

14. William Schnieder, "Putting the 'Clint' in Clinton," *Washington Post,* 28 May 1995, C1.

15. James L. Nolan, Jr, "Political Discourse in America's Past and Present Culture Wars," in James L. Nolan, Jr., ed., *The American Culture Wars: Current Contests and Future Prospects* (Charlottesville, Va., and London: University Press of Virginia, 1996).

16. See James Davison Hunter, *Evangelicalism: The Coming Generation* (Chicago: University of Chicago Press, 1987); and Melinda Bollar Wagner, *God's Schools* (New Brunswick, N.J.: Rutgers University Press, 1990).

17. See, for example, Michael Weisskopf and David Maraniss, "In a Moment of Crisis: The Speaker Persuades," *Washington Post,* 13 August 1995, A1, part of a series in the *Washington Post* titled "Inside the Revolution: Holding it Together."

18. Gianfranco Poggi, *The State: Its Nature, Development and Prospects* (Cambridge: Polity Press, 1990), p. 138.

19. Ibid., p. 120.

20. William Connolly, *Legitimacy and the State* (Oxford: Basil Blackwell, 1984), p. 223.

21. See Poggi, *The State,* pp. 4–7, where he argues that "coercion is the defining feature of the political form of social power," which in the modern context is a less visible but no less real basis for state power.

22. Stanton Peele, *Diseasing of America: Addiction Treatment Out of Control* (Toronto: Lexington Books, 1989), pp. 221–22.

23. Ibid.

24. "Lawmakers to Receive Sensitivity Training," *New York Times,* 25 November 1992, B, 6:1.

25. Gabriel Escobar, "Sensitivity Training for D.C. Officers Is Called Insulting," *Washington Post,* 14 October 1992, D1.

26. Christina Hoff Sommers, quoted by Walter Olson, "When Sensitivity Training Is the Law," *Wall Street Journal,* 20 January 1993, A13.

27. Lynn Chu, cited in ibid.

28. Andrew Martin, "Man Charges Harassment at Sensitivity Training," *Chicago Tribune,* 8 September 1994, 2C, 1:2.

29. Ibid.

30. Ibid.

31. "The FAA Learns the Hard Way," *Chicago Tribune,* 26 September 1994, 1, 16:1.

32. Ibid.

33. From the author's field notes, Miami (Dade County) Drug Court proceedings, 30 January 1995.

34. From the author's field notes, Oakland, California, Drug Court, 9 February 1995.

35. Artie Anderson and Luis Altamirano, interview with the author, 30 January 1995, Department of Human Resources, Office of Rehabilitative Services, Diversion and Treatment Facility in Dade County, Florida.

36. Lois McNay, Foucault: A Critical Foundation, (Cambridge: Polity Press, 1994), p. 95.

37. Judge Gerald S. Bakarich, interview with the author, Sacramento, California, 10 February 1995.

38. From the author's field notes of a visit to Impact House, the Los Angeles Drug Court treatment facility, 5 August 1994.

39. Jürgen Habermas, *Legitimation Crisis* (Boston: Beacon Press, 1973), p. 101.

40. Ibid.

41. John Scharr, "Legitimacy in the Modern State," in *Legitimacy and the State,* ed. Connolly, p. 117.

42. Ibid.

43. Ibid., p. 109.

44. As Robert Bellah, Richard Madsen, William Sullivan, Ann Swidler, and Steven Tipton explain in *Habits of the Heart: Individualism and Commitment in American Life* (Berkeley: University of California Press, 1985), "While the culture of manager and therapist does not speak in the language of traditional moralities, it nonetheless proffers a normative order of life, with character ideals, images of the good life, and methods of attaining it. Yet it is an understanding of life generally hostile to older ideas of moral order. Its center is the autonomous individual, presumed able to choose the roles he will play and the commitments he will make, not on the basis of higher truths but according to the criterion of life-effectiveness as the individual judges it" (p. 47).

Selected References

Abbot, Grace. *The Child and the State*. New York: Greenwood Press, 1938.

Angle, Paul M., ed. *The Complete Lincoln-Douglas Debates of 1858*. Chicago: University of Chicago Press, 1991.

Arendt, Hannah. "What Was Authority?" In *Authority*., edited by Carl J. Friedrich. Cambridge, Mass.: Harvard University Press, 1958.

Aristotle. *The Rhetoric and Poetics of Aristotle*. Translated by W. Rhys Roberts. Introduction by Edward P.J. Corbett. New York: Modern Library, 1954.

Badie, Bertrand, and Pierre Birnbaum. *The Sociology of the State*. Translated by Arthur Goldhammer. Chicago: University of Chicago Press, 1983.

Beetham, David. *The Legitimation of Power*. Atlantic Highlands, N.J.: Humanities Press International, 1991.

Bell, Daniel. *The Coming of Post-Industrial Society: A Venture in Social Forecasting*. New York: Basic Books, 1973.

———. *The Cultural Contradictions of Capitalism*. New York: Basic Books, 1976.

Bell, Peter A. "The Bell Tolls: Toward Full Tort Recovery for Psychic Injury." *University of Florida Law Review* 36 (1984): 333–412.

Bellah, Robert, *The Broken Covenant: American Civil Religion in Time of Trial*. Chicago: University of Chicago Press, 1975.

Bellah, Robert and Phillip Hammond. *Varieties of Civil Religion*. New York: Harper & Row, 1980.

Bellah, Robert, Richard Madsen, William M. Sullivan, Ann Swidler, and Steven M. Tipton. *Habits of the Heart: Individualism and Commitment in American Life*. Berkeley: University of California Press, 1985.

Bendix, Reinhard. *Max Weber: An Intellectual Portrait*, 2d ed. Berkeley: University of California Press, 1977.

Benson, Peter L., and Dorothy L. Williams. *Religion on Capitol Hill: Myths and Realities*. San Francisco: Harper & Row, 1982.

Berger, Peter, and Thomas Luckmann. *The Social Construction of Reality*. New York: Anchor Books, 1966.

Berger, Peter. "Toward a Sociological Understanding of Psychoanalysis." *Social Research* 32 (1965): 26–41.

Berger, Peter. *The Sacred Canopy: Elements of a Sociological Theory of Religion.* Garden City, N.Y.: Doubleday & Co., 1967.

Bremner, Robert H., ed. *Children and Youth in America: A Documentary History,* 3 vols. Cambridge, Mass.: Harvard University Press, 1971.

Brubaker, Rogers. *The Limits of Rationality: An Essay on the Social and Moral Thought of Max Weber.* London: George Allen & Unwin, 1984.

Caplow, Theodore. *American Social Trends.* New York: Harcourt Brace Jovanovich, 1991.

Cassirer, Ernst. *The Myth of the State.* New Haven, Conn.: Yale University Press, 1979.

Church, Robert. "Moral Education in the Schools." In *Morality Examined,* edited by Lindley J. Stiles and Bruce D. Johnson. Princeton, N.J.: Princeton Book Company, 1977.

Collier, James Lincoln. *The Rise of Selfishness in America.* Oxford: Oxford University Press, 1991.

Connolly, William. *Legitimacy and the State.* Oxford: Basil Blackwell, 1984.

Diagnostic and Statistical Manual of Mental Disorders: DSM-III-R. Washington, D.C.: American Psychiatric Association, 1987.

Diggins, John P., and Mark E. Kann. *The Problem of Authority in America.* Philadelphia: Temple University Press, 1981.

Dionne, E. J. *Why Americans Hate Politics.* New York: Simon and Schuster, 1991.

Durkheim, Émile. *Selected Writings.* Edited by Anthony Giddens. Cambridge: Cambridge University Press, 1972.

Elshtain, Jean Bethke. *Meditations on Modern Political Thought.* New York: Praeger Publishers, 1986.

Emirbayer, Mustafa Kemal, "Moral Education in America, 1830–1990: A Contribution to the Sociology of Moral Education." Ph.D. diss. Ann Arbor: University of Michigan Dissertation Services, 1990.

Fingarette, Herbert. *Heavy Drinking: The Myth of Alcoholism as a Disease.* Berkeley: University of California Press, 1988.

Foucault, Michel. *Discipline and Punish: The Birth of the Prison.* New York: Vintage Books, 1979.

———. *The Foucault Reader.* New York: Pantheon Books, 1984.

Friedman, Lawrence M. "Rights of Passage: Divorce Law in Historical Perspective." *Oregon Law Review* 63 (1984): 647–69.

———. *Total Justice.* New York: Russell Sage Foundation, 1985.

———. "Civil Wrongs: Personal Injury Law in the Late Nineteenth Century." *American Bar Foundation Research Journal,* nos. 2–3 (1987): 351–77.

———. *The Republic of Choice: Law, Authority, Culture.* Cambridge: Harvard University Press, 1990.

Geertz, Clifford. *Local Knowledge: Further Essays in Interpretive Anthropology.* New York: Basic Books, 1983.

Gergen, Kenneth J. *The Saturated Self: Dilemmas of Identity in Contemporary Life.* New York: Basic Books, 1991.

Giddens, Anthony. *Capitalism and Modern Social Theory: An Analysis of the Writings of Marx, Durkheim and Max Weber.* Cambridge: Cambridge University Press, 1971.

———. *Modernity and Self-Identity: Self and Society in the Late Modern Age.* Cambridge: Polity Press, 1991.

Glendon, Mary Ann. *State, Law and Family: Family Law in Transition in the United States and Western Europe.* New York: North-Holland Publishing Co., 1977.

———. *Abortion and Divorce in Western Law: American Failures, European Challenges.* Cambridge, Mass.: Harvard University Press, 1990.

———. *Rights Talk: The Impoverishment of Public Discourse.* New York: Free Press, 1991.

Gross, Martin L. *The Psychological Society.* New York: Random House, 1978.

Habermas, Jürgen. *Legitimation Crisis.* Boston: Beacon Press, 1973.

———. "How Is Legitimacy Possible on the Basis of Legality?" In *Tanner Lectures of Human Values* 8 (delivered at Harvard University, 1 and 2 October 1986). Cambridge: Cambridge University Press, 1988.

Hellweg, Susan A., Michael Pfau, and Steven R. Brydon. *Televised Presidential Debates: Advocacy in Contemporary America.* New York: Praeger Publishers, 1992.

Herman, Ellen. *The Romance of American Psychology: Political Culture in the Age of Experts.* Berkeley: University of California Press, 1995.

Herring, Terri Krivosha. "Administering the Tort of Negligent Infliction of Mental Distress: A Synthesis." *Cardoza Law Review* 4 (1983): 487–518.

Hersh, Richard H., John P. Miller, and Glen D. Fielding. *Models of Moral Education.* New York: Longman, 1980.

Hinck, Edward A. *Enacting the Presidency: Political Argument, Presidential Debates, and Presidential Character.* London: Praeger Publishers, 1993.

Horwitz, Allan V. "Therapy and Social Solidarity." In *Toward a General Theory of Social Control,* edited by Donald Black, vol. 1. New York: Academic Press, 1984.

Hughes, Robert. *Culture of Complaint.* Oxford: Oxford University Press, 1993.

Hunter, James Davison. *American Evangelicalism.* New Brunswick, N.J.: Rutgers University Press, 1983.

———. *Evangelicalism: The Coming Generation.* Chicago: University of Chicago Press, 1987.

———. *Culture Wars: The Struggle to Define America.* New York: Basic Books, 1991.

Hunter, James Davison. *Before the Shooting Begins: Searching for Democracy in America's Culture Wars*. New York: Free Press, 1993.

Hunter, James Davison, and Stephen C. Ainlay. *Making Sense of Modern Times*. New York: Routledge & Kegan Paul, 1986.

Hyde, Alan. "The Concept of Legitimation in the Sociology of Law." *Wisconsin Law Review* (1983): 379–426.

Ingber, Stanley. "Rethinking Intangible Injuries: A Focus on Remedy." *California Law Review* 73 (1985): 772–856.

Jamieson, Kathleen Hall, and David S. Birdsell. *Presidential Debates: The Challenge of Creating an Informed Electorate*. Oxford: Oxford University Press, 1988.

Kaestle, Carl. *Pillars of the Republic: Common Schools and American Society*. New York: Hill & Wang, 1983.

———. "Moral Education and Common Schools in America: A Historian's View," *Journal of Moral Education* 13, 2 (May 1984): 101–11.

Kloppenberg, James. "The Virtues of Liberalism: Christianity, Republicanism, and Ethics in Early American Political Discourse," *Journal of American History*, 74, 1 (June 1987): 9–33.

Kramer, Rita. *Ed School Follies*. New York: Free Press, 1991.

Kraus, Sidney. *The Great Debates: Background—Perspective—Effects*. Bloomington: Indiana University Press, 1962.

Kuhn, Thomas. *The Essential Tension*. Chicago: University of Chicago Press, 1977.

Lantry, Terry L. "An Expanding Legal Duty: The Recovery of Damages for Mental Anguish by Those Observing Tortious Activity." *American Business Law Journal* 19 (1981): 214–26.

Lasch, Christopher. *Haven in a Heartless World*. New York: Basic Books, 1977.

———. *The Culture of Narcissism*. New York: W. W. Norton & Co., 1978.

———. "For Shame: Why Americans Should Be Wary of Self-esteem." *New Republic*, 10 August 1992, pp. 29–34.

Leukefeld, Carl G. and Frank M. Tims, eds. *Drug Abuse Treatment in Prisons and Jails*. National Institute of Drug Abuse (NIDA) Research Monograph 118. Washington, D.C.: U.S. Department of Health and Human Services, 1992.

Lipset, S. M. "Some Social Requisites of Democracy: Economic Development and Political Legitimacy." *American Political Science Review* 53 (1958): 69–105.

———. *Political Man: The Social Bases of Politics*. New York: Anchor Books, 1960.

Lipset, S. M., and William Schneider. *The Confidence Gap: Business, Labor, and Government*. New York: Free Press, 1983.

Luhmann, Niklas. *Political Theory and the Welfare State*. Translated by John Bednarz, Jr. New York: Walter de Gruyter, 1990.

MacIntyre, Alasdair. *After Virtue: A Study in Moral Theory*. Notre Dame, Ind.: University of Notre Dame Press, 1984.

Marlowe, Douglas Bryan. "Comments: Negligent Infliction of Mental Distress: A Jurisdictional Survey of Existing Limitation Devices and Proposal Based on an Analysis of Objective versus Subjective Indices of Distress." Villanova Law Review 33 (1988): 781–833.

Marx, Karl. *On Society and Social Change*. Edited by Neil Smelser. Chicago: University of Chicago Press, 1973.

———. *The Marx-Engels Reader*. Edited by Robert C. Tucker. New York: W. W. Norton & Co., 1978.

Mecca, Andrew, Neil Smelser, and John Vasconcellos. *The Social Importance of Self-esteem*. Berkeley: University of California Press, 1989.

Merelman, Richard M. "Learning and Legitimacy." *American Political Science Review* 60 (1966): 548–61.

Miller, Richard S. "The Scope of Liability for Negligent Infliction of Emotional Distress: Making 'the Punishment Fit the Crime.' " *University of Hawaii Law Review* 1 (1979): 1–47.

Mills, C. Wright, and Hans Gerth. *Character and Social Structure: The Psychology of Social Institutions*. London: Routledge & Kegan Paul, 1954.

Nolan, James L., Jr., ed. *The American Culture Wars: Current Contests and Future Prospects*. Charlottesville, Va. and London: University Press of Virginia, 1996.

Peele, Stanton. *Diseasing of America: Addiction Treatment Out of Control*. Toronto: Lexington Books, 1989.

Poggi, Gianfranco. *The Development of the Modern State: A Sociological Introduction*. Stanford: Stanford University Press, 1978.

———. *The State: Its Nature, Development and Prospects*. Cambridge: Polity Press, 1990.

Polsky, Andrew J. *The Rise of the Therapeutic State*. Princeton, N.J.: Princeton University Press, 1991.

Purpel, David, and Kevin Ryan. *Moral Education: It Comes with the Territory*. Berkeley, Calif.: McCutchan Publishing Corporation, 1976.

Ranney, Austin. *The Past and Future of Presidential Debates*. Washington, D.C.: American Enterprise Institute for Public Policy Research, 1979.

Rice, John Stedman. *A Disease of One's Own: Psychotherapy, Addiction, and the Emergence of Co-Dependency*. New Brunswick, N.J.: Transaction Publishers, 1996.

Rieff, Philip. *The Triumph of the Therapeutic*. Chicago: University of Chicago Press, 1966.

Rieff, Philip. *The Feeling Intellect: Selected Writings.* Chicago: University of Chicago Press, 1990.

Riesman, David. *The Lonely Crowd: A Study of the Changing American Character.* New Haven and London: Yale University Press, 1961.

Roth, Guenther, and Wolfgang Schlucter. *Max Weber's Vision of History: Ethics and Methods.* Berkeley: University of California Press, 1979.

Scaff, Lawrence A. "Fleeing the Iron Cage: Politics and Culture in the Thought of Max Weber." *American Political Science Review* 81 (September 1987): 3.

Schaar, John H. "Legitimacy in the Modern State." In Legitimacy and the State, edited by William Connolly. pp. 104–133. Oxford: Basil Blackwell Publisher, 1984.

Schluchter, Wolfgang. *The Rise of Western Rationalism: Max Weber's Developmental History.* Berkeley: University of California Press, 1981.

Schur, Edwin. *The Awareness Trap: Self-Absorption instead of Social Change.* New York: Quadrangle/ The New York Times Book Co., 1976.

Seligman, Adam B., *The Idea of Civil Society.* New York: Free Press, 1992.

Sennett, Richard. *The Fall of Public Man: On the Social Psychology of Capitalism.* New York: Vintage Books, 1976.

Shafir, Gershon. "The Incongruity between Destiny and Merit: Max Weber on Meaningful Existence and Modernity." *British Journal of Sociology* 36 (1984): 4.

Sheldon, Charles Ward. *The Political Philosophy of Thomas Jefferson.* Baltimore: Johns Hopkins University Press, 1991.

Smolla, Rodney A. "Let the Author Beware: The Rejuvenation of the American Law of Libel." *University of Pennsylvania Law Review* 132 (1983): 1–94.

Sykes, Charles. *A Nation of Victims: The Decay of the American Character.* New York: St. Martin's Press, 1992.

Szasz, Thomas. *Law, Liberty, and Psychiatry.* Syracuse, N.Y.: Syracuse University Press, 1963.

———. *The Therapeutic State: Psychiatry in the Mirror of Current Events.* Buffalo, N.Y.: Prometheus Books, 1984.

Thernstrom, Stephen. *Poverty and Progress: Social Mobility in a Nineteenth Century City.* Cambridge, Mass.: Harvard University Press, 1964.

Tocqueville, Alexis de. *Democracy in America.* 2 vols. New York: Alfred A. Knopf, 1945.

Towey, Joseph P. "Negligent Infliction of Mental Distress: Reaction to Dillon v. Legg in California and Other States." *Hastings Law Journal* 25 (April 1974): 1248–65.

Trilling, Lionel. *Sincerity and Authenticity.* Cambridge, Mass.: Harvard University Press, 1972.

Tucker, James. "The Therapeutic Corporation: Social Control in a Post-Bureaucratic Organization." Ph.D. diss., Department of Sociology, University of Virginia, August 1992.

Twiford, J. Rainer. "Emotional Distress in Tort Law." Behavioral Sciences and the Law (Spring 1985): 121–33.

Tyack, David, Thomas James, and Aaron Benavot. *Law and the Shaping of Public Education, 1785–1954.* Madison: University of Wisconsin Press, 1987.

Vatter, Harold G. and John F. Walker. *The Inevitability of Government Growth.* New York: Columbia University Press, 1990.

Weber, Max. *From Max Weber: Essays in Sociology.* Edited by H. H. Gerth and C. Wright Mills. New York: Oxford University Press, 1946.

———. *The Protestant Ethic and the Spirit of Capitalism.* Translated by Talcott Parsons. New York: Charles Scribner's Sons, 1958.

———. *Economy and Society.* 2 vols. Edited by Guenther Roth and Claus Wittich. Berkeley: University of California Press, 1978.

Westerhoff, John H. *McGuffey and His Readers: Piety, Morality and Education in Nineteenth-Century America.* Nashville: Abingdon Press, 1978.

Wolfe, Alan. *The Limits of Legitimacy: Political Contradictions of Contemporary Capitalism.* New York: Free Press, 1977.

Wrong, Dennis. *Max Weber.* Englewood Cliffs, N.J.: Prentice-Hall, 1970.

Wuthnow, Robert. *Meaning and the Moral Order: Explorations in Cultural Analysis.* Berkeley and Los Angeles: University of California Press, 1987.

Wuthnow, Robert, J. D. Hunter, Albert Bergessen, and Edith Kurzweil. *Cultural Analysis: The Work of Peter L. Berger, Mary Douglas, Michel Foucault and Jurgen Habermas.* New York: Routledge & Kegan Paul, 1984.

Zilbergeld, Bernie. *The Shrinking of America.* Boston: Little, Brown & Co., 1983.

Ziskin, Jay. *Coping with Psychiatric and Psychological Testimony.* 3d ed. Vol. 1. Venice, Calif.: Law and Psychology Press, 1981.

Index

CPSIA information can be obtained at www.ICGtesting.com
Printed in the USA
LVOW040524171112

307679LV00009B/13/P

9 780814 757918